Beyond the Stars
Volume 4

Beyond the Stars:

Studies in American Popular Film
Volume 4

Locales in American Popular Film

edited by

Paul Loukides
and
Linda K. Fuller

Bowling Green State University Popular Press
Bowling Green, OH 43403

Dedication

As is perhaps appropriate for a work on locales, this book is dedicated to Albion College and to the many special people who have entered my life through its doors.

Paul Loukides

To the many men in my life—husband, three sons, father-in-law, brothers-in-law, cousins, friends, neighbors, colleagues, students, and many friends of these many men, who helped this feminist make a case for defending "maleness."

Linda K. Fuller

Contents

A Foreword for Film Scholars

The *BEYOND THE STARS: Studies in American Popular Film* series was begun with a sense that the study of American movie conventions of plot, character, material objects, locales and thematic or ideological motifs across the boundaries of genre—as well as within those boundaries—could lead to new insights into the relationship between popular film and the complex social matrix of American life.

With four volumes of the series now completed, it seems clear that the close analysis of the patterns of American film—in what might be called "film convention studies"—has at least begun to show its potential as a critical tool for looking at the symbiotic relationship between movies and the greater society.

Although a number of papers within the *Beyond the Stars* series are structured around a core premise of film genres as a primary classification tool for the study of popular film, the series itself, including this volume, demonstrates how the study of the conventions of films (plot, character, locales, material objects, thematic motifs) in and of themselves, is a fruitful and illuminating approach to the great body of films which do not fall comfortably into any usefully exact genre classification.

For the film scholar interested in the symbiotic relationship between popular film and American life, the study of film conventions offers the kind of historical perspective that is a requisite component of the study of American popular culture. Because individual film conventions of plot, character, material objects, locales and themes/ideologies can be documented with some precision, they can offer particularly telling clues into the interaction between the world of film and the social environment which created and consumed those films. That is, we can, with some precision, document the first car chase, the first mammy figure, the last appearance of running board-riding cops, the growth, maturation and death of anti-fascist films or anti-communist films, the history of Arabs or Jews or Native Americans, or ethnic Irish in the movies. We can conceivably find every use of ballparks as locales, or document the number of swimming pools or penthouse apartments or fifth floor walk-ups from decade to decade. We can measure the amount of firepower used in action films from year to year, or examine the changes and constants of fashions of formal and informal wear and uniforms. The study of film conventions allows us to do content analyses and examinations of the social context and historical moment of mixed racial romances and marriages, the uses of cocaine and other drugs, or the appearance of baptisms and funerals.

The documentation and study of film conventions, like the study of film genres, is based on identifying patterns within the broad field of popular film. Film conventions, like all other cultural patterns, have social roots and thrive or die in the complex and everchanging social environment which they both reflect and help create. Whether we trace the evolution of the Western, the changing forms of musicals, or ways in which conventions of character, or places, or thematic motifs have altered or remained fixtures within the flow of films made for the popular American audiences, we are concerned with identifying and interpreting patterns which have been created through time.

In this volume of the *Beyond the Stars* series, the subject of the various individual essays are discrete conventions of movie locales, but the subject of the volume as a whole—as with the other books in the series—is the viability of film convention studies as a tool for the study of film and American culture.

The dominance of the "genre approach" to the study of American popular film is apparent not only in the bibliographies of film scholarship, but also in the ways film scholars have traditionally thought about groups of films. While it is clearly convenient to group films into genres and sub-genres like "buddy films," "big caper films," "atomic monster films," "Vietnam films," "post-modern Westerns," and so forth, finding and using genre classifications is premised on looking at groups of whole films rather than at those parts of films which movies of several genres or sub-genres might have in common.

Put another way, film convention studies focus on the stock components of movies like stereotyped characters, common plot devices, the presentation and uses of material objects, commonplace locales, and the basic themes and ideologies that appear in dozens, or sometimes hundreds of films.

Because film convention studies seeks to identify the uses of the various conventions across groups of films from given years or decades rather than from within genres, it affords the popular culturist a means of probing a wide range of films that might not otherwise appear to have much in common. When scholars like Jack Shaheen or Donald Bogle document the images of Arabs or Blacks in American film, they are working out patterns which are not based on a few dozen films where Arabs or Blacks are necessarily central figures; rather, they are examining hundreds of films where Arabs or Blacks appear in roles ranging from minor to central. The same is true for writers like Howard Good, Kathy Merlock Jackson and Stephen Pendo, who have documented and illuminated the presentation of journalists, children, and aircraft across a wide range of film types.

Although the scope of film convention studies is perhaps its greatest asset, the need to try to be inclusive in the documentation and analysis of various film conventions often presents the film scholar with the daunting—but not impossible—prospect of trying to find particular conventions across great bodies of films. For example, it is a relatively limited task to look at the role of the schoolteacher in the Western, even though there are thousands of Westerns. It is much more difficult to focus on the conventional role of the schoolteacher in films of the 1950s and 1960s or the Silent Era, since teachers may appear in detective films, comedies, family melodramas or virtually any type of movie. Whether the goal might be to examine cultural images of teachers or automatic weapons or cities, or Cinderella stories, the problems faced by the scholar of film conventions are compounded by the sheer mass of film that Hollywood has produced and the paucity of relevant indices. The researcher interested in film adultery, or instances of car chases, or images of sailing ships, or Singapore as locale, or the anti-business motif in American films, or the temperamental redhead as a character type, or any of hundreds of other film culture conventions, does not yet have access to encyclopedias of film conventions. For a few of the hundreds of film conventions, some prior scholarship at least offers a starting point; for others, there is only the willingness of individual film scholars to search out the gold of particular conventions from the stream of popular film.

The *BEYOND THE STARS* series was begun with the modest hope that there would be enough film scholars interested in the conventions of American film to add substantially to the documentation and analysis of the five basic types of film conventions across and within the lines of genre. With more than 75 essays appearing in the series and more than a thousand films cited in the essays and filmographies, the series seems to have at least partially fulfilled one of its purposes.

If the works presented within the volumes of *BEYOND THE STARS* serve to demonstrate the utility of the film convention approach to popular film and American culture, then the efforts of its authors and editors will go beyond the cumulative worth of the essays that appear within the series. It is our hope that others will follow the faint path that we have tried to broaden and lead us to new insights into the patterns of American film and American culture.

Introduction
Conventions of Locale in Popular Film

Paul Loukides
and
Linda K. Fuller

It is perhaps a testimony to how little we really pay attention to the locales of film that so few places from the movies seem really memorable. Locales, except when they are developed in ways which make them special, typically function as unquestioned backgrounds within the movie world. Like all the commonplaces of our culture, the most ubiquitous and traditional conventions of film tend to be taken as "givens" within the reality of the movie world. The conventions of American popular film—whether of character, plot, objects, themes, or locales—are, by their very nature, both familiar and rarely noticed.

It may be that because so much of our daily lives is spent within very real conventions of locale that we scarcely question, or pay attention to, the filmic conventions of place. Within our everyday world, bedrooms and bathrooms, dining rooms and kitchens, auto garages, fast food restaurants, business offices and factories, freeways and suburban streets, farms and bars, London and laundromats are typically environments with whole complexes of built-in expectations as to what belongs and does not belong within a particular setting. Basketball in the dining room, campfires in the office, swimsuits in the subway, sheep in a suburban yard, big screen television sports in funeral homes are all clearly possible, but they would offend our sense of place and the proprieties—that is, the conventions, of those places.

In film, as in our everyday world, conventions of locales typically have quite fixed, and even rigid conventional parameters which have scarcely been studied by popular culturists. With the possible exception of those locales traditionally linked to particular film genres like the town and landscape of the classical Western, or the nightclubs, apartments and city streets of the gangster film, surprisingly little has been written about the conventions of locales and their importance as part of the cultural matrix of popular film. Examining the conventions of film locales, and the ways in which those conventions of place are used

1

in film, can help reveal whole sets of cultural assumptions within the films which Americans create and consume.

Although locales in film are often reflections of the commonplace world in which we live, or are taken directly from the real world in films shot on location, this does not necessarily mean that the conventions of movie locales are mere statistical accidents (given x number of films, some number will likely be shot on suburban streets, some other number will include shopping malls, yet others might include auto garages). Rather, the conventions of film locales reflect the cultural attitudes of both film makers and film audiences and the kind of nominal expectations that we share for common or even extraordinary places that our lives and our knowledge of film engender in us. As filmgoers, we are conditioned to recognize that night-time cemeteries are dangerous places for outdoor romance, that Western gunmen are much more likely to shoot it out in the saloon or the street than in the general store or the schoolhouse yard. We know that gothic mansions on a stormy night are risky, that Mexican villages will be poor, and on and on through whole litanies of conventions tied to movie places.

Whether we look at the conventions of suburban houses, small towns, cities like New York or Chicago or Budapest, stripjoints or urban parks, we are likely to recognize conventions so deeply embedded in our cultural assumptions as to be both unremarkable and universal in film.

Like stock characters and everyday plot conventions, the conventions of locale are such ordinary stuff that they typically occasion notice only when they are deliberately or accidently broken. The air conditioner that appears in a few frames of *High Noon*, or the boom mike that seems to hang from the sky in an open field in *Billy Jack* contravene the conventions on which those films are based. The machinegun attacks on bedroom couples in both *Godfather* and *Godfather II*, the shower slashing in *Psycho*, the plane attack in *North by Northwest*, or the suburban mayhem of *Halloween* once had an enhanced ability to shock because they broke the conventions of safety commonly associated with bedrooms, bathrooms, bucolic fields and middle class suburban enclaves.

Like all conventions, the conventions of locales are subject to change as both the society and movies change. Bathrooms, hot tubs and showers, while still used as sanctuaries and as locations for sensuality and sex, seem to have become much more dangerous places than either dining rooms or family rooms, as films like *Psycho, Dressed to Kill*, and *Fatal Attraction* have helped transform them into places of entrapment and mayhem in the movies.

The movies might well have also helped make basements into places where dangers lurk among the shadows. The place of resting vampires in scores of films, and the focal point of horror in dozens of psycho-horror movies like *Psycho* and *Silence of the Lambs*, the basement—whether in a Transylvania castle or suburban house or urban apartment building, is not a neutral place in the movies. The movie basement is a dark place, the place where monsters wait.

Movie-made conventions of locale, like the commonplace assumptions about the real world that we tend to share, are richly connotative. For example, from at least the time of *White Heat*, industrial areas—factories, warehouses, mills, garages, refineries and junk yards—have been frequently used as locations for dramatic shoot-outs. In films like *Robocop* and *Robocop II, Darkman, Lethal Weapon, Terminator* and *Terminator II, Dirty Harry, The French Connection* and *Batman*, bleak industrial landscapes have served as both a dramatically useful location and as visual metaphors. Large enough to allow maneuvering and flight, filled with menacing shadows, hiding places, cover, weapons of opportunity and indigenous dangers, the industrial locale is a child's dream of the perfect place to play guns. As visual metaphors, the industrial landscape offers a dehumanized environment tied to capitalism, technology, and the corrupting pursuit of wealth and power. In films like *Robocop*, where the corruption of civil society is directly tied to capitalism without conscience, or in the *Terminator* films, where the menace to human existence derives from a technology gone amok, the shootout on the factory floor visually locates corruption in the physical environment of the industrial landscape.

The study of the conventions of film locales—a part of what might be called "film convention studies"—across the borders of genre as well as within those boundaries can lead us to new insights into the relationship between popular film and the complex phenomenon which we call American life. The sheer number of film titles tied to locations perhaps suggests the evocative power of locales in the American mind. Whether tied to geographic places, public spaces, or more personalized, private locations, film titles bound to locales number in the hundreds.

Among geographic locations—places that might be found on a map—are movie titles and films centered around countries, states, cities, counties, neighborhoods, even streets. From *Good Morning, Vietnam* to *To Russia, with Love*, to *Passage to India* and *Burma Road*, from *California Dreaming* to *Kansas*, to *The Texas Chainsaw Massacre* and *The Man from Colorado*, from *Vera Cruz* to *Niagara* and from *Macon County Line* to *Flying Down to Rio*, from *Brighton Beach Memoirs* to *Slaughter on 10th Avenue, Nightmare on Elm Street* and *A Miracle on*

34th Street, the evocative power of geographic locations has been used repeatedly in movie titles.

Other kinds of locales are also well represented in film titles. Houses, for example, rate nearly thirty entries in Maitlin's *TV MOVIES*, ranging from the generic *House Across the Bay* to the *House Across the Street* to *The House of the Seven Gables* and the *House of Usher*. Boats (*Mutiny on the Bounty, Titanic, Posideon Adventure, Lifeboat*), eating places and bars (*Mystic Pizza, Porky's, Ballad of the Sad Cafe*), space and fantasy places (*The Man from Planet X, Journey to the Center of the Earth, It Came from Outer Space, Westworld*) as well as generic places like *The Big House, Field of Dreams,* and *Hometown, U.S.A.*, rate scores of entries each.

The question, of course, is whether there is any particular significance in the very large number of films in which locales are mentioned in the title. A related question is whether film titles and the use of place names within those titles has anything at all to do with the conventions of locales within the movie tradition. The answer to both questions seems a tentative "Yes."

A quick survey of place or location—centered titles suggests that place or location names, like filmic locations themselves, are most often used for evocative or connotative effect. Whether we think about *Nashville* or *Casablanca* or *Manhattan* or *Philadelphia Story* or *The Boston Strangler,* the place in the title brings with it a set of widely shared cultural assumptions about the places named. Nashville is not Topeka, just as Casablanca is not Rome. The Connecticut Kid would be a different person than the California Kid, and a "Home" of Cards, or of Usher, or of Seven Gables would be different places than the houses of those same names. *A Trip to Bountiful* promises a different experience than a *Trip to Flint,* and *Badlands* offers a potential viewer something different than *Grand Canyon* or *Niagara*. In war films, the places of battle, whether real or created, seem to tap historical echoes—as in *Bataan, Sands of Iwo Jima, Pork Chop Hill, Hamburger Hill, Tobruck,* or *The Battle of the Coral Sea*. In dozens of films the connotative power of place names is used to suggest something about the hero, as in *The Man from Snowy River, The Man from Frisco,* from Hong Kong, from Laramie, or *The Man from the Alamo*.

Like the visual and dramatic conventions of locales, place titles offer filmmakers and film viewers a quick shorthand access to widely shared conventions and assumptions. As with place titles, locales in films are typically instantly recognizable and familiar, their readability depending on visual (and sometimes auditory) cues as simple (or complex) as a familiar landmark (the Eiffel Tower, the Golden Gate

Bridge, the Manhattan Skyline) or a film title, or a combination of cues that helps differentiate potentially confusing sites from one another. A desert with tanks, peopled with characters dressed in khaki, places us differently than the same desert with horses and cowboys. Characters in Medieval garb on a modern urban street are either actors, party-goers, or time travellers; the same crew in a dark forest is in a 14th-century forest.

Yet as easily as we read locales in film and translate place titles into a set of expectations about particular movies, the conventions of film locales are anything but simple and fixed. The 17 essays which appear in *BEYOND THE STARS IV: Conventions of Locales in American Popular Film*, closely examine the conventions of international borders, the Mideast, the New South, newsrooms, beaches, churches, swimming pools, ballparks, highways, fight arenas, Western saloons, Latin America, homemakers' spaces, futuristic cities, men's rooms, New Orleans, and the Southwest; collectively, they reveal the huge diversity and complex history of the conventions of locales in a broad range of Hollywood films.

The essays in this collection serve to suggest quite how rich and complex a subject film locales offer. Among the geographical places discussed, the range extends from the Old West to futuristic cities. Jay Boyer documents the earliest days of the Western's conventions as he recounts how early filmmakers sought out and used the various landscapes of Arizona in the early years of the Western. New Orleans, the subject of Mark Charney's essay, offers an exemplary case of a particular American city being used as a convention-laden locale: New Orleans in film is a city of witchcraft, corruption and illicit passion. Carol Ward examines the image of the "New South" in scores of films spanning some 20 years and finds that the "New South" of the movies is a place haunted by its own traditions and history. In an essay on international borders in film, Carlos Cortes shows how borders have been used in the "writing and rewriting of U.S. history" in American movies, and how borders become the focal setting for personal, intellectual and international conflicts in film. Barbara Obadashian outlines the recurrent elements of some 40 years of the sub-genre of American road films and sees in them a "quintessential American archetype" where the road is a destination, a way of life, a metaphor for alienation and rebellion. In "South of the Border," Brooks Robards looks at 60 years of images of Latin America in film and shows how the elements of an "exotic and yet familiar" area are conventionalized in films as different as the 1930 Latin musicals and the "pseudo-documentaries" of the 1980s. Jack Shaheen makes a strong case that the movies inherited 19th-century English attitudes toward Arabs and

"Ayrab-land." He documents how the "Ayrab-land" of contemporary films is virtually the same landscape that film goers have seen for more than 70 years in spite of the huge social changes that have transformed the Middle East. Colleen Tremont suggests that while futuristic films like *Batman*, *Total Recall* and *Bladerunner* owe a historic debt to Fritz Lange's *Metropolis*, the dystopia which they create suggests a darker and more pessimistic vision of the future than Lange's.

The essays dealing with public and ritual spaces reveal how some of the conventions of these kinds of locales are dealt with in American movies. Using an examination of the cycle of 1960 "beach movies" as the core of her essay, Kathy Merlock Jackson discusses beaches in films, finding that they are used "as a place for solitary reflection; as a place of romance and sex, often illicit; and as a place of danger and threat." Terry Lindvall deals with images of churches in some 75 years of American film, ranging from romantic comedy to horror and science fiction, and shows the ways in which churches represent "a set of subtle, substantial, and strategic symbols." In tracing the filmic conventions of ballparks in the movies over the course of the more than 70 years in which they have served as the venue for baseball films, Doug Noverr makes a convincing case that the conventions of ballparks have undergone substantial change. Where early films treated ballparks as backgrounds where particular action took place, more recent films have attempted to evoke the mythic dimensions of the ballfield as a place where important rituals are inacted. Edward Reccia, in his essay on boxing films, also focuses attention on the ritualist dimensions of the conventional locales of the boxing film—particularly the boxing ring itself, where rituals of violence, suffering, defeat and redemption are acted out in the public eye. The western saloon, which Diana Reep discusses, may be among the most familiar conventional locales in the movies. Reep sees in this well known part of the western's iconography "the indoor setting for the same cloak of barbarism and law that is taking place on a grand scale in the outdoor setting…the saloon mixes both the Eastern promise of order…and the Western threat of unbridled lawlessness."

The last portion of this collection deals with more private arenas and the commonplace spaces of work and leisure. Linda K. Fuller's treatment of men's rooms in popular film suggests that the rise of the Women's Movement has seen an increase in the use of men's rooms as bastions of male privacy and as spaces where men gather to be men. In his essay on swimming pools in popular film, Greg Metcalf shows that swimming pools are rarely neutral places; rather, they are either locations for sensuality and sex or focal points for violence and conflict, depending on whether the pool is dominated by women or by men.

Norma Green recounts more than 50 years of American fascination with newsrooms, which she argues are shown not only as places where news is readied for press or camera, but also as the site for actions ranging from floods to fistfights, fires and mayhem. In Thomas Sobchack's account of the space of melodrama, "the rooms women inhabit in these films not only limit their world, but display the limitations the world places on them."

The essays in this volume cover only a small portion of the conventions of locales which are so much a part of American film. Farms and suburbs, prisons and stripjoints, restaurants and factories, children's rooms and hair dressing salons, and dozens—perhaps hundreds—of other stock locations remain to be represented. But the purpose of this volume has never been to capture some illusive or comprehensive American locale; rather, the intent has been to focus attention on the ways in which the conventions of locale reflect—and perhaps distort—the world in which we live as citizens and movie goers.

Paul Loukides
Albion College

Linda K. Fuller
Worcester State College

Geographical/ Conceptual Places

No Fit Place for Any Man, Woman, or Child: Depictions of Arizona in Our Earliest Films

Jay Boyer

The cameraman of a production company I've been researching wrote home to Philadelphia to his wife. He was writing from Prescott, Arizona. He'd been making movies on location in the Southwest for nearly a year. He detailed in his letter the beauties and natural wonders of the region, then asked her to join him. She refused to come. She thought she preferred to stay where she was, thank you just the same. She had heard about that part of the country. She wrote back, "Mother was talking to someone about my going to Arizona and he told her that he had been there and that it was no fit place for any man, woman, or child to be. He says that the mountains throw off a substance called lava: that, if it falls on one's face, it stings worse than a dozen bees. If this is true, please write at once and don't tell me it is alright if it is not, for that would only be endangering my health. Write and let me know just the situation."

The year was 1913 and her fears seem ludicrous, if not downright comic, for he was hardly writing from an untamed wilderness. By 1913, Prescott, in fact, was a mix of frontier settlement and modern town, and it prided itself on being at once one of the oldest communities in the state and a fairly progressive place to live. It had been the first capitol of the Arizona Territory. In May of 1864 then Secretary of State Goodwin gave the town its name, looking to William Hickling Prescott, author of *History Of The Conquest of Mexico* for his inspiration. By the end of 1864, Prescott had its own hotel, the Jackson, a restaurant, stores, two doctors, and a billiard saloon; but most important to its growth, it had its own security. Fort Whipple was nearby for its citizens' protection.

Two years later the capitol was moved to Tucson, and after that, to Phoenix, the capitol of the state today, though Prescott continued to grow without losing much of its initial frontier atmosphere. Rich mineral deposits west of Prescott in the Copper Basin, as well as those to the south near the Hassayampa River, drew miners, while the area's good flat land drew farmers, cattlemen, and sheep herders.

11

By 1913 the Prescott area had a population upwards of 5000, and, like so many Western towns, with the coming of the railroad it had become immediately linked with Wall Street and with the Industrial Revolution as well. Yet it hadn't completely lost its initial character. Its population numbered merchants and professional people and a predictable assortment of the gainfully employed; primarily, however, the people of the area still took their living from the land or from animal husbandry of one kind or another, and continued to live their lives much as they had before the turn of the century. There were starting to be chain stores and the like, but older merchants like James L. Gardner still did business more or less like always. On the shelves of Gardner's General Store could be found brands like Pillsbury, Swift, and Carnation, goods acquired by wholesalers Rinkle and Peacock from their warehouses in El Paso. But there's no evidence that they sold better than the more established brand names, brands Gardner's had been carrying for years, such as the gunpowder black Gunpowder Tea or rich yellow wheels of locally produced cheese or coffees with names like Mocha or Java or Lyons. Gardner's relied primarily on the ranchers for its trade, and stockmen or their wives still came to town only once or twice a month for supplies, often on large drays drawn by Percheron horses. Gardner's was like many of the older stores in the area. It extended credit generously, delivered the goods on time, billed the customer once a month, and with each bill came either a sample of the store's candy for the wife and children, or a house cigar for the husband.

At Ruffner's livery stable in 1913 you could still rent a barouche for formal occasions as well as a team of black horses; of course, Ruffner could also help you acquire a gas driven auto. You had only to call him and make an appointment. Telephones were common place, as were cars. Most of the streets were paved. You could drive up and down the mains streets and find evidence of civic organizations and fraternal lodges and teachers with their schoolchildren and a variety of new churches and businesses, but there was also the stately Bank of Arizona that had become a fixture on the corner of Gurley and Cortez Streets, as had the Winsor Restaurant which had earned a reputation several states broad for its family style meals of fried chicken.

Despite its homey town square and its blocks of middle-class residences, either of which could have as easily been located in Ohio or Indiana as in the Southwest, parts of the town still had a decidedly "Western" flavor. There were still clear signs of what had once been Chinatown, a hotbed of sin and cowboy debauchery, and located on the first block of South Montezuma Street was a series of cattlemen's bars. Before the great fire of 1900 which burned down much of the infamous

Whiskey Row, there were at least 30 working saloons in Prescott, an astounding number for a town its size, and many of the saloons that had been rebuilt kept up the tradition of liquor served "Prescott style." You could take your poison there two ways, by the glass or by the flask. A glass cost 15 cents, if you wanted hard liquor. But the second glass cost less: figure two for a quarter. And as for the flasks, they came in two-bit and four-bit sizes. These Prescott flasks were easily recognizable the minute you walked through the door. They were made of glass the color of amethyst, and these round, short-necked bottles stood in rows behind the man behind the bar.

In other words, by 1913, Prescott was like much of Arizona. It was a—sometimes uneasy—mix of the old and the new, with an emphasis on the latter. But that's not the impression you might have gotten from how the state was portrayed in the motion pictures that were being made on location in the state. And that's important. Much of America's first exposure to a newly formed state such as Arizona came through the motion pictures being made there on location, and its the first of these pictures that I mean to consider in this article. I want to begin by briefly discussing the first film companies to work in the state, the Independents, the AMPC, the Lubins and the Seligs, with particular attention to the Western Selig Polyscope Company and the films they produced in the Prescott area in 1913. Like many of the Westerns of the period, the films they produced seem to have put the working cowboy before the rest of America as a last remnant of frontier life; and, they offered up a landscape in which rugged men regularly triumphed over evil and treachery. But they did more than that. Their plots and storylines may have identified Arizona with noble resistance to the cultural and social changes taking place in the East, and, at least occasionally, created on the screen a mythical region where self-determination and self-definition were still plausible.

Making Movies in Arizona

The first films to be made in Arizona were probably shot between 1906 and 1909 by "Independents" in flight from "the Edisons." None of their films exist today, nor is there a solid written record of their production, which is sad but understandable. The films were being made with camera equipment that was in flagrant violation of patents claimed by Thomas Alva Edison, and since 1897 he'd been doing his best to put an end to this in ways both legal and not. The operations were surely hurried, catch-as-catch-can, and by modern standards, few copies were being struck at a time. Surely the few prints that ever existed, since they were printed on nitrate base film stock, have long since turned into a fine red powder in attics and storage bins across the country. And the records of their production, what records there were, have disappeared as well. There was no good reason to keep copious records, after all. The less paperwork you had on hand, the fewer records the Edison lawyers might subpoena.

It's reasonable that Arizona would have been attractive to film makers on the run. Not fully a state until 1912, it must have seemed lawless, relatively speaking. Its weather and sunshine were certainly inviting enough. And its exotic and varied terrain must have piqued the curiosity of city-bound audiences east of the Mississippi. City-bound, overcrowded, industrialized, the audiences for these early Southwest films surely found a momentary escape in the area's prototypically Western vistas.

By 1911, these same scenic wonders were drawing the makers of travelogues to Arizona. One of the film producers to specialize in such fare was the Co-Operative Film Manufacturing Company of Los Angeles. In the summer of 1911, its crew traveled throughout Arizona, taking "travelogues" as they went, and by the end of that same year, three Phoenix men, John Coyle, Robert Turnbull, and Arnold Smith tried to establish a permanent film production unit in the state in order to make more of the same. They called themselves the Arizona Motion Picture Company, the AMPC. The company seems to have been short-lived, and its films of the cacti near Camelback mountain in Phoenix and of the mining camps at Winkleman don't seem to have taken the motion picture industry by storm, but Coyle, Turnbull, and Smith were able to find a New York film distributor, which suggests that Arizona was beginning to get national attention in this newly born medium.

Arriving in 1912, one of the first theatrical film companies to come to Arizona was the Lubin Company. It must have seemed at the time to be but one more stage of the growing company's expansion. A German immigrant, its founder, Siegmund "Pop" Lubin, had settled in Philadelphia around the turn of the century and set up shop as an optician, then branched out from his optician's parlour to the grinding of camera lenses, and, never satisfied, branched out yet again to the making of movies. Soon he gave up his optician's practice entirely and began making films in earnest. He moved across the street from one of Philadelphia's first motion picture theatres, Brandenburg's Dime Museum, where he built a well-equipped production studio as well as a sophisticated lab, and set to work. It didn't take Lubin long to see that depending upon your movies alone for a steady income could be a hit and miss proposition, so to ensure a constant flow of cash he set up a movie pirating operation in his basement.

Lubin kept his employees busy there making positive prints of other studios' work, films which he then sold as his own at a discount. Between the films he made and the films he pirated, Lubin became a rich man, and he must have enjoyed some dubious standing in the motion picture industry by the time he was offered the chance to make his production part of the Motion Picture Patent Company, the largest and most powerful conglomerate of film makers in America at the time. He was, if nothing else, a force to be reckoned with.

By 1910, Lubin had moved his operation out of the city to a 500-acre estate at Betzwood, Pennsylvania, and, within a few years, he was looking to expand his operation still farther. About 1911, he began sending small troupes of movie makers to the South and to the West for a few months each year; and thanks to their success, he considered keeping at least one troupe in the West year round.

In 1912 he sent such a troupe to Arizona. The Lubin group arrived in Douglas, Arizona on February 22, 1912, after taking the El Paso and Southwestern Railroad from El Paso, Texas, where they'd been making films along the Texas border and in Juarez since December, 1911. Their intention was to make similar films in the Douglas area, particularly in Douglas's sister city, Agua Prieta, Mexico, which was—both literally and figuratively—little more than stone's throw from the center of Douglas proper.

The company's El Paso work included "The Handicap," "A Mexican Courtship," and probably at least the first reel of "The Revolution." During its stay in El Paso, the Lubins seem to have specialized in films about Mexican revolutionaries, Mexican treachery and the like, capitalizing on the topicality of Mexico's political unrest, and they surely intended to continue this when they arrived in Arizona. But they may have thought twice once they got there. Things along the Arizona-Mexican border were turning ugly. In El Paso, the Lubins had never been far from the 18th Infantry stationed at Fort Bliss. In Douglas, they were on their own.

They had no sooner settled into Douglas than stories began to appear in the local newspaper, the *Douglas Dispatch*, about the dangers afoot in the area. The ominous sounding prose of this March 1, 1912 *Dispatch* article telling of Americans who had been apprehended across the border and charged with insurrection seems to have been in keeping with the mood of the day:

In the inflamed eye of public opinion in the little town across the border, the Americans were thought to have some sinister purpose, with the backing of the United States government. One report across the line is that they were spies sent out to ascertain the topography of the sister republic. The fact that they were fully armed, even to carrying big sabers, and marched along the right-of-way of the Narcozi line, makes this story laughable to the well-informed Mexicans, who laugh at the idea of the proceeding in this manner, so sure to land them in trouble.

The Lubins left Douglas in March and traveled north, leaving the Tucson and Phoenix areas in the summer when the desert heat grew too much for them and headed toward the mountains. They finished out their summer and early fall in the northwest part of the state, high in the mountains near Prescott, arriving in July; then, as the snows approached, they headed south toward Nogales.

In the next year, while the Lubins were working in New Mexico, Prescott attracted yet another motion picture company, the Selig Polyscope Company, this one a semi-permanent company that seems to have made more than 50 films in and around the Prescott area between 1913 and 1914 alone. The Seligs were led by actor/producer/director William Duncan. Although he arrived in Prescott with only 15 other players, the company would later consist of upwards of 50 actors and crew, including Tom Mix, Eugenie Besserer, Bessie Eyton, Myrtle and Marshall Stedman, Rex De Rosselli, Charles Clang, "Baby" Lillian Wade, Lillian Hayward, and Frank Weed.

The Seligs arrived in Prescott on 4 January, 1913, and occupied the make-shift studio building that the Lubins had used the past summer, then gradually came to occupy the famous Diamond S Ranch, a semi-working ranch that employed some of the best wranglers in the area. Occasionally they produced two- and three-reel Westerns. Their bread and butter, however, was the split-reel cowboy shoot 'em up, and it's for these films, particularly those starring Tom Mix, that they've earned their place in motion picture history, such as it is. What George Fenin and William Everson say about these Mix films in *The Western* is much what motion picture history seems to have concluded about the company as a whole: "Committed to quantity, he had no time to develop his own screen personality, or to enlarge the scope of the films themselves."

No one would want to argue that the Arizona branch of the Selig company was raising the level of cinematic art, but their prodigious output of Arizona movies was depicting and defining the newly founded state of Arizona for many movie goers living east of the Mississippi more fully than any motion picture company had done before; and its telling that this was probably the case even after the Selig company folded and was absorbed by Fox, for a number of these Arizona Westerns seem to have remained in distribution, some having been re-edited and issued as serials.

Arizona as Depicted by "The Seligs"

Many of the Westerns produced by the company the locals called "the Seligs" seem to me to have been indistinguishable from Westerns being made by other companies in other states during the period. Good guys and bad; swift, violent action; the triumph of right over wrong— many of the Westerns the Seligs produced followed the fundamental patterns of the split-reel and one-reel Westerns of the day: crime, pursuit, retribution. Some of their Westerns departed from such standard fare, though, and it's these I want to briefly consider. To begin with, they departed insofar as they focused on romance of one sort or another. Too, they seem to have employed comedy more fully than most standard Western plotting. They seem to have addressed contemporary social issues—if somewhat obliquely. And they seem to have been more concerned with the East than one might anticipate.

A good example of how these films set up a simple opposition between East and West is to be found in "Bud's Heiress" (1913). At a glance, the storyline seems to have been little more than an excuse to give the horsemen and cattlemen on Selig's Diamond S Ranch the chance to do their stuff before the camera. Two sisters, Ruth (Myrtle Stedman) and Flo (Florence Dye), come from the East to spend their summer vacation on the Diamond S Ranch and are quickly given a taste of cowboy ingenuity. The car they hire to drive them to the ranch from the train station breaks down. Led by Bud Wilson (William Duncan), several of the wranglers on the ranch discover the trouble, lasso the auto, and drag it to the ranch as if it were an errant steer. To welcome the girls, the cowboys put on a show of rodeo stunts, winning their admiration. And by the end of the film, two of the cowboys have won their hearts as well.

This is similar to what occurs in "Taming A Tenderfoot." City-born and bred Willy B. Clever (Lester Cuneo) is sent West by his wealthy father. The film is subtitled "A City Man Has Troubles In The West," and this turns out to be the case. The cocky Willy soon learns that he's no match for the challenges of Arizona ranch life and returns to the East.

It may be a tribute to the popularity of this storyline that it was used in more than one-reelers. In fact, a variation on it was used as well in what was surely the company's biggest, most expensive production during their residence in Arizona—a two-reeler entitled "The Cowboy Millionaire" (1913). The Selig Polyscope Company had first produced the story in 1909. It had been released under the same title shortly before the end of that year, October 21. In this much shorter form, it had proved to be one of the company's biggest successes, and the company intended to capitalize on its popularity in producing this re-make on location. It promised the audience the story they were familiar with along with a large, authentic cast of "Cowboys, Indians, Onlookers, Pedestrians, Policemen, Theater Goers, Etc."

In the first reel, the foreman of the Diamond S. Ranch, Bud Noble (Carl Winterhoff) and his men are in town on a Saturday afternoon. This is their half-day off, and they take advantage of the time and relax by bulldogging steers, busting broncos, and generally causing havoc on the main streets of Prescott. The celebration is brought up short, though, for Bud learns in telegram that he has just inherited an estate of one million dollars from his uncle. The telegram instructs him to come East to Chicago to meet with his uncle's attorney.

In Chicago, Bud seems at first to be entirely out of his element. His cowboys clothes and simple Western manner make him appear to be something of a bumpkin. But he quickly catches the eye of the attorney's stenographer (Winnifred Greenwood), and almost immediately persuades her to marry him.

As the second reel begins, a year has passed. Bud has traded in his spurs for spats and Bud and his wife have become caught up in the momentum of Chicago's high society. They spend their time going to theaters, parties, dances, clubs. But Bud is bored with the social life, and, on an impulse one evening he wires the Diamond S Ranch: "This high-brow life is killing me. Am sending you special train. Bring the whole outfit, horses and all. The town needs excitement. Come and help wake it up."

The film follows Bud and his Arizona cowboys through a series of misadventures. An outing to the theater ends when the cowboys react to the villain with six-guns. A cruise on Bud's yacht brings on an epidemic of sea-sickness. It soon becomes clear that an Arizona cowboy is apt to be as out of place in the big city as a tenderfoot would be on a ranch. Bud decides to send them home; they have no place in Chicago, and, for all intents and purposes, they really have no place in his life any longer.

Such a simple opposition between lifestyles is to be expected, given the era. In the American psyche there were still sharp distinctions between industrialized regions of the country and regions where the economy was premised upon usage of the land. But what interests me most about the films produced by the Seligs is the degree to which they seem to define Arizona in terms of the East. That is, Arizona is less often depicted as a landscape with its own virtues and faults than it's depicted in opposition to an America that exists east of the Mississippi. Indeed, it's as if the films have difficulty conceiving of Arizona without employing Eastern life by means of comparison.

This may help to account for how some of their films handle such matters as Prohibition and suffrage, two of the most controversial issues of the day. Most of us associate Prohibition with the Roaring Twenties and the National Prohibition Act, the Eighteenth Amendment to the Constitution passed in July 1919, better known as the Volstead Act, but Prohibition was a hotly contested issue in this county long before that. Particularly since the turn of the century, Prohibitionists had declared alcohol consumption to be a menace to health and industrial efficiency and had lobbied to have it outlawed. For the first few years of the century they enjoyed most of their victories at the state and local level. By 1913, they were looking toward Prohibition at the national level. The Prohibitionists had gained many political ears and newspapers were carrying stories of Congressional legislation aimed at supplementing and strengthening state and local Prohibition laws that were already on the books, with an eye toward doing still more.

These Prohibitionists were no more ambitious than their sister suffragettes. Building on the groundbreaking work of Susan B. Anthony and Elizabeth Cady Stanton, organizations at both state and local levels were vying to obtain the vote for women. In 1912 and 1913, a number of regional organizations were gaining national attention for their work in this regard, among them the Mississippi Valley Conference and the Southern Women's Conference, and by 1913 a number of these organizations had come together to bring about the Congressional Union—later to become the powerful National Woman's Party.

In other words both Prohibition and suffrage were topical, and the Seligs seem to have employed them fairly regularly, often mixing physical action with broad, slapstick comedy. Like virtually all forms of social change, suffrage and Prohibition were generally identified in these storylines with women, and with Eastern women in particular. Regularly, these women were brought into contact with two-fisted Arizona cowboys, and with predictable results. In "The Suffragette" (1914), for instance, the suffragette of the title, Samantha Roundtree (Myrtle Stedman), comes to town to lecture in the public square on "Votes For Women." When a couple of cowboys, Waggy Bill (William Duncan) and Bill's best friend, Whooping Pete (Lester Cuneo) learn of this they decide to teach the outsider a lesson. They gather a group of local ranch hands, dress up as indians, swoop down upon her lecture, and carry her away to the mountains. There, the cowboys tie her to a tree and begin piling brush at her feet as though they are savages about to burn her at the stake. While this is going on, Bill, their leader, slips away, changes into his own clothes, and comes back on the scene as Samantha's salvation. He runs off her tormentors and releases her, and is surprised to find that she's slightly more grateful than he'd anticipated. She is so grateful, in fact, that when he gets her back to town she refuses to let him go. Having found a real man at last, she puts aside her interest in suffrage and turns her interests toward marriage. The film ends with Bill being spirited out of her clutches by Whooping Pete and other riders just in the nick of time.

This same mentality is to be found in the films dealing with Prohibition. Hard-drinking and drunkenness are to be found in most of the films the Seligs produced. Arizona men are generally depicted as hard-drinking cowboys who, as the cliché would have it, work and fight as hard as they drink. The storylines which introduce Prohibitionists into their midst are generally romantic comedies, with the Prohibitionist being portrayed as a woman from the East. None of this is taken very seriously. The attraction of the cowboy to the woman, and of the woman to the cowboy, as well as the opposition of their values and lifestyles, is often little more than an excuse to begin a series of comic chases and gags. This is true, for instance, in "Matrimonial Deluge" (1914). A middle-aged ranchman, Dan Clark (William Duncan) tries to court a Prohibitionist, Mandy Dawson (Myrtle Stedman). When he shows up drunk at her house one night, she throws a bucket of water on him and tells Dan that she never wants to see him again. To show her she's not the only woman in the world, Dan advertises for a wife in the newspaper. The cowboys on the ranch discover the replies he's received and answer them as a prank. They promise marriage to each applicant and make appointments for Dan to meet all the women at the same time and place. They then let Mandy in on the joke. She's there to watch as the women, believing Dan has made fools of them, chase him into the hills. The film ends as his friends confess that they're behind the confusion; to make amends, each cowboy takes on a woman to be his wife.

Like suffrage and Prohibition and other forms of social change, organized religion is often depicted as an Eastern phenomenon in early Westerns; and here too romance is sometimes an issue. But comedy is rarely employed. The storylines tend toward action/adventure, and there seems to be a curiously serious side to these storylines. Arizona is not simply depicted as being antithetical to the East, it's depicted as an arena in which civilized—read Eastern—men can establish or reaffirm their masculine identity. In "The Cattle Thief's Escape" (October 1, 1913), for instance, Reverend John Morrison (William Duncan), who's been educated for the ministry in the East, comes into cattle country with the intent of spreading the gospel. He falls in love with Rosie Craig (Myrtle Stedman), the daughter of a prominent ranchman. Rosie has any number of suitors among the ranch's working cowboys, and to discourage Morrison from pursuing her they attack him as a group. The minister surprises them by being quite good with his fists, but one of the cowboys, a halfbreed, Peter Becker (Tom Mix) will not relent. Becker makes it looks as if Morrison has rustled cattle, having actually rustled them himself. When Pete's scheme is discovered, the injured parties try to take the law into their own hands. Morrison points out that they have recovered their cattle, and he persuades them to set Becker free.

There's a certain redemptive quality assigned to Arizona in a few of these Selig Westerns. It would go too far to say that the state is held out as post-lapsarian Eden, or even as virgin land in which renewal and self-determination are always possible. But Arizona is occasionally portrayed as a landscape in which a man can break with his past and define himself anew. The storyline of "Howlin' Jones" (1914), subtitled "A Henglishman Becomes Westernized," deals with a British nobleman who flees his family responsibilities in favor of becoming a cowboy on Arizona's Diamond S Ranch. The first few lines of the promotional material sent out by the Seligs to advertise the film surely suggest the spirit of the film itself:

Occasionally the first son of an English family wishes he were second, preferring the gay and easy life to the pressure of a coronet, and many an available candidate for the house of peers has quietly slipped away to some far corner of the earth, to lose himself in preference to entering the world of politics and submit to the irksome conventions of its social obligations. So it came about that Howland-Jones (who is in reality Lord Howland), comes to America, incognito, and slides down *into the great lone land of Arizona, to try out himself, get next to the people, and incidentally a lot of other "varmits," and try to earn his own living at some occupation not quite as laborious as golf or as dangerous as polo, as extravagant as bacharat (sic), or as assinine (sic) as sitting in the club windows, watching the ladies crossing Picadilly, on rainy days* (italics mine). The cowboys underestimate the foreigner; they don't see past his monocle, his knickerbockers, his cane. They decide to have some fun at his expense by putting him aboard a bronco so fierce that it defies all but the finest of riders. Jones survives the test; he triumphs, in fact, then he settles down in Arizona—"for the love of the new land he has found so congenial."

The chance for a civilized man to define himself through his own mettle in "a lone land" seems to have been employed in a number of the Selig one-reelers, albeit with variations. For example, in "Buster's Little Game" (December 17, 1913), a young boy, Buster Holmes (William Duncan), goes East to get a university education. When he returns to the ranch six years later, he both looks and acts like a tenderfoot and he is soon the butt of a number of jokes. Only the ranchman's daughter, Helen Blake (Myrtle Stedman) seems to sense that he has what it takes to find his place among the cowboys. He gets her to promise to marry him when he can ride the most vicious "outlaw" bronco on the place. His successful ride wins him not only her hand, but the respect of the other cowhands and his self-respect as well.

Although the theme of redemption is sometimes used, Arizona is more often depicted less as an alternative to the East than as its antithesis. And when one thinks of the place Arizona occupies in the American psyche today, perhaps that raises as many questions as it answers.

Arizona and the American Psyche

In a way, it's ironic then that much of what early movie-goers saw was Prescott, particularly the older and more infamous sections of the town, for the record suggests that the Seligs rarely went beyond shooting in Prescott or the areas adjacent to it. It's ironic that the state they put before the American public was in many ways circumscribed by their reluctance to travel farther.

Or maybe not. The image of Arizona they put before the American public was circumscribed in yet another more salient way, one that had little to do with topography. To a surprising degree, the state existed on the screen as little more than an ill-defined antithesis to what the East had to offer, and, to a greater degree than we generally assume, that may still be true today. One has only to consider the way its been depicted in motion pictures over the last 50 years or so, or how it promotes itself to the rest of the country even now. Often in the American psyche, Arizona may still be defined more clearly by what it isn't, than by what it is.

Selig Polyscope Films Made in Prescott, Arizona
1913-1914

A Canine Matchmaker: Leave It to a Dog
A Cure for Carelessness: A Touch that Makes the Whole World Kin—11/14/13
A Dip in the Briney: Fun Afloat and Ashore—12/24/13
A Friend in Need: Don't Give Notes—1/23/14 [?]
A Gunfighter's Son: A Colorful Story of the West
A Matrimonial Deluge: One of the Dangers of Advertising
A Pair of Stockings: Dexterous Footwork—5/13/14 [?]
A Rough Ride with Nitroglycerine: A Story of Oil Fields and Explosives
A Ticket to Happiness: Deceit Outdoes Itself—5/19/14
An Embarrassed Bridegroom: Showing that Clothes Are Essential to a Wedding
An Apache's Gratitude: Saving a Good Samaritan
At Cross Purposes: Fussed by a Face—1/2/14 [?]

The Bank's Messenger: A Drama of the West
Bill's Birthday Party: A Comedy of Western Boots and Eastern Slippers
Bud's Heiress: A Story of the Famous Diamond S. Ranch
Buster's Little Game: The Comeback Surprises the Ranchers—12/17/13
By Unseen Hand: A Sun-Glass Mystery—1/7/14
The Capture of 'Bad Brown': The Comedy Drama of a Western Bad Man—
    9/25/13
The Child of the Prairie: How the Waif Found Her Own—11/13/13
"The Conversion of Mr. Anti: A Wise Man Changes His View:—11/6/13 [?]
The Cowboy Millionaire: A Comedy Drama Masterpiece—2/3/13
The Cattle Thief's Escape: A Minute to Get Out of Sight—10/1/13
Cupid in the Cow Camp: Via Mail Order—11/26/13
The Deputy's Sweetheart: The Story of a United States Marshall
The Evil She Did: A Shadow for Declining Days—5/6/14 [?]
The False Friend: Parted by a Forged Letter—9/30/13
The Good Indian: A Saving Service Rewarded
Good Resolutions: How the Victoria Cross Was Redeemed—1/1/14
His Father's Deputy
How Betty Made Good: A Toast Lifted in Water
How It Happened: Reflecting One of the Curiosities of Circumstantial Evidence
Howlin' Jones
The Jealousy of Miguel and Isabella: Tried by Fire and Triumphant
Juggling with Fate: Showing How One Many Plays Many Parts
The Little Sister: The Gold Dust Girl
The Living Wage: An Ever Present Problem—1/6/14
Made a Coward: The Fear of the Desert
Marian, the Holy Terror: Fortuitous Accidents—5/12/14
Marrying Gretchen: Cupid Takes Odd Turns—5/5/14
The Marshall's Capture: A Story of Desert Places
Mother Love Vs. Gold: Outlaws Outwitted—12/23/13
Mounted Officer Flynn: A Heavy Hand Outwits a Precious Pair—11/25/13 [?]
The Policeman and the Baby: How a Little One Terrorized a Big One—9/26/13
    [?]
Range Law: An Excellent Diamond S. Ranch Drama
Religion and Gun Practice: The Way of the West
The Rejected Lover's Luck
The Rustler's Reformation: Fixing a Father-in-Law—12/1/13
Sallie's Sure Shot: A Tale of Devotion and Dynamite
Schoolmarm's Shooting Match: How the Bond of Bachelors Was Cemented—
    11/7/13
The Senorita's Repentance: How Love Played with Life
The Sheriff and the Rustler: Two Men Game to the Last
The Sheriff of Yavapai County: Depicting the Rescuing of a Gambling Victim
    from Himself
The Shotgun Man and the Stage Driver: How a "Hold-Up" Was Avoided
The Suffragette or the Trials of a Tenderfoot

Taming a Tenderfoot: A City Man Has Troubles in the West
The Taming of Texas Pete: Making a Bad Man a Good 'un
Teaching Father a Lesson: Parents Should Have Consideration—5/20/14
Tony and Maloney: Love Laughs at Free Lunches—2/6/14 [?]
Two Sacks of Potatoes: Villains Outwit Themselves—10/29/13
When May Weds December: Look Out for the Affinity—10/28/13
With Eyes So Blue and Tender: Visualized Sentiment of an Old Song—
    12/16/13 [?]
Within the Hour: A Thief Repents Truly—12/3/13 [?]

Witchcraft, Corruption, and Illicit Passion:
Filming in the Big Easy

Mark J. Charney

The March 5 edition of *The Times-Picayune* quotes Robert Lemer, location manager of *The Big Easy* and *Blaze*, as saying, "You can't turn on the television and not see L.A. When we come to New Orleans, we're coming for a specific look." In the past, films made in and about New Orleans, such as *Easy Rider* (1969), *A Streetcar Named Desire* (1951), *Hush, Hush, Sweet Charlotte* (1965), and *Pretty Baby* (1978), use events in the city (Mardi Gras, Jazz Festival, or Superdome playoffs) or the city's southern/plantation heritage to offer general, often exaggerated descriptions about the South or to represent primal urges looming under the surface of controlled southern gentility. In *Hush, Hush, Sweet Charlotte*, for example, director Robert Aldrich presents a generic antebellum South replete with mansions, "Big Daddy's," and hoop skirts, on the surface indistinguishable from most other stereotypical southern plantation settings (*Gone With the Wind, The Beguiled*), whereas films like *Streetcar* and *Pretty Baby* reveal a darker, more honest side of the city, using New Orleans to attempt to represent realistically and/or symbolically the decay of southern values and the decline of southern naivete.

In *Streetcar*, director Elia Kazan films New Orleans from the perspective of a group of New Orleanians who live on Elysian Fields, a street whose name ironically suggests a passage to Heaven, to trace the decline of a woman who clings desperately to the prestige of her southern heritage; in *Pretty Baby*, Louis Malle uses the Columns Hotel on St. Charles Avenue as his central location for a whorehouse which encourages the marriage between an eccentric photographer and a 12-year-old girl. Both films depict a Louisiana of decadent values and perverse compromises. In *Streetcar*, Blanche Du Bois is sacrificed by her sister Stella for a brutal, sensual husband who both repels and attracts her, while the 12-year-old in *Pretty Baby* is sacrificed by a mother who values her own material gain and future security over her daughter's virginity. Louisiana in *Streetcar* and *Pretty Baby* is a southern province that ironically prides itself on its individuality, no matter how

25

destructive, and New Orleans is the city within the state that represents the influence of capitalism and the influx of tourism. The Napoleonic code, particular only to the state of Louisiana, becomes a way for Stanley in *Streetcar* to maneuver his sister-in-law to admit financial and moral defeat, and for the mother in *Pretty Baby* to sell her daughter to a photographer who is obsessed with her beauty and innocence.

In both films, directors Kazan and Malle film New Orleans in tight frames, emphasizing as realistically as possible the civilization that has encroached upon the city, increasing its claustrophobic nature and emphasizing the incestuous relationships of its inhabitants. The sumptuous settings and spacious lawns of films such as *Hush, Hush, Sweet Charlotte* are replaced by tight, cramped quarters where people live on top of one another, making privacy impossible. Neither the Kowalskis in *Streetcar* nor the prostitutes in *Pretty Baby* can have a conversation or a passionate moment without being overheard and misunderstood by those people who surround them. The diffused, low key lighting and the compressed space of each movie force viewers to share the characters' feelings of intrusion and paranoia which they ultimately come to associate with Louisiana and New Orleans. And both directors blame the corruption of the city itself—at least partially—for the tragic fate of their protagonists.

But neither *Streetcar* nor *Pretty Baby* presents a New Orleans as dark or as abstract as that of Dennis Hopper's influential film *Easy Rider*. In *Easy Rider*, Wyatt, also known as Captain America (Peter Fonda), and his sidekick Billy (played by Hopper himself), make Mardi Gras the celebration around which they organize their cross-country trip. Although the film cynically implies that America is a country which ultimately prevents rather than encourages individuality, it is at Mardi Gras in New Orleans where Captain America realizes that the duo's search for freedom will most certainly fail. Mardi Gras, which to both Wyatt and Billy initially indicates the fulfillment of a spiritual journey, eventually symbolizes everything Wyatt has learned to despise—crass materialism, weakened values, and dishonest human interaction.

Wyatt, at least, understands this almost as soon as he enters the city limits of New Orleans. Sitting in the ante-room of a plush, stereotypical house of pleasure in the red light district, much darker than the lush red and green interiors in *Pretty Baby*, he has a momentary flashforward in which he sees his own death. Roaming the streets of the Mardi Gras celebration, Wyatt and Billy encounter garish, pagan-seeming rituals where drinking, drugs, and crowds lead the two protagonists and their prostitutes to a cemetery. Leaning on a mausoleum, the foursome divide hits of acid Wyatt receives earlier from a commune leader who advises him to take the hallucinogen at just the right time. Wyatt, who was reluctant to leave the commune they visited on their way to the city, hopes that the acid trip will bring to New Orleans at least a little of what he and Billy had expected— some sense of spiritual freedom lacking elsewhere in the country. The images that follow, a montage of death, sacrifice, sex, loneliness, and torture, reveals especially to Wyatt that he and Billy have failed in their search for America. As in *Streetcar* and *Pretty Baby*, the New Orleans of *Easy Rider* encourages its characters' decline. Outside of the city, both Wyatt and Billy are shot randomly by Louisianians who object to their long hair and motorbikes, an ironically fitting end for a character such as Wyatt who realizes after Mardi Gras that he and Billy have "blown it." The New Orleans of *Easy Rider* teaches Wyatt that death is preferable to compromise.

Since the mid-1980s, however, films set in New Orleans no longer concentrate on presenting the city realistically or even using the city symbolically to represent the loss of innocence that began with the end of the Civil War. Recent films set in New Orleans have increased the emphasis on the city's "specific look" and decadent atmosphere, often depicting New Orleans more as a hub of metaphorical and supernatural evil than as a city of realistic crime and shifts in southern values. In such films as *No Mercy* (1986), *Zandalee* (1990), *Angel Heart* (1987), and *The Big Easy* (1987), directors Richard Pearce, Sam Pillsbury, Alan Parker, and Jim McBride, respectively, present New Orleans as a city whose charm masks a steamy undergrowth of corruption. This corruption, often inspired by witchcraft or other supernatural forces, encourages characters to uncover primitive forms of evil and elicit the decadent passion lurking beneath the city's celebratory appeal. Ultimately, this discovery enlightens each character's self-awareness, which not only permanently changes his or her perspective, but also ultimately makes the crime inseparable from the city.

Richard Pearce in *No Mercy* offers the most traditional portrayal of New Orleans. The characters he describes are either good or evil, and the conflict he creates does not delve too deeply into the supernatural. Pearce sets New Orleans in sharp contrast to inner-city Chicago where protagonist Eddie Jilette, played by Richard Gere, works as an undercover cop with his best friend Joey. When Joey is brutally stabbed by New Orleans crime lord LoSado (Jeroen Krabbe), Eddie travels to the Big Easy to exact vengeance upon the murderer. The trip from Chicago to New Orleans is more than just a mere 1,500 miles; for Eddie, it is a time warp spiralling him back to the antebellum South. His first vision of "the city that care forgot" is the spacious backyard of Paul Devereux's (William Atherton) stately southern mansion, where the ladies of the family graciously offer Eddie mint juleps. Black servants stand at attention waiting for a Devereux command, and wealthy members of the clan, apparently oblivious to the murderous humidity, play tennis or lounge around the pool and sculptured gardens. In contrast to the muted colors of the Devereux estate, Eddie dresses in black. This immediately labels him as outsider, symbolizing his direct and honest demeanor especially compared to the soft-spoken, double-talking southerners. When Devereux emphasizes to Eddie that "It's different down here. You don't know New Orleans. They don't even talk like us," the viewing audience recognizes that the Chicago undercover cop not only stands against LaSado; he is battling the enigmatic New Orleans way of life. Only by understanding and breaking the rules of the city can Eddie triumph over this adversary.

The New Orleans' police in *No Mercy* are just as corrupt as the wealthy Devereux family or the evil LaSado, but ultimately they are less threatening because of their ape-like behavior and corresponding IQ's. After Eddie pursues clues which lead him through the tattoo parlors and strip joints of Bourbon Street, he finds himself followed by a policeman who attempts to frighten the out-of-town cop with violent redneck language: "This is my town.... You cross me and I'll personally grease the pole that slides you into a tub of shit." Later when Eddie is arrested on false charges, the same policeman warns him about the differences between the North and the South: "I don't know how you do things in Chicago and I don't intend to find out, but it doesn't work down here." Eddie, sensing the none-too-subtle subtext of the cop's insult, replies, "They're still pissed off about losing the war." In spite of the police force's crusade to ban Eddie from New Orleans, his Chicago wiles and Northern street-smart attitude help him to elude the overweight, undereducated Southern law officers. In fact, Eddie has more trouble crossing the river into Algiers than he does escaping the bumbling traps set by the *Smokey and the Bandit* police stooges in New Orleans.

It is in Algiers that Eddie discovers the motive for LaSado's crimes. Having purchased Michel Duval (Kim Basinger) as a young girl from her desperate mother, LaSado keeps her for himself as a sexual slave. Her attempts to escape her captor and "rightful owner by Louisiana law" have inspired a full-scale gang war. Before he ventures to the wild and dangerous suburbs of Algiers where LaSado retains complete control, Eddie listens to warnings from frightened police who rarely venture into the untamed area: "You go asking questions in

Algiers, they'll cut your tongue out and throw it in the river." Pearce creates in Algiers a visual metaphor for the corruption of the entire Southern way of life. He films the area using orange low key lighting to emphasize New Orleans' grimy, threatening nature, and he fills the streets with bars, tattoo parlors, and warehouses converted into centers for covert operations. The Devereux's of New Orleans may conduct business in Algiers, but you would never catch them there; instead, Algiers is the home of the black and lower-class white henchmen— misfits in the Reconstructed South who pay homage to LaSado, the "carpetbagger" controlling their lives.

Handcuffed to Michel through a series of inappropriate, almost screwball comedy turn-of-events, Eddie temporarily escapes from Algiers and the evil LaSado into the swamps of Louisiana, more to initiate him into the stereotypical conventions associated with New Orleans than to further the plot of the movie. During his swamp journey, Eddie learns to catch crabs, eat crawfish, and speak broken Cajun; through his association with Michel, he internalizes enough about the city to battle LaSado and win. The final showdown in a deserted Algiers hotel owes more to the Western genre than to the Southern conventions exploited earlier in the film. After the mandatory love scene between Gere and Basinger, Eddie defeats LaSado's army of New Orleanians and sweeps Michel from one form of servitude into another even less appealing—that of the wife of a Chicago cop. Their eventual union at the end of the film does not reflect a marriage of the old with the new. Rather, their relationship implies that Michel is saved by abandoning the outdated morés of a defeated Southern society to live an advanced and progressive Northern way of life. She finds salvation in the arms of Chicago.

In Sam Pillsbury's *Zandalee*, drug-trafficking crimes and Western showdowns are secondary when compared to crimes of passion. Unlike *No Mercy, Zandalee* tells the story of three Lousianians who need no introduction into the moral and cultural complexities of New Orleans; instead, each character suffers partially because of the influence of New Orleans upon their lives. Set in the heart of the French Quarter, *Zandalee* recounts the tired love triangle of two Baton Rouge buddies, Thierry Martin (Judge Reinhold) and Johnny Paul Gregory Collins III (Nicholas Cage), and the woman who comes between them (Erika Anderson). Thierry, once a poet and professor, has taken over his father's business— Southern Comm—upon the old man's death. The shift in professions, from artist to businessman, has made Thierry a self-professed "paraplegic of the soul," unable to write or make love to his sexually frustrated wife, Zandalee. Although she immediately dislikes Johnny when he rudely introduces himself to her in the kitchen of her and

Thierry's Quarter home, he senses her sexual dissatisfaction, seeing in her the inspiration for creativity without which, he claims, "You are truly unable to go straight up the devil's ass, look him right in the face, and smile." Their inevitable affair is both violent and sacreligious (Zandalee and Johnny have sex in a confessional, after which he screams, "Thank you Father"), and leads ploddingly to the death of both Thierry, who dies from love, and Zandalee, who dies from guilt. At the end of the film, Johnny is left, dead lover in his arms, heading toward the impressive cathedral in the heart of Jackson Square where he had anally raped Zandalee earlier in the film.

Pillsbury rounds out this thin excuse for a plot with lots of local French Quarter scenery, much less violent and supernatural than the fictionalized Algiers, but eccentric and bizarre all the same. Characters speak in soft, gentile, southern accents ("heah" for here; "cayh" for care), and many casually use New Orleans' slang, such as "making groceries" for going shopping. Pillsbury even uses local favorites such as Becky Allen in bit roles to give the city what he considers an honest flavor. As a transitional device, Pillsbury films Zandalee running through the Quarter where she encounters New Orleans' prisoners who collect trash, odd mimes in white face and full clown regalia, and punks suspiciously resembling characters from *Sid and Nancy*. With the exception of one scene, she surprisingly never runs into what the Quarter is actually full of—tourists. The dress shop in which Zandalee works is simply a cinematic excuse to trade quips about the city with her gay crossdressing friend, who she consistently tries to suit in a dress appropriate for the Sweetheart's Ball. The quips range from playful statements attacking the city ("You're getting seriously lethargic even for New Orleans") to judgments made about New Orleans' relationship to the world at large (Zandalee: "The quarter's a pit." Gay friend: "It's not just the quarter, honey; it's everywhere").

But although *Zandalee* contains no references to witches, spiritual possession, or supernatural murders, the sexual relationship between the title character and Johnny Collins serves as a metaphor for the corruption of the city itself. One of the first places they go together, for example, is a bar which features oral sex shows on stage and a clientele from *Deep Throat*. Bums on the street mumble New Orleanisms— "Where y'at darlin'? Ya got something for me?—while prisoners from the local jail spout philosophy as Zandalee runs by —"Nothin's as good as they say it is darlin'." After a night in which Zandalee bar hops in the Quarter, she returns to Thierry pleading to experiment with anal intercourse, justifying her behavior by what she just seen: "They have strange and wonderful secrets on Bourbon Street."

The short-lived and destructive relationship between Zandalee and Johnny parallels what Pillsbury sees as life in New Orleans. Their lovemaking—and that is the extent of their development as lovers—is a series of sado-masochistic grunts and grinds. Zandalee is pulled into alleys, onto washing machines, and within confessionals, while Johnny mumbles, "We're gonna fuck like animals in the alter of the primal" and "Stick my dumb coonass prick inside of you with your husband in the next room." All three characters revert to primal stages when the film builds towards its climax in the Bayou. Thierry shoots a gun indiscriminately while yelling in forced Cajun dialogue, "You come to the back woods, the back woods they come to you"; Zandalee admits, "I guess I'm just still white trash"; and Johnny drinks Dixie beer and slaps Zandalee in an attempt to convince her that she loves him. The New Orleans of *Zandalee* presents a thin veneer of civilization—couples at least go inside or into dark alleys to have anal intercourse: the Bayous of Louisiana strip the three of their manners, leaving them alone to make love and shoot guns anywhere.

At the end of the film, when Zandalee runs in front of the gun intended for Johnny (a drug lord we've never met yells, "You got to make accounts payable man"), audiences realize that she chooses death over the New Orleans way of life. Because Johnny's debts are never a major plot point in the film, the shooting at the end implies corruption even worse that the evil LoSado in *No Mercy*. LoSado ultimately represents a specific evil, a character whose death signals the end of one strain of corruption. Audiences have no idea who kills Zandalee, which suggests that indiscriminate violence may strike randomly at any time on any street corner in the French Quarter. Ultimately, then, the city that helped to destroy her husband and her own commitment to morality is less preferable to Zandalee than dying. As her gay friend approaches Zandalee's limp body in tears and a spiffy silk gown complete with a feather boa, Pillsbury can expect audiences to feel no sense of regret. Once free of New Orleans, Zandalee can face her spiritual maker. It is Johnny, earth bound and tied to a city both corrupt and corrupting, that audiences really pity.

In Alan Parker's *Angel Heart*, Northern private detective Harold R. Angel (Mickey Rourke), travels to New Orleans, this time from the alien environment of New York. Like Eddie in *No Mercy*, Angel must learn the New Orleans way of life that Zandalee and her men know so well before he is able to locate for the mysterious Louis Cyphre (Robert de Niro) the elusive singer Johnny Favorite. His search leads him to the stately Devereux-like home of Margaret Cruzmark (alias Madame Zora, played by Charlotte Rampling), a New Orleans' native whose father exerts as much influence in New Orleans as LaSado does in Algiers. Margaret's previous romantic ties with Favorite and her affection for the supernatural lead Angel into a maze of voodoo parlors and satanic rituals. The more Angel learns about New Orleans, the more he longs to return to the security of New York: "I ain't up on all this voodoo shit. I'm from Brooklyn."

Many of the shots depicting New Orleans in *Angel Heart* are interchangeable with those in *No Mercy* and *Zandalee*—darkly-lit streets, tap-dancing black street performers, steamy bars, the occasional streetcar, and the fat, xenophobic cops. The exchanges between Louisiana policemen and Angel especially seem lifted from Pearce's film. When Angel begins to uncover a series of ritualistic murders inexplicably tied to Johnny Favorite, an obese New Orleans cop announces, "You play jump rope with the Louisiana law and I'll stuff your big city smarts right up your ass." Another warns him of the potential danger of associating too closely with blacks: "Angel, we don't mix with jigaboos. The colored folks keep to themselves." Angel replies, "Well, hey, I ain't from down here." Prejudiced, violent, and cowardly, the New Orleans policeman is so obsessed with genitalia and bathroom humor that he has little time for actual detective work, even if such work wouldn't harm his own vested interest in organized crime.

Unlike *No Mercy* and *Zandalee*, *Angel Heart* is full of complex references to the supernatural, from the mysterious shots of ceiling and window fans, bloody walls, and black-hooded figures to the dreams and hallucinations Angel experiences once in the South. Angel's quest leads him from the parlors of Margaret Cruzmark to the backroads of Voodoo Mambo Queen Evageline Proudfoot. Favorite's daughter Epiphany (Lisa Bonet) participates in bloody chicken rituals, and even a local musician, Toots, understands that a chicken foot signals impending danger. Only Angel, the outsider, cannot translate the voodoo codes that are immediately discernible to the general New Orleans natives. Each of the deaths in the film indicates an association with the grotesque and supernatural: a syringe jabbed through Dr. Fowler's eye; genitalia stuffed in Toots' mouth; a heart ripped from Margaret's breast; her father boiled in his own pot of gumbo. The real suspense in the film lies not with Angel's eventual discovery that he is Johnny Favorite, a singer who made an agreement with the devil to achieve his popularity, but with the detective's efforts to decipher an entire language of voodoo ritual. The discovery of his true identity is only possible when Angel first uncovers the corruption that lurks beneath the antebellum surface of Southern gentility. Parker's vision of the South is ultimately more threatening than Pearce's or Pillsbury's; the New Orleans of *Angel Heart* has made a pact with the devil himself.

In Jim McBride's *The Big Easy* the protagonist is not the outsider, like Eddie Jilette or Harry Angel, but insider Remy McSwain, one of the youngest detectives ever to make lieutenant on the New Orleans police force. The outsider in *The Big Easy* is Anne Osborne (Ellen Barkin), the assistant District Attorney, whose association with the New Orleans lieutenant will not only initiate her into an entirely different way of life, but will also banish her self-professed sexual inadequacies. McBride uses the romance between Remy and Anne to perpetuate the city's lawless atmosphere and celebratory code of behavior. When Anne fails to recognize that the term "wiseguy" means member of the mafia, for example, Remy asks smugly, "You're not from here, are you?" When she hesitates to dance at Tipitina's, Remy chidingly reminds her, "This is New Orleans—the Big Easy. Down here dancing is a way of life." When Anne expresses displeasure at the extra "benefits" Remy receives from New Orleans businessmen for his increased police protection, Remy replies confidently, "I'm not defending anything. This is New Orleans dahlin'. Folks have a certain way of doing things down here." Anne's initiation into the New Orleans way of "doing things" introduces her to Dixie beer, gumbo, crawfish etoufee, and cajun dancing, but beneath the surface of the city lies a complex network of police corruption—almost a feudal caste system where those who want police protection must pay for it.

McBride organizes the conflict in *The Big Easy* around this police corruption, and he uses Remy as the protagonist who learns from outsider Anne that falling into the New Orleans way of life ultimately undermines the ethics of the police profession. Quaid plays Remy with a cocky assurance that wins both Anne and the audience's affection at first. His immediate sexual conquest over the once frigid Anne supports Remy's assertion that "New Orleans folks have a certain way of doing things down here," and his playful attitude with fellow policemen makes his job seem more like a hobby than a profession. Through Remy, McBride depicts New Orleans as a city of family values and celebrations, from the "Where y'ats" exchanged casually on the streets to the Cajun music played on the McSwains' front porch. But Remy's easy charm and slick demeanor mask a lack of moral fibre that symbolizes the entire city. Although the young detective gracefully frees himself from illegal compromise and unethical practices through the redemptive quality of Anne's love, the rest of the city remains corrupt and self-destructive.

The plot of *The Big Easy* traces Remy's search to uncover the criminals who are responsible for a series of random murders around the city. Seemingly associated with the voodoo rituals of Daddy Mention (one of the victim's hearts is ripped from his chest, supposedly to give the murderer his strength) and the mafia connections of the Tandino family, the deaths in *The Big Easy* indicate both criminal and supernatural elements. Remy's rocky relationship with Anne illustrates the police force's tendency to accept under-the-counter payment (the "Widows and Orphans" fund) in exchange for the protection already promised by law. As Remy begins to develop a moral conscience, he and Anne discover that the police, on the surface a bunch of "good ole' boys," are connected to the systematic murders. Ultimately he finds that members of his own force have been committing the crimes and justifying them by implicating criminals and voodoo masters they feel would be better off dead. The police plan to abscond with the final shipment of heroin, thus setting them up for life. Remy, of course, stops the corrupt policemen, losing his best friend on the force in the process, backs out of the "Widows and Orphans" fund, and marries Anne at the end of the film.

McBride's condemnation of the corruption lurking beneath the easy atmosphere of New Orleans is in many ways a harsher indictment of the city than that in *No Mercy, Zandalee,* and *Angel Heart. No Mercy* ultimately deteriorates into a western battle between good and evil, *Zandalee* suggests that city influence can corrupt an relationship initially based on love, and *Angel Heart* borrows from the horror genre to bind together the characters of Harry Angel and Johnny Favorite. *The Big Easy* manages to capture some of New Orleans on film, from dinner at Mosca's to the Blaine-Kern Mardi Gras Warehouse on the Mississippi River. But like *No Mercy, Zandalee,* and *Angel Heart, The Big Easy* depicts a New Orleans in which the rules differ from those in other cities—for the worse. In spite of the fact that McBride allows Anne to influence Remy, she confronts her potential as a woman in the arms of a lieutenant whose every step and Cajun slur embodies the city. Remy may have regained his moral conscience, but Anne, because of the New Orleans influence, regains her ability to appreciate life. On the surface, the New Orleans in *The Big Easy* may seem more realistic and appealing than the southern caste system in *No Mercy,* the predictable love triangle in *Zandalee,* and the satanic supernatural influences in *Angel Heart,* but it has become just as mythic and shallow.

Tracing the presentation of New Orleans in just a few of the films made about and within the city reveals that contemporary filmmakers have moved away from using the city's southern roots to describe New Orleanians as possessing genteel accents associated with the deep South, and to emphasize garish plantation style mansions which house corruption and barely control the primal urges of the occupants within. Depth of character and solid plot development of films such as *A*

Streetcar Named Desire, Pretty Baby, and *Easy Rider* are sacrificed for sensationalism associated with supernatural, violent aspects of the city. Unlike recent films that playfully attack Los Angeles or New York, while at the same time ultimately romanticizing the cities (*L.A. Story, Grand Canyon,* and all Woody Allen movies), movies about New Orleans falsely depict the city almost as a character which both initiates and perpetuates sexual, violent, and supernatural evil, a city where Mardi Gras occurs year 'round and corruption lurks inside every shucked oyster.

Filmography

Year	Film	Director
1938	*The Buccaneer*	Cecil B. DeMille
1938	*Jezebel*	William Wyler
1941	*The Flame of New Orleans*	Rene Clair
1946	*New Orleans*	Arthur Lubin
1950	*Panic in the Street*	Elia Kazan
1951	*A Streetcar Named Desire*	Elia Kazan
1957	*Long Hot Summer*	Martin Ritt
1958	*Bucanneer*	Anthony Quinn
1958	*King Creole*	Michael Curtiz
1958	*Mardi Gras*	Edmund Goulding
1964	*Hush, Hush, Sweet Charlotte*	Robert Aldrich
1965	*This Property is Condemned*	Sydney Pollack
1965	*The Cincinnati Kid*	Norman Jewison
1966	*Hotel*	Richard Quine
1966	*Hurry Sundown*	Otto Preminger
1968	*Number One*	Tom Gries
1969	*Easy Rider*	Dennis Hopper
1971	*Five Easy Pieces*	Bob Rafelson
1971	*Longstreet*	Joseph Sargent
1972	*Live and Let Die*	Guy Hamilton
1973	*Gator Bait*	Ferd and Beverly C. Sebastian
1974	*Hard Times*	Walter Hill
1974	*Obsession*	Brian de Palma
1975	*Going Home*	Herbert B. Leonard
1976	*French Quarter*	Dennis Kane
1978	*Pretty Baby*	Louis Malle
1978	*Murder at Mardi Gras*	Ken Annakin
1979	*Hardcase*	John Moxey

1980	*Concrete Cowboys*	Burt Kennedy
1981	*Cat People*	Paul Schrader
1983	*Hobson's Choice*	Gilbert Cates
1983	*Tightrope*	Richard Tuggle
1985	*Down by Law*	Jim Jarmusch
1986	*No Mercy*	Richard Pearce
1986	*Shy People*	Andrei Konchalowsky
1986	*Sister, Sister*	Bill Condon
1987	*The Unholy*	Camilo Vila
1987	*Angel Heart*	Alan Parker
1987	*The Big Easy*	Jim McBride
1988	*Fletch Lives*	Michael Ritchie
1988	*Johnny Handsome*	Walter Hill
1988	*Heart of Dixie*	Martin Davidson
1989	*Blaze*	Ron Shelton
1989	*Miller's Crossing*	Joel Coen
1989	*Traveling Man*	Fred Baron
1989	*Tune In Tomorrow*	Jon Amiel
1990	*Zandalee*	Sam Pillsbury
1990	*Hot Steps*	Gerry Lively
1990	*Black Lake, Dry Ice*	Chip Ellinger
1990	*This Gun for Hire*	Lou Antonio
1990	*The Barry Seal Story*	Roger Young
1990	*The Awakening*	Mary Lambert
1991	*JFK*	Oliver Stone
1991	*Storyville*	Mark Frost
1991	*Love and Curses, New Orleans Style*	Gerald McRaney
1991	*Netherworld*	David Schmoeller
1991	*The Gate to Nothing*	Massinno Lantini
1991	*A Woman's Secret*	Aristide Massaccesi
1991	*Delta Heat*	Michael Fischa
1992	*Passion Fish*	John Sayles

International Borders in American Films:
Penetration, Protection, and Perspective
Carlos E. Cortés

In the final sequence of Jean Renoir's World War I classic, *Grand Illusion* (1937), two French army lieutenants (Marechal and Rosenthal) attempt to reach sanctuary in Switzerland after escaping from a German military prison. As they plod slowly and agonizingly across the vast, open, snow-covered valley, under fire from a German patrol, they engage in the following subtitled dialogue.

Marechal: "Are you sure that over there is Switzerland?"
Rosenthal: "No doubt."
Marechal: "It looks the same."
Rosenthal: "What do you want? The border is man-made and invisible...nature doesn't give a damn."

Suddenly the German patrol stops firing. Its commander has judged that the two Frenchmen have crossed that mysterious, unseen line. The international border has brought them safety.

In this dramatic concluding sequence, the border between Germany and Switzerland becomes the main, though invisible, character. Neither the French escapees nor the pursuing German soldiers can see the border, but they all recognize it. They cannot touch it, but they honor and respond to it. The border—simultaneously a goal to be reached, an obstacle to be penetrated, and ultimately a protection to be cherished— dominates the film's conclusion.

The international border—including the idea of the border—has played a vital role in motion pictures since their inception. This has certainly been true of American movies, which have continuously used the border as a primary theme, compelling context, or even active character. In some cases the border itself plays a central role. In other cases the *idea* of the border informs the film or challenges the characters.

Because of the unique nature of international borders, filmmakers have found it convenient to draw upon them for a variety of film functions. The border has served as a divider between nations, which protagonists seek to penetrate. It has served as a form of protection, sometimes illusory, between individual antagonists and antagonistic nations. And it has served as a locus of perspective, whose presence is viewed in differing and often conflicting manners by individuals, groups and nations.

In titles of American movies, "border" has consistently meant the U.S.-Mexican border. *Bordertown* (1935), *Border Incident* (1949), *Borderline* (1950), *Border River* (1954), *Borderline* (1980) and *The Border* (1982) all deal with Mexico. Most of these films involve smuggling—of people or drugs. All carry the verbal weight of that particular border as a problem or contributor to problems (Maciel 1990). Implicitly and sometimes explicitly, that border has served as a movie-hyped threat to U.S. society—a funnel for criminals, refugees and undocumented immigrants rather than as a political protector of a mythological American way of life.

Other movie titles have used place names as metaphors for an international border, thereby preparing audiences for some kind of border experience. *The Tijuana Story* (1957) pulls potential American audiences' eyes toward the south to the U.S.-Mexican border, lets viewers know that they are in for a border tale, and suggests that sordidness will be involved. *Niagara* (1953) turns audiences' visions toward the north to the U.S.-Canadian border, but the title cloaks the film in an air of mystery, leaving prospective viewers unsure whether they are in for a romance, a comedy, or a melodrama, but suggesting that the relentless, pounding, nation-separating falls either will play a role or will provide a pulsating backdrop to the movie's events. *El Norte* (1983) also keeps audiences' eyes focused to the north, but moves their bodies south into Latin America, so that they are viewing the United States from below the border. In this case the film impels viewers to experience the film through the eyes of two Guatemalan refugees, whose goal is to reach *el norte* (*norteamérica*—the United States). To do so, they must cross two international borders, first from Guatemala into Mexico, later from Mexico into the United States, as well as deal with numerous inter-cultural borders.

This essay will address two recurring questions concerning the use of international borders in American motion pictures. First, how have American films used borders in their writing and rewriting of U.S. history? Second, how have borders been employed in American movies to examine personal angsts, intercultural relations and international conflicts?

Borders in the Movie Rewriting of U.S. History

Nations have struggled over borders. In some cases this has meant struggles over the location of the border. In other cases it has involved the creation of borders by newly-independent nations or the elimination of borders of nations being eradicated. Finally, it has meant attempting to keep people within borders. Three themes in U.S. history have achieved particular film longevity in engaging this dimension of international borders: the Civil War; the Texas Revolution; and the Indian Wars.

The issue of the border permeated the Civil War itself. Could the Confederacy create and maintain an international border between itself and the United States, from which it had seceded, or would the Union defeat the Confederacy, preserve a single nation, and turn that international border into a transitory phenomenon? This border question has provided a subtext for all Civil War movies from *The Birth of a Nation* to *Gone with the Wind*, from *The General* to *Glory*.

But some Civil War movies have used the border in an even more instrumental role. Two films, *The Raid* (1954) and *The Horse Soldiers* (1959), illustrate that role. Both involve the sending of troops across the border into enemy territory not to gain land, but to create military and psychological havoc by proving that the border could be penetrated and by demonstrating that the border provided no security for civilians. Moreover, the two movies offer alternative perspectives, providing Union and Confederate views of borders.

In *The Horse Soldiers*, a Union cavalry unit rides south into Confederate territory, creates the requisite amount of havoc, and then escapes back behind Union lines. In *The Raid*, a comparable Confederate attack occurs. The twist, however, is that the Confederates do not move north across the Union border, but penetrate the border south from Canada, ransacking a Union town before escaping back into Canada, where the border again provides safe harbor. Two borders, two perspectives, two forays, two territorial penetrations, two exposures of political borders as illusory protection, and two escapes back across an international line.

The 1836 Texas Revolution, too, was fought in part over a border issue fostered by an independence movement. The issue—would Texas, then part of the Mexican province of Coahuila, succeed in winning its independence and create a border between itself and Mexico? Or would Mexico be able to subdue the rebellion and solidify its national borders?

Movies on the Texas Revolution have differed dramatically from those on the Civil War. Unlike Civil War movies, which have presented both Union and Confederate perspectives, American movies on the

Texas Revolution have predictably focused almost exclusively on Anglo-Texan perspectives. And while Civil War movies have often dealt with the border itself, including giving audiences the vicarious thrills of riding with Union and Confederate raiders in their border-penetrating forays, Texas Revolution movies have usually focused on a metaphorical international border, the Mexican mission known as The Alamo.

The Battle of The Alamo was fought in San Antonio in March 1836, between Texas revolutionaries within the mission and Mexican troops outside of the mission, with the Mexicans emerging victorious. One month later, at the Battle of San Jacinto, the Texans turned the tables, defeating the Mexican army and extracting a treaty recognizing Texas independence (although the treaty was rejected by the Mexican Congress). Yet the Alamo walls in a losing fight, not the San Jacinto plains in a winning battle, have survived as the metaphor for this border struggle.

From *The Immortal Alamo* (1911) and *The Martyrs of the Alamo* (1915) to *The Last Command* (1955) and *The Alamo* (1960), Texans (always portrayed as brave, skillful, and honorable) vainly defend their walls/borders against Mexican troops (usually portrayed as cowardly, incompetent, and sadistic), who ultimately penetrate the walls of that metaphorical border. Not until 1969, in *Viva Max!*, did American movies present an alternate, fictionalized perspective. In that film, a bumbling present-day Mexican general, acting on his own, secretly crosses the U.S.-Mexican border and non-violently recaptures The Alamo in a comedy of errors, although he ultimately has to return it to the United States.

Which brings us to American Indians (Native Americans). More than 400 treaties between different American Indian civilizations and the U.S. government have established myriad reservations (officially, "internal nations") within the United States. This, of course, has involved the creation of borders. And as with almost all borders, this has meant disputes. (For example, the Navajos and Hopis are currently contesting the border between their neighboring nations/reservations.)

Over the course of American movies' long love-hate relationship with American Indians and the process of U.S. westward expansion, filmmakers have often engaged border issues. In such army-and-Indian or cowboy-and-Indian movies, borders have embodied multiple meanings. Principally they have stood for escape from imprisonment, the return to Indian roots, Indian reincarceration, intercultural violation, and occasionally interracial union.

Movie Indians have often U.S. government-imposed borders as a type of prison to be challenged. In *Apache* (1954), the brave, resourceful

Masai manages to escape from a train carrying him to imprisonment behind a Florida reservation's borders and wages a one-man war for himself, his wife and his child-to-be in order to establish personal turf, on which he grows a cornfield as his own family border. In *Ulzana's Raid* (1972), Apaches again rebel against the reservation border, breaking out from their confines. Even Canadian movie Indians flee from reservation borders, such as the Cree in *Pony Soldier* (1952).

But escape from imposed borders has not always been enough. Return to their own historical-cultural borders sometimes became the ultimate goal of movie Indians. For example, that is what drives the Indians of John Ford's *Cheyenne Autumn* (1964). Relocated to a distant place by the federal government, a Cheyenne band struggles against brutal weather, hostile whites, and the pursuing army in a courageous attempt to return to its homeland, 1,500 miles away. Using *Cheyenne Autumn* as a kind of *mea culpa* for all of the Indians he had slaughtered throughout the years of his westerns, a latter-day Ford lamented in an interview that he had:

...killed more Indians than Custer, Beecher, and Chivington put together...Let's face it, we've treated them badly—it's a blot on our shield; we've cheated and robbed, killed, murdered, massacred and everything else, but they kill one white man, and God, out come the troops. (Sinclair)

If movie Indians want to escape from U.S.-imposed borders and return to their own historical borders, then U.S. troops must put them back in their place. So rounding them up (or wiping them out in the process) becomes a third border-related Indian movie theme. In *Apache*, *Ulzana's Raid*, *Cheyenne Autumn*, and myriad other westerns, the army or some vigilante group sets out to restore order—meaning forcing Indians back behind the official government borders. Usually the military succeeds: Masai is tracked down in *Apache*, although the film ends without showing what the army will do with him; not so in *Ulzana's Raid*, as the army patrol wipes out the rebellious Apaches. (Interestingly, Burt Lancaster plays both the stalwart Masai in *Apache* and Apache-chasing army scout McIntosh in *Ulzana's Raid*). Sometimes the Indians appear to triumph (at least during the time frame of a particular film). For example, in *Cheyenne Autumn*, although the army corners the survivors of the trek just 300 miles from their goal, the Secretary of the Interior tells them that he will plead their case and support their desire to return to their homeland. The Indian victory is more explicit in *Fort Apache* (1948), when the Apaches wipe out a pursuing army unit (although a tacked-on postscript indicates that the unit's heroic "last stand" inspired other army troops to triumph in the Indian wars).

Some movie Indians seek external international borders rather than internal homeland borders as a refuge. In *Winterhawk* (1976), when two of his braves are killed in a white ambush, a Blackfoot leader retaliates by abducting a young white sister and brother and heading for the safety of the Canadian border. After various clashes with the pursuing white posse, Winterhawk voluntarily returns the two young people to his pursuers. Then, in a double border crossing, Winterhawk heads into Canada, while Clayanna, the young white girl who has fallen in love with him, decides to remain with Winterhawk, thereby simultaneously breaching racial and cultural borders (Cortés 1991).

But even borders, particularly reservation borders, do not always provide absolute Indian refuge from marauders, including the U.S army. Particularly in movies of the 1960s and 1970s, when the old west often served as a metaphor for the war in Vietnam (particularly the My Lai massacre), the army does the penetrating of borders and the slaughtering of innocents. In such movies as *Little Big Man* (1970) and *Soldier Blue* (1970), Indians find that borders, even U.S. government-imposed and guaranteed borders, provide no more safety for Indians than they did for Confederate civilians in *The Horse Soldiers* or Union civilians in *The Raid.*

Hollywood's revisiting of U.S. history, then, has been replete with international borderiana. As lines to be defended, to be penetrated, or to be eradicated, borders have played a continuous role. As real or illusory walls, borders have framed dramatic conflict. As context or character, as goal or protection, borders have served a key role in Hollywood's exploration of the formation and reformation of our nation.

Borders as Symbols of Personal and Intercultural Conflict

In *Paths of Glory* (1957), a French army unit is sent on a suicide attack against an impregnable German stronghold, the Ant Hill, during World War I. To succeed, they must penetrate the temporary German battlefield border.

In *The Professionals* (1966), a wealthy American railroad magnate hires four American soldiers of fortune to "rescue" his wife, who presumably has been abducted by one of Pancho Villa's commanders during the Mexican Revolution. To succeed, they must penetrate the U.S.-Mexican border.

In *Hold Back the Dawn* (1941), World War II European refugees congregate in the Mexican border city of Tijuana, waiting and hoping for the opportunity to enter the United States. To succeed, they must obtain permission to penetrate the border.

In *Julia* (1977), author Lillian Hellman travels through pre-World War II Nazi Germany in order to smuggle money to an underground organization that is trying to purchase freedom for Jews trapped in Germany. To succeed, she must penetrate two borders—both into and out of Germany.

In the autobiographical *Midnight Express* (1979), American Billy Hayes, imprisoned in Turkey for drug smuggling, seeks to escape both from prison and from the country. To succeed, he must penetrate two borders—the prison walls and then the Turkish frontier.

In *The Sea Chase* (1955), German Captain Karl Ehrlich seeks to sail his clunky old freighter from Sydney, Australia, back to his homeland when World War II breaks out. To succeed, he must penetrate the British naval blockade to reach his nation's border.

These six films exemplify the many ways that the border has functioned as a critical element in American film. Moviemakers have used international borders as rich, tension-laden locales for examining personal angsts, intercultural relations, and international conflicts. To raise and dramatize these issues, makers of these six films adopted a variety of strategies for drawing upon international borders to establish a context of confusion and indeterminacy or to suggest the dialectical interplay of fear and security. As a symbol of restraining oppression or as a sought-after goal of prospective freedom, the international border has served as a filmic convenience for tapping primordial viewer reactions to externally-imposed, particularly governmentally-imposed, limits.

In its examination of war, *Paths of Glory* treats the border as a transitory, undefinable divider of nations, personified by two armies facing each other across a huge, meaningless expanse of land. That borderland consists of three temporary territories, each with its mini-boundaries of trenches and barbed wire: French-occupied territory; German-occupied territory; and the separating "no-man's-land," which becomes alien and dangerous for soldiers of either side. When French soldiers are ordered to attack the heavily fortified Ant Hill, they realize that they will have difficulty even getting out of French territory, have little chance of crossing no-man's-land, and have almost no hope of penetrating German territory. Worse yet, each step forward, each yard gained, and each barbed wire obstruction crossed mean less chance that the French soldiers will be able to make it back to the relative safety of their own trenches. Too much success—penetration—increases the likelihood of the ultimate failure, death.

The border in *Paths of Glory* serves a dual function. In military terms, the soldiers' assigned goal is to cross the unofficial military border to capture a German position. In personal terms, their true goal is not victory but survival, to return across that border with their lives.

The border in *The Professionals* is equally murky, but for other reasons than in *Paths of Glory*. Not a transitory military frontier, but one carved by politicians, it separates the united States and Mexico. Yet in visual movie terms, the politically-etched official desert border stands more open and traversable than *Path's* militarily-etched, trench-marked unofficial battlefield border.

The desert border also carries with it a different set of challenges: once the professionals have penetrated the border and reached interior Mexico, how can the "fab four" rescue team carry out its mission, capture the girl, and get back to the border with her lover, Captain Jesús Raza, in pursuit? No physical barriers will stand in their way once they have arrived at the border. Reaching the border will be their dilemma. The almost-undetectable border serves as an unseen goal of safety in their flight.

In *The Professionals*, the open, desolate, unmarked, unpoliced U.S.-Mexican border of the 1910s suggests the miscibility of the two nations' histories and destinies, as well as its easy penetrability (whether by gunmen or immigrants). In contrast, in *Hold Back the Dawn*, the closed, crowded, vividly marked, firmly guarded border of the 1940s dramatizes the increasing significance of that political border as a national and historical divider.

Dawn's European refugees confront the same U.S.-Mexican international border that faced *The Professionals*, but with a quarter-century temporal chasm and a rural-urban physical chasm. The refugees have already reached the border by getting to Tijuana. They can see it and touch it, but without U.S. government approval they cannot cross it. How can they take that last step, legal entry into the United States? The physical presence of the border simultaneously invites and oppresses, raises both hopes and frustrations. Constant shots of the border checkpoint are juxtaposed with the refugees' increasingly desperate conversations.

This sets the stage for the scheme of charming Romanian gigolo Georges Iscovescu, who romances Emmy Burton, an unsuspecting American teacher, into marrying him during her visit to Tijuana. In this way he can gain legal admission into the United States. But before he manages to enter the country, the scheme is exposed. However, the now love-smitten Georges steals a car, crashes through the border gate, and eludes police to reach Emmy, who has been hospitalized because of an automobile accident. Although Georges is captured and deported to Mexico, the movie ends happily with a final border crossing, this time a legal one by the reunited lovers.

Lillian Hellman, too, reaches an international border in *Julia*. Clearly and even more ominously marked than the one facing *Dawn*'s refugees at Tijuana, the border crossing from France into Nazi Germany carries overtones of dread. Questioned by suspicious German border guards, Hellman must confront her own personal border—her internal frontier of fear. Should she return to the train that will take her across the border and plunge her deep into the heart of Nazism, or should she read the German border guard's mood as a last-chance warning to turn back?

Resisting her border-heightened terror, Hellman proceeds on to Berlin, knowing that she will never again be free from fear until she crosses the next border, the one *out* of Germany. After a tension-filled stop in Berlin, where she surreptitiously delivers money to her friend, Julia, Hellman reboards the train. But not until she passes the border sign, this time indicating her exit from Germany, can she (and audiences) breathe easily.

No such signs come into view for *Midnight Express*' Billy Hayes in contemporary Turkey. With hashish strapped to his body, Billy goes to the Istanbul airport, where he receives an exit stamp on his passport, the normal sign that the international border has been successfully crossed, and climbs on the tram carrying him to the normality of airplane boarding. But this is October 1970, and times are not normal. Fearing terrorism, Turkish officials are body-checking passengers for bombs just before they board the plane. The international frontier has suddenly vaulted from the airport terminal to the airplane stairs, and Billy fails in this second attempted border crossing, as the body-check reveals his stash of drugs.

Sentenced to 30 years imprisonment, Billy now faces a dual border—the prison walls that obstruct him from escape and the political borders that obstruct him from true freedom. The movie never shows the international border, but the border as quest remains implanted in Billy's mind and in the minds of viewers. It is *the* goal. The movie ends in 1975 with Billy breaking out of prison, not crossing the international frontier. But the prison walls symbolize the political border, and the final titles confirm that Billy did, in fact, succeed in escaping from Turkey.

In contrast, *The Sea Chase*'s Captain Karl Ehrlich fails to bring his freighter, the Ergenstrasse, back to Germany. Docked in Sydney, Australia, at the time of Hitler's invasion of Poland and with Ehrlich realizing that the British will probably impound his ship, he guides the ship out of the harbor under cover of dense fog. An outspoken opponent of Nazism, Ehrlich had been demoted from cruiser commander because of his criticism of Hitler's regime. Yet the proud, nationalistic Ehrlich dedicates himself to taking his ship "home" to his country's sacred borders.

Once at sea, the Ergenstrasse becomes a target of the chagrined British navy. With daring and imagination, Ehrlich evades his pursuers and manages to reach the North Sea. However, within a figurative arm's reach of his goal, the German border, Ehrlich is cornered and the Ergenstrasse is sunk. As in the case of *Midnight Express*, a postscript—this time the narration of the pursuing British commander—suggests that Ehrlich probably survived the sinking and may have personally reached his border goal.

Whether explicit or implicit, clear or fuzzy, marked or unmarked, official or unofficial, guarded or unguarded, real or metaphorical, threatening or tempting, international borders have provided gripping locales for American movies. Fimmakers have used borders to address questions, generate tensions, explore personal angsts, and examine conflicts. Moreover, by manipulating borders—and audiences' coded responses to borders—filmmakers have been able to draw viewers into the human dilemmas of movie characters confronting the various meanings of borders.

The Conflicted Border Revisited

Of all international borders employed by American moviemakers, the U.S.-Mexican border remains the reigning screen symbol of "borderness."

For Hollywood, Mexico has been an ideal movie arena—a geographically contiguous, perceptually mysterious, and often turbulent nation with a physically identifiable, linguistically challenging, and culturally different people. And Mexicans have been the perfect vehicles for the filmic structuring of Anglo-American challenges, responses, dilemmas, resolutions, and ideological expositions. (Cortés 1989)

Whether as a contested border in Alamo films, a violent border in Mexican revolution films, an obstructionist border in cops-and-immigrants films, or a crime-infested border in mystery films, that 2,000-mile international dividing line has continuously served as a provocative locale. Two films, Orson Welles' *Touch of Evil* (1958) and Richard "Cheech" Marín's *Born in East L.A.* (1987), embody the complexities and contradictions implicit both in this particular border and in its movie treatment.

In *Touch of Evil*, the border both divides and unites. It divides politically, separating the United States and Mexico. But it also unites the two sides of the frontier—the twin cities of Los Robles—in cross-cultural depravity. Moreover, the international political border heightens the intercultural personal border between the two protagonists—Mexican narcotics inspector Mike Vargas and American police captain Hank Quinlan.

Sequences ricochet back and forth across the border. Dynamite is planted in an automobile parked in Mexico, but it does not explode until the car crosses the border into the United States. Seeking safety during her husband's investigation into local Mexican crime, Mike's American wife crosses the border into the United States and checks into a motel. Yet the border follows her, as she is assaulted by a group of young Mexicans, whose criminal family owns the American motel.

Separated by nationality as their nations are separated by the border, Mike Vargas and Hank Quinlan are also separated by identity and symbolism. Simultaneously an American lawman and an accomplice of Mexican border mobster Joe Grande, Quinlan becomes the movie representative of border culture. In contrast, Vargas symbolizes national government intervention in that distant culture (Vargas even opines, "Border towns aren't real Mexico"). Quinlan embodies the inchoate nature of the border, perhaps any distant political borderland. Vargas personifies the efforts of central governments to control not only their borders, but also those distinct cultures that emerge in borderlands. At the movie's end, Quinlan is shot and killed on the border, one movie moment of national triumph over borderland localism.

Born in East L.A. provides an alternative take on the same border. As in *Touch of Evil*, the border separates the two nations. But in contrast to *Touch of Evil*'s porous border, which functionally unites Mexican and American social systems, *Born in East L.A.*'s protected border rigidly divides (or at least tries to divide) the two societies.

The border's reverberations even reach Los Angeles, where Guadalupe Rodolfo ("Rudy") Robles, a young, third-generation Chicano, is picked up in a U.S. Immigration and Naturalization Service raid and is deported to Tijuana. Lacking any documentation (he had left his wallet at home), Rudy cannot convince U.S. border officials that he is an American and therefore has the right to return to the United States. Instead, he is forced to sneak back across the border into his own country.

He ultimately succeeds. To the backing of Neil Diamond singing "They all come to America," Rudy, his El Salvadoran lover, some new Chinese pals, and hundreds of other would-be-Americans march across a rugged, rural part of the border despite the futile efforts of two border patrolmen to stop them. At least for the moment, "the people" (as in "Power to the People") have caused the border to disappear.

Politicians may create international borders, law enforcement agents may guard them, and armies may go to war over them. Individuals may view borders as avenues or obstacles, as promises of security or threats of imprisonment, as lines to be penetrated or to be defended. As long as human beings both draw lines to separate peoples into nations and contest the meaning of those lines, borders will continue to furnish rich, riveting, and revealing locales for moviemakers and moviegoers.

Works Cited

Cortés, Carlos E. "Hollywood Interracial Love: Social Taboo as Screen Titillation," in Paul Loukides and Linda K. Fuller (eds.), *Beyond the Stars: Studies in American Popular Film*, Volume 2, *Plot Conventions in American Film*. Bowling Green, OH: Bowling Green State University Popular Press, 1991.

_____. "To View a Neighbor: The Hollywood Textbook on Mexico," in John H. Coatsworth and Carlos Rico (eds.), *Images of Mexico in the United States*. La Jolla: Center for U.S.-Mexican Studies, U of California, San Diego, 1989.

Maciel, David. *El Norte: The U.S.-Mexican Border in Contemporary Cinema.* San Diego: Institute for Regional Studies of the Americas, San Diego State U, 1990.

Sinclair, Andrew. *John Ford.* NY: Dial P, 1979.

Filmography

Year	Film	Director
1935	*Bordertown*	Archie Mayo
1941	*Hold Back the Dawn*	Mitchell Leisen
1948	*Fort Apache*	John Ford
1949	*Border Incident*	Anthony Mann
1950	*Borderline*	William Seiter
1952	*Pony Soldier*	Joseph M. Newman
1953	*Niagara*	Henry Hathaway
1954	*Apache*	Robert Aldrich
1954	*Border River*	George Sherman
1954	*The Raid*	Hugo Fregonese
1955	*The Last Command*	Frank Lloyd
1955	*The Sea Chase*	John Farrow
1957	*Paths of Glory*	Stanley Kubrick
1957	*The Tijuana Story*	Leslie Kardos
1958	*Touch of Evil*	Orson Welles
1959	*The Horse Soldiers*	John Ford
1960	*The Alamo*	John Wayne

1964	*Cheyenne Autumn*	John Ford
1966	*The Professionals*	Richard Brooks
1969	*Viva Max!*	Jerry Paris
1970	*Little Big Man*	Arthur Penn
1970	*Soldier Blue*	Ralph Nelson
1972	*Ulzana's Raid*	Robert Aldrich
1976	*Winterhawk*	Charles B. Pierce
1977	*Julia*	Fred Zinnemann
1978	*Midnight Express*	Alan Parker
1980	*Borderline*	Jerrold Freedman
1982	*The Border*	Tony Richardson
1983	*El Norte*	Gregory Nava
1987	*Born in East L.A.*	Cheech Marin

On the Road Again:
An American Archetype

Barbara Odabashian

Just as no art form is more closely identified with America than popular film, no cinematic convention is more historically and culturally significant than the overwhelmingly popular and omnipresent sub-genre, the road film. It is the quintessential American archetype. Deriving from the myth of the western frontier that expresses a desire for the escape from physical boundaries and old world societal barriers, the representation of the road in American film traditionally depicts a quest for freedom.

The archetype of the hero undergoing a journey has taken many cultural forms; in American film this archetype has been glorified by our romance with the road and with the automobile. In times when we are in the process of redefining or at least reexamining society's values as a whole, the hero reigns as "king of the road." The central focus of the true road film is on the road itself as a place to live or way of life rather than on the road as a means to another destination. The road as primary destination is similarly a pattern in American literature as evidenced in the works of Walt Whitman and Jack Kerouac. The development of the roles of the highway and the automobile as prime movers in American society is a by-product of American technology and economic power. Combining art and technology, the highway thus becomes a logical focus for American filmmakers.

Life on the road—successful or disastrous, pleasurable or self destructive—is the final and desired destination of the protagonists of a unique category of road film. This category is composed of films in which the highway serves as a metaphor for the protagonists' alienation from the social establishment. Within this singular category of road film we find heroes of the absurd who choose to exist in a condition of constant motion rather than accept the status quo. By using or seeking the so-called freedom of the road to escape the prohibitions and restrictions of society, they consciously accept or even choose the road as an alternative way of life. Indeed these literally on-the-go protagonists make a rather dramatic, if ironic, social statement in their choice of

50

mobility over stasis. In the latter part of the 1960s there were two American road or highway films (made only two years apart) that stunned their audiences and caused endless debate: *Bonnie and Clyde* (1967) and *Easy Rider* (1969). A disturbing precursor to *Bonnie and Clyde* appeared at the half century mark: *Gun Crazy* (1950); a remarkable descendant appeared at the beginning of the last decade of the century: *Thelma and Louise* (1991). Throughout cultural history, the fictional journey has provided a means of identifying our heroes and, correspondingly, the contemporary values of society. As historical periods change, so do the hopes and fears of individuals and members of society, so do our heroes. Since film may be to the twentieth century what theatre was to the sixteenth century or the novel to the nineteenth, it is particularly propitious and advantageous to review the history of this remarkable category of American road film, albeit in microcosm by comparing these particular parallel films, to obtain a close-up picture of the problematic nature of certain American values as we enter the last decade of this century.

As prologue to a discussion of the huge impact of these road films in the 1960s, a work in the preceding decade should first be considered: *Gun Crazy* (1950), directed by Joseph H. Lewis, a road film that appears to be a forerunner to *Bonnie and Clyde*. In *Gun Crazy*, the two protagonists, Annie Laurie Starr (Peggy Cummins) and Bart Tare (John Dall) are most alive when they are on the road. Indeed their life is the road. They marry, and they become armed robbers; their automobile becomes their home, and the road their way of life. Foreshadowing the desires of Bonnie and Clyde, it is the thrill, the danger, of the life of crime that appeals to Laurie, who seeks to escape the drudgery and tedium of everyday life. Instead of settling down to a normal job and home, they take to the gun and to the road. Although Bart repeatedly wants to quit the life of crime, his passion for Laurie stops him. She, in turn, is excited by the freedom of their fast-paced life. In truth, despite Bart's fears, neither he nor she seems capable of settling down or fitting in to a normal home life.

She is definitely not a homebody; from their very first meeting on, she, literally and metaphorically, wears pants. At one point, Laurie and Bart dress like cowboys, he with white hat and she with black, to rob a bank; they even wear gun holsters as part of their "costumes." Indeed they are play cowboys with shooting skills that are only seen in the fantasy world of the West found in Amerian films. The only apparel that truly suits Laurie and Bart, however, is the body of an automobile. The only role they are truly suited for is that of armed robbers rather than honest, average citizens. The only place they really feel at home is on the road.

When Bart begins to get anxious that their life is "a nightmare," Laurie convinces him to do one final job so that they will have enough money to go away, and to split up for a while. During the big job, Laurie kills two people, but Bart does not know that she has killed anyone. They drive to the second getaway car and Laurie gets out of Bart's car to drive away down the road on her own. Bart drives off first. They are both driving in opposite directions in convertibles. Bart stops his car and turns to look back at Laurie; she stops her car and turns to look at him. Bart turns his car; Laurie turns her car. He gets out of his car and runs to her car and gets in the driver's seat with her; they embrace. They are both—literally and metaphorically—in the driver's seat, in a close embrace; kissing and driving as one, they take off together. The road is their passion; their passion, the road. This choreography of vehicles on the highway is the old dance of love. The two are inextricably intertwined. Bart and Laurie cannot live without each other or the road.

When they are forced to hop a freight train and return to Bart's hometown as a last resort, to hide from the police, Laurie feels ill at ease in his sister's home. Laurie does not trust Bart's "own sister" (who wears an apron and stands at a stove), and then, while they are eating dinner, Bart's old boyhood friends drive up to the house to persuade him to surrender. Their only hope is to get back on the road. In the end, they are chased by the police on a highway leading to the mountains where Bart and his friends "hunted" as young boys. The camera shoots down on the car from above as they race along the highway. There is a symbolic shot of Bart's face from below, with the camera shooting up through the steering wheel of the car so that the wheel frames Bart's face. The car steers around road construction blocking the highway, blocking their seeming road to freedom. Finally, they come—literally and metaphorically—to the end of the road. They run hand in hand into the woods, where they are tracked down by Bart's friends, and, when Laurie tries to shoot them, he shoots her, and in turn is shot by his own friends. Once they are forced off the highway, their death is inevitable.

The highway or the open road does not bring these protagonists the freedom or escape they so desperately desire; instead the road signifies their position as outsiders in terms of the legitimate constructs of home or society. Again, these are people who claim the road as their home, but these are also people who cannot find a home off the road or at the end of the road. These are people who are trapped in their cars on the "open" road. The protagonists of *Gun Crazy* are the protagonists of *film noir*. They are alienated from home and society and obsessed with sex and violence.

Combined qualities of fatalism and greed, cynicism and selfishness are the prime characteristics of *film noir* protagonists that reflect the psychological, cultural, and political malaise of post-war America in a historical period dominated by rules of rigid social behavior, sexual repression, and political isolationism. The films of this period are a far cry from those of the war period that reflect home and communal values, self sacrifice and nurturing love, and patriotic idealism. However, the films of the late forties through the fifties have much more in common with the following decade, the sixties, a time when societal values, sexual roles, and political boundaries were being tested and reevaluated, although the latter period was characterized by, at least, a strong desire for change, futile or not, rather than a despair born of a natural cynicism.

In the 1960s two significant road films dramatically characterized the decade: *Bonnie and Clyde* (1967) and *Easy Rider* (1969). Arthur Penn's *Bonnie and Clyde* is the quintessential American film, a film considered to be a landmark work by film students and filmmakers alike, whereas Dennis Hopper's *Easy Rider* can essentially be considered a remake or a shadow of the former. Oddly enough, Jean-Luc Godard was interested in the script of *Bonnie and Clyde* although the deal was never made for him to direct what turned out to be such an all-American film.[1] Godard went on to make a different but equally sensational and significant road film of his own, *Weekend* (1967), that questioned and criticized French and American values via a highway littered with human and vehicular wreckage. (In turn, *Weekend* can perhaps be considered the granddaddy of the Australian "Mad Max" films with their post-apocalyptic vision of the future.)

There is some question about whose vision dominated *Bonnie and Clyde*.[2] Was it the creation of director Arthur Penn, leading man/producer Warren Beatty, screenwriters David Newman and Robert Benton, or film editor Dede Allen? No matter, however, who the force was behind the film, its vision is singular. This is a film that has two "heroes," Bonnie and Clyde, a woman and a man, who undergo a journey together. They both initially undertake the quest because America is in a state of economic and social depression in the 1930s. They are frustrated with the condition of their lives and want to make something of themselves. Substitute political "oppression" for "depression" and let the rest ride, and we are en route to the sixties.

When they first meet, Clyde identifies Bonnie as a waitress. He is right, and she hates admitting that is what she is. He promises to make her rich and famous, and they ride off in a stolen car. It is not long before their first "joy ride" comes to a screeching halt. Clyde is impotent; he says that he is no "ladies' man." In the end she makes him potent by making him famous in her poems; Clyde is turned on by her "story" of their lives being published in the newspaper. However, their fame is not the fame of Odysseus or of Beowulf; their fame is of no benefit to society. They accidentally do good to a poor citizen here and there, but Clyde has no idea what to do with his life except rob banks and run from the police, and Bonnie goes along for the ride.

Even their violence is accidental. Clyde commits the first petty robbery to provide proof of his true identity to Bonnie, who is skeptical. Next he sets out to rob a bank but ends up dragging the teller out to Bonnie to confess that the bank has crashed and there is no money to be taken. Then he goes to rob a grocer's with shopping list in hand, only to be attacked by a butcher with a big knife and be forced to strike back with the handle of his gun. Finally, in his second attempt to rob a bank with the aid of a new, young accomplice, C.W. Moss, Clyde and Bonnie exit the bank only to find that C.W. has parked the car. But comedy turns to melodrama when this comic delay leads to an officer jumping on the car. Clyde kills him by shooting him in the face through the car window.

The movie posters blazed: "They're young...they're in love...and they kill people." Archetypically, a hero can undergo a journey in which he performs extraordinary feats (both physical and mental) in order to save a kingdom and marry its princess. Or the hero can undergo a journey in which his dying serves as a sacrifice to restore his kingdom to its proper state. Or the hero can undergo a journey in which he leaves home as a young, immature man and returns an older, wiser man ready and able to serve his country well. Do Bonnie and Clyde save a kingdom? No. Do they die? Yes, but their deaths do not serve a sacrificial purpose and do not restore the health of their country. Do they gain wisdom on their journey so that, when they return home, they can come to the aid of their fellow countrymen? No. Indeed Bonnie's mother tells her that she does not want her daughter to come home now that she is a criminal wanted by the police, and Bonnie is shocked. And, when Bonnie asks Clyde what he would do differently if given a second chance, he replies that he would live in one state and commit robberies in another, and Bonnie realizes that, in addition to no longer being able to return home, she is on a journey with a man who is going nowhere. Clyde has no idea at all what a true hero's journey entails; Bonnie only has a glimmer of an idea that they are on the wrong track and that glimmer comes much too late.

Bonnie and Clyde "see" themselves as heroes, but in fact they are only heroes in the world of movies or fiction, not the world of reality. They portray themselves as American folk heroes, as in the scene with the farmer and his helping hand when Clyde offers them his gun to shoot out the windows of the home that the bank foreclosed; "We rob banks," boasts Clyde. Their fame, however, is based on rumor rather than on actual deeds, on newspaper "hype," which they foster themselves. They send "self-portraits" made by camera to the newspapers along with Bonnie's autobiographical poems. On a purely cinematic level, *Bonnie and Clyde* is primarily a movie about movies and secondarily a movie about movie genres, specifically, the western. The key to this film and its heroes lies in its disturbing yet exciting revision of this traditional mode. Like the typical western hero, Bonnie and Clyde stand outside the social establishment, but they stand so far out that these "heroes" can no longer benefit or influence society in a positive fashion.[3]

Dennis Hopper's *Easy Rider* also has two heroes; this time the heroes are both male. It is the 1960s, and the heroes undertake a journey across America in search of freedom.[4] The blurb on the film poster solemnly intones: "A man went looking for America and couldn't find it anywhere...."

The film opens with our heroes, Wyatt/"Captain America" (Peter Fonda) and Billy (Dennis Hopper), making a drug deal to "finance" their American quest. They have five days to get to Mardi Gras. Ironic, too, is the fact that their journey goes from the West to the East—the opposite of the traditional American journey, the journey west to the American frontier. The two heroes ride together just like in the good old westerns, and one of them is dressed in a fringed leather frontier jacket and the proper hat. But they ride motorcycles (not horses), and the other is dressed in a jacket and helmet emblazoned with the American flag (perhaps an ironic reference to the flag carrying cavalry of the epic westerns). And, of course, they both wear sunglasses. (To shade them from what, one wonders.) They seem to have as much difficulty "seeing" the truth, as others do seeing beyond or beneath their disguises.[5] They ride through classic American scenes, John Ford "western" scenes—Monument Valley. But these heroes die ignominiously by the side of the road (shades of Bonnie and Clyde). Is Hopper making some sort of bad joke about tragic heroes? I believe, rather, the joke is on America.

Wyatt and Billy make it to Mardi Gras even though on the way their newly found "friend," George Hanson (Jack Nicholson), is bludgeoned to death by rednecks in the dark of the night while he is asleep. They do achieve their literal goal, but to what purpose? Immediately after they leave New Orleans they are killed on the road. They are killed by rednecks who seek to frighten them with a "show" of violence, but in the movies "appearance" is reality. After Billy is mortally wounded when his motorcycle is shot from under him, the rednecks intentionally shoot Wyatt, "Captain America," to cover up the senseless brutal deed.

Bonnie and Clyde are killed by the side of the road when they stop to help a "seeming" friend, C.W.'s duplicitous father, change a tire which does not really need changing. (He is putting on a "show" of helplessness in order to render them truly helpless.) They are ambushed by the law, the Texas Ranger and his confederates, and die the death they had both foreseen (underscored visually by Dede Allen's emphatic editing of their final stunned and mutual glances).

What Clyde, in particular, does not clearly see, however, is that he is not the hero he imagines himself to be. It is not for nothing that at the end of this movie Clyde pops out one of the lenses in the sunglasses he has inherited (Blanche's sunglasses). (Earlier, first his brother, Buck, is shot in the eye; then Buck's wife, Blanche, is shot in the eye. Also one of the headlights of the getaway car is shot out.) Clyde ends up wearing sunglasses with only one lens, not unlike the singular "eye" of the camera. Clyde can only see clearly out of one eye; his vision is 50 per cent. He knows enough to be critical of American society, but he does not "see" how to fix it. Clyde and Bonnie, like the two buddies in *Easy Rider*, are killed on the road because they have no real destination in life and no real home to which they can return.

Bonnie and Clyde hype their own "myth" rather than really become heroes. Wyatt and Billy are "cowboys," not cowboys with white hats and white horses but cowboys with helmets and motorcycles. But what does it mean when our modern/cinematic symbols of freedom—the automobile, the motorcycle—fail us? Did we deceive ourselves in thinking that the technology of the future would set us free? The car and motorcycle are visible technological symbols of freedom; they signal the peculiarly American promise of the open road. In the "road" pictures of the sixties, however, these cinematic vehicles "double" as symbols of entrapment.

In the sixties many Americans, in particular young Americans, began to believe they had been deluded into thinking they were free and began searching for true freedom. But in the end many of them found themselves facing the same dilemma as Bonnie and Clyde—frustrated with the status quo but unable to see a clear way out. Reviewing the state of the hero's journey through the medium of motion pictures, we can clearly see that these road films reflect a point of view popular among a highly visible, and certainly vocal, portion of the American population, the view that in the sixties America becomes a society capable of trashing its heroes along with its hopes and desires. Or, in the words of Wyatt aka Captain America, "We blew it."

Exploring the highways and byways of cinema and culture, these road films provide us with a topical/topographical map of certain significant sociological and cultural factors/features in America's past and present. A new era begins, in the last decade of the twentieth century, with the road film *Thelma and Louise* picking up where *Bonnie and Clyde* and *Easy Rider* left off. Ridley Scott's *Thelma and Louise* (1991) mirrors the earlier films in suggesting the need to escape the repression of established society (though the emphasis this time is on gender rather than economics) and the desire to search for personal freedom and autonomy (though the outcome this time is nihilistic rather than "revolutionary" or politically idealistic). The egomania of the 1980s has apparently cost Americans their sense of irony, the ability and desire to observe their own too human flaws from an objective distance or rational perspective. *Thelma and Louise* is exhilarating because of the natural intensity of the two lead actors, Geena Davis and Susan Sarandon. If not for them, however, the brightly colored picture presented by the director, Ridley Scott, is bleak. These women hurl themselves against a wall of destruction without stopping for a moment to comprehend the real futility of their road trip. These women do not voluntarily undertake a journey, but are forced by the spectre of male violence to retaliate against a sexist society, and then run like hell. They believe they have no choice; they are the sisters of Clyde Barrow, whose only idea for a new way of life, if given the opportunity, is to live in one state and rob in another. They choose to drive off the road and off the edge of the Grand Canyon because they are outmanned. The ending of *Bonnie and Clyde* is much less macho; the two lovers go for a ride on a fine country day into town, and stopping to help C.W.'s father change a tire, they are, pathetically, gunned down by a hail of bullets. They are ambushed/martyred by a bankrupt (morally and economically) society, but, in the end, at least Bonnie sees the error of their ways, of trying to escape society's oppression by going on the road and living by the gun. Neither Thelma nor Louise truly sees the error of their ways; their solution to the gender crisis in America is to gun their car over the edge of the precipice and into thin air. Who's macho now?

   Thelma and Louise opens with a black and white image as the camera pans right from a scenic expanse to a long dirt road receding into the mountains from the plains. As the camera fixes on the scene, the light comes up; then, as the credits roll, the scene grows dark against the blue of the sky until the image fades to black. This silent show says it all; light dawns for Thelma and Louise on the road only to turn to darkness and death. They are going on a weekend trip, driving to a cabin in the mountains in a sky blue 1966 T-Bird Convertible. Louise, a waitress, tells a customer who lusts after Thelma, "She's running away with me." In turn, Louise asks Thelma, "How come Darryl [her husband] let you go?" Thelma answers, "Because I didn't ask him." She is afraid to tell her husband about the road trip because he does not want her to do anything but hang around the house. Before they get into the car, they take a photo of themselves together: "Smile." This polaroid picture of the two (headshots of Louise with sunglasses and Thelma without) is placed at an angle against the expansive blue sky and clouds that cover the top three-quarters of the movie poster for *Thelma and Louise*. Depicted beneath the wide sky is the landscape of Monument Valley, and coming straight out from the mountains in the center of the poster is the black asphalt highway. The poster proclaims, "Somebody said *get a life*...so they did."

The first stop they make is the Silver Bullet, a "cowboy" bar; Louise remarks, "I haven't seen any place like this since I left Texas." It is at the Silver Bullet that Thelma is taken out to the parking lot by a guy, Harlan, who calls the women "kewpie dolls," who then beats her and attempts to rape her. Harlan continues to be verbally abusive and macho even though Louise points a gun at him. She shoots him, and his dead body ends up sprawled against the hood of a car. Thelma and Louise drive off in the dark and the rain with the white top of the convertible up and the big trucks honking as they veer in front of them on the highway. Later, they meet up with the obscenely gesturing driver of a long silver tank truck that looks like a "silver bullet." Eventually they invite him to pull over by the side of the road, and, when he refuses to apologize for his sexist behavior, they aim their guns at his truck and the "silver bullet" goes up in smoke. The "silver bullet," of course, connotes the mythic sexual power of the male.

In this film, once the two women leave home, they are either on the highway or never very far off it, except, of course, at the end when they drive off the canyon rim. They stop at the Motor Inn and from the window of their room we can see the traffic go by on two levels of the highway as the women argue about what to do. Louise gets on the phone to her boyfriend, Jimmy, to get him to send her life's savings, and we see the trucks go by in the mirror next to her on the wall and we hear, in the background of their conversation, the sounds of traffic, and then the words of a song, "I'm going down the lonesome highway before I die."

Also, throughout the film, we keep seeing cowboy images or images from western movies. In addition to Louise's cowboy jacket and boots, her boyfriend, Jimmy, wears a cowboy shirt and the young boy Thelma picks up, J.D., wears a big white cowboy hat. (Later in the film, Thelma "borrows" Louise's black cowboy jacket with white embroidery.) When they first start out on their road trip, there is a scene of cattle grazing by the side of the road and again, later, they see cowboys herding cattle as they are driving in the midst of John Ford country. Later on, when they pull into a gas station, there is a cowboy on a white horse in the background. Even above the bed where Thelma and J.D. make passionate love, there is a long oblong picture of a wagon train. All these visual references to the mythic West serve as a painful reminder of the contrast between traditional American folk heroes and Thelma and Louise (between the cultural worlds of the western movie and the road film).

When they are nearing the end of the road, Thelma says, "I know this whole thing was my fault." Louise responds, "You ought to know by now it wasn't." Chased by a "posse" of cop cars, they drive off the highway through laundry lines and over dirt fields. Thelma lights up a cigarette and passes it to Louise, "You're a good friend." Louise replies, "You, too. You're the best. How do you like the vacation so far?" Then, just before they drive straight up to the edge of the Grand Canyon, Thelma says, "You're a good driver." In the end, Louise reaches over and kisses Thelma on the lips; the two hold hands and Louise guns the car over the edge of the canyon. Unlike Bonnie and Clyde, they do not send their pictures to the newspapers to immortalize themselves; the polaroid picture of the two of them, smiling, can be seen lying on the back seat of the car.

Even though the film ends with a freeze frame of Thelma and Louise in their 1966 T-Bird soaring in the sky, there is nothing uplifting about this ending. The film ends with a silent thud. Ironically, in the midst of all the bright sunlight, and dramatically lit colors of the night skies, and the expanse of the wide open road, Ridley Scott has made a film as mentally claustrophobic as any *film noir*. Only in this case, the feeling of claustrophobia is belied by all the shots of the wide open plains and the mountain ranges, again, the traditional scenery of Hollywood westerns. Thelma and Louise may appear to be floating in the heavenly blue sky above, but they are, in reality, poised for the longest and hardest fall of them all.

If *Thelma and Louise* is seen as a feminist road film, it does not portend well for the women of America despite the elation of some film critics.[6] Ultimately, what Thelma and Louise do not share is the most significant aspect of their relationship. Although they realize what roles they do not want to continue to play in life, in their relationships with men, they do not seem to know what they do want. Louise tells her boyfriend, Jimmy, that she loves him, but "it's time to let go of the old mistakes." Thelma tells her husband, Darryl, that he is not her "father." They only get to make half of the heroic journey, however; they do not become fully mature and respected citizens of society rather their emotional development is arrested at an early stage. Holding hands, as if they were children, Thelma and Louise jump off the veritable cliff; once again they are head off at the pass by a dominantly patriarchal society, by a "posse" of men representing the law of the land. Once again, for the protagonists of the road film, their only freedom has been a fleeting illusion, found only on the highways of America; once again, they have been forced off the road, and cut off in the prime of their lives, by the powers that be.

When Louise stares out at the panorama of what is America in Monument Valley, she sees that there is nothing or no place in this country for her. For a while, Thelma and Louise pretend at belonging by changing costume. Thelma gives up her "feminine" clothes (her flowery terry robe and white dress) and helpless manner, and Louise trades in her nurse's (the waitress) uniform and mothering behavior, and they both wear pants (blue jeans) along with the men's hats they have picked up along the way. Louise looks in the rear view mirror to put on some lipstick and then throws it away. She gives all her silver rings and jewelery to an old man with a white beard in exchange for his old straw hat, which she then wears for the rest of the journey, whereas Thelma adopts the cap of the obscene truck driver, which has the emblem of the American flag on the front. (Louise's last name is Sawyer; she is wearing an old straw hat à la Tom Sawyer and, by her own behavior and performance, she does persuade Thelma of the desirability of staying on the road and even taking the driver's seat.) It is important to note that, although Louise starts out as the dominant partner, Thelma adopts that role half way along. In the end, however, they become equal partners. They also share "masculine" tasks; Louise is the better driver, and Thelma the shooter. They "get a life," but it is delusional in nature, merely an optical illusion on the distant horizon of the American highway. *Thelma and Louise* is a cry in the dark for the women of America; standing in the middle of Monument Valley, in the middle of the night, Thelma asks Louise, "What's going on?" The reply: "Nothing."

The frustrated optimism of the 1960s represented in *Bonnie and Clyde* and *Easy Rider* has developed into the desperate nihilism of the 1990s represented in *Thelma and Louise* and other road films such as David Lynch's *Wild at Heart* (1990) and Gus Van Sant's *My Own Private Idaho* (1991). Captain America concludes, "We blew it." In the sixties there had existed the possibility of political, social, and economic freedom, even though the dream was not realized. So far the films of the nineties paint a completely different picture. Thelma warns Louise: "Don't blow it." At the beginning of the 1990s there is not even a glimmer of "liberty and justice for all," so Thelma's notion of not blowing it is to "keep going," because she does not "remember ever feeling this awake." If these road films attempt to provide us with cultural maps of America's past and present, perhaps they may even serve as guides to the future. Film history attests that the appearance of these films at least strongly suggests that we are entering an era of social and political discontent and conflict. As we approach the turn of the century, the recent outcrop of this singular category of American road film does not augur a better future.

Notes

[1]The screenwriters, Newman and Benton, admired François Truffaut's films and first offered their script to him. Although he thought it was "an excellent script," he, in turn, in a letter (7 September 1964) to their agent, Elinor Jones, recommended that they offer it to Jean-Luc Godard: "I am convinced that he [Godard] would be absolutely the man for the job,...and what he might well give you is an American *Breathless*" (*Correspondence 1945-1984*, ed. Gilles Jacob and Claude de Givray, trans. Gilbert Adair [New York: The Noonday Press, 1990] 251-52).

[2]Among the many discussions of *Bonnie and Clyde*, I find these two to be the most pertinent, and therefore acknowledge in advance any debt I may incur in the following discussion: Pauline Kael, *Kiss Kiss Bang Bang* (Boston: Atlantic-Little, Brown, 1968) 47-63; Edward Murray, *Ten Film Classics: A Re-Viewing* (New York: Frederick Ungar, 1978) 149-66.

[3]See Leo Braudy's discussion of "Westerns and the Myth of the Past" (124-39), "Truffaut, Godard, and the Genre Film as Self-conscious Art" (163-69), and "The Transformation of Genre: Film and Society in the 1970s" (169-81) in *The World in a Frame: What We See in Films* (Garden City: Anchor Books, 1977).

[4]See the socio-cultural analysis of "The Sixties" (68-97) and, specifically, of *Easy Rider* (95-97) by Leonard Quart and Albert Auster in *American Film and Society Since 1945* (London: Macmillan, 1984).

[5]See Braudy's comparison of the clothes of Brando in *The Wild One* (Laslo Benedek, 1953) and of his "costumed descendants" Fonda and Hopper in *Easy Rider* (222-23).

[6]In particular, see Manohla Dargis's emphasis on the creation of "a paradigm of female friendship" in "Roads to Freedom," *Sight and Sound* July 1991: 14-18.

Selected Filmography

Year	Film	Director
1950	*Gun Crazy*	Joseph H. Lewis
1956	*The Searchers*	John Ford
1967	*Bonnie and Clyde*	Arthur Penn
1967	*Weekend*	Jean-Luc Godard
1969	*Easy Rider*	Dennis Hopper
1971	*Two-Lane Blacktop*	Monte Hellman
1979	*Mad Max*	George Miller
1981	*The Road Warrior*	George Miller
1985	*Lost in America*	Albert Brooks
1986	*Something Wild*	Jonathan Demme
1990	*Wild at Heart*	David Lynch
1991	*Thelma and Louise*	Ridley Scott
1991	*My Own Private Idaho*	Gus Van Sant

South of the Border:
Hollywood's Latin America

Brooks Robards

Walt Disney's classic cartoon *The Three Caballeros* (1945) provides a good introduction to how Hollywood uses Latin America as a locale. The film is a travelogue of Latin nations, and the opening credits summarize some of the conventions of the Latin setting: bright colors, cacti growing in an open landscape; men with sombreros riding donkeys; and tile-roofed adobe houses lining the hills.

Our guide Donald Duck receives a giant gift-wrapped package from his friends in Latin America, and inside are a host of presents, each from a different Latin nation. But first Sterling Holloway, as narrator, offers a quick geography lesson with a map of South America.

The first present Donald opens contains a reel of film that transports us first not to Latin America, but to the South Pole. In this film-within-a-film, we meet an adventurous penguin named Pablo and in the blink of an eye pass Cape Horn and the Straits of Magellan; sail by Lima, Peru; turn left near Quito, Ecuador; and finally land in the Galapagos Islands. After snacking on a banana, Pablo hops into a hammock strung between palm trees, grabs a fan and reaches for the cold drink supplied by a tortoise-waiter.

Next we cross the snow-capped Andes to arrive in the Amazon jungle, where "Professor" Holloway provides us with background on the exotic birds found in nearly a dozen different Latin nations. In Brazil we find Spanish-style adobe churches, dew-bedecked orchids, shuttered windows and wrought-iron balconies. In Mexico, we discover a land of guitar music, piñatas, serape-draped cowboys, luscious live-action bathing beauties and bull-fights.

While the geography is occasionally a bit fuzzy, this celluloid synopsis of the Latin landscape is surprisingly accurate, down to its Galapagos-based penguin. Besides cataloguing many of the conventions of Hollywood's version of Latin America, *The Three Caballeros* represents part of a wave of Hollywood interest in Latin America in the late 1930s and 1940s.

Hollywood's fascination with the Latin settings, however, dates back even earlier to the silent era when according to Allen L. Woll and Randall M. Miller, "pseudo-documentaries" of the 1910 Mexican Revolution were shown in U.S. theatres (243). The line between fact and fiction in these movies was not always clear, and Woll and Miller recount how Pancho Villa himself signed a contract with Mutual Film Corporation to have his battles recorded (243). Latin locales have continued to play a significant role in Hollywood movies, sometimes reflecting an idealized, romantic vision of what is in fact a large and disparate group of nations and other times reinforcing a rather negative set of stereotypes of the Latino as a stock movie character.

Hollywood's early fascination with its neighbors to the South—in particular Mexico, since it shares a border with the U.S.—is understandable. North Americans sometimes call Latin America their backyard. But because early movies about Latin America often relied on narrative and character stereotypes of violence and villainy, they were greeted with less than enthusiasm by Latins themselves. The Mexican government threatened to ban an unflattering Hollywood version of its country in 1922. When *Girl of the Rio*, starring Dolores Del Rio and Leo Carrillo and set in a border town, was released in 1932, protests spread, with Panama, Nicaragua and Spain joining Mexico to complain.

According to film historians, the popularity of Latin America in movies in the 1930s—and 1940s when *The Three Caballeros* was made—may have been an extension of Franklin Delano Roosevelt's Good Neighbor Policy and one later motivated by more specific strategic concerns related to World War II. In any case, it is clear that political considerations have provided a significant texture to Hollywood's version of Latin America from early on.

With its emphasis on music and dance, *The Three Caballeros* comes out of a tradition of movie musicals with Latin settings epitomized by Thornton Freeland's *Flying Down to Rio* (1933). Rick Altman traces the South-of-the-Border craze back to *Rio Rita* (1929), starring Bebe Daniels and John Boles, and estimates that musicals with Latin settings averaged one a year during the 1930s. After Carmen Miranda's American debut in *Down Argentine Way* (1940), Hollywood produced more than two dozen Latin musicals during the 1940s.

If the European arena developed unpleasant associations before and during the war years, Latin America seemed like a new frontier: exotic and yet familiar; replete with a varied and spectacular scenery; a place for adventure but one nevertheless tied to European social and cultural traditions because of its Spanish heritage. With much of it below the equator and tropical in climate, the Latin American landscape also exuded a Before-the-Fall sense of sexual freedom.

In *Flying Down to Rio*, bandleader Gene Raymond meets Brazilian aristocrat Dolores Del Rio in Miami and follows her to Rio. Raymond's sidekick is Fred Astaire, in his first appearance with Ginger Rogers. The movie's adventure motif is reinforced narratively by emphasizing the trip down to Rio—with a stop in Port au Prince, Haiti—and by framing key landmarks, like Sugar Loaf Mountain, in cinematic postcards. The spectacular finale puts dancing beauties on the wings of airplanes, with the Rio skyline and beaches in the background.

Once the conventions of the Latin locale in the musical were established, the music and dancing alone could be suggestive enough to signal the setting. By the time Astaire appeared in *You Were Never Lovelier* (1942) with Rita Hayworth and bandleader Xavier Cugat, the travelogue approach of *Flying Down to Rio* was no longer necessary. The Buenos Aires, Argentina, setting is signaled by an establishing overhead pan of the city, with its European-flavored monuments and squares, at the beginning of the movie. The rest of *You Were Never Lovelier* unfolds inside Hayworth's parents' elegant house and garden, or her father's hotel office.

Director Vincente Minnelli took the Latin locale in another direction with his musicals *Yolanda and the Thief* (1945) and *The Pirate* (1948), making the most creative use of Latin motifs, according to Altman (188). Both films emphasize the exotic and romantic dimensions of a Latin landscape through a vivid, artificial color palette and the use of narrative devices like dream sequences to help transform the setting into a self-consciously imaginary world. After *Nancy Goes to Rio* (1950), Hollywood turned to other popular locales, like Paris.

The Latin craze was not confined to musicals. At its peak in 1939, three memorable movies outside that genre had Latin settings. Two are adventure melodramas—John Farrow's *Five Came Back*, with Lucille Ball in an atypical role, and Howard Hawks' *Only Angels Have Wings*, starring Cary Grant and Jean Arthur. William Dieterle's *Juarez*, starring Betty Davis and Paul Muni, is a biopic. According to Woll and Miller, *Juarez* so impressed the President of Mexico when it was released that he requested it be shown in the Mexican Palace of Fine Arts. It was the first time a film was accorded such an honor (247).

These three films—along with *The Treasure of the Sierra Madre* (1948), the John Huston classic starring Humphrey Bogart—are important to a discussion of Latin locales because they suggest dimensions of the Latin setting that remain latent in musicals. The headhunter-infested

Amazon jungle of *Five Came Back* and the Andean peaks of *Only Angels Have Wings*, where condors threaten the mail planes, help establish a dark side to the exotic tropical landscapes of Latin America.

Using Mexico as their backdrop, *Juarez* and *The Treasure of the Sierra Madre* point toward aspects of the frontier world of the western. Both have settings that are in some ways interchangeable with the North American Southwest or Far West—arid, rocky, agrarian, with an austere topography of mountains and/or plains.

The *Treasure of the Sierra Madre* has the same donkeys, Latin-style music and porticoed piazzas used in musicals to signify a Latin world. In Huston's film, however, they become indicators of an environment of disorder, debauchery and alienation. Although Woll and Miller suggest *Juarez* "avoided the blatant stereotypes of the Mexican and revealed a newfound sympathy toward Latin characters" (247), it could be argued that the movie, which tells the story of violent, third-world revolution, simply glorifies aspects of the same old stereotypes.

In the western, Mexico plays an important role as a setting. As the place to which John Wayne and Claire Trevor escape at the end of John Ford's classic, *Stagecoach* (1939), Mexico signifies the land on the other side of the border. Both physically and metaphorically, it is the same as the region in the U.S. that it adjoins—and yet different. In westerns ranging form John Ford's *Rio Grande* (1950) to Howard Hawks's *Rio Bravo* (1959) and *El Dorado* (1967), it is a place the central characters move in and/or out of. It is the primary locale less often, as in Robert Aldrich's *Vera Cruz* (1954), where Burt Lancaster and Gary Cooper are part of a plot to oust the Emperor Maximillian; or Sergio Leone's spaghetti western, *A Fistful of Dollars* (1964), where an Italian-produced Mexican setting takes on an eerie, almost Fellini-esque quality.

In the musical, a Latin setting provides a pleasant interlude of escape, a taste for adventure, an interval of sensuous indulgence. In westerns, it represents a more permanent and desperate form of escape. "You are like the wind, blowing over the land and passing on," one of the Mexican villagers tells Yul Brynner in *The Magnificent Seven* (1960), directed by John Sturges. Most of the seven hired gringo gunmen don't survive the attack by bandits on the village they are protecting.

If, as Thomas Schatz suggests, the landscape of the West "depicts a world of precarious balance in which the forces of civilization and savagery are locked in a struggle for supremacy" (47), the Mexico of the western suggests a resolution of that struggle that is ultimately without solace. When the North American outlaws of Sam Peckinpah's *The Wild*

Bunch (1969) engage a band of Mexican bandits in battle, there are no real winners in the bloodbath that follows. The Mexican world of the western is a permanent reminder of the hero's alienation.

Less often, westerns incorporate a Latin setting that isn't Mexican. In William Castle's *The Americano* (1955), Glenn Ford heads to Brazil with a shipment of Brahma bulls. In George Roy Hill's parodic *Butch Cassidy and the Sundance Kid* (1969), Paul Newman and Robert Redford head for Bolivia as a last resort, after being told, "Your time is over and you're gonna die bloody. All you can do is choose where." The first animal they see is a llama instead of a burro, and the fact that they can't speak Spanish keeps them from holding up a bank. In both movies, the replacement of a Mexican setting comments on the conventions of the genre.

Constantin Costa-Gavras's *Missing* (1982) is the first of a series of movies with Latin settings in the 1980s that reinvent the "pseudo-documentary." Based on a true story, *Missing* chronicles the search for a young expatriate North American who disappears during the Chilean coup that overthrew Salvador Allende. Gone are the more obvious markers of a Latin setting found in the musical and the western. In their place come tanks and soldiers, and a rather generic urban landscape of hotels, buses and embassies.

The irony of this move toward authenticity, in which real events are manipulated to make a political statement, is that in some ways it ends up repeating the kinds of Hollywood stereotypes that enraged Latins in the industry's early days. The Latin world of *Missing* is violent, mysterious, alien. While the U.S. Embassy becomes a convenient villain in the end, North American values, as embodied by Jack Lemmon and Cissy Spacek, prevail.

Roger Spottiswood's *Under Fire* (1983) opens disconcertingly in Chad with elephant-riding soldiers. It is not entirely inappropriate to read this preliminary trip to Africa as a commentary on the travelogue approach to Latin locales used in some musicals. The scene shifts almost immediately to Nicaragua, where Spottiswood combines the rapidly disintegrating urban landscape of Managua just before the overthrow of Somoza with a more idyllic Sandinista-style guerrilla camp in the mountains.

The movement of Nick Nolte and Joanna Cassidy from corrupt, almost post-nuclear urban setting to romanticized rural camp and back again provides an interesting subtext to the movie's version of Nicaraguan politics. As in *Missing*, the plot's resolution comes when the central characters leave the movie's Latin setting and go home to the United States.

Oliver Stone's *Salvador* (1986) clearly returns to the travelogue format used in *Flying Down to Rio* and *The Three Caballeros* by starting in Los Angeles. Journalist buddies James Woods and James Belushi, as reprobate as any of the Wild Bunch, drive down to El Salvador on the Pan American highway instead of flying or going by boat. As in *Missing* and *Under fire*, the landscape is a bleak one, littered with helicopters, tanks, soldiers, burnt-out buildings and dead bodies. Stone's version of Latin politics, more simplistic than Spottiswood's, uses women as the chief signifier of a primitive and therefore purer Latin culture, where streams are for washing clothes and people still ride donkeys and sleep in hammocks. Once again, the central character escapes to the United States, but this time he tries, unsuccessfully, to take his Latina woman with him.

Less explicitly political are several 1980s movies that try to portray Latin America as almost pure landscape. John Boorman's *The Emerald Forest* (1985) uses the Brazilian jungle as a backdrop to the search for a young boy kidnapped by an Amazon tribe. Roland Jaffe's *The Mission* (1986) returns to the eighteenth century to tell the story of a Jesuit outpost in the Brazilian jungle. A utopian vision of a Central American rain forest provides the plot for Peter Weir's *The Mosquito Coast* (1986). All three capitalize to some extent on the growing fascination of U.S. environmentalists with Latin America. John McTiernan's Arnold Schwarzenegger vehicle, *Predator* (1987), exploits related concerns. His approach is much more transparent, however, since the Central American jungle is literally turned into an alien creature that must be wiped out by Schwarzenegger and his team of CIA mercenaries.

Even as brief an examination of Latin American locales as this one makes clear that the ways in which Hollywood uses Latin settings are surprisingly similar at very different times in its history and in very different genres and types of movies. The romantic notion of Latin America as an Eden-like world established by musicals in the 1930s and 1940s finds its analogues in some of the pseudo-documentaries and environmentalist movies of the1980s. Even the darker visions of the Western can be seen to represent an extension of similar notions. Its arid, violent landscapes suggest a locus of extremes similar to the lush, tropical settings of Latin musicals.

The Hollywood version of Latin America is first and foremost a land of the imagination. Sometimes a celebration, sometimes a crude compilation of stereotypes, sometimes an ideologically motivated tract, it is bound by an abiding set of attitudes about the people of Latin America and their relationship to the U.S.—their neighbor.

Works Consulted

Altman, Rick. *The American Film Musical*. Bloomington: Indiana UP, 1987.

American Film Institute Catalogue of Motion Pictures Produced in the United States. 3 vols. to date. NY: R.R. Bowker, 1971-1988.

Cawelti, John. *The Six-Gun Mystique*. 2nd ed. Bowling Green, OH: Bowling Green State University Popular Press, 1984.

Halliwell, Leslie. *Halliwell's Filmgoer's Companion*. 9th ed. NY: Charles Scribner's Sons, 1988.

Maltin, Leonard, ed. *Leonard Maltin's Movie and Video Guide*. 1992 ed. NY: Signet, 1992.

Video Hound's Golden Movie Retriever. Detroit: Visible Ink P, 1991.

Woll, Allen L. and Randall M. Miller. *Ethnic and Racial Images in American Film and Television*. NY: Garland Pub., 1987.

Filmography

Year	Film	Director
1929	*Rio Rita*	Luther Reed
1932	*Que Viva Mexico*	Sergei Eisenstein
1933	*Flying Down to Rio*	Thornton Freeland
1934	*Viva Villa*	Jack Conway
1935	*Under the Pampas Moon*	James Tinling
1936	*Rose of the Rancho*	Marion Gering
1936	*Hi Gaucho!*	Thomas Atkins
1936	*The Dancing Pirate*	Lloyd Corrigan
1936	*The Gay Desperado*	Rouben Mamoulian
1938	*Tropic Holiday*	Theodore Reed
1939	*Stagecoach*	John Ford
1939	*Five Came Back*	John Farrow
1939	*Only Angels Have Wings*	Howard Hawks
1939	*Juarez*	William Dieterle
1940	*Down Argentine Way*	Irving Cummings
1941	*Blondie Goes Latin*	Frank Strayer
1942	*Ship Ahoy*	Edward Buzzell
1942	*You Were Never Lovelier*	William Seiter
1944	*The Falcon in Mexico*	William Berke
1945	*Yolanda and the Thief*	Vincente Minnelli
1945	*The Three Caballeros*	Norman Ferguson
1945	*The Bullfighters*	Mal St. Clair
1946	*Notorious*	Alfred Hitchcock
1946	*Holiday in Mexico*	George Sidney

1947	*Out of the Past*	Jacques Tourneur
1948	*The Pirate*	Vincente Minnelli
1948	*The Road to Rio*	Norman Z. McLeod
1948	*The Treasure of the Sierra Madre*	John Huston
1950	*Rio Grande*	John Ford
1950	*Borderline*	William Seiter
1950	*The Bullfighter and the Lady*	Budd Boeticher
1952	*Viva Zapata!*	Elia Kazan
1954	*Vera Cruz*	Robert Aldrich
1954	*The Naked Jungle*	Byron Haskin
1955	*The Wages of Fear*	Henri-Georges Clouzot*
1955	*The Americano*	William Castle
1958	*Touch of Evil*	Orson Welles
1959	*Rio Bravo*	Howard Hawks
1959	*Virgin Sacrifice*	Fernando Wagner
1960	*The Magnificent Seven*	John Sturges
1961	*The Last Sunset*	Robert Aldrich
1961	*Operation Eichmann*	R.G. Springsteen
1962	*The 4 Horsemen of the Apocalypse*	Vincente Minnelli
1963	*Fun in Acapulco*	Richard Thorpe
1964	*The Night of the Iguana*	John Huston
1964	*A Fistful of Dollars*	Sergio Leone*
1964	*That Man from Rio*	Philippe De Broca*
1964	*The Pink Panther*	Blake Edwards
1965	*The Sons of Katie Elder*	Henry Hathaway
1966	*The Professionals*	Richard Brooks
1966	*...And Now Miguel*	James Clark
1966	*Grand Prix*	John Frankenheimer
1967	*El Dorado*	Howard Hawks
1967	*In Cold Blood*	Richard Brooks
1967	*Tarzan and the Great River*	Robert Day
1968	*A Bullet for the General*	Damiano Damiani
1968	*Villa Rides*	Buz Kulik
1969	*Hook, Line & Sinker*	George Marshall
1969	*Easy Rider*	Dennis Hopper
1969	*Butch Cassidy and the Sundance Kid*	George Roy Hill
1969	*The Wild Bunch*	Sam Peckinpah
1970	*The Great White Hope*	Martin Ritt
1971	*Bananas*	Woody Allen
1973	*Interval*	Daniel Mann
1974	*Bring Me the Head of Alfred Garcia*	Sam Peckinpah
1977	*Sorcerer*	William Friedkin
1977	*Alambistra*	Robert M. Young

1978	*Dona Flor & Her Two Husbands*	Bruno Baretto*
1978	*The Boys From Brazil*	Franklin Schaffner
1979	*Bye Bye Brazil*	Carlos Diegues*
1981	*Pixote*	Hector Babenco*
1982	*The Border*	Tony Richardson
1982	*Fitzcarraldo*	Werner Herzog*
1982	*Missing*	Constantin Costa-Gavras
1982	*Last Plane Out*	David Nelson
1983	*Under Fire*	Roger Spottiswood
1983	*Romancing the Stone*	Robert Zemeckis
1984	*Blame It On Rio*	Stanley Donen
1984	*Against All Odds*	Taylor Hackford
1984	*The Evil that Men Do*	J. Lee Thompson
1984	*Toy Soldiers*	David Fisher
1985	*Latino*	Haskell Wexler
1985	*The Official Story*	Luis Puenzo*
1985	*The Emerald Forest*	John Boorman
1985	*Kiss of the Spider Woman*	Hector Babenco*
1986	*The Mission*	Roland Joffe
1986	*Salvador*	Oliver Stone
1986	*Miss Mary*	Maria-Luisa Bemberg*
1986	*Three Amigos*	John Landis
1986	*The Mosquito Coast*	Peter Weir
1987	*Catch the Heat*	Joel Silberg
1987	*Predator*	John McTiernan
1987	*Sweet Country*	Michael Cacoyannis
1987	*Let's Get Harry*	Alan Smithee
1988	*Walker*	Alex Cox
1988	*Moon Over Parador*	Paul Mazursky
1988	*Old Gringo*	Luis Puenzo*
1990	*Wild Orchid*	Zalman King

*Notes foreign-produced (wholly or in part; primarily Latin) films with wide distribution and/or influence in the United States.

The Arab World as Place

Jack G. Shaheen

Men are short of vision, and they see but that for which they look. Some look for evil and they find evil; some look for good and it is good they find.

Conversation between an Arab
guide and novelist Gertrude Bell,
(*The Desert and the Sown*
by Gertrude Bell, 1907)

Introduction. This essay provides an overview of selected feature films which focus on the Arab world as place. The distinction of settings, embellished by costumes, properties, and music in which the action occurs, will be documented and discussed. For more than two decades this writer has researched the manner in which Arab locales are depicted in more than 400 motion pictures. Included are analyses of representative films from specific regions.

Most films do not display the diverse geographic areas of the Arab world. Instead, moviemakers project a "seen one, seem 'em all" setting—a mythical "Ay-rabland," which typically has no geographical, social or political reality.

Ever since cameras started cranking, moviemakers have conjured up and presented to viewers distorted landscapes vis-a-vis "Ay-rabland." This illusory setting functions as a make-believe theme park complete with shadowy, topsy-turvy sites, patronized by us all. By interweaving central myths, the abhorrence of Arabia has embedded itself firmly in the psyche of viewers. Acting as a producer's flashcard—jackals howl when the moon is full—Hollywood's fictive, sterile and corrupt desert culture imitates yesteryear's distorted representations of Africa-as-dark continent.

Supplementing Ay-rabland are instruments of amusement and violence, found in the moviemaker's "Instant Ali Baba Kit." Property supervisors stock the kit with **khanjars** (curved daggers), lengthy whips, imposing scimitars, magic lamps, magic sapphires, enchanted roses, **bakhur** (incense), mosaic chairs and tables, giant feather fans made of ostrich and peacock flumes, feather-backed dias', pillows embroidered in brilliant designs, Turkish baths, "Asses milk baths," hubble bubble pipes, decorative coffee pots, burning incense in brass lanterns peppered with punched out designs, ornate copper and brass trays, thinly veiled

72

litters held aloft by elephants carrying queens and princesses, ropes and snakes which pop out of baskets when flutes are played, World War I switchboards, sunglasses and Rolexes.

Before contemplating screen portraits, we should remember that our impressions of the Arab world have derived from European, especially British and French societies. Portraits of Arab nations were brought to America's shores by colonists who were seeking economic opportunity and freedom from discrimination. And their attitudes were shaped by more than 500 years of religious and political struggles between Europe and the Arab and Turkish worlds (Hamilton 1271).

In the late nineteenth and early twentieth centuries, European writers were both fascinated and repelled by Arabia. The legacy of their writings in travel books, guides, and memoirs are evident in today's motion pictures (Mabro i).

It should be noted that "Americans, in general, have an abysmal understanding of the world." Also, they "show little appetite for increasing their understanding," says *U.S. News and World Report* editor, David Gergen (Serfaty 52). Americans know "less basic geography than the citizens of Sweden, West Germany, Japan, France and Canada, and considerably less than they knew forty years ago," says Gergen (Serfaty 53). When we group different Mideast nations as one and the same, this sometimes leads to serious repercussions. In 1980, at the height of the Iranian hostage crisis, a national opinion poll revealed that "70% of the Americans surveyed identified Iran, the Persian nation, as an Arab country, and 8% admittedly could not identify it. Imagine what effect this misperception had on American attitudes toward Arabs at the time" (Slade 144).

As a result of Fulbright-Hayes Lectureship grants and several speaking tours sponsored by the United States Information Service (USIS), I have lived and traveled extensively throughout the region, having visited 15 nations in North Africa, Southwest Asia and the Arabian peninsula. Prior to my sojourns, which began in the early 1970s, I, like most Americans, had considered the region to be uncultivated. My sentiments were shaped not from personal experiences, but from a constant diet of allegorical panoramas on silver screens. I was not aware that the region was one-and-a-half times as large as the United States. Nor did I know that approximately 250 million Arabs lived in 21 nations, which stretch from the Straight of Hormuz to the Rock of Gibraltar. Eventually, I came to discover that, like America, the Arab world accommodated diverse citizens: farmers, mechanics, bakers, artists, engineers, homemakers, storekeepers, doctors, lawyers, educators and business persons.

I have come to know a people who share religion, heritage and history. Many business and government leaders attended college in the West, which may help to explain why the region hosts more than 100 Rotary and Lion's Clubs. Most Arabs living in villages and cities reside in homes or apartments. The majority are poor, not rich; most do not dwell in desert tents; most have never seen an oil well or mounted a camel and none live in palace harems or take excursions on "magic carpets." Their dress is traditional or western; the variety of their garb and lifestyle defies stereotyping.

Geographically, Arabia is at the center of our modern civilization; it's the point where Asia, Europe and Africa come together. There is no single Arab nation. There are, instead, distinct peoples who reside in three distinct areas: North Africa (Algeria, Djibouti, Egypt, Libya, Mauritania, Morocco, Sudan, Somalia, Tunisia); the "Fertile Crescent" (Iraq, Jordan, Lebanon, occupied Palestine and Syria); and the Arabian Peninsula (Bahrain, Kuwait, Oman, Qatar, Saudi Arabia, United Arab Emirates and the Republic of Yemen).

Strategically, the area is important because it holds two-thirds of the world's known oil reserves. In 1991, as a result of Operation Desert Shield and Desert Storm, more than half a million young American men and women went to the area. Also, this region is where the first civilizations originated. The land gave the world an alphabet, writing, agriculture and the three major monotheistic religions. The Arab world is a history rich with scholars and a common language steeped in devotion. Most Arabs are Muslims, but two million Arab Jews and 15 million Arab Christians live in the region (Hayes 1).

In the movies, these Arab realities are ignored; make-believe settings dominate motion pictures. Some film titles accent abracadabra-fantasy-type locales, others focus on "exotic" cities, and still others highlight desert ruins and outposts, which act as efficient backdrops for sex-and-slaughter-in-sand scenarios.

For almost 100 years, scores of scenarios have been played out in deserts (the sand dunes appeared bonafide but in many films the rocky hills were Californian), ragged black and white tents, cafes, slave markets, oases and palm trees, ruins, forts, hotels, tombs and oil wells. *The Sheik* (1921) helped initiate the theme: "uncivilized Arabs fighting in savage deserts." In *The Sheik*, the protagonist, Ahmed, helps auction off Arab women and then abducts a European damsel. Explains Ahmed: "When an Arab sees a woman he wants, he takes her!"

Historically, wasteland settings reveal routine melodramas which feature Arabs vs. British forces and/or legionnaires. Armed with up-to-date weapons, rifles, machine guns and a few tanks, the outnumbered forces fire away at hordes of charging Arabs wielding sabers. Conversely, in *Beau Sabreur* (1928), the obese Sheikh El-Hamel employs advanced technology. He frustrates western heroes by desert mines, which he explodes in a secret chamber by means of an electric switch.

Years later, even Elvis Presley had difficulty coping with scoundrels in the sand. In *Harum Scarum* (1965), at the "Palace of Jackals," Elvis survives the "death of a thousand cuts." The Arab female assassin warns him about a land with "oil," but without "cars" or an "airport." She adds: "When you come to our country you will be stepping back two thousand years." *Paradise* (1982) focuses on savage Arabs who, in 1823, attack a caravan enroute from Baghdad to Damascus. Led by the Jackal, who chopped off the head of an American woman, the knaves gallop through the desert in pursuit of two western youths. The dressed-in-black Jackal is determined to take and rape the young English heroine. Why does he fail? Because two chimps wearing burnooses, and an American youth, out-smart him.

At times, scene designers augment desert vistas by inserting mountain hide-outs, alleyways, **suqs** (market places), caves, dingy old prison cells and dungeons. In Arabian Nights fantasies, producers play to camel stops in and around ancient Arabia, particularly Baghdad. Viewers are treated to lavishly gaudy sets, complete with harem quarters in gleaming marble palaces topped with shining cupolas. **Mabkharas** (incense burners) and Egyptian/Aztec decor, are as mixed as the characters' accents, melding civilizations as different as Chinese, Indian and Persian.

Confused free-for-alls feature plenty of action in the "Land of the Cyclops;" appearing are rich-colored carpets, stationary and airborne, nasty ghouls, giant two-headed birds of prey, 12-headed monsters, mechanical horses and serpent-women. In *The 7th Voyage of Sinbad* (1958), an evil magician places an Arab woman in a large basket, tosses in a snake, garbles magic words and out pops a blue-faced serpent-woman, complete with four arms.

The Thief of Baghdad (1924) helped introduce fantasy abracadabra fables, such as *Arabian Adventure* (1979). Baghdad, "the dream city of the ancient East," is featured in both films. In *Thief*, however, religion plays a positive role. Mosques and Holy Korans are as significant as imaginative settings. The protagonist's innumerable adventures culminate, when, mounted on a winged horse, the thief topples a dragon and sea spider. In *Adventure*, the heroic prince topples both rebel troops and metal monsters. *Thief*'s panoramas are impressive: the Cavern of Enchanted Trees, Citadel of the Moon, the Midnight Sea and Mountains of Dread Adventure yield exciting visual treats. The final frames in both films show the heroes saving Baghdad; they triumph in flying carpet duels and fly off with the beloved princesses.

Images of a thousand disappointments and delights enter the collective conscience as falsification and myth. Often, exotic fairy-tale atmospheres are supplemented by the Egyptian desert, countryside and rivers. Cinematographers show houseboats and steamships and **feluccas** (small sailboats) skimming effortlessly over the Nile. Near river banks, grass and mud-brick huts appear in the shadows of the Sphinx, pyramids, obelisks, temples and other Egyptian ruins. Desert excavation sites feature ancient scrolls, Egyptologists' studies (where else to conceal the mummies?), and underground treasure tombs complete with secret passages, inscribed hieroglyphic curses and skeletons tucked between coffins underneath pyramids.

In **suqs**, antiquated taxis, overstuffed limousines and trucks dispute narrow streets with **arbanas** (one horse-carriages), herds of camels, sheep and donkey carts. The melee sends "the milling crowd dashing for cover; carts of goods are overturned and clouds of dust envelop the scene," writes Professor Linda L. Lambe (Lambe 8). "The everyday clamor and swirl of confusion is multiplied," says Lambe, when charlatans hawk slaves and goods on unsafe narrow, dark and dusty streets. To illustrate the influence settings have on viewers, one of Lambe's brightest students remarked, after viewing clips from a number of Arab films in class: "The pushy open-market vendors, the harem girls, the snake charmer, and the fanatical Islamic swordsman.... Surely such things are actually present in the Middle East" (Lambe 25).

Middle Eastern music—cymbals, flutes, violins, **derbukes** (drums or bagpipes made of animal skin), tambourines, and lutes—alerts viewers to anticipate other properties of destruction: evil medallions ("it means death to whoever holds it'), concealed poison in rings, branding irons and stretching wheels of anguish ("punishment of the slow death") prevail in torture chambers, and venomous darts and "poison asps" dominate Sultans' dwellings.

Hypodermic needles are vogue in several contemporary films. In *Black Sunday* (1977) a Palestinian terrorist disguised as a nurse pokes an Israeli intelligence agent with a poisoned hypodermic needle. In *Trenchcoat* (1983), Arab sheikhs inject the kidnapped American heroine with a hypodermic and in the *Black Stallion Returns* (1983), an Arab cur thrusts an Arabian stallion with a hypodermic (Michalek 7).

Producers augment Ay-rabland's landscapes and Instant Ali Baba Kits with unsightly stock characters in sundry silhouettes and sizes. Costumers reveal Arab women as either being clad very heavily or very scantily. They often appear as enslaved vixens in the marketplace's auction block, or as bending belly dancers in cafes and courtyards; seldom are they seen as being loved or as loving others. Although harems no longer exist in the region—"the word 'harem' simply means the segregated part of the house where strange men do not have access— costumers display harem maidens in satin or transparent slacks with tight-fitting vests which highlight as much bosom as possible. The girls don tassels and wear coquettish tiny black, blue and white veils, often semitransparent (Mabro 3).

Because some costumers perceive women as men's slaves, not as men's partners, they adorn Arab women from head to toe with yards of black cloth. This bundles-of-black fixation conveys a warning to possible suitors: the woman's attractiveness is "tainted with the blackness of sin." Like Americans, many Arabs elect to wear one fashion in the privacy of the home, then another style of clothing when mingling in a public place. The women who wear scarves, veils, and cloaks in public do so out of love and modesty. Some wear this mode of dress for religious, economic and sexual reasons, or as a form of political protest. Customs and style of dress are not dictated in the region; many opt to put on Western-style clothing, which range from blue jeans to Parisian dresses. Others opt to put on the veil, the **hijab**, a head scarf that covers head, neck and part of the face, and the **abaya**, a cloak to cover the body. Interestingly, costumers only place Arabian garb on women-of-the west when these distressed heroines are being made ready to fend off Arab scoundrels seeking to seduce the spotless super stars.

Excluded from screen wardrobes are exquisitely designed clothes from Syria, Morocco, Jordan and other nations. Beautifully embroidered Palestinian dresses which reveal "the history of Palestine," contain representative examples of patchwork, of cross-stitch, and of the elaborate crouching associated with cities. For women of Bethlehem, for example, "the costumes reflected "their standing in society—their economic status, whether married or single, the town or area they were from" (Grutz 38). A colorful **jilayah**, or coat from Galilee—"appliqued with bright patches of red, green, and yellow taffeta" and embroidered in a myriad of vivid patterns—hints at "origins that might date back to Joseph's coat of many colors," writes Grutz (35).

As for men, symbols of treachery are found in their head-gear and worry beads. The Arabs call worry beads or prayer beads the **misbaha**. Scenarios frequently show a tricky Arab man contemplating dastardly deeds, moving the beads—made of wood, coral, amber, plastic, glass, mother-of-pearl or almost any other hard material—rhythmically between thumb and index finger so that one bead clicks against the next one. What viewers fail to comprehend is that each bead represents a reference to God and in Arabic there are 99 such expressions. A 33-bead **misbaha** would require the cycle to be repeated three times.

Costumers cover the heads of male Arab characters with black and white or red and white **kuffiyehs**. On heads of others, they place red fezes with or without tassels, multi-colored turbans and tarboushes. Often, they cover wily character types with white **thobes** ("walking bedsheets"), which blaze with slated sunlight in casbahs; the caricatures prance about in pointed **babouche** slippers. Covering the man's body are khaki-colored fatigues, or striped and checkered robes; the robes and some **kuffiyehs** resemble glaring tablecloths pinched from Italian restaurants. If not attired in pajama-type **thobes**, costumers show men wearing fashionable suits with red fezzes, turbans, or lengthy **kuffiyehs**, a sight I have yet to see.

When cinematographers focus on Cairo and other North African municipalities, viewers are initially introduced by the mosques' slender minarets gleaming in the background. Shady cafes and puzzling bazaars follow; they function as symbols of backwardness. Most screen **suqs** resemble not the reality—a wide variety of restaurants and shops with friendly proprietors—but emulate Hollywood's *Algiers'* casbah settings. Cinematic images reveal mazes of crooked cobblestone walkways swallowing up unsuspecting tourists as well as Western thieves who seek temporary sanctuary from the law. Uneven stone steps lead to shadowy and hidden passageways where beggars squat before graffiti on walls.

Consider the similarities of *Algiers* (1938, a re-make of the French film, *Pepe le Moko*, 1936) and *Casbah* (1948, a re-make of *Algiers*). In both films, Algeria's lower depths appear as a decrepit thicket—a sweeping maze of narrow winding passages. In *Algiers*, the narrator cautions, "There is not one casbah, but hundreds; there are thousands. It's easy to go in, but not so easy to come out." Several French policemen explain the area to a recently arrived inspector. "The reality of the casbah is something stranger than anything you could have dreamed," says one." It's like "entering another world; a melting pot for all the sins of the earth," says another. Warns the third: It's "the filth of centuries."

Algiers and *Casbah* begin with the muezzin's call to pray, followed by sounds of an upbeat Parisian tune, and a haunting Arabic melody. The implication here is the clash of cultures. In *Algiers*, the narrator cautions, the "casbah's population includes many...drifters and outcasts...and criminals." Confirms a policeman: "it's always been that way." *Casbah* opens with an Algerian guide gliding western tourists off a bus. He advises: It's "not wise to be left alone in the streets of the casbah." Nor is it wise to trust *Casbah*'s Arab counselor, whose blatant flirtations aggravate Western tourists.

The scenarios focus not on Algerians in love, but on romance between the French couple, Gabrille and Pepe. Says *Algiers'* narrator: "Supreme on these heights rules one man, Pepe le Moko, wanted by the French police." Pepe loathes the casbah; he's repulsed by his environment—beggars, whores, corrupt merchants, thieves—and longs to return to "marvelous" Paris "where they speak French."

Gabrille does not say to Pepe, "take me **to** the casbah"; instead she silently screams, get me **out** of the casbah. Pepe concurs. "Gotta get out of here. The dirt and the noise, day in and day out." In *Casbah*, Pepe explodes, "It's like being in a grave. I can't stand much more of it." To him, death offers more freedom than the casbah. Both films conclude with the inspector saying to the fatally wounded Pepe, "I'm sorry Pepe, he (the inspector's colleague) thought you were going to escape." Says Pepe, "And so I have, my friend." The scene is played *outside* the casbah, by the ship, with Gabrille on board, bound for Europe.

At times, directors transfer the action to seaports, complete with hodgepodge costuming, language and geography. Consider *Morocco* (1930) and *Song of Scheherazade* (1947). In *Morocco*, the few women who appear don not **abayas,** but Spanish garb; they speak not Arabic, but Spanish. *Scheherazade* opens with two Russian soldiers, Rimsky-Korsakoff and a count, discussing their upcoming liberty in "Morocco, a Spanish port." *Scheherazade*'s producers and writers project Morocco, an Arab nation, as Spain. Although flamenco dancing accompanied by the penetrating Moorish tunes of the **cante jondo** with its rhythms separated by slight pauses is of Arab origin, viewers hear not Arabic songs of the Moors, but traditional Russian and Spanish songs accompanied by flashy dance routines (Salloum 3).

The Arabs of Morocco appear briefly in two scenes, as vendors mulling about in the background. Also, serving a Spanish family is "Hassan, the little Arab boy," who is mostly invisible, always silent. Although Korsakoff's opera, *Scheherazade,* was inspired by the tales of a beautiful "Arabian" woman, in this film, the beautiful Cara, a Spanish lass, arouses Korsakoff's passion.

Why did filmmakers transform locales and characters? Did they think American viewers would not accept the film's hero, Russian composer Korsakoff, romancing an Arab woman? Whatever the reasons, consider an early scene which takes place inside the Cafe Oriental; Cara wears a veil. A male patron inquires what other patrons ask: "How'd a nice girl like you come to be in a (bad) place like this?" The implication here? The Spanish Cara is better than other women, mostly Moroccan, who work at this seedy spot. When Cara departs the Cafe' Oriental, she tosses off the veil, confirming her emancipation.

Romance and adventure among the sand dunes is the theme of the Kalem Company's, *Captured by Bedouins* (1912). In *Bedouins*, the Egyptian desert is a treacherous setting for westerners and Arabs alike. Filmed at "Luxor, Egypt, on the Nubian Desert," the film opens with Doris, the American heroine, visiting the Sphinx. Here, she is "discovered by prowling bedouins" and taken to their "native village" where she's held captive inside a straw hut, resembling a tepee. Doris' suitor, an Englishman by the name of Lieutenant Grieg, poses as an Arab and rides to the rescue. States the title card, "A Strange Arab," as Grieg's face is covered with black polish. A shoot 'em up ensues, creeping bedouins on camels versus khaki-clad Egyptian soldiers with fezes on horses. During the melee, Grieg and Doris hide behind a camel (in a Cowboy-versus-Indian film, a horse or covered wagon serve as protection) and fire away at charging bedouins, who eventually retreat.

Opulent tents in mountain ranges complete with sand dunes, represent Samari, a mythical Arab nation, in *I Cover the War* (1937). In *War*, "fanatic tribesmen" reappear; they pine for rifles to use against the British. When an American newsreel producer arrives, the British officer, wearing pith helmet and khakis, greets him, saying: "Welcome to Samari. Although why in the world you should come here, I don't know."

Several scenes focus on the "Oasis Hotel," and the **suq** where veiled women saunter and bearded beggar spies dwell. Additional action occurs inside the British compound and at Muffadi's, the rebel leader's, tent encampment. On entering his tent, Muffadi wears a fez and a white western suit; his followers are mute. Moments later he greets his comrades wearing a burnoose and flowing robe; they cheer. Muffadi rides off with his "horde of tribesmen" to attack the compound. But the Arab's reign of terror ends as British pilots arrive in time to drop bombs on the charging "horde."

The British and Americans topple Arab hordes in *Adventures in Iraq* (1943). Here, "the wastelands of Iraq," complete with "devil worshippers," and Ali-Babble dialogue are featured. Opening frames show a plane encountering technical difficulties and being forced to land. Suddenly, "Arab tribes that lie in the foothills and come out only to rob and kill," kidnap three westerners, Tess, Doug and George. Previously, George had warned Doug: "Don't land here. Try to find a place with some civilization." Look, says George, "a castle in this godforsaken wilderness." The castle, complete with "sacrificial altar," is a "palace and fortress, all in one." Boasts castle-keeper Sheikh Ali, "many nations covet my oil." Ali considers Hitler's Germany a possible market for his kingdom's oil.

Several scenes show Iraqis bowing before a serpent carved in a wall, which represents "the image of Satan." Explains Ali: "The religion of my people has always been primitive idolatry and superstition." Boasts Ali, "We know very well we are barbarians." Wearing a turban with his western suit, Ali apologizes for the "medieval punishment" about to be inflicted on the captors. Tess and Doug are forced to tolerate the crowd's insults and threats as they are carried through the **suq** on chair lifts. *Iraq* concludes with the western hostages being rescued not by the Foreign Legion but by Captain Carson of the United States Air Force, who arrives in the nick of time. When the Iraqis hesitate to release the prisoners, Carson orders his pilots to dump a few bombs on Gotsi, the Iraqi fictional kingdom. On seeing the telling effects of U.S. firepower, Sheikh Ali capitulates, bowing to the "superior force."

Many desert films later, western heroics are again displayed in *Abbott and Costello Meet the Mummy* (1952). Cameras focus on Egypt's pyramids, complete with secret passageways and hidden treasures, tombs and a sacred medallion. The story concerns Klaris, a prowling mummy, who still lives after 4,000 years in musty wrappings. Tagged "bandages with eyes," Klaris is kept alive by drinking a mysterious elixir. Although it's simple for writers to terminate shifty Egyptian villains, it's arduous for them to annihilate skulking mummies. In *Mummy*, however, property masters set off a dynamite charge in the tomb's sacred temple, destroying the tattered Klaris and revealing the legendary treasure. To preserve the legend of Klaris, Abbott and Costello transform the temple into a nightclub. *Mummy* concludes with interior shots of the duo's new establishment, "Cafe' Klaris." Here, disguised as mummies, more than a dozen band members perform.

Nearly three decades later, Egypt's cities, tombs, and desert remain menacing backdrops for Westerners who conduct research on Pharaohs. In *Sphinx* (1981), no sooner does Erica, the American Egyptologist, clear customs in Cairo, she is harassed on the street by assertive Egyptian youths begging for cigarettes. Other adolescents pinch her buttocks. Erica's problems accelerate when she announces herself at a **suq**'s antique shop; she is greeted by the murdered body of an unscrupulous art dealer; he was killed with a saber. In her hotel room, fearful of being robbed, and doubting the security of the hotel's safe, she tucks away her valuables.

Filmed in Egypt, most of the action in *Sphinx* takes place in and around Luxor, especially the gigantic monuments of the Valley of the Kings. Here, Erica befriends Ahmed Khazzan, an official of the antiquities division of the United Nations. She also stumbles onto a smuggling operation designed to relieve Egypt of all the treasures left in the country's tombs and museums. Prior to rescuing Erica from a sealed tomb, the dying Ahmed explains: "Egypt's great natural resource? Death."

In order to record Egypt's historic landscapes, producers from many nations visit Cairo, the cinematic center of the Arab world. Yet, Egyptian officials and imagemakers are concerned because they believe Hollywood does not project their nation and its peoples in a fair or favorable light. *Sphinx*, for example, is banned in Egypt because of a highly improbable scene in which an Egyptian policeman tries to rape Erica inside the police shed at Saqqara, a busy archaeological tourist attraction. This attempted rape scene was not in the screenplay shown to Egyptian authorities; after *Sphinx*'s film crew left Egypt, producers shot the scene in Europe and added it to the footage (McDougal 23).

As with *I Cover the War* and *Adventures in Iraq*, American ingenuity, air power, up-to-date armaments and desert forts are featured in films focusing on Palestinians. In *Prisoner in the Middle* (1974), a B-52 bomber on a routine mission to the Middle East, develops mechanical trouble and goes off course. A nuclear warhead is accidentally jettisoned, landing on the Jordanian side of the Jordanian-Israel border. On leave in Jerusalem, Colonel Stevens, a U.S. officer, is asked to locate and "deactivate" the warhead. Israeli troops also seek the device. Desert scenes focus, not on Israelis and Jordanians, but on unshaven Palestinian "terrorists" clad in fatigues and wearing red and white, or black and white **kuffiyehs**. When asked by Stevens what they plan on "doing with that thing," the Palestinian Major replies: "Very simple, use it. One bomb, no Jews."

The action begins in the desert with Israeli girls singing on a school bus. Suddenly, Palestinians shoot off a rocket and subsequent frames reveal bloodied bodies of innocents and a toy bear. Property supervisors often use toys and dolls among rubble when producers opt to show Palestinians slaughtering children, especially in films such as *Wanted Dead or Alive* (1987) and *Death Before Dishonor* (1987). *Prisoner's* Israeli soldiers deride the Palestinian villains as either having "hash" for sale or being "too busy making love with their sheep to do business." The contemporary Jordanian desert setting reveals Palestinians on camels committing barbaric acts, similar to primitive deeds carried out by Indians in Hollywood's early Westerns. They not only slaughter schoolgirls but one rapes an Israeli woman. An Israeli soldier is torn apart when Palestinians tie his arms to two horses. Also, the screenplay contends that more than 15 Palestinians are not sufficiently strong or bright enough to load the captured warhead onto the back of a pick-up truck. *Prisoner* concludes at an abandoned fort where the outnumbered Israelis, assisted by Colonel Stevens, terminate scores of Palestinians.

An American soldier directs his guns at Kuwaitis in *Best Defense* (1984). *Defense* features Wylie Cooper, an American officer stationed in Kuwait; Cooper pokes fun at dumb Kuwaiti soldiers with Italian accents. The unfit soldiers are unable to steer an innovative U.S. tank; they play with themselves in locker rooms. The producers opt not to show a progressive and highly developed Kuwait, complete with modern highways, mosaic twin water towers, museums, beach resorts, hotels, gardens or arabesque government buildings. Instead, Officer Cooper belittles Kuwait, which is represented on screen by gobs of camels and untidy street people mulling about in messy **suqs**. In one scene, uniformed American officers and Arabs in **thobes** appear on a reviewing stand; a U.S. officer repeatedly stumbles when trying to explicate commonalities. "Kuwait and America share a common heritage. Like. Ah...Ah...Ah...Your desert. We, (Americans) too, have deserts."

Defense shows the Iraqi air force dropping bombs on Americans and Kuwaitis. The scenario further confuses viewers when Kuwaiti women dressed in black, and youths, toss stones not at the invading forces, but at Officer Cooper. He grunts to the Kuwaiti soldiers, "pull out your prayer rugs." Cooper then points the tank's guns on Kuwaiti youths: "Okay, you desert rats, now you die." Interestingly, *Best Defense* is based on Robert Grossbach's 1975 novel, *Easy and Hard Ways Out*, which concerns Vietnam and North Vietnamese aggression.

Settings shift from the desert to eastern Mediterranean locales in *Navy Seals* (1990). The viewer encounters "scum-bag" Palestinians wearing **kuffiyehs**. Here, "these cheese-dicks" shoot at a U.S. helicopter and kill one crewman and capture another. Also, action occurs aboard ships, in warehouses, "Arab strongholds" in Lebanon's dungeons and fortresses, and in Beirut, the "ass-hole of misery." In *Seals*, Palestinian "ragheads" and "fuckers" seize American-made Stinger missiles, "the ideal weapon for terrorist actions." Thus, the movie focuses primarily on bombed out Beirut where the SEALs destroy both the missiles and the "terrorists."

Initially, the SEALs, disguised as Palestinians, land "somewhere in the Arab world." The "somewhere" is represented by a fortress where American prisoners are held. Advanced U.S. weaponry is employed to blow up "a piece of shit" and "his assholes." Their hideout is engulfed in flames. Next, still in search of the missiles, the SEALs board a merchant ship "off the coast of Syria." Arab passengers on deck intermingle with "terrorists," sheep and goats. One wonders whether the producers intended to have viewers judge the Arab travelers by the company they keep. Midway through the film, producers insert a television set. A late-breaking news item is projected in order to enforce the "Arab lands as violent places" theme; the TV newscaster reveals "Algerians" have attacked "a civilian aircraft."

Final frames reveal the defeated "terrorists" chasing after the SEALs in a Mercedes. Missiles destroyed, the SEALs look to rendezvous with their submarine. One SEAL sighs, "Looks the same. It all looks the same."

In the credits, *Seals'* producers extend "thanks to the Department of Defense and the Department of Navy." But, according to J.P. Mitchell, Commander, U.S. Navy and Assistant Chief of Information, "The Navy did not formally cooperate with Orion Pictures' *Navy Seals*." Added Commander Mitchell, "Quite recently the Navy denied support to another SEAL movie. Support was denied not only because of the inaccurate portrayal of the Navy SEAL community but also because of the negative portrayal of Arabs in the Middle East."

Summary. The Middle East Peace Conference, beginning in 1991, provides moviemakers with opportunities to unlearn stereotypical depictions of the region. They could challenge students and the general public by developing and presenting scenarios which display a wide range of costumes, properties and landscapes. Continued representation of the Arab world, complete with mythical, Ay-rabland settings and Instant Ali Baba Kits, benefits no one. As President John F. Kennedy said: "The great enemy of truth is very often not the lie, deliberate, contrived and dishonest, but the myth, persistent, persuasive, and realistic" (Shaheen 10).

The most distorted and misunderstood aspect of the Arab world is that its landscapes have markedly changed since the early 1900s. The trouble is that the screen images of Arabia have not changed in the past 90 years—except to worsen. Consider this scene extracted from a late-1940s *Movietone* newsreel entitled, "Immigrants Arrive in Palestine." Summing up Palestine as place, the narrator states: "These Jewish immigrants found a hostile land, filled with swamps, snakes, scorpions and Arabs." The insinuation here being, Palestine was a parched land populated by barbaric peoples awaiting civilized conquerors to enter (AMC Channel, May 1991).

Repetitious and negative images of Palestine and other Arab nations literally sustain adverse portraits across generations. There is a commanding link between make-believe aberrations and the real world. Unless moviemakers take time to become informed about genuine landscapes, Arab settings on movie screens will continue to exhibit properties of terror such as guns, bombs, tanks and air bases. Viewers will proceed to see alongside camels, goats and donkeys, sleek limousines, complete with tinted windows. The sleek automobiles let them (villains in **thobes** and/or fatigues) see you, but you can't see them. And Arabesque military forts, complete with basement torture chambers, will continue to supplement ornate twelfth-century palaces.

Scholars and imagemakers understand that there is a dangerous and cumulative effect when static and offensive pictures remain unchallenged. Yet, as of this writing producers remain adamant; they selectively structure Ay-rabland as outlandish "over there" scenes for stale camel-operas. Perhaps ignorance and fear of the "different" prevents them from projecting more accurate pictures. Perhaps filmmakers are not conscious of their own motives or messages.

Stereotyped settings may be slow to fade away, because so much of the cinematic library dates back for generations. Most probably, previous panoramas served as the imagemaker's visual lesson plan. Exposed to scores of past portraits, perhaps producers realized Arabian expanses were effortless to clone. Also, dreary Ay-rabland may remain attractive to cinematographers because their clichéd vistas have gone largely unchallenged, a result of complacency about the misrepresentation of the region. Or, perhaps, imagemakers simply do not care that the Arab world emerges as a dissimilar environment.

Donned in different garb and speaking a different language, Arabs continue to be shown as shadowy types, worshiping a "different" deity. Nearly all peoples are lumped together as a mass of wretched beings in need of mental modification. Myopic emphasis on desert dunes, where Western heroes vanquish Arab villains, are reminiscent of open plains scenes where just-like-us Cowboys overpower "different" Indians. Note scholars Miller and Woll, "From the silent era to today, the Arab image has stalked the silent screen as a metaphor for anti-Western values." Sharply "etched in black," Arabs appear as "lustful and exotic villains to Western heroes and heroines" (Miller and Woll 179).

Ay-rabland's inhabitants herald an almost Satanic presence. Lurking behind Saharan landscapes, Arabs "live by sword and intrigue" and function as ultimate un-assimilable aliens," threateningly different from us (Ibid). Author Robert J. Lifton explains the possible consequences of selective framing, "It's much easier to make an enemy out of somebody who looks different, who is from a different race, a different background, a different religion" (Lifton PBS).

How much longer must viewers wait before imagemakers unlearn their Ay-rabland? When might they expect to see rational pictures? Fresh scenarios could illuminate, not darken, perceptions. The ultimate result would then be an image of the Arab world as neither hell or heaven, but as a fitting component of planet earth.

"Men (and women) hit only what they aim at," writes Thoreau. "Therefore, though they fail immediately, they had better aim at something high." Because the telling effects of insidious settings narrow our vision and blur reality, moviemakers could not aim higher than by working to dispel unsightly portraits of the Arab world. It becomes ultimately an issue of conscience and morality.

Works Cited

Note. The author selected representative films based on the number of film titles for each of the regions discussed.

North Africa: 78 titles, total. 59 titles relate to Egypt: Mummy, 13, Cleopatra, 9, Nile, 8, Egypt/Egyptians, 8, Cleopatra, 9, Pharaoh, 5, Sphinx, 2, Suez, 2, Tomb, 1, Pyramids, 1, and Scarab, 1. And 18 titles relate to Morocco, (18) Morocco, 9, Tangier, 6, Casablanca, 3.

Abracadabra Arabs and Settings: 33 titles, total. Sinbad, 9, Aladdin, 7, Ali Baba, 5, Harem, 5, A Thousand and One Nights, 4, Hajji Baba, 1, Magic Carpet, 1, Sultan, 1.

Arabian Peninsula: 17 titles, total. Arabian/Arab, 9, Arabia, 8.

Fertile Crescent: 16 titles relate to Iraq: Baghdad, 12, Babylon, 3, Iraq, 1.

Desert: 38 titles, total: Desert, 28, Sahara, 7, Sand(s), 2, Bedouins, 1.

Bell, Gertrude. *The Desert and the Sown*. London, Heinemann, 1907.

Cortés, Carlos E. "Pride, Prejudice and Power: The Mass Media As Societal Educator On Diversity." A research paper by Professor Cortés, to be published in *Prejudice, Polemic, or Progress?* 4 James Lynch, Celia Modgil, Sohan Modgil, eds.

Grutz, Jane W. "Woven Legacy Woven Language." *Aramco World Magazine* Jan.-Feb. 1991: 35.

Hamilton, Marsha. "The Image of Arabs in the Sources of American Culture." *Choice* Apr. 1991: 1271.

Hayes, John R., ed. *The Genius of Arab Civilization*. New York UP, 1975: 1.

Lambe, Linda L. "Hollywood's Arab Other." From Lambe's paper presented at the annual Arab American University Graduates Conference (AAUG), Washington, D.C. 3 Nov. 1989: 8, 25.

Lifton, Robert J. Comments on *PBS's Faces of the Enemy* documentary telecast in St. Louis, MO 28 May 1987.

Mabro, Judy. *Veiled Half-Truths*. New York, I.B. Tauris & Co Ltd., 1991, i.

McDougal, John M. "When the setting calls for pyramids, filmmakers avoid Egypt." *The Christian Science Monitor* 23.

Michalek, Larry. "The Arab in American Cinema: A Century of Otherness." *Cineaste* Vol. XVII, No. 1, 1989: 7.

Miller, Randall M., and Allen L. Woll, eds. *Ethnic and Racial Images in American Film and Television.* New York, Garland, 1987: 179.

Mitchell, J.P. Personal correspondence with the author, letter dated 12 Sept. 1990.

Movietone Newsreel. American Movie Channel. The author viewed the segment late May 1991. The exact time and date are excluded because page two of the author's notes is missing.

Salloum, Habeeb. "Arab Influences in Spanish Music, Song and Dance." *Middle East Dance and Culture Association* 3 Aug. 1991.

Serfaty, Simon, ed. David Gergen's essay, "Diplomacy in a Television Age." *The Media and Foreign Policy.* New York, St. Martin's, 1991: 52, 53.

Shaheen, Jack G. "The Media's Image of Arabs." *Newsweek* 29 Feb. 1988: 10.

———. "The Persian Gulf Crisis Gives Scholars a Chance to Encourage More Accurate Depictions of Arabs." *Chronicle of Higher Education* 31 Oct. 1990: B1, 3.

Slade, Shelly. "The Image of the Arab in America: Analysis of a Poll on American Attitudes." *The Middle East Journal* Spring 1981: 144.

Wall, James M. "Israel is Losing the Living Room War." *The Christian Century* 27 Jan. 1988: 75.

Filmography

Year	Film	Director
1912	*Captured By Bedouins*	Kalem Company
1921	*The Sheik*	George Melford
1924	*Thief of Baghdad*	Raoul Walsh
1928	*Beau Sabreur*	John Waters
1930	*Morocco*	Josef von Sternberg
1937	*I Cover the War*	Arthur Lubin
1938	*Algiers*	John Cromwell
1943	*Adventures in Iraq*	D. Ross Lenderman
1947	*Song of Scherazade*	Walter Reisch
1948	*Casbah*	John Berry
1955	*Abbott and Costello Meet the Mummy*	Charles Lamount
1965	*Harum Scarum*	Gene Nelson
1974	*Prisoner in the Middle*	James O'Connor
1979	*Arabian Adventure*	Kevin Connor
1981	*Sphinx*	Franklin J. Schaffner
1982	*Paradise*	Stuart Gillard
1984	*Best Defense*	Willard Huyck
1990	*Navy Seals*	Lewis Teague

1935	*The Last Outpost*	Louis Gasnier
1937	*Ali Baba Goes to Town*	David Butler
1937	*Slave Girl*	Charles Lamont
1939	*Beau Geste* (Other versions: 1926,1966, 1977)	William Wellman
1939	*The Four Feathers* (Other versions: 1915,1929)	Zoltan Korda
1941	*Outlaws of the Desert*	Howard Bretherton
1942	*Road to Morocco*	David Butler
1944	*Ali Baba and the Forty Thieves*	Arthur Lubin
1949	*Bagdad*	Charles Lamont
1958	*Desert Hell*	Charles M. Warren
1963	*Captain Sinbad*	Byron Haskin
1964	*John Goldfarb, Please Come Home*	J. Lee Thompson
1979	*Ashanti*	Richard Fleischer
1984	*The Ambassador*	J. Lee Thompson
1986	*Iron Eagle*	Sidney J. Furie
1985	*Jewel of the Nile*	Lewis Teague
1987	*Ishtar*	Elaine May
1990	*Duck Tales The Movie: Treasure of the Lost Lamp*	Bob Hathcock
1991	*The Sheltering Sky*	Bernardo Bertolucci

Metropolis Redux:
Visual Metaphor and the Urbanscape
Colleen M. Tremonte

Dateline: Gotham City—The city planning commissioner is on the take. Zoning regulations, building codes, height limitations, and setback requirements are unheard of devices. As a result, development is out of control and the physical environment assumes a sinister character reminiscent of a 21st-century Dickens tale.

(Pearson 206)

What Clifford Pearson vividly captures in his reportorial, almost curt, description of *Batman*'s Gotham City is one of the central aspects of narrative construction in contemporary action/adventure films: the use of the urbanscape to explore the displacement of a populace within its own borders. Telescoping the idea of the "city" corrupt and in need of repair, this urbanscape complicates the spectator's consideration of individual and/or cultural identity. Purposely evoking images of a dualistic urbanscape such as that of Fritz Lang's 1926 classic *Metropolis*, films such as *Blade Runner, Batman, RoboCop*, or *Black Rain* construct a landscape that queries the implications of contemporary society's appropriations of technology.

Visualized predominantly through the built figures of architectural structures and forms, the action/adventure urbanscape within these films operates as metaphor by articulating a vision of a techno-world fraught with ethical and/or moral ambiguity. Often, within this landscape, identifiable configurations (gothic edifices and neoplastic corporate offices) will mirror the antagonism of the populace, with the grimly painted streets amid which they stand functioning as "doubles" for the citizenry.[1] Furthermore, such configurations, and the objects contained therein, directly and/or indirectly delineate the mythic dimension of the hero/antihero who, in circular fashion, is usually equated with the body politik. Any disruption of the movement of bodies between these configurations or any disruption of spatial arrangement of objects within them, including that prompted by the appropriation of consumerized "toys," works discursively to convey the skewed and corrupted reality of the filmic world.

89

Metropolis, one of the first films to employ urban set design discursively, provides the touchstone against which many contemporary urbanscapes may be measured. In this silent film, Lang, himself a student of architecture, establishes a generic syntax which visualizes sound through a select composition of built figures (expressionistic sets) and a select sequencing of shots (such as montage, jump-cut, and cross-cutting).[2] Consequently, the viewer not only *sees* but *hears* the motion of the pistons through the superimposition of one machine upon another; not only *sees* but *feels* the halting, chorus-like gestures of the laborers. A living analogue of the people who move within and between the boundaries of the upper and lower cities—of Freder, Maria, Rotwang, and Fredersen—*Metropolis* provides the two-tiered prototype of futuristic urbanscapes: the upper city—a grandiose street of skyscrapers alive with an incessant stream of air taxis and cars; the lower city—a cavernous, cinderblock shut off from the daylight. The end result is the intentional "schisming" of the body of the city, of an industrial/machine society which separates the corporate rulers from the manual laborers.[3]

The narrative centers on the conflict between the upper city, the domain of corporate manager Fredersen and the elect, and the lower-city, the home of the exploited workers who operate the monstrous machines. The scenario begins with clandestine, rebellious activities led by the virtuous Maria; various standard and stock complications (kidnapping, floods, a mad-scientist, Rotwang, who creates a humanlike, woman robot) further the plot which concludes with hero-son Freder's sudden epiphany, the need to mediate between the "heart" and the "hands." Playing with an obvious good versus evil motif, *Metropolis* does not indict mechanization (or automation) in and of itself but, rather, its abuses. Once the workers and the city are saved, another vision of the metropolis is spawned, one of managed utopia. Implicit in this vision is the recognition of the paradoxical nature of the city: the potential to be controlled by that which we create to house ourselves.

In the extrapolated collage time of Ridley Scott's *Blade Runner* (1982), the convoluted timelessness of Tim Burton's *Batman* (1989), the imploded present of Paul Verhoeven's *RoboCop* (1987), Irvin Kershner's *RoboCop II* (1989) or Sam Raimi's *Darkman* (1990), the impinging "now" of Scott's *Black Rain* (1989), or the speculative near-future of Verhoeven's *Total Recall* (1990), the vision of the city is not only dichotomized, it is schizophrenic: *Metropolis* redux par excellence. By combining Lang's earlier stylistic innovations with the fragmentary visions, forms, and techniques of contemporary society, these films explore the eroding sense of cultural and/or individual identity within a technologized and alienating world. In each, the hero/antihero finds himself alienated from the very place which grounds his identity, from the city—Los Angeles, New York, Detroit, Gotham. Moreover, in each, the city lies in decay or teeters on the brink of destruction, implicitly or explicitly, as a result of corporate or mob greed fueled by consumer greed run amok.

In *Blade Runner*, for example, Rick Deckard (Harrison Ford) finds himself, as does the whole of Los Angeles, indirectly controlled by the actions of the Tyrell Corporation which produces and markets replicants, bio-engineered, off-world slaves. As Eldon Tyrell tells him, "Commerce is our goal here at Tyrell." Deckard casts himself in the role of "killer" (a *blade runner* whose task is to "retire" renegade replicants) rather than that of "victim" because he wants to survive. *Black Rain* finds its hero/antihero Nick (Michael Douglas) surrounded by similarly ambiguous market constraints, only now the competing forces are the mob and the "suits" (the hierarchical police departments). Traveling from the bowels of New York to the unsettling landscape of urban Osaka, Japan, Nick—the ugly American, the lone cowboy—finds himself embarked on a quest for self-integrity in an alien city. And while not as immediate in its *realism*, the devastation and malfeasance of Gotham City are just as *real* to the viewer. Ostensibly caused by multiple crime organizations, such as Boss Carl Grissom's, Gotham's deterioration is, nonetheless, aggravated by the greed of its citizenry; a lone Batman (Michael Keaton) not only fights crime *on* the streets of Gotham, he also fights the citizens of the streets who are willing to be bought off by Joker.

In the most recent of action/adventure films, those in which the hero is technologized and in which the fight for the city literally becomes a question of property acquisition, this type of corporate, mob, and/or consumer greed is complicated. In the *RoboCop* films, both Detroit and Murphy/Robocop (Peter Weller) fall prey to the "privatization is best" and "let's build a beautiful Delta City" slogans of OCP (Omni Consumer Products). In *Darkman*, Peyton/Darkman suffers the same fate as the riverfronts and streets of the city—victim to Strack's commoditization ploy. Even *Total Recall*'s Mars colony nears doom as a result of greedy entrepreneurship while a confused Quaid/Hauser (Arnold Schwarzenegger) decides whether to suppress or to liberate the "city on the hill"—the city over Venusville.

Ultimately, the urbanscape concretizes the symbiotic relationship between the "coporeal body" of the individual hero/antihero and the social/political body of the collective community, revealing characters to be as much *of* the city as *in* the city. Bodily assaulted and seemingly schizophrenic, protagonists like Deckard/Roy, Batman/Wayne, Murphy/Robocop, Peyton/Darkman, or Quaid/Hauser suffer the same punishment inflicted on the city and its inhabitants. Gripped by an apathy which parallels the larger populace's disconcern and fragmentation, *Blade Runner*'s Deckard suffers his physical and emotional disequilibriums in stoic silence. The antithesis to his predicament, like the city's, comes in the form of the runaway replicants (epitomized in Roy Batty) who long for life and identity. Similarly, *Batman*'s Bruce Wayne exhibits a known aloofness and an insularity which mirror Gotham City's own indifference; his alter ego—Batman—stoically endures the throes of criminal injustices and activities, as does Gotham. Among the throngs we find yet another antithesis to the city and to the hero: Wayne/Batman's nemesis, Jack Napier. A villain resurrected in the disfigured body of Joker, Napier reveals yet another aspect of the hidden pathos of the city.

Contrapunctually, *Black Rain*'s Nick suffers the physical assaults of the city in enraged rebellion: he is a good cop gone bad through compromise and need (Nick is under investigation by the internal affairs department for taking confiscated drug money). Fighting both the punks in the streets and the suits at the office, Nick sees New York as "one big gray area." His only possibility of redemption lies outside this swamp, in surrogate territory; that is, Nick can reclaim his identity as a good cop by stepping outside his personal displacement in New York into a cultural displacement in Japan.

The body-city metaphor is most explicit, however, in action/adventure films like *RoboCop* and *RoboCop II*, where "the human body, the corporate body, the body politic, the social body" literally converge in personage of Robocop/Murphy: the penultimate, computerized police officer (Codell 12). As "[t]he nexus of hi-tech production and consumerism as an end-in-itself" (he is a cyborg) (12), Robocop/Murphy externalizes the assault against the city differently than Deckard or Batman; in him the audience *objectively* perceives the overt equation between city/technology/humanity. Turning this measure back in on itself, *Darkman* and *Total Recall* not only externalize the body-city image in respect to technology, they *internalize* it in a nonpsychological manner. Like Deckard, Batman, and Robocop/Murphy, *Darkman*'s Peyton Westlake and *Total Recall*'s Quaid—and their alter egos, Darkman and Hauser—suffer the bodily assaults *of* the city *for* the city. Unlike Deckard and Batman, they do not battle existent inner demons or repression but, rather, imposed psyche infections.

Quaid/Hauser can only rescue the interplanetary lower-city (Venusville) and himself after successfully defeating the purposeful subjugation of his mind/body to a higher techno-consumer order, the voluntary memory implant. Unlike Robocop/Murphy, who must overthrow OCP's unsolicited directives against the unsuspecting trust of the body politik, Quaid must overthrow his own directives. Peyton's predicament parallels Quaid's in that he must fight against the directives and potentials of science and medical technology: the artificial skin. Ultimately, the pain of his disfigurement is manageable only through medical control, by surgically severing the sensory nerves where they enter the brain—the same fate which awaits the unsuspecting city. Unfortunately, the cost is high, as the doctor explains:

When sensory input is lost, the mind grows hungry. Starved of its regular diet of input, it takes the only remaining stimulus it has—the emotions—and amplifies them, giving rise to alienation, loneliness...

Ironically, then, though Peyton does reclaim the city by ridding it of its cancer—the villainous Strack—he fails to reclaim his own earlier identity. Hence, technology cannot save Darkman from his pain and loneliness.

As well as signaling the symbiotic relationship between the body of the hero and the body of the city, these films' urbanscapes work as visual metaphors in that they invariably articulate a vision of society while concurrently conveying the hero/antihero's placement/ displacement within that vision. In *Blade Runner*, director Scott selectively and meticulously converts a named locale and time (Los Angeles, November 2019) into a nihilistic nowhere and everywhere. The city is a "polluted megapolis," a "thronged, overfreighted world" riddled with "earthquake-defying skyscrapers that reek of soullessness" (Demsey 33). Playing with established generic codes and a combination of visual cues (variations on tonalities of light and compact detailed-images), Scott paints a city which metaphorically represents the darkness and ambiguity of both Rick Deckard and the society in which he lives. And as in *Metropolis*, this landscape suggests a misappropriation of technological knowledge, objects, and artifacts which divides the city's inhabitants into victims (both humans and replicants) and victimizers (Tyrell, police, blade runners). Afterall, as police captain Bryant tells Deckard when recruiting his help in "retiring" renegade "skin jobs": "You know the score. If you're not cop, you're little people."

As in the opening scenes of *Metropolis*, the opening sequence of *Blade Runner* finds a combination of overhead long shots sweeping across a skyline crowded with buildings standing toe-to-toe and broken by the streaking of "air taxis" (patrol car/planes). An upward pan of the Tyrell Corporation, a monolithic edifice whose center line suggests the ascending path of a ziggurat temple, again recalls the upper city's skyscrapers and transom lines of *Metropolis*. However, this sequence also inverts the pristine look of the upper-city as Tyrell's squat-topped corporate headquarter ironically echoes the devouring machine of *Metropolis*'s lower city. Amid the rain-sheathed night, aerial flares cast an iridescent orange glow and electric billboards flash intrusive blue and white hues. Structurally, this scene challenges the spectator's own visual and emotional responses to the landscape, similarly to the "Voight Kampt" test used to discriminate replicants from humans. We find a city collapsing under its own weight evoked in the confused image of a

tenebrous, phosphorescent city [which] spreads from horizon to horizon and spews rolling fire-balls into the twilight; creepy, vertiginous views down skyscraper canyons to arterial streets...pulsating with a forest of beings who look human but seem robotic. (34)

Technology is no longer agency alone, a tool for changing the urbanscape; it is now agent, merging with the city.

The structural relationship between the cityscape and the narrative becomes fully evident when we realize that actions develop only as a consequence to Deckard's hunt for the replicants. His coursing along the trash-littered streets and between or within specific buildings—police headquarters, the Tyrell Corporation, his apartment, J.F. Sebastian's apartment—reiterates the interplay of architectural configurations and place in Deckard's ethos. A man seemingly at ease with his dis-ease, Deckard appears to be a "man of the streets." When he is first picked up by the police (while eating noodles at a sidewalk sushi bar), he feigns ignorance of the street "lingo—cityspeak—a mishmash of Japanese, Spanish, German and what have you." Yet, as a voice-over narration reveals, Deckard has an intimate if antagonistic acquaintance with the city and its people.

Later, Deckard is identified within interior spaces that have been exteriorized to become part of the street scene through the select sequencing/montage of shots. In these rooms, as Janice Rushing and Thomas Frentz note, " 'Nature' has virtually disappeared, and the line between outside and indoors seems insignificant as light rarely penetrates the dark, smoky haze of either" (68). Deckard's apartment, for example, shot on location at Frank Lloyd Wright's Mayan-influenced Ennis Brown house (Dempsey 34), stands illuminated by the flashing lights of billboards and the reverberating sounds of the traffic that infiltrate through the windows. In it, as in the city, Deckard appears alienated and detached, never quite at home. Cluttered with objects (he has to search for a clean glass in which to offer Rachel a drink), furniture (including a piano), and low-ceilings (creating a sense of claustrophobia), the apartment becomes an extension of the streets rather than a protective escape from them.

Two other exteriorized interior spaces work to blur the distinction between architectural structures and the urbanscape, as well as to reveal Deckard's character: Tyrell's office and Sebastian's apartment. The waiting office of the Tyrell corporation, the lone, open room in the film, unfolds as does Fredersen's corporate office in *Metropolis*. The only noticeable piece of furniture, a sparse, elongated table/desk, is dwarfed by the sheer excess of the openness of the area and by the ample, if obscured, lines of a picture window. A mixture of lean art deco and neoforties haute couture, this room stands juxtaposed to the throbbing city below (it's the only room in which dusk-flecked sunlight streams), and it bespeaks the very sterility which strangles both the city and Deckard. Framing shots of Deckard and Tyrell trapped between the window and the table, which again call to mind Fredersen's positioning in *Metropolis*, signal the corruption and ambiguity which result from the need to control the city. The same effect is inversely achieved in Sebastian's apartment, a tenement decked and jeweled in the costume of an operatic stage or in the fashion of a masked ball. Awash in genetic "toys" and dolls which bespeak of consumer-technology's attempts to supplant human relations, this apartment encapsulates the implosion and stasis of the city. Marked by wrought iron-grill work and lattices, the lobby of the building, through which one passes to gain admittance into Sebastian's domicile, resembles the very streets from which it seeks to separate itself.

Through repeated scenes of Deckard's movement between the streets, his apartment, and Sebastian's reified toyshop, an alternation that continuously gathers momentum, the film connects the images of the urbanscape until they literally come together in one: the rooftop of the tenement building that witnesses the reversal of the hunter and the hunted in climactic hand-to-hand combat. Though Deckard first enters the tenement in search of the remaining replicants, he exits as prey. Roy stalks Deckard, forcing him (and the audience) to address the question of his existence (just as he has forced Tyrell to answer for the consequences of bio-genetic god-playing). Presented as a montage of interior shots which burst outward, the entire sequence again focuses the spectator's attention on the blurred distinction between inside space and outside space. As the rain gives way to a blue sky at Roy Batty's death, symbolically depicted in the release of the dove, the scene poetically reiterates the disruption which may result when "technologically" driven "truths" possess the city and its populace.

Burton's *Batman* presents another example of the urbanscape as visual metaphor constructing character ethos. A veritable maze of "nighttime canyons" (Kael 83), of dark alleyways guarded by towering and crowded skyscrapers, Gotham City is a collage within a collage, an eclectic stew of early brownstone buildings mixed with modern brutalism and of gothic architecture tempered with Italian futurism. *Looking* and *feeling* as if it has been designed by thousands of architects over hundreds of years, this city expresses an almost nihilistic vision of the world. The Gotham City Cathedral, for example, which stretches Antonio Gaudi's *Sagrada Familia* into a giant skyscraper (Pearson 206), symbolizes the a-religiosity and secularization of the city and its inhabitants. The fascist design of City Hall, which stands catty-corner to the machinelike design of the Flugelheim Museum, envisions what art critic Jeanne Silverthorne has dubbed "a postmodern Hades" (12).[4] The result: a conflated sense of ahistoricity in which everyone's past is brought to bear on the present; a space in which myth and modernity are fused, blurred, and transformed into a postmodern nightmare—a city swallowing its own populace.

Again working with syntactic codes *Batman*, like *Blade Runner*, appropriates some of the conventions and narrative devices of *Metropolis*. The opening pan of large, creature-like edifices—City Hall, the Flugelheim Museum, the cathedral—clearly establish the context in which the people exist and through which Batman and Joker move. A convergence of the upper and the lower city, dank Gotham houses both the corporate managers, now cast in the guise of crime bosses and government officials, and a seemingly self-exploiting citizenry. Once again the battle for the city takes the viewer on a labyrinth-like journey through sinuous bowels, a maneuver which is again complemented by the movement into and between architectural configurations. For example, the film's climatic closing, in which Batman scales the heights of the cathedral in hot pursuit of a fleeing Joker and a captured Vicki Vale, repeats nearly verbatim Freder's pursuit of Rotwang and the captured Maria in *Metropolis*'s closing sequence.

Identified within the spacious yet oppressive rooms of the Wayne mansion while his alter ego is identified on the streets of Gotham, Bruce Wayne defines the typical mythic creature who moves easily between two worlds. A recluse of sorts, Wayne feels displaced in his own home and among his own possessions (as does Deckard); there are even some rooms, such as the formal dining room, that he never uses. He is, however, completely at ease in his protective cave dwelling, a literal extension of the physical ground of Gotham and a metaphorical extension of the city. In a similar manner, those rooms that articulate Joker's ethos—the subterranean basement/workshop, littered with cut-up fragments of photographs (the same mad-cap and sinister milieux of Rotwang and Sebastian), and the ordered disorder and coherent disjunctiveness of the Flugelheim Museum—betray the precariously controlled psychotic bent of his personality. Even the stock sterility of Boss Grissom's corporate office/apartment, which Joker later possesses, conveys a sense of narcissistic artificiality. Cast in cement and glass, in art deco designs and shapes, this interior space articulates a conscious rejection of traditional values and signals the ironic futility of art and technology as commodities. This room again finds the outside brought indoors through the meticulous framing of "the bad guys," when Grissom and Joker stand trapped in front of a picture-window and streamlined desk. The fractured view afforded through the window reiterates the sense of separation and vulnerability of the city.

The primacy of Batman and Joker, however, depends less upon their placement within architectural configurations than upon their ability to manipulate the technological "toys"—from television broadcasts to flying batmobiles—which consumerism has privileged to its logical end: to own and appropriate the "city." In this respect, each object in the environment becomes a player in the turf war, in the fight for technological management of the environment. For example, when Vale and Knox wander into the museumlike trophy room at the Wayne mansion, they are surrounded by objects and artifacts of punitive nature and ritual grandeur. The objects (armor shields, tribal masks) represent traits which Wayne finds attractive and which signal the human endeavor to subdue a people and the land. Prominently situated at the far end of the room, however, hangs a more contemporary tool of environment management, a wall-size two-way mirror. Empowered by the consumer status afforded by Bruce Wayne's wealth, Batman has access to a whole world of electronic surveillance and gadgetry. Part hero, part voyeur, Wayne/Batman's schizophrenic nature is then solidified through a number of demonstrations of his technological prowess: spying on Vale and Knox via the mirror; eavesdropping on Commissioner Gordon and his guests via hidden video cameras; and literally flying through the streets protected by the armored bat costume and vehicle.

Joker, the world's first "fully functioning homicidal artist" who "make[s] art until someone dies," similarly embraces postmodern consumer technology in his attempts to control the city. After his own disfiguring mishap, Joker seeks to appropriate the all of Gotham. And like Batman, his technical prowess manifest itself in deliberate actions: tainting consumer products and pirating airwaves. Ironically, Joker's attempts to "own" the streets of the city remain restricted to the tools, vehicles, and costumes of past technologies. For example, when Batman breaks into the Fluggelheim Museum to rescue Vale from Joker's treachery, Joker can only covetously exclaim, "Get me those wonderful toys!" Hence, despite its apparent comic-book texture and fairy-tale ending (the narrative culminates in a duel between the road warrior and the dark knight for the fair maiden), *Batman* still calls our attention to the consequences of a city disrupted by technology and consumer greed.

Black Rain, on the other hand, marks the inversion of the gothic dreariness of a *Blade Runner* or *Batman*, from complete film noir darkness to one of balanced luminosity. The opening shots follow our "hero" Nick as he rides his motorcycle across a bridge into the city, an orange haze breaking behind skyscrapers and dancing across the river's surface. A symbol of rebellion and prowess, the bike (a technological toy which becomes a technological tool) epitomizes Nick's identity and displacement. His moves between the congregation of bikers, his apartment, and police headquarters further suggest there is no one reality, no black and white. Hence, rather than betraying a vision of the world dark and sinking under its own weight, the film presents a world prismed into multiple grays.

Just as the motorcycle becomes an essential aspect of Nick's ethos, so too does it becomes his tool for managing the city and appropriating the landscape. After "collaring" Sato in New York (this chase scene takes the viewer through the metaphoric slaughterhouse of the mob—the massacre at Scalari's—to the literal one of the hanging carcasses), Nick learns he must hand Sato over to the Japanese police. Accompanied by Charlie, he begrudgingly arrives in Osaka only to be duped into releasing Sato. Committed to finding his prey (lest IAD thinks he is in on the deal), Nick tries to work the territory, but the absence of his tools (his bike and handgun) impedes his ability to get the "lay of the land." His misunderstanding of the landscape parallels his continuous misassessment of the situation. For example, when Masa refuses to divulge information being gathered at a crime site, Nick decides that he and Charlie will walk to the hotel. Their "twenty minute walk" turns sinister as the empty streets and burnished chrome buildings become the playground for their harassment by a local gang traveling, not surprisingly, on motorcycles. It is only later, after Charlie is killed (by Sato's motorcycle cronies), that Nick begins to recognize his misjudgment and misassessment.

Culling generic images to create both cityscapes, New York and Osaka, Scott carefully hones the gray areas away until the viewer faces a black and white dilemma—the initial conflict between Nick and himself becomes one of right and wrong (significantly, he and Masa take their "collar" in alive). As in other action/adventure films, the opening aerial shots of Osaka pan an orange tinted, smog-filtered, industrial zone while the closing scenes move us into the relatively, climate-clean countryside.

As in *Blade Runner*, Scott likewise spends the narrative forward by exteriorizing those interior spaces which delineate Nick's ethos: in both New York and Japan, Nick moves between police headquarters, a restaurant or club, and an apartment. Hence, though critics may find Scott's "shots...counterproductive" (Kauffman 31), the intrusion of the city into interior rooms echoes a prevailing vision of sterility and corruption.

The ironic employment of generic images and codes of the urbanscape, the self-referentiality of the conventions, distinguishes later action/adventure films, such as *RoboCop*, *Darkman*, and *Total Recall*. Note how the *RoboCop* films juxtapose the crime-riddled, drug-infested streets of Detroit against the model, and apparently visionary, "Delta City"—yet another "collection of white, windowless monoliths" (Codell 12). Within and between *RoboCop* and *RoboCop II*, there is a continuous interspersement of images which divide the urbanscape into a Dantesque canvas by night and a Hooper still by day. Parallel shots and repetitions force the viewer to see Detroit's underworld in respect to Detroit's upperworld, and to conclude neither is acceptable. For instance, *RoboCop* opens with Murphy and his partner Lewis on duty in the "hell" district of the city, where they are ambushed by Boddicker, the evil drug-lord. That the action takes place in an abandoned steelmill which becomes the equivalent of the abandoned inner city is not as significant in and of itself as when juxtaposed against the occupied (OCP) corporate building. Parallel shots, alternating between the meeting room equipped with the model of Delta city and the steelmill, reiterate the opposition of Detroit/reality and Delta City/illusion. Just as does vice-president Jone's art deco office, the postmodern building which houses OCP conveys an image of contemporaneity and corporate greed which meets that of the drug kings and the warehouse. Both spaces suggest a conscious rejection of history, tradition and values.

Darkman and *Total Recall* also find the metropolis metaphor rejecting history, tradition, and values. Strack, the evil industrialist from *Darkman*, prominently displays the model of his project in front of wall-length windows, in the middle of his trendy and modernish office (tres *Metropolis*). An obvious comic book sketch of the fight for the city, *Darkman* works its frames and shots around the visible darkness of night and the visible brightness of day—a juxtaposition which borders on distraction. Gone are the ambiguous shades and tints of *Black Rain*; back are the clear delineations of *Metropolis*. As a lost Peyton maneuvers through the streets by day disguised as those he seeks, and a found Darkman passes unaware by night, the contest becomes one of moral integrity (especially as it translates into the need to love and protect his girlfriend, Julie Hastings). Not surprisingly, the final scene of the film has Darkman scaling the heights of a half-completed high-rise in search of his fair damsel held by the evil entrepreneur. The final question has been answered at a sacrifice: the city (and Julie) has been saved, but Darkman has failed to restore his former self.

In *Total Recall* the parallel to Lang's *Metropolis* falls between the upper world of colonized Mars, as aligned with Earth 2084, and Venusville, the lower world of Mars. Lying pristine and glittering, fully automated and still profit-motivated, Earth and the upper world of Mars find people careening through concourses built along geometrically drawn lines and planes of steel, concrete, and glass. Not unexpectedly, the narrative unfolds in a manner similar to *Metropolis*, with johnny-cabs, hovering skyscrapers, and a tram that extends the length of the screen. Again the upper city skyline marks the efficiency and ordered vision of a future city maintained by the exploitation of technology and humans; we learn such beauty can only be maintained through the exploitation of the Mutants.

Finally, as in *Blade Runner*, *Batman*, and *Black Rain*, the interior rooms in these films delineate character ethos, only now the spaces embody the *absence* of the hero/antihero. When Robocop/Murphy visits his former home, he discovers it emptied of everything, including his identity; Douglas Quaid/Hauser is "Recalled" to Mars because he has neither a significant home nor identity. Even Peyton/Darkman lives in a collapsing, vacant warehouse (one highly reminiscent of his burnt out laboratory) which symbolizes a former self. Always this hero/antihero finds his dislocation or displacement wrought and exacerbated within the confines of interior walls which are representative of the larger city.

As visual metaphor, the urbanscape provides the action/adventure film with a mechanism for structure and a manner for discourse. Its employment of a generic syntax enables the viewer to identify and define both character ethos and narrative plot, for within and against it the idea and the personality of the hero/antihero is continuously shaped, reiterated, and changed. But, perhaps, more importantly, such a landscape lies fertile with queries and proclamations of technology's actual and potential influence on a society. As it constructs the filmic world, the urbanscape challenges the viewer to reconsider, if but for the briefest moment of entertainment, his or her own position in relation to the city.

Notes

¹For further discussion on the doubling motif (though not as associated with the landscape) see J.P. Telotte's "Human Artifice and the Science Fiction Film," *Film Quarterly* 36, no. 3 (Spring 1983): 44-51.

²Rick Altman defines "generic syntax" as established genre codes, as the repetition of recognizable situations, themes, and/or icons. Arising from the "conflation of a series of similar texts...[which] make it easy to understand the text in a predetermined way," these codes make it less likely that the urbanscape "will be construed in [any] different, non-generic way" (101). For further discussion see Altman's *The American Film Musical*. Bloomington and Indianapolis: Indiana UP, 1987. 3-5, 131.

³Critics note that *Metropolis* does not necessarily object to the structure of a machine society (which borders on fascism) but, rather, to the unbalanced worker-employer relationship. It simply calls for better labor arbitration/mediation.

⁴Set designer Anton Furst cites architectural references ranging from Otto Wagner (the Flugelheim Museum) and Louis Sullivan to contemporary Japanese architect Shin Takamatsu (the Axis Chemical Factory). See Pilar Viladas' "Batman: Design for the Bad Guys," *Progressive Architecture* 70 (Sept. 1989): 21-22.

Works Cited

Altman, Rick. *The American Film Musical*. Bloomington and Indianapolis: Indiana UP, 1987.

Codell, Julie. F. "Murphy's Law, Robocop's Body, and Capitalism's Work." *Jump Cut* no. 34 (1989): 12-26.

Dempsey, Michael. Rev. of *Blade Runner*. *Film Quarterly* 36 (Winter 1982-83): 33-38.

Jameson, Fredric. "Postmodernism and Consumer Society." *The Anti-Aesthetic: Essays on Postmodern Culture*. Ed. Hal Foster. Washington: Bay P, 1983. 111-25.

Kael, Pauline. "The City Gone Psycho." *The New Yorker* 65 (10 July 1989): 83-85.

Kauffman, Stanley. Rev. of *Black Rain*. *The New Republic* (16 Oct. 1989): 31-32.

Pearson, Clifford A. "Urban Fright." *Architectural Record* 78 (Jan. 1990): 206.

Rushing, Janice Hocker and Thomas S. Frentz. "The Frankenstein Myth in Contemporary Cinema." *Critical Studies in Mass Communications* 6 (1989): 61-80.

Silverthorne, Jeanne. "The Cave." *Artforum* 28 (Sept. 1989): 12-14.

Telotte, J.P. "Human Artifice and the Science Fiction Film." *Film Quarterly* 36, no. 3 (Spring 1983): 44-51.

Viladas, Pilar. "Batman: Design for the Bad Guys." *Progressive Architecture* 70 (Sept. 1989): 21-22.

Filmography

Year	Film	Director
1926	*Metropolis*	Fritz Lang
1982	*Blade Runner*	Ridley Scott
1984	*Terminator*	James Cameron
1984	*Tight Rope*	Richard Tuggle
1985	*Fear City*	Abel Ferrara
1987	*RoboCop*	Paul Verhoeven
1987	*Running Man*	Paul Michael Glasser
1987	*Wall Street*	Oliver Stone
1988	*Red Heat*	Walter Hill
1989	*Batman*	Tim Burton
1989	*Black Rain*	Ridley Scott
1990	*Darkman*	Sam Raimi
1990	*Hardware*	Richard Stanley
1990	*RoboCop II*	Irvin Kershner
1990	*Total Recall*	Paul Verhoeven
1991	*Circuitry Man*	Steven Lovy
1991	*Terminator II: Judgement Day*	James Cameron

The Southern Landscape
in Contemporary Films

Carol M. Ward

Historians have been talking about the "New South" since Reconstruction and the "Sunbelt South" since the 1970s, but popular imagination refuses to allow the mythology of the Old South to die. Although Jimmy Carter's presidency in the 1970s rekindled curiosity about Southern manners and mores, the stereotypes that gained currency—the redneck and the good ole boy (both personified in popular films by Burt Reynolds)—were far from accurate and certainly less than flattering. As the economic landscape of the South changed with the influx of tourists, retirees, and businesses, foreign and domestic, the movie versions of the South continued to exploit the old stereotypes, albeit sometimes with interesting variations. The 1980s saw the rise in the number of films being made in the South as state film commissions were established to lure filmmakers away from the traditional centers of production in Hollywood and New York (Florida is now the third most popular filmmaking site). This shift in production resulted in a new crop of films set in the South dealing with Southern characters, history and themes, revealing America's continuing fascination with the literature and culture of the region.

An examination of these recent "Southerns" discovers some recognizable trends that have helped to distill what qualities and characteristics the South represents in the popular imagination. Primarily, the South is perceived as a place haunted by the past, either the personal past of the protagonist or the social history of the region. A strong, almost oppressive sense of place—the family and the community—permeates these often nostalgic portraits. The hazy golden-hued cinematography signals the mist of memory; the voice-over narration and flashback structure herald the mythologizing of the past; the montage of old black and white photographs recalls the ghosts of former selves; the pervasive graveyards provide intimations of mortality. These visual and narrative motifs, in combination or separately, identify the Southern locales in such diverse films as *Paris Trout, Shag: The Movie, Rambling Rose, Miss*

Firecracker, Everybody's All-American, and *Prince of Tides,* among others.

The cinematography, settings, and art direction conspire to evoke a kind of timelessness, so that even stories set in the present seem to be taking place in an indeterminate past, as if the South were stuck permanently in the 1950s (witness David Lynch's two films set in the South, *Blue Velvet* and *Wild at Heart*). A critic of *Bull Durham* is surprised at one point to notice a calendar with the 1987 date: "Up to that point, it has been possible to think that this is a folksy, if unusually electric period piece, from its sepia-tinted opening photographs of back alley baseball to Annie Savoy's bobbysoxed stride through the twilight streets of Durham into the local stadium" (Combs 269). Whereas other regions feature stories set in the present, emblematic of the alienation and rootlessness of contemporary life, the South is the place in America where history happened, where families and communities still exist, where pastoral values flourish. The present in the South is a mere platform from which to take excursions into the past. In the rare exception to this rule, as in *sex, lies, and videotape* set in contemporary Baton Rouge, recognizable Southern locales are so subdued as to be almost invisible. This insistence on history is indicative of the refusal of people, Southerners included, to believe that the South has changed, has become modern, has overcome many of the problems of the nineteenth century and discovered many of the problems of the twentieth century.

The history that is most associated with the region, a legacy of the Old South, is the ignominious record of racism inherited from the days of slavery. In these contemporary films the battlefield has shifted from the Civil War to Civil Rights as filmmakers discover (finally) the struggle of Blacks to gain equality in American society. Just as it took about twenty years for filmmakers to return to the Vietnam war, so this recent concern for the Civil Rights movement allows audiences a safe cushion of time between the actual events and the movie versions and reflects more about today's problems with race relations than about what happened in the 1960s. When Hollywood wants to find out what went wrong with race relations in America, it turns to the South for solutions. Although racial tensions and overt hostilities are being experienced all over the United States, few communities being exempt from these serious problems, the South seems disproportionately represented in films with racial violence and bigotry. As young Southern poet Gregory A.Sellers comments, "The South is only a magnification of what the whole nation is—racist, violent, xenophobic" (Ingalls B4).

Even more ironic is the failure of these films to deal with current racial problems, as the stories (often based on actual incidents) are safely set in the haze of history and presented with the politically correct perspective of 20-20 hindsight. Since many of the events dramatized occurred between twenty and thirty years ago, their value as history lessons to a younger generation is doubtful. They seem calculated in a way to make white audiences feel that such problems are safely in the past, that as a more enlightened public we could surely avoid such blatant examples of bigotry; for older black audiences they function as a sort of nostalgic memory of the bad old times when the battles were righteous and the cause was clear.

An interesting collary to the struggle for civil rights presented in these contemporary "Southerns" is the struggle of women to gain autonomy and freedom. In the land of the most feminine of women, the country of Scarlett O'Hara and Blanche DuBois, it seems heretical to speak of women's liberation. Although white women were placed on pedestals to prevent them from being molested by black men and a war was fought ostensibly to protect them from violation, recent filmmakers have perceived the link between racism and sexism and discovered the role of white patriarchy in perpetuating both. History is reinterpreted to reveal this spiritual bond between Blacks and the Southern white woman, to explore the underlying connections between the fight for civil rights and the demands of feminism.

The role of women is particularly interesting in the Southern film since women often dominate the screen and the narratives in a manner rare for American films in general. Since Southern films often portray the life of a whole community, a range of women's roles is possible, from the scheming ambitious Southern Belle, to the wise matriarch, to the steel magnolia, to the spunky artist who must escape the South to prosper. Contrary to the stereotype of the feuding belles, friendship between women is cherished and often plentiful in what could qualify as female "buddy films" (*Steel Magnolias, Fried Green Tomatoes, Shag: The Movie,* for instance). Perhaps because of the legacy of the genteel South stereotype and Faulkner's lawyers, men in Southern films are not all violent; there are some tortured intellectual and poetic souls who look to women for inspiration and strength. Although these characters tend to romanticize their women and attempt to perpetuate the pedestal of worship, the women themselves are feisty and realistic survivors of a crippling system of sexism—latent or active.

While not all of the films made about the South deal with the issues of history, racism, and sexism, the majority do touch upon these important themes in some degree, using the Southern landscape to explore such contemporary issues safely distanced by the obscurity of the region and the mythologizing process. The film that typifies how filmmakers use Southern history and landscape more for their purposes than for the presentation of historical fact is *Mississippi Burning*. In a scathing critique of this backward-looking perception of the Civil Rights movement, the *Motion Picture Guide Annual* critic places the film in a historical context:

> During the last eight years there has been an alarming increase in racial tension, resentment, and violence in the United States. The Howard Beach incident, the Tawana Brawley case, and the reaction of some whites to the Jesse Jackson campaign have reopened the old wounds of American racism. This development, combined with the general apathy toward, attacks on, and outright subversion of key civil rights statutes by the Reagan administration, has brought about a renewed tolerance and tacit approval of bigotry, to the extent that a presidential candidate could openly provoke the racist instincts of frightened whites to get votes while the mainstream media turned a blind eye (the Bush's campaign's use of the Willie Horton issue). Given this alarming trend, a major motion picture designed to remind viewers of the horrors perpetrated against people of color just 25 years ago should have been one of the most important films of the year. (111)

Instead, *Mississippi Burning*, according to this and other reviewers, sensationalizes the action surrounding the FBI investigation of the 1964 murder of three Civil Rights workers, insists on telling the story from a white perspective, depicts every white Southerner as "a slobbering racist animal," and portrays the Blacks as helpless victims instead of the leaders that they were in the historical incident. Originally envisioned by its producer Fred Zollo as "a modern western, a John Fordian story, truly good vs. evil," *Mississippi Burning* spends too much time visualizing violence and destruction and not enough time developing the characters (Davis 36). British-born director Alan Parker refers to the character played by Frances McDormand as "the only white Southern character who has any kind of sensibility or any kind of integrity with regard to having a problem with the racism they're born with"—a comment that reveals the oversimplification of complex issues and the holier-than-thou attitude that plague the film as a whole (Davis 38).

This character also demonstrates Parker's connection of racial bigotry to the repression of women. Although the woman helps the FBI agent (Gene Hackman) solve the mystery and implicates her own bigoted husband in the process, she must pay for her collaboration with the enemy by suffering physical abuse, social rejection, and the destruction of her home by the KKK. Although the protection of white women has often been used as an excuse for violence against black men, as *Mississippi Burning* demonstrates, if women step out of line, they too will be punished with similar violence. Ironically, here it is the former Southern good ole boy sheriff who uses his charm to convince her of the higher principles at stake and thereby endangers her life. Unfortunately, the film implies that she would not have acted on her own without the encouragement of the noble male who brought out her better instincts.

A more realistic version of the related problems of racism and sexism can be found in *The Long Walk Home*, a quiet antidote to the bombast of *Mississippi Burning*. The parallels between the family's maid (Whoopi Goldberg) and the proper Junior League housewife of the 1950s (Sissy Spacek) are developed dramatically as the two women and their families are caught up in the turmoil of the Montgomery bus strike. Spacek comes to the gradual realization that the power that she first wielded in her marriage, the power over home and children, is called into question when she defends her maid against the racist actions of a local policeman and later when she violates the strike by driving the boycotting maid to work. Lying to her husband to keep her rebellious actions from him, she is put in a position of subterfuge not uncommon to black servants from the days of slavery. When Spacek follows her emerging social consciousness by becoming an official driver for the strikers, she must endure the violence of the racist white men, just as surely as if she were Black. The bond between the women—Black and white—is solidified historically in the film by Spacek's photograph of herself as a child with her Black nanny and by Spacek's daughter's narration: "There is something special about someone who changes and who changes those around her." The use of any narration at all, hardly necessary to the clarity of the plot, seems calculated to give meaning and context to the events of the historical narrative. A child during the action of the movie, the daughter/narrator is peripheral to the plot, never seen as an adult, but only heard as a disembodied voice that interprets events for the modern viewer, assuring us that the events are significant, again asserting the Southern film trait of a mandatory historical perspective.

A potentially more controversial alliance, of Black male and white female, is the basis for *Driving Miss Daisy*, Australian director Bruce Beresford's Oscar-winning film adaptation of Alfred Uhry's successful play. Through the interaction of the worldly black chauffeur (Morgan Freeman) and a wealthy Jewish widow (Jessica Tandy), the film subtly charts the course of social change from 1948 to 1973 as it filters into the insulated world of Atlanta society. But the filmmakers carefully avoid the romantic subtext between these two longtime companions; their age and the difference in their races dictate that their relationship remain chaste despite their deep friendship. What ultimately brings them together is not sex but their common status as outsiders. When they are stopped by state troopers on their way to Mobile, Daisy's wealth and social position cannot prevent the troopers, representative of white male authority, from humiliating them both, him for being Black and her for being Jewish.

Any possible sexual context is also eliminated in *A Gathering of Old Men* (retitled *Murder on the Bayou* for video sales), while a similar white noblesse oblige attitude is expressed, this time by Holly Hunter toward "my people" and "my land." Believing that her social status in the community and her race will protect her from prosecution, she offers to confess to a murder that she did not commit so that her favorite sharecropper (Lou Gosset, Jr.) will not be lynched by angry redneck Cajuns. The South's history of racial violence is evoked as all the old black men in the community sit in a cemetery reminiscing about victims of racism; the voices of those men confuse the real killer, who is hiding nearby, into thinking he is hearing the voices of his ancestors urging him to stand up to the whites by telling the truth. The use of different narrative voices fosters a communal spirit that the film, based on Ernest Gaines's novel and Charles Fuller's script, demonstrates in the plot. Directed by German filmmaker Volker Schlondorff, this made-for-TV film projects a sense of anticlimax about the events. The redneck was killed because he was "living in the past," when such violence against Blacks was tolerated. The Black men's unity behind the accused man surprises the whites, who think it is "a little late to be getting militant." Hunter's patronizing attitude, although well-meaning, is also outdated when this Black man is perfectly capable of taking care of himself.

The pervasiveness of patriarchy is symbolized in *Paris Trout* as an epidemic of rabies, which first infects the young Black girl who is later brutally shot down in her own home by the sadistic racist Trout (brilliantly played with unusual restraint by Dennis Hopper). As the economic leader in the small Georgia town, Trout maintains power over the blacks by his financial loans and over his wife (Barbara Hershey) by a reign of psychological terror and physical brutality. The wife is carefully paralleled through the film with the dying Black child, as both are victims of Trout's violence. As the white male jury sits in judgment on him for the murder of the Black girl, the power of patriarchy is at its zenith; in the 1950s on the verge of the Civil Rights movement, he is pardoned for his crime. After two murders (including the sacrificial slaughter of his invalid mother) and Trout's ultimate suicide, his wife pronounces the film's benediction, the "oldest lesson of the South:" "It is easier to bury than to forget." The Southern film would have us believe that the South is full of such graveyards.

Whether or not a particular Southern film focuses on Civil Rights, Black characters tend to function as the soul or conscience of the white characters. The white football hero's alter ego in *Everybody's All-American* is a black high school athlete (Carl Lumbly) who, because of his race, does not get a college or professional football bid. Instead, he becomes a successful restauranteer, by necessity and also by choice. Even when he is given a chance by the Gray Ghost (Dennis Quaid) to try out for a pro team, he decides there are more important things in life than football, like Civil Rights activism, so he fights to integrate lunch counters. His story intersects the main plot occasionally to remind the white man that fame is fleeting and there are many ways to win in the game of life. Eventually, he hires the Ghost's wife (Jessica Lange) to run some of his restaurants in an interesting reversal of fortunes. In *The Long Walk Home*, Whoopi Goldberg is often framed visually as a sort of silent shadow to Sissy Spacek as Spacek's political awareness evolves. In *Heart of Dixie* an Alabama coed (Ally Sheedy) is politicized when she sees a young Black man attacked and beaten by whites at an Elvis Presley concert for wanting to dance to the new music. Even in the quirky *Mystery Train* by Jim Jarmusch, the black hotel clerk (played by R&B great, Screaming Jay Hawkins) and his sidekick serve as a sort of anchor and provide comic perspective for the three intersecting plots involving Japanese tourists, an Italian widow who sees the ghost of Elvis, and a band of misfits in Memphis, Tennessee. In Bruce Beresford's production of Josephine Humphrey's novel *Rich in Love*, the youthful heroine's mother (Jill Clayburgh) is inspired by her Black maid's daughter to explore her freedom and leave her family behind. This tendency to use Black characters as white consciences, however, denies Blacks their autonomy and individuality; they remain significant not for what they think or do but for how they affect the white characters.

In these and other Southern films, white men are depicted mainly in association with violence, as bigoted rednecks, jocks, politicians, lawmen. Even well-meaning men eventually cause, perpetuate, or helplessly witness violence (the lawyer in *Paris Trout*, the narrator/cousin in *Everybody's All-American*, Tom Wingo in *Prince of Tides*). In most Southern films, the women are the moral, strong, engaging, and complex characters. Always the home of the most interesting and notorious women in the country, the South still produces its share of beautiful, sexy, and ambitious belles—Kim Basinger, Cybill Shepherd, Julia Roberts, Andie MacDowell, Faye Dunaway, Donna Rice, Marla Maples, to name a few.

110 Beyond the Stars

Their filmic/fictional counterparts must at some point confront that ghost of the past that haunts every Southern woman: Scarlett O'Hara Hamilton Kennedy Butler. Scarlett represents the unreconciled impulses of women toward independence and autonomy on the one hand and total child-like dependence and helplessness on the other. The Southern Belle personifies the schizophrenia experienced by many modern women as they are torn between the security of the pedestal and the expression of their individual competence in the world outside the home and family. In Southern films, these contradictory impulses are often embodied by different characters, providing alternatives for the heroine to explore. In several movies—*Miss Firecracker, Heart of Dixie*, and *Shag*—specific references to the Old South of *Gone with the Wind* reveal the filmmaker's awareness of the contemporary Southern woman's struggle to free herself from the Southern Belle stereotypes of the past.

In *Miss Firecracker*, Holly Hunter plays an orphan who attempts to gain her social salvation by winning the Miss Firecracker contest that her idealized belle cousin had won years before, as shown in the old home movies of this impressive event. The security of the Southern Belle tradition is expressed through Elain (Mary Steenburgen), the former beauty queen who thrives uneasily on the worship of her family, husband, and community. Although she gives a speech about how much she has enjoyed her life as a beauty, Elain seems aware that being beautiful brings limitations; it is not the salvation that her cousin Carnelle (Hunter) wants it to be.

Carnelle represents the dilemma of the New Southern woman. As her name indicates, her sexual appetites have earned her the reputation of a "Miss Hot Tamale," and it is this social judgement of her that she is trying to rectify as she so desperately seeks to fulfill the old beauty codes of the ideal Belle. But Carnelle has a vitality that is not appreciated by her relatives or by the town that likes to look down on her, morally and socially. During the beauty contest, she watches her main competition perform the "I'll never be hungry again" monologue from GWTW in her authentic Scarlett frock. The tears that fill Carnelle's eyes come as much from her incipient awareness that she cannot match the perfection of this belle as they do from the emotional power of the speech and all that it inspires in every Southerner. Her talent, a tap dance to "The Star-Spangled Banner," lands her in last place. That "Yankee" national anthem celebrating the union of the states cannot compete with the lure of the GWTW "Dixie"; she is too forward-looking in this land of look behind. Carnelle literally falls on her face as she parades down the runway in her dead aunt's faded and rotting evening gown. When she confronts Elain about keeping the treasured red dress from her, Carnelle puts aside her ugly duckling child's hat, realizing that she does not want to live in the past all of her life as Elain does. Going out to watch the fireworks light the night sky, Carnelle achieves the "eternal grace" that she had sought as she is transformed into an adult—one who has confronted her past, put it behind her, and looks forward to a new future.

In *Heart of Dixie*, based on Anne River Siddon's novel *Heartbreak Hotel*, Maggie DeLoach (Ally Sheedy) is torn between two different visions of womanhood: the traditional Southern Belle, represented by her sorority sister Delia (Virginia Madsen), and her unconventional beatnik friend Aiken Reed (Phoebe Cates). Steeped in Southern tradition and engaged to the son of a wealthy Southern gentleman, Maggie is intrigued by Aiken, whose very name suggests the longing for change that Maggie feels. Spritely Aiken smokes in class, wears black clothes, performs modern dances, uses birth control, goes after any man she wants, gets pregnant, moves to New York City for a new life, and drinks out of the "colored" water fountain in defiance of racial codes. She appeals to the wild individualistic part of Maggie's personality, the side that has been repressed by the stereotypical roles forced on the proper Southern lady.

Delia also appeals to Maggie because of her style of wildness, one that fits into the Southern Belle code. Instead of Aiken's refreshing sexual honesty, Delia manipulates men by her teasing sexuality. She steps right out of a Tennessee Williams' play, wearing a slip, smoking a cigarette, sporting a new Kim Novak hairdo, drinking beer at a disreputable strip joint in Phenix City, dancing provocatively by herself until soldiers circle around her like animals in heat. As in *Rambling Rose* and *The Butcher's Wife*, the Southern woman does not seem to know that a slip is made to be worn under a dress and not by itself. She sees no need for a career, since marriage to a successful man is her ultimate goal. In order to pursue a career in journalism, Maggie surrenders the security that her boyfriend Boots offers to a more than willing Delia, who steps in to fulfill her fantasy of being mistress of Tara.

In a key scene in the movie, Maggie gives Delia a copy of an article against racism that she knows will stir up controversy. When Delia is crowned Honeysuckle Queen amidst a bevy of beauties in hoopskirts and boys in Confederate uniforms, she uses her acceptance speech to warn Maggie: "When you mix one hundred years of tradition, gentility, and good ole Southern honor with friendship, you get a way of life you know you could never turn your back on. Because if you betray that which you say you love, you only betray yourself." After bringing all the pressures of tradition to bear on Maggie, she leads the crowd in a moving rendition of "Dixie." Knowing that she will become an outcast and lose all the advantages she has as a white and as a woman in a patriarchal racist social structure if she defies tradition to follow her moral idealism, Maggie maturely stands by her decision to publish the article and fight for racial equality.

In a lighter look at Southern society, *Shag: The Movie* presents a group of graduating high school senior girls out for a last fling together at the beach. Drawing on the conventions of beach movies, of recent *Dirty Dancing* spinoffs, and of teen romance, *Shag* still manages to confront some of the issues of the Southern film. The four teenaged girlfriends are hemmed in by restrictive codes of behavior forced upon them by their mothers, popular magazines, and social peer pressure, as well as their own internalized standards of proper female behavior. The senator's daughter Luann (Page Hannah) is most imbued with these rules; her mother advises her before the girls head out for their adventures, "Don't change clothes in a gas station, don't wear dark lipstick, try to learn something about Southern history, don't wear bermuda shorts (they're trashy), try to be gracious, and above all, remember who you are." Luann tries to uphold these upper class standards of the Southern lady that she plans to become; as she tells the other girls when they arrive at Myrtle Beach during the Sun Fun Festival, "We can have fun but we cannot be wild." "Wild," of course, is the Southern doublespeak for "sexual."

On the other end of the spectrum, Bridget Fonda plays an ambitious would-be Belle named Melaina (a role she reprises in *Doc Hollywood*), who plans to secure her future by winning the Miss Sun Fun contest. For her contest routine she practices a risqué interpretive dance number wearing a bikini and sporting a Confederate flag. Appalled by such heresy, the traditional Luann convinces her to adopt the manners if not the standards of the proper Southern lady as she coaches her performance of Scarlett's "I'll never go hungry again" speech. In the hedonistic environment of Myrtle Beach, being judged by a teen rock heartthrob, Melaina has no chance to win the contest with her traditional speech and conservative one-piece swimsuit. The "greaser" who dares to perform a sexy tap dance routine to "Dixie" while wearing a rebel flag bikini is chosen. Although the old forms will not suit the fast-paced modern world, Melaina gets the last laugh when her Southern Belle resiliency and sexuality manage to land her a talent agent and a trip to Hollywood despite her loss.

Caught between the proper Southern lady and the rebellious Southern Belle, Carson (Phoebe Cates) discovers her true sexuality in a passionate encounter with a modern day Rhett Butler (Robert Rusler), discarding her rich but dull fiance (Tyrone Power, Jr.) in the process. With refreshing honesty, she can finally admit: "I've been wild all along and didn't know it."

Implied in all these films is a rejection of the Southern Belle mystique that constricts the women to certain narrowly defined roles of behavior. As long as they stay within the boundaries of proper behavior, they are safe; if they dare to question the roles or to express divergent views/behavior, they risk becoming social outcasts, losing everything that had privileged them. There seems to be no middle ground in these films; in order to find one's true self, the facade must be broken, the past must be put aside, the codes must be rejected. The actress (or in these films, the beauty queen) is an appropriate image of the experience of the Southern Belle. Southern women are put on display for their poise, congeniality, talent, and physical attractiveness, external traits that are valued above character, intellect, and individuality. The code of manners is so elaborate that all Southern women become actresses, fulfilling the requisite forms with or without conviction.

As these recent Southern films demonstrate, filmmakers seem conscious of the legacy of Southern literature and films, conscious of the stereotypes that have evolved from the works of Margaret Mitchell, Tennessee Williams and William Faulkner. How they handle these stereotypes, however, presents another dilemma: is the film merely imitating its predecessors or is there a degree of irony and awareness in the presentation? The problem of how to read these stereotypes and conventions can be seen in contrasting reviews of *Miss Firecracker*, to select one film of many that inspire such conflicting interpretations. In analyzing the black character Popeye Jackson (played by Alfre Woodard), one reviewer sees the movie version of Beth Henley's play basically as recycled Tennessee Williams: "Woodard is either directed or allowed to cartoon herself in a way that might have given even Butterfly McQueen pause, and all the characters are offered up for detached observation like carnival show freaks" (*1990 Motion Picture Guide Annual* 154). In the *Variety* review, on the other hand, Woodard is praised for "revivifying ethnic stereotypes such as bugged-out eyes into a hilarious, original character" (22). Are stereotypes being challenged, redefined, reclaimed or are they merely being perpetuated? As discussed, *Miss Firecracker*, *Heart of Dixie*, and *Shag* all contain conscious references to GWTW that help define the heroine's romantic situation. Similarly, *Doc Hollywood* creates a self-professed "Hee Haw Hell" that satirizes and transforms the country bumpkin stereotypes of the Southern backwoods, although it is hard in this film to tell whether the parody is conscious or accidental. Indeed, it is a fine line that many of these productions walk, but most of the stories contain within them an awareness of the Southern mythology, providing the audience a means through which to understand and critique the stereotypes and conventions.

Ironically, the South, presented as a place haunted by tradition and history, has become the film industry's landscape for exploring contemporary problems of racism and feminism. Hollywood filmmakers have traditionally believed that they should not set a film in the South unless the story was going to be about "The South." William Faulkner insisted that his stories were about the eternal verities and were applicable to all humans; why can't fimmakers invent interesting stories about real people who happen to live in Atlanta, or Charlotte, or Montgomcry, instead of returning to GWTW for a cast list? Without presenting a totally homogenized view of Southerners, this new Southern could find the quirky elements in local characters as have many documentary filmmakers (like Errol Morris, Ross McElwee, Steven Roszell, Heather McAdams). Certainly the self-proclaimed "redneck, punk, drag queen" Bradley Harrison Picklesheimer in McAdams's documentary portrait is much more inventive than the cliched town fairy thrown into *Doc Hollywood* for local color and cheap laughs. The real New South contains fascinating, unique individuals, people who have been shaped by history, by social circumstances, and by regional identity. Perhaps as more filmmakers come to this New South to make movies, they will tell those stories instead of recycling the stale stereotypes mired in past ignorance and prejudice.

Works Cited

Combs, Richard, Rev. *Bull Durham, Monthly Film Bulletin* Sept. 1989: 269.
Davis, Thulani. "Civil Rights and Wrong." *American Film* Dec. 1988: 34-38, 54-55.
Ingalls, Zoe. "A Southern Poet Seeks to Fathom Racial Prejudice." *The Chronicle of Higher Education* 13 Nov. 1991: B4.
Rev. *Miss Firecracker. 1990 Motion Picture Guide Annual* 22.
Rev. *Miss Firecracker. Variety* 19 Apr. 1989: 22.
Rev. *Mississippi Burning. 1989 Motion Picture Guide Annual* 111.

Partial Filmography of Southern Films

Year	Film	Director
1972	*Deliverance*	John Boorman
1972	*The Legend of Boggy Creek*	Charles B. Pierce
1972	*Sounder*	Martin Ritt
1973	*Gator Bait*	Ferd and Beverly Sebastian
1974	*The Autobiography of Miss Jane Pittman*	John Korty
1974	*Buster and Billie*	Daniel Petrie
1974	*Cockfighter*	Monte Hellman
1974	*Conrack*	Martin Ritt
1974	*Macon County Line*	Richard Compton
1975	*Hard Times*	Walter Hill
1975	*Mandingo*	Richard Fleischer
1975	*Nashville*	Robert Altman
1975	*Return to Macon County*	Richard Compton
1976	*The Bingo Long Traveling All-Stars and Motor Kings*	John Badham
1976	*The Drowning Pool*	Stuart Rosenberg
1976	*Drum*	Steve Carver
1976	*Gator*	Burt Reynolds
1976	*Kudzu*	Marjorie Short
1976	*Sounder, Part II*	William A. Graham
1977	*Greased Lightning*	Michael Schultz
1977	*Return to Boggy Creek*	Tom Moore
1977	*Smokey and the Bandit*	Hal Needham
1978	*It's Grits*	Stanley Woodward
1978	*Pretty Baby*	Louis Malle
1979	*Carny*	Robert Kaylor
1979	*The Great Santini*	Lewis John Carlino
1979	*Norma Rae*	Martin Ritt
1979	*Wise Blood*	John Huston
1980	*Coal Miner's Daughter*	Michael Apted
1980	*Little Darlings*	Ronald F. Maxwell
1980	*Smokey and the Bandit II*	Hal Needham
1981	*Cannonball Run*	Hal Needham
1981	*The Night the Lights Went Out in Georgia*	Robert F. Maxwell
1981	*Sharky's Machine*	Burt Reynolds
1981	*Soldier Girls*	Nicholas Broomfield & Joan Churchill
1981	*Southern Comfort*	Walter Hill
1982	*Cat People*	Paul Schrader
1982	*Six Pack*	Daniel Petrie

1982	*Swamp Thing*	Wes Craven
1982	*Vernon, Florida*	Errol Morris
1983	*The Big Chill*	Lawrence Kasdan
1943	*The Lords of Discipline*	Taylor Hackford
1983	*Smokey and the Bandit 3*	Dick Lowry
1983	*Stroker Ace*	Hal Needham
1984	*Cat on Hot Tin Roof*	Jack Hofsiss
1984	*The River*	Mark Rydell
1984	*The Slugger's Wife*	Hal Ashby
1984	*A Soldier's Story*	Norman Jewison
1984	*Streetcar Named Desire*	John Erman
1984	*Tightrope*	Richard Tuggle
1984	*Writing in Water*	Stephen Roszell
1985	*Belizaire, the Cajun*	Glen Pitre
1985	*The Long Hot Summer*	Stuart Cooper
1985	*Marie: A True Story*	Roger Donaldson
1986	*Blue Velvet*	David Lynch
1986	*The Color Purple*	Steven Spielberg
1986	*Crimes of the Heart*	Bruce Beresford
1986	*Down By Law*	Jim Jarmusch
1986	*A Gathering of Old Men* (or, *Murder on the Bayou*)	Volker Schlondorff
1986	*Huey Long*	Ken Burns
1986	*'Night Mother*	Tom Moore
1986	*No Mercy*	Richard Pearce
1986	*Sherman's March*	Ross McElwee
1986	*Shy People*	Andrei Konchalovsky
1987	*Angel Heart*	Alan Parker
1987	*Athens, GA—Inside/Out*	Bill Cody
1987	*The Big Easy*	Jim McBride
1987	*Ernest Goes To Camp*	John Cherry
1987	*Matewan*	John Sayles
1988	*The Accidental Tourist*	Lawrence Kasdan
1988	*Big Business*	Jim Abrahams
1988	*Biloxi Blues*	Mike Nichols
1988	*Bull Durham*	Ron Shelton
1988	*Clara's Heart*	Robert Mulligan
1988	*Ernest Saves Christmas*	John Cherry
1988	*Everybody's All-American*	Taylor Hackford
1988	*Heartbreak Hotel*	Chris Columbus
1988	*Meet...Bradley Harrison Picklesheimer*	Heather McAdams
1988	*Mississippi Burning*	Alan Parker
1988	*School Daze*	Spike Lee
1989	*Blaze*	Ron Shelton
1989	*Driving Miss Daisy*	Bruce Beresford

1989	*Glory*	Edward Zwick
1989	*Great Balls of Fire*	Jim McBride
1989	*Heart of Dixie*	Martin Davidson
1989	*In Country*	Norman Jewison
1989	*Miss Firecracker*	Thomas Schlamme
1989	*Mystery Train*	Jim Jarmusch
1989	*sex, lies, and videotape*	Steven Soderbergh
1989	*Shag: The Movie*	Zelda Barron
1989	*Steel Magnolias*	Herbert Ross
1990	*Chattahoochee*	Mick Jackson
1990	*Daughters of the Dust*	Julie Dash
1990	*Days of Thunder*	Tony Scott
1990	*Ernest Goes to Jail*	John Cherry
1990	*The Long Walk Home*	Richard Pearce
1990	*Modern Love*	Robby Benson
1990	*Paris Trout*	Stephen Gyllenhaal
1990	*Wild At Heart*	David Lynch
1991	*The Ballad of the Sad Cafe*	Simon Callow
1991	*The Butcher's Wife*	Terry Hughes
1991	*Cape Fear*	Martin Scorsese
1991	*Doc Hollywood*	Michael Caton-Jones
1991	*Ernest Scared Stupid*	John Cherry
1991	*Fried Green Tomatoes*	Jon Avnet
1991	*JFK*	Oliver Stone
1991	*Paradise*	Mary Agnes Donoghue
1991	*Prince of Tides*	Barbra Streisand
1991	*Rambling Rose*	Martha Coolidge
1991	*The Silence of the Lambs*	Johnathan Demme
1992	*Memphis*	Yves Simoneau
1992	*Mississippi Masala*	Mira Nair
1992	*My Cousin Vinny*	Jonathan Lynn
1992	*One False Move*	Carl Franklin
1992	*Passion Fish*	John Sayles
1993	*Rich in Love*	Bruce Beresford
1993	*Sommersby*	Jon Amiel

Public/
Ritual
Spaces

Frankie and Annette at the Beach:
The Beach Locale in American Movies
and Its Dominance in the 1960s
Kathy Merlock Jackson

Americans have long felt an attraction to the sea and its landscape counterpart, the beach; thus, it is not surprising that beach scenes have appeared frequently in the movies. At the same time in which silent movies were finding their audience, the beach resort was gaining popularity as a vacation spot, a phenomenon depicted by Mack Sennett in his Bathing Beauties comedies. Although in the years that followed, beaches took on other connotations in the American mindset—most notably, as a place for battle and bloodshed during war depicted in movies such as *Beach Red* (1967), *The Longest Day* (1972), and *Apocalypse Now* (1979)—Americans have traditionally associated beaches with leisure time, escape from everyday routine, summer homes, and vacations, and this image has proved to be the key way in which beaches have been portrayed in the movies. Over the years, the beach setting, captured by the use of camera shots featuring groups, couples, or solitary individuals against a backdrop of sand and crashing waves, has become a mainstay in American film with literally thousands of movies featuring beach scenes. Of these, certain ones stand out, by virtue of their popularity, vision, or effect on the collective American consciousness. An analysis of key films featuring a beach locale, particularly the popular American International Pictures' beach party movies of the 1960s, shows what meanings movie audiences have come to associate with beaches through seeing them in the movies. It also sheds light on the ways in which cinematic beaches reflect cultural values and trends.

Key Beach Scenes in Movies of the 1940s and 1950s
Although the term "beach movie" was not coined until the 1960s, many earlier movies contained important beach scenes. A few of the most memorable occurred in the 1940s and 1950s. In 1940, Alfred Hitchcock released *Rebecca*, which tells the story of a naive young woman who feels overshadowed by the memory of her husband's beautiful and accomplished first wife and goes to a secluded beach to

121

think. Set in Monte Carlo and Cornwall, *Rebecca* shows the beach as a place of solitude where one goes to be alone and reflect.

Other movies portrayed the beach as a place for sexual encounters. In the 1946 film *The Postman Always Rings Twice*, Cora Smith, played by screen siren Lana Turner, dons a provocative white two-piece bathing suit during a midnight interlude at the beach with her husband Nick (Cecil Kellaway) and Frank Chambers (John Garfield), a drifter who is sexually attracted to her; later, she and Frank engage in rough, intense lovemaking and carry out a plot to kill her husband. The beach scene, which had difficulty getting past the movie industry's censorship board, was popularized in the August 1945 issue of *Life* magazine in an article titled "Love at Laguna Beach," which included six photographs of Turner and Garfield in their swimwear. Writing in *The Dame in the Kimono*, Leff and Simmons note, "In one shot, Turner wrapped her arm around the prone Garfield; in another, moodily lit from behind, they were mouth to mouth: 'A torrid kiss by moonlight seals the couple's reconciliation,' *Life* panted" (Leff and Simmons 133). In another key film, *From Here to Eternity* (1953), Deborah Kerr proclaims, "I never thought it could be like this. No one ever kissed me the way you do," as she engages in a wartime extramarital affair with Burt Lancaster, complete with a sultry embrace on the Hawaiian beach as the waves cascade around them. This passionate scene has arguably become one of the most recognizable in all of American cinema.

In other movies, the beach setting carried danger. In the well known 1954 movie *Creature From the Black Lagoon*, a prehistoric gillman stalks an Amazon lagoon, thereby creating fear and hysteria. Writing many years later, horror writer Stephen King recalls the effect that this movie had on him:

I remember only one scene clearly from the movie, but it left a lasting impression. The hero ([Richard] Carlson) and the heroine (Julia Adams, who looked absolutely spectacular in a one-piece bathing suit) are on an expedition somewhere in the Amazon basin. They make their way up a swampy, narrow waterway and into a wide pond that seems an idyllic South American version of the Garden of Eden.

But the creature is lurking—naturally. It's a scaly batrachian monster that is remarkably like Lovecraft's half-breed, degenerate aberrations—the crazed and blasphemous results of liaisons between gods and human women....This monster is slowly and patiently barricading the mouth of the stream with sticks and branches, irrevocably sealing the party of anthropologists in. (King 103)

Drawn to the monster that he calls "my Creature," King notes that he responded to it in the same way that every writer of horror fiction hopes the audience will: with total emotional involvement (King, 104). King was not alone. *Creature From the Black Lagoon* created a horrific image of the evil that lurked in the sea, one that many found memorable. *On the Beach* (1959) also depicts the beach as a dangerous place. This film, starring Gregory Peck, Ava Gardner, Fred Astaire, and Anthony Perkins, carries a strong anti-war message: it tells of the ordeal of the last surviving people on earth who await certain death due to radioactivity.

All told, *Rebecca, The Postman Always Rings Twice, From Here to Eternity, Creature From the Black Lagoon,* and *On the Beach* proved to be important films. They set the stage for the major ways in which beaches would be depicted in future movies: as a place of solitary reflection; as a place of romance and sex, often illicit; and as a place of danger and threat.

The Dominance of the Beach Locale in Movies of The 1960s

The popularity, and perhaps notoriety, of the beach scenes in *Rebecca, The Postman Always Rings Twice, From Here to Eternity* and *Creature from the Black Lagoon* may have contributed to the proliferation of beach locales in movies of the 1960s, for it was then that the beach setting truly came into its own in American cinema. The trend began in 1960 with MGM's blockbuster film *Where the Boys Are,* featuring four coeds from a Midwestern university who drive hundreds of miles to Ft. Lauderdale for spring break to seek sunshine and, more importantly, encounters with the opposite sex; they find both. In another popular film, *Gidget Goes Hawaiian* (1961), a perky, wholesome teenage girl finds love amid the sea and sand. Box-office attractions Elizabeth Taylor and Richard Burton, playing the roles of a liberated artist and well-meaning but misguided married minister respectively, find illicit romance on the coast at Big Sur in *The Sandpiper* (1965). In all of these films, the beach becomes the setting for forbidden sex, either premarital or extramarital. Added to these is an array of beach horror films, spawned by *Creature From the Black Lagoon,* in which monsters rise mysteriously from the sea, most notably *The Horror of Party Beach* (1964) and *The Beach Girls and the Monster* (1965). The beach locale also became the site of other types of horror. Alfred Hitchcock's thriller *The Birds* (1963), which chronicles a series of attacks of flocks of birds, is set in a seaside community, as is *Last Summer* (1965), a film that culminates with the shocking rape of a shy teenager at Long Island's Fire Island by people she trusted as her friends. Given the popularity of beaches in 1960s movies, it was not surprising to see them in star vehicles, such as *One-Eyed Jacks* (1961) with Marlon Brando and *Blue Hawaii* (1961) with Elvis Presley. The beach even became a key element in a popular documentary *The Endless Summer* (1966), which follows two surfers to beaches all over the world in search of the perfect wave. In all, over a hundred movies released during the 1960s, many of them "B" movies, featured a beach locale in a prominent way, thereby forming one of the decade's most important film settings.

The American International Pictures' Beach Party Movies and Reasons for Their Popularity

Perhaps best reflective of the 1960s trend of beach locales in film was an entire beach genre: a series of lighthearted beach party movies released by American International Pictures between 1963 and 1967. Set on the California coast and starring teen heartthrobs Frankie Avalon and Annette Funicello, these pictures, carrying such memorable titles as *Beach Party* (1963), *Muscle Beach Party* (1964), *Bikini Beach* (1964) *Beach Blanket Bingo* (1965), *How to Stuff a Wild Bikini* (1967), received uniformly awful reviews. *Time*, for example, called *Beach Party* "unoriginal" and reported that "in comparison, it makes Gidget's Roman misadventures look like a scene from *Tosca*" (*Time*). *The New York Times* claimed that anyone who lasts through *Muscle Beach Party*, is "a double-eyed stoic" (*New York Times*). In its review of another American International release, *The New York Times* reported, "*How to Stuff a Wild Bikini*—yep, that's the title.... And anyone who wanders inside expecting the worst will not be disappointed. For here, finally and in color, is the answer to a moron's prayer" (Thompson 48). A later article called the same movie "the worst film of the last two and maybe the next two years" (*New York Times*).

Despite their lack of critical recognition, the American International beach party movies became box-office hits. Churned out cheaply and quickly with a usual filming schedule of only two weeks, the beach movies made a considerable profit for American International and its founders, president James H. Nicholson and executive vice-president Samuel Z. Arkoff. *Beach Party*, for example, cost a modest $500,000 to produce and the same amount to promote and returned an estimated $6 million; *Bikini Beach*, made for $600,000, took in approximately ten times that much (Lewis 85). Given American International's propensity for making money, Nicholson and Arkoff had a nickname for their company: "the Jolly Green Giant of Hollywood" (Ransom 91).

The 1960s popularity of beach settings in movies in general and American International's beach party films in particular raises several questions. Why did the beach locale, although present in other eras, prevail so strongly in the 1960s, and what does its dominance suggest about the collective mindset of the time? Also, why did American International's beach party movies, despite scathing reviews, flourish at the box office? An analysis of these questions reveals much about the cultural milieu of the 1960s as well as meanings movie audiences have come to associate with the beach locale.

Before addressing the content of the popular American International beach pictures, it is useful to consider social factors of the 1960s that led to their popularity. Movies reflect culture, and certainly the prominence of beach setting in 1960s movies reflects the rise of the beach as a vacation spot. In post World War II America, the work week was shortened and paid vacations became standard, measures that gave Americans more leisure time (Braden 287). Along with this came a travel boom. Sociologists observed Americans' growing devotion to recreation and noted that vacations away from home, while once considered a luxury for the middle class, had become a necessity (Leepson 533). The democratization of travel was brought about primarily by the automobile (Braden 287). By the 1960s, due to the affluence of the postwar years, more Americans than ever before owned their own automobiles, and 80 percent of all travel was by automobile (Kando 230). Also, thanks to a $50 billion program for highway construction spearheaded in 1954 by President Dwight D. Eisenhower (Heppenheimer 12), by the 1960s an extensive system of interstate highways was built. This, along with the evolution of roadside motels, restaurants, and gas stations, made it possible for Americans to travel long distances faster and more conveniently (Braden 325). These conditions led to a dramatic increase in beach vacations, which in the opinion of many fulfilled the requirements of a perfect vacation. When polled, Americans have indicated that their vacation satisfaction is related to a tourist spot's opportunities for relaxation, leisure, and escape (Lounsbury and Hoopes 1), requirements easily fulfilled by a sojourn to the beach.

The popularity of American International's beach movies also reflects an important fashion trend: the two-piece and, later, bikini bathing suits. In July 1963, the mainstream *Saturday Evening Post* featured on its cover an attractive blond sporting a white net two-piece bathing suit. The accompanying article noted that although American women had not yet embraced the bikini, the two-piece bathing suit was continuing to gain ground as it had for the past three years, thereby enabling the bathing suit industry to sell two hundred million dollars' worth of merchandise the previous year (Trombley 30). By 1967, however, the bikini had arrived. Designed by Piscine Molitar, the two-piece bathing suit with little more than an inch-wide bra and G-string bottom was introduced in Paris in 1946, at the same time as the explosion of the first atomic bomb on the Pacific island of Bikini (Calasibetta 499). It was dubbed "bikini" for its shock value and the sensation that it created on Riviera beaches (Calasibetta 499). Although bikinis were slower to catch on at American beaches, by 1967, 65 percent of the youth set donned them, and the mature seemed ready to follow (Aboulker 49). Observing the trend of briefer swimwear in the 1960s, William Trombley wrote, "But the real bonanza is still the female body bared to public view near a body of water" (Trombley 30). American International's beach movies of the 1960s did just that, giving audiences, as Harry and Michael Medved point out, "an excuse for watching whole squadrons of starlets exposing their bodies in a socially acceptable setting" (Medved 135).

The beach movie craze also points directly to the youth culture and the movie industry's attempt to satisfy it. The postwar American baby boom lasted from 1946 to 1964 and produced approximately 76 million babies, a full one-third of the population (Jones 2). By the 1960s, many baby boomers had reached their adolescent and teenage years, and the nation was dominated by a youth culture. While the key audience for movies has always been the young, in the 1960s, this segment made up an even greater proportion of the overall population and of the movie audience. In the 1960s, the most frequent and enthusiastic moviegoer was single and between the ages of 16 and 24; this age group made up a staggering 76 percent of the motion picture audience (Considine 6). Aware of the demographics of the primary movie audience, the National Association of Theater Owners made known what had been a driving preoccupation: to attune itself to the desires of the vital youth audience (Considine 6-7). The beach movies, which promote a message of surfing all day and swinging all night and carefully omit any mention of high school, law, church, or parents, were aptly designed for a youth audience. Further, the beach movies parallel the youth trend of beach music, best exemplified by the Beach Boys. During the same period that American International Pictures released its beach party movies, the Beach Boys reached music stardom with such hits as "Surfin'," "Surfin' Safari," "Surfin' U.S.A.," "Surfer Girl," and "California Girl."

The popularity of American International's beach pictures also reflects several realities of the movie industry in the 1960s. In 1946, there were only 100 drive-in theaters in the United States, a number that swelled to over 4,000 by the 1960s (Levy 83). Drive-in exhibitors were howling for more movies—"good, bad, or indifferent"—to attract their predominant audience of the under-25 crowd (Levy 81-83). Beach movies fit the bill.

A more pressing concern in the movie industry centered around the developing medium of television. As television continued to erode the movie theater audience, film studios and exhibitors looked for ways to lure people back into the theaters. This resulted in a relaxation of the movie industry's earlier censorship codes. As *From Here to Eternity* and *The Postman Always Rings Twice* proved years earlier, audiences respond to lovers in bathing suits embracing on the beach. American International took notice of this fact but avoided controversy. The company's beach films, complete with their bikini-clad teenagers, carefree surfing songs, frantic dances, and sexual innuendos, took advantage of the film industry's new freedom while at the same time conformed to traditional values. American International's formula, as conceived by the company's president James Nicholson, appealed to young audiences. It is described as follows:

Lots of boys and girls in scanty clothes come to the...beach...in a cute conveyance of some kind. They pile out, turn on radios and begin to dance wildly around. Unknown to the kids, the girls' behinds, or "fannies," as they are called in the industry (the camera direction "Fanny Shot" has a legitimate place in the jargon of film making, right along with "Angle On," "POV," and "Now Take a Picture Of"), are being lovingly examined by a middle-aged male through some sort of optical device. Cut to the beach where the sleeping arrangements are being worked out. The way they work out is that the boys and girls sleep *in two separate places*.... These two places are not separated by very much, however, and the boys make manly attempts to get in bed with the girls but are not successful. (Ransom 90)

As one American International executive described, in the beach movies, "Sexiness is always present...but there is no sex" (Ransom 90). Thus, "We get approved by everybody" (Ransom 90). The beach movies, then, are reflective of a loosening of the film industry's code and at the same time an adherence to traditional moral values.

The box office success of American International's beach movies also provides a casebook study of innovative marketing in the film industry. According to company president Nicholson, "70% of a picture's appeal is in the title" (Levy 81). Thus, he would test the effects of various titles on a sample of young people, and if a title seemed to click, he hired people to write a script and churn out a film. In particular, he was aiming for the 19-year-old male, reasoning that younger teens would attend a movie geared to an older audience and that girls would acquiesce to the entertainment choices made by their dates (Levy 82). With this strategy, films such as *Beach Blanket Bingo* and *How to Stuff a Wild Bikini* were born. Another marketing technique was to advance book a film to open simultaneously at several theaters all over town, thereby suggesting to the audience that the movie was hot property and everyone was rushing to see it (Levy 83). (Often, too, this meant that many people would see a film before a particularly negative review appeared and discouraged potential audience members.)

Clearly, American International's beach movies function as important artifacts of the movie industry and culture of the 1960s. They also provide insight into the meanings that movie audiences have come to associate with the beach setting. The beach movies are not known for their scintillating plots; instead, a basic formula prevails: Frankie, played by Frankie Avalon, and his steady girlfriend Dee Dee, played by Annette Funicello, drive to the beach happily singing. Once they arrive, it becomes clear that they will not be engaging in an isolated romantic interlude. Much to Frankie's dismay, the gang is there too, and, at Dee Dee's insistence, they work out separate sleeping quarters for the males and females. In an aside to the audience, Frankie registers his disbelief at this arrangement. On the beach, Frankie, Dee Dee and their friends enjoy a carefree life of surfing, singing, and dancing. At one point, a ridiculous older male, in the form of, perhaps, an anthropologist studying their mating rituals or a land developer trying to get them to leave the beach, intrudes upon their private world. Around the same time, a motorcycle gang wearing black leather jackets and headed by a bumbler named Eric Von Zipper enters their territory, and Von Zipper proclaims his love for one of the female surfers. Various interactions among the different personalities take place as the surfers strive to maintain their turf. Along the way, Dee Dee tries to persuade Frankie to settle down and marry her, and he resists, saying he prefers the carefree life. Frankie then gets interested in another woman, thereby prompting Dee Dee to get jealous and hook up with another man; this makes Frankie jealous. To add to the plot, the surfers engage in some offbeat new activity, be it skydiving, muscle-building, or karate, with Frankie and Dee Dee taking on danger in order to impress one another. By the end of the movie, the surfers realize that the ridiculous male who invaded their beach actually has a heart and is not so bad after all, and Eric Von Zipper, in a slapstick routine, is carried off by his gang members. Frankie and Dee Dee get back together, with Dee Dee continuing to affirm her credo: "A girl needs a ring before she can swing" (Levy 93). The surfers dance on the beach to a fast rock and roll tune as the movie's credits roll.

In the American International beach movies, the beach becomes a backdrop for relationship studies. Traditionally, the beach has been associated with relationships that are quickly formed but shortlived and transient. Lois Banner notes that beaches have

occupied an ambiguous place in the minds of Americans. They were places of anonymous meeting, outside of the regular confines of American culture, away from "conventional restraints." They mixed together friends and strangers in new and novel combinations. They were close to nature and the relaxing forces of sun and fresh air, away from the accustomed circles that monitored behavior. At them conventional mores were easily loosened. (Banner 265)

Given this, the beach setting for Frankie and Dee Dee provides several associations. Note that although Frankie and Dee Dee have a steady relationship, once they arrive at the beach, it is immediately threatened, thereby causing them to link up briefly with other partners. The cause of their rifts is always the same: Dee Dee's requests for marriage and commitment, which seem inappropriate and ironic in a beach setting marked by transience and lack of responsibility. Frankie responds with a true beachcomber's answer: "I want it easy and I want it free."

The beach setting provides another irony. Contrary to expectation, while at the beach and away from social restraints, Dee Dee does *not* loosen her sexual morals; if anything, she becomes even more chaste. So what effect does this have on the audience? Will an audience that has come to associate a beach setting with eroding morals be disappointed by the American International formula, especially when the movies' promotional campaigns tend to stress sand, surf, and sex? According to one American International executive, no:

Kids realize that sex play exists, but they don't like to get involved with it.... A boy watching a movie and sitting next to a girl with whom he's necking will be embarrassed. Even today's dance steps are pretty damn puritanical. The greatest sex play we've had in the beach pictures is a kiss or two stolen behind a surfboard. Or a lingering underwater kiss that ends comically because Boy and Girl have to come up for air. If they tarry beneath a palm tree, a falling coconut will disable the Boy while Girl comes to her senses. Any punishment comes from Nature—not from parents. (Levy 82-83)

The beach setting of the American International beach party movies provides a sexually charged atmosphere where scantily clad young people—totally isolated from the restrictive social factors of parents and school—surf, sun, sing, dance, and romance. Sex never takes place, but the beach setting carries with it a certain anticipation, the possibility that it always could. For young people in the movie audience of the 1960s, this was paradise if there ever was one.

The popularity of the American International beach pictures led to many imitators, among them 20th Century Fox's *Surf Party* (1964) with Bobby Vinton, thereby solidifying the 1960s as the golden years for the beach in film. Although the popularity of the beach party pictures did not last long, it did help to establish the beach as an important film setting, one that has prevailed, although not as frequently as in the 1960s, in the decades since. The discussion of a few key films shows the directions that beach setting in movies took in subsequent years.

The Beach Setting in Movies After the 1960s

After the 1960s, the dominance of image of the beach as a party site began to wane, although its legacy remained, particularly in the form of remakes and sequels. In 1988, Frankie Avalon and Annette Funicello resurrected their roles as Frankie and Dee Dee in *Back to the Beach*, which features the two as middle-aged parents and pokes fun at their earlier beachcombing days. *Spring Break* (1983), *Where the Boys Are* (1984), and *Shag* (1989) are inspired by both the 1961 original of *Where the Boys Are* and the American International beach party movies. Set in Ft. Lauderdale, Florida, the first two provide opposite sides of the same coin: *Spring Break* tells the story of the annual teenage mating ritual from a male point of view while *Where the Boys Are* describes the female perspective. Both are set in the 1980s and treat sex more graphically that their 1960s' predecessors. *Shag*, on the other hand, is set in 1963 and takes a more nostalgic view. It focuses on the demure character of Carson (Phoebe Cates), who is about to graduate from high school in Spartanburg, South Carolina and marry a wealthy, safe but ultimately boring guy from her hometown. Three of her friends whisk her off to Myrtle Beach for a final fling, and there she falls for and has sex with a brash Yankee college student, someone very unlike herself. The beach setting in these movies conforms to previous depictions of the beach as a place for parties and sex, and one in which even conservative, conventional people tend to go wild.

However, this traditional image was giving way to the portrayal of the beach as less frivolous, more reflective place. This trend can be evidenced by films such as the immensely popular *Summer of '42*, released in 1971. This nostalgic film uses a beach setting to chronicle the coming of age of 15-year-old Hermie (Gary Grimes), who while spending the summer at his family's vacation house at an island off of the New England coast becomes infatuated with Dorothy (Jennifer

O'Neill), a friendly, attractive woman of 22 whose husband goes off to fight in World War II. Thus, a beach setting provides the backdrop for an unlikely relationship between a teenager and an older, married woman. In one of the most memorable scenes in the film, a very self-conscious Hermie goes into a drug store to buy his first condom, an activity that seems more likely in a carefree summer place than in a more restricted city environment. Distraught when she receives a telegram informing her that her husband has been killed in battle, Dorothy has sex with Hermie and later departs from the island, leaving Hermie to walk alone along the shore and reflect upon his memorable summer and what it has taught him about life, love, sex, and death. In essence, *Summer of '42* uses a beach setting to address the theme of sexual awareness, a key concern during the sexual revolution of the late 1960s and 1970s. The beach setting of *Summer of '42* is also crucial for another reason: it establishes the beach as a place, away from everyday conventions, where people unlike one another are brought together and form unlikely relationships.

This theme is carried out in a number of popular films. In *The Heartbreak Kid* (1971), a newly married man (Charles Grodin) on his honeymoon in Miami Beach falls in love with a gorgeous woman (Cybil Shepherd) while his bride nurses a sunburn in her hotel room. In *10* (1979), a middle-aged Hollywood songwriter (Dudley Moore) becomes obsessed with a beautiful woman (Bo Derek). While she is on her honeymoon at a beach resort, he saves her husband's life, which gains him a rare moment of intimacy with her. *The Flamingo Kid* (1984), starring Matt Dillon, couples a teenager from a poor Bronx neighborhood with a highrolling car dealer who is the gin rummy champion at a ritzy Long Island beach club. When Jeffrey (Dillon) takes a summer job as a cabana boy at the beach club, flashy Phil Brody (Richard Crenna) takes him under his wing, thereby prompting Jeffrey to reject his father's working-class values until he learns the truth about Brody's questionable character. In all of these movies, the vacation beach setting reflects the erosion of moral and social conventions, thereby bringing together people who in their ordinary lives would never have been linked.

This is also a key theme in *Beaches* (1988). In this film, Hilary Whitney, the daughter of a upper-class attorney from San Francisco sits crying under the boardwalk in Atlantic City because she is lost. She is rescued by CC Bloom, a feisty girl from a lower-class Bronx family whose mother is determined to make her a star. The two girls become instant friends and vow to keep in touch, which they do through the frequent exchange of letters. As years pass, the two enter very different lifestyles. CC, played by Bette Midler, becomes a brassy, well-known jazz singer, and Hilary, played by Barbara Hershey, a lawyer like her father. Although their friendship is marked by periods of tension, it endures, only to be threatened by Hilary's developing a fatal heart virus. During what she knows will be the last summer of her life, Hilary, a single parent, asks CC to spend time with her and her daughter at her beach home, and CC does, thereby sealing their friendship. As the film's title suggests, the beach setting carries significance. Because CC and Hilary meet at a vacation beach where people stay for a while before returning to their everyday lives, the expectation is that their friendship will be, like the beach setting, marked by transience. Thus, their friendship is threatened from the onset; the transience of the beach, marked by Hilary's premature death, prevails. However, the beach also carries with it a sense of renewal. By spending their last summer together at a beach, CC and Hilary have come full circle. CC carries with her fond memories of their friendship kindled at the beach, ones triggered each time she sings her popular show song "Under the Boardwalk."

In 1975, one of the all-time most successful films featuring a beach setting was released, *Jaws*, based on the novel by Peter Benchley and directed by Steven Spielberg. This film opens with two teenage lovers, giddy from drink, cavorting to the beach at a summer resort in Long Island, New York for a midnight swim. The young woman, apparently the victim of a shark attack, does not return. Spielberg's film, which follows an expert shark hunter (Robert Shaw), an ichthyologist (Richard Dreyfuss), and the town's police chief (Roy Scheider) on their quest to kill the man-eating shark, characterizes the sea in much the same way as *Creature from the Black Lagoon*: as a place of threat and terror. However, the more sophisticated special effects of *Jaws*, in particular its frightening 25-foot mechanical shark, made for an even more intense emotional response. *Jaws* fits into one of the most successful film cycles of the 1970s, the disaster film. As Americans coped with the disaster in their own lives caused by an economic recession, they watched films such as *The Poseidon Adventure*, *The Towering Inferno*, and *Earthquake*, all of which addressed the classic conflict between man and nature. *Jaws* captures this conflict in a beach setting. The success of *Jaws*—one of the biggest blockbusters of the decade—spawned a number of imitators, among them *Blood Beach* (1981), directed by Jeffrey Bloom. In Spielberg's own *1941* (1981), he opens with a scene jokingly reminiscent of *Jaws*, featuring a nude female swimmer bounding into the surf as threatening music plays in the background.

Conclusion

The beach setting has been a mainstay in American film, culminating with the popularity of the American International "beach films" starring Frankie Avalon and Annette Funicello in the 1960s. While the beach has provided the backdrop for a diverse assortment of plotlines and genres, films set at the beach seem to have one element in common: they address relationships. At the beach, waves come in and wash away the sands. Thus, the beach has characteristically been portrayed as a place of transience: people pass through, staying perhaps a week or two or a summer, before returning to their ordinary, conventional lives. In many cases, the beach setting breaks down traditional cultural, moral, or socio-economic barriers and draws together unlike people who would not have been linked otherwise. Thus, relationships formed at the beach are sometimes illicit and generally shortlived or threatened. The seaside lovers in films as diverse as *The Postman Always Rings Twice, From Here to Eternity, The Sandpiper*, and *Jaws* are doomed. In the American International Films, Frankie and Annette's permanent relationship undergoes stress each time the two visit the beach. The friends in *Beaches* maintain their unlikely friendship, but its inception at the beach suggests that it is doomed, a prophecy fulfilled by Hilary's early death.

Ultimately, the beach setting has been used in American films in three ways: as a place of solitary reflection; as a place of romance and sex, often illicit; and as a place of danger and threat. Beach scenes in films, then, either conform to these images or provide an element of surprise by going against the popular expectations.

Thus, the beach has become more than a simple setting for sun and fun. It has become a filmmaker's shorthand for relationships that are either threatened, or shortlived.

Works Cited

Aboulker, Florence. "Brief, Briefer, Briefest." *Time* 2 June 1967.

Banner, Lois W. *American Beauty*. Chicago and London: U of Chicago, 1983.

Braden, Donna R. *Leisure and Entertainment in America*. Dearborn, MI: Henry Ford Museum and Greenfield Village, 1988.

Calasibetta, Charlotte. *Fairchild's Dictionary of Fashion*. New York: Fairchild Publications, 1975.

Considine, David M. *The Cinema of Adolescence*. Jefferson, NC and London: McFarland, 1985.

Heppenheimer, T.A. "The Rise of the Interstates." *American Heritage of Invention and Technology* Fall 1991.

Jones, Landon Y. *Great Expectations: America and the Baby Boom Generation.* New York: Ballantine Books, 1980.

Kando, Thomas M. *Leisure and Popular Culture in Transition.* St. Louis: C.V. Mosby, 1975.

King, Stephen. *Danse Macabre.* New York: Everest House, 1981.

Leepson, Marc. "Tourism Boom." *Editorial Research Reports* Vol. II, No. 3, 21 July 1978.

Levy, Alan. "Peekaboo Sex,or How to Fill a Drive-In." *Life* 16 July 1965.

Lewis, Richard Warren. "Those Swinging Beach Movies." *Saturday Evening Post* 31 July 1965.

Lounsbury, John W. and Linda L. Hoopes. "An Investigation of Factors Associated with Vacation Satisfaction." *Journal of Leisure Research* Vol. 17, No. 1, 1985.

Medved, Harry and Michael. *Son of Golden Turkey Awards.* New York: Villard Books, 1986.

Ransom, J. "Beach-Blanket Babies." *Esquire* July 1965.

Rev. "How to Stuff a Wild Bikini." *The New York Times* 29 Jan. 1967, sec. II.

"Surf Boredom." *Time* 16 Aug. 1963.

Thompson, Howard. " 'Wild Bikini' Appearing in Neighborhoods." *New York Times* 12 Jan. 1967.

Trombley, William. "The Big Boom in Bathing Suits." *The Saturday Evening Post* 13 July-20 July 1963.

Filmography

Year	Film	Director
1940	*Rebecca*	Alfred Hitchcock
1946	*The Postman Always Rings Twice*	Tay Garnett
1953	*From Here to Eternity*	Fred Zinnemann
1954	*Creature From the Black Lagoon*	Jack Arnold
1959	*On the Beach*	Stanley Kramer
1961	*Blue Hawaii*	Norman Taurog
1961	*Gidget Goes Hawaiian*	Paul Wendkos
1961	*One-Eyed Jacks*	Marlon Brando
1961	*Where the Boys Are*	Henry Levin
1963	*Beach Party*	William Asher
1963	*The Birds*	Alfred Hitchcock
1963	*The Longest Day*	Andrew Marton, Bernhard Wicki, Ken Annakin
1964	*Bikini Beach*	William Asher
1964	*Horror of Party Beach*	Del Tenney
1964	*Muscle Beach Party*	William Asher
1964	*Surf Party*	Maury Dexter

1965	*Beach Blanket Bingo*	William Asher
1965	*The Beach Girls and the Monster*	Jon Hall
1965	*Last Summer*	Frank Perry
1965	*The Sandpiper*	Vincente Minnelli
1966	*The Endless Summer*	Bruce Brown
1967	*Beach Red*	Cornel Wilde
1967	*How to Stuff a Wild Bikini*	William Asher
1971	*Summer of '42*	Robert Mulligan
1972	*The Heartbreak Kid*	Elaine May
1975	*Jaws*	Steven Spielberg
1979	*Apocalypse Now*	Francis Ford Coppola
1979	*10*	Blake Edwards
1981	*Blood Beach*	Jeffrey Bloom
1984	*Blame It on Rio*	Stanley Donen
1984	*The Flamingo Kid*	Garry Marshall
1984	*Where the Boys Are*	Hy Averback
1987	*Back to the Beach*	Lyndall Hobbs
1988	*Beaches*	Garry Marshall
1989	*Shag*	Zelda Barron

Holy Architecture:
Cinematic Images of the Church
Terry Lindvall

What good is a road if it doesn't lead to a church?

Repentance (1987)

Crossing across the geography of film genres is the silent structure of the church building. As a convention, it has proven remarkably adaptable to romantic comedy, drama, western, horror, and even science fiction and slapstick comedy. It functions as a stable set piece in the furniture of a film, the small country church planted against a rural landscape or a majestic Gothic Cathedral looming over the middle ages. Its significance, however, spreads beyond its denotative existence as a religious meeting place; the image of the church building is immersed, even baptized, in motive views of communication. Its place of action in a film narrative enables it to affirm, reaffirm, correct, challenge, or subvert both the meaning of the scene or character, and the meaning of its own existence.

The church is often an invisible visible space in films. It exists; it is there; but it seems to merely decorate or embellish the background. It functions as more than innocent backdrop; it functions as a set of subtle, substantial and strategic symbols in the discourse of film. This study draws it out as a significant figure on the landscape of film. By seeking to isolate and define prevailing types of images, we may sort the images into groups according to the vehicle used to convey the particular tenor of the church. It is through this agent or medium expressed that the subject of the metaphor can be adequately displayed and compared.

If there is a deep structure to the various surface connotations of the church image it may be found etymologically. The Greek word *ekklesia* denotes the assembly or the church. It represents the gathered people of God called out into a saved community, of saints enjoying a dynamic, organic relationship with God. The term *church*, however, signifies in contemporary jargon the building, the structure in which religious people meet. It stands as bulwark symbol of many different

136

colors: of hypocrisy, of social elitism, of sanctuary, of spiritual and supernatural power. The organic nature of an assembled people has ossified into the organizational structure that we now call (correctly or incorrectly) a church. The congregation is either the outworking or infusing of that image's meaning in flesh and blood. The kind of members of the body of believers shapes how one perceives and acts toward the structure.

The true fellowship, *koinonia*, denotes organism rather than organization—a Christian community of sinners versus a society of self-righteous prigs in a cult of respectability. Civil religion can fashion the image of the church, reconstructing it into a country club of Pharisees. In contrast, Biblical metaphors of the church, derived from the letters of the Apostle Paul, include tropes that might not be readily conspicuous to the modern, or postmodern, observer: the Body of Christ, the Bride of Christ, the flock of Christ, the household (*oikos*) of God, and the living temple of the Holy Spirit. All indicate a dynamic and personal relationship of God to His people. The hollowing of these images into the facades of buildings is not due simply to the two-dimensional nature of film; rather, the identification of people with their meeting houses led to a fusion and confusion of the two as one. The Church then dropped off its connection to the people and took on the loci of the people. With the advent of bishops, deacons, presbyters, and other "professionals" the church became more hierarchical and institutional. Thus the institutional image overshadows the personal, charismatic one. The Church as social organization, as part of the ever notorious military/industrial/corporate complex, smothers the aspect of community. The structural, corporate image hovers as an institution of power in the social matrix. Luther's distinction in his controversy with the Papacy focused upon the visible and invisible body of Christ. The visible is data for empirical description and analysis. Since the enlightenment, it is easier to measure and evaluate the visible, particularly when it takes on such a concrete, wood, hay, and brick actuality.

In *The Image*, Kenneth Boulding argues that attitudes and behaviors toward an object are determined by the subjective perceptions of representations of that object, by the composite portrait of that object in the public mind. Thus concerns about the portrayals of minority or religious groups in the media rise out of the prevailing dominant representations (e.g. Keyser, Friedman, Boggs, etc.). The question of how the media elite, as Rothman and Lickert call them, the gatekeepers of meaning, portray the church will be our interest here.

The sign of the Church building in film bears diverse meanings, connoting the assembly of God's people, a place of sanctuary, a source of the supernatural, a hypocritical structure, and a variety of other significant notions. Our initial task is to identify the aesthetic and rhetorical dimensions of these images. It is beyond the scope of this preliminary essay to place the collection of types into historical/economic/social perspectives. That worthy assignment goes to other studies less general in nature. This inventory of tropes is not exhaustive, nor mutually exclusive. Rather, I have collected and marshalled observations of seemingly recurring representations, gleaning meanings from the references, their context, and the actions/words that take place within their realms.

The images examined here rarely fit the metaphors applied by the Christian Scriptures; such notions as the church being the Body of Christ, or His Bride, or a vine are rare. Rather the dominant signified motifs circle around the significance of the edifice itself. The church in the twentieth century art form of cinema is an organization, not an organism. It is a place, rather than people. One goes to church or looks at a church, rather than is part of a church. To be a member does not connote the living imagery from St. Paul's epistles of being an eye or foot of a physical body, but being a statistic on a membership roll. If there is a correlation between a biblical description and a cinematic representation it may be in the image of God's people being living stones. The construction material of church buildings may not be that mortal or animated but it does indicate the multiplicity of parts needed to make up the residence of God.

People worshiped God not on the mountain top nor necessarily in the temples, but in fellowship. Film translates the church not as the gathering of the faithful, but as a small, white-front country church or as the towering Cathedral of Notre Dame. Henry R. Sefton points out how "occasionally pagan temples were taken over and adapted by the Christians for their own worship....Such adaptation has been described as 'turning the temple inside out' " (Dowley 151). The process of cathedral being redesigned into a movie theater as portrayed on the cover of a 1960s *Esquire* magazine is countered by the reverse process of "converting" the movie theater into a church, as represented in Robert Zemeckis' *Back to the Future*, where a XXX porno-theater is turned into, as the marquis reads, an Assembly of Christ church. The den of iniquity and devils, as the theater was frequently decried in the twenties and thirties, is now reconverted into a holy place. Yet, as any student of religious history knows, a road goes two ways. A road to Jerusalem is also a road away from Jerusalem.

Denominations do not figure into the houses of God, much. Of course, Ingmar Bergman (whose knight meets a wonderfully allegorical

and chess-playing Death in a medieval confessional in *The Seventh Seal*)
cannot escape his father's Lutheranism, even in attempting to smother it
in cold unbelief in *Winter Light* or burn it in hellfire in *Fanny and
Alexander*. Luis Bunuel's oppressive Roman Catholic ecclesiastics
cojoin bourgeoisie society in an insidious conspiracy and secrecy (drawn
according to the lines of Kenneth Burke's pyramidic hierarchy of
mystery). Martin Scorsese's Roman Catholic roots and Paul Schrader's
Calvinism do not come into their films gently. *Mean Streets* (and to
some degree *The Last Temptation of Christ*) and *Hardcore/Light of Day*
respectively are not far away from the hearts of their creators'
upbringing. Quakers in *High Noon* and *Friendly Persuasion* and the
Amish in *Witness* provide intercultural events for audience members not
familiar with less well known communities of faith.

The thematic symbol analysis that this study applies has resulted in
a typology of signifying categories for the church as follows: (1) Social
Structure; (2) Political Institution; (3) Center of Hypocrisy; (4) Museum
or Empty Building; (5) Supernatural Fortress; (6) Sanctuary; (7) Locus
of Romance; (8) Source of Healing and Transcendence; (9) House of
God and People of God. (This study does try to exclude Biblical and
biographically religious films, from *One Foot in Heaven* to *Marjoe* or
The Mission, or films where the dominant or primary location is the
church, such as in *Hallelujah, Going My Way, The Bishop's Wife* or
Winter Light. The few exceptions to this restriction are so apt that we
couldn't refuse admittance.)

A Modest Typology
Social Structure
The significance of the church building to its congregation was
paramount in earlier ages. Often, as Gombrich pointed out, it was "the
only stone building anywhere in the neighborhood; it was the only
considerable structure for miles around, and its steeple was a landmark
to all who approached from afar" (Gombrich 126). The structure slipped
from this truly high and mighty position to the modern age where it
became akin to the Stock Exchange, the Court House, the High School,
the Country Club—basically part of the furniture of a given society.
When the Little Rascals play hooky from church in *The Little Sinner*, it
is not much different from playing hooky from Miss Crabtree and the
schoolhouse. As a social structure in film, the church building provides a
backdrop for weddings, funerals, baptisms, and carries the weight of
tradition in its diverse ceremonies. The rare appearance of a white
Western country church in Lawrence Kasdan's *Silverado* shows up in a
show down, a stable backdrop for good guy Kevin Kline in his climactic

mainstreet duel. It stands preeminent over the hotel, bank, saloon, and the events of the town run by crooked sheriff. It is probably the only building not controlled by the fascist state. In contrast, in *The Russia House*, the National Cathedral in Washington D.C., still under construction, stands by silently as part of the social/political landscape of the Capitol. In *The Big Chill*, Kasdan opens with the funeral of a suicide being conducted in an ordinary church, friends filling the pews in this Baby Boomer comedy. So too do all the darkly selfish acquaintances appear at the church funeral service to pray for themselves in the black comedy, *Heathers*. The funeral in *Out of Africa* is conducted in a small chapel, that merely squats against the magnificent scenery of the continent's preeminent and imposing landscape.

The church is the locus of information and direction for her people. Even in a B grade adventure like *Street Justice*, the hero (presumed dead after hiding out for several years) returns to his church to find the whereabouts of his wife and daughter. (We are told that this is also the church where Frank Sinatra got married.) Historically, the church would often keep birth, baptism, and marriage records, so became a source of key and important information. It served as the focal point of social, as well as religious life.

The stately cathedral in the early Middle Ages sustained a marked contrast between the lofty and the humble, the elaborate center of authority and the simple, even primitive homes of the people. Yet it was the people's center. Under the rounded arches of Norman style, one found a functional place of worship. Every nook and cranny of the building was designed for a purpose, coordinating sundry activities, including worship, art gallery, theatre, library, school, market place, civic center. Crouse indicated that since it was

the house of people as well as the house of God, and because medieval art emphasized the unity of all knowledge, the cathedral was meant to be a mirror of the world. The carvings were naturalistic and detailed representations of beasts, Bible stories, and allegories of vices and virtues. The structure of society was represented in carvings of the hierarchies of both church and state which portrayed ministers, knights, craftsmen, peasants, and tradesmen in the various activities. Theology was reflected in the structure of the building; the upward striving towards God; the cross-shape; and the altar situated in the east, facing Jerusalem. Every detail of the creed—from the Trinity to the creation, and from the passion of Christ to the Last Judgement—appeared in sculpture and stained glass. The harmony represented by such a structure signified the ideals of medieval art and thought. (Dowley 293)

Yet its place in the community was not singularly religious in purpose. Henry Sefton explained that, "As the largest building in the town it was a natural meeting-place for social activity and even trade. At Chartres the transepts of the cathedral served as a kind of labor exchange, and the crypt beneath the church was always open for the shelter of pilgrims and the sick. The sounds of services often mingled with the greetings of friends and the haggling of traders" (Dowley 291). The secular guilds and trades were involved in special carvings and windows, all classes of society represented and participating in the building or rebuilding and use of the church edifice.

Medieval art expressed a coherent system of values and a view of the universe based on an understanding of Christianity. Its purpose was to point to the spiritual reality that underlay the material world. Medieval artists used symbolism and allegory to present their ideas.

Will Durant remarked that in the thirteenth century: "Pictures and ornaments in churches are the lessons and scripture of the laity." Pictures, statues, architecture, poetry, hymns, legends and the theatre were all needed to teach those who could not read. These artists created a highly developed system of symbols in which most things had a spiritual as well as a literal meaning (Dowley 290).

The church was the center of goodness, and for various good works. Some films carry on this notion of the church as center of activity for the community. Dick Van Dyke in *Cold Turkey* leads his neighbors in a campaign to stop the city from smoking. Disney's pleasant and diversionary *North Avenue Irregulars*, depicts ordinary citizens, mostly housewives and their minister, working out of their headquarters in a church to successfully thwart local bootleggers.

The church is commonly portrayed as an essential element in black culture. The black church which welcomes Peter Boyle in *The Dream Team*, until he identifies himself as Jesus, is a hand-clapping, enthusiastic inner city congregation. In the zany *Blues Brothers*, Jake (John Belushi) receives a vision from God in a wildly charismatic church service led by the "Rev" (James "I feel good" Brown) singing and dancing to vibrant and zesty Negro spirituals. The swinging spirited worship gets the congregation jumping, leaping and praising God. A blue light engulfs and illumines Jake (effecting a ecstasy of flipping and cartwheeling) on how to raise money for the only home he's ever known, the orphanage, leading him and his partner Elwood (Dan Akroyd) on a "mission from God." Nothing can stop them, neither Army, State Highway Patrol, Air Force, or Marines on their mission. The church is the site of revelation and inspiration, of energy and life and music, of social community.

The haunting, sad and airy flute in *Boudu Saved From Drowning* serves as musical complement to the sublime image of the church spire of Sainte Chappelle in Jean Renoir's playful film. The spire of the chapel inspires; it leads upward and heavenly, bestowing the desire to soar above the earth. This satiric attack of upper middle-class society (effetely copied in *Down and Out in Beverly Hills*) portrays a tramp rejecting the extravagant and immoderate life style of his rescuers, and returning to his blessed, impoverished way of drifting. His sweet escape from the trappings of possession (and what appears to be his death to others who know not where he has gone) is punctuated with a final freeze frame of the church spire. He joins those, who like the fox have no hole to call his own, for a better life, one under the light of Providence and not the shadow of culture.

The cathedrals and churches were integral parts of all human activity. They held together the fabric of society, weaving all the threads into its own social tapestry. Thus if one wanted to be baptized, marry or bury (hatched, matched and dispatched), one would call on the church.

Film images reaffirm the role of the church in carrying on these social functions, even if with a less religious import. The holy sacrament of baptism is performed ironically in the House of God in such films as *The Godfather* with a wry juxtaposition of the sacred and the profane, the baptism of an innocent intercut with the butchering of rival mobs. The indictment of ecclesiastical powers ignorant of or contaminated with earthly, machiavellian powers happens as the church performs its social religious function, baptisms.

In *Once Around*, Holly Hunter's family, being torn apart by her generously unbridled husband Richard Dreyfus, fights over the scheduled time for their newborn baby's baptism. Over the dinner table argument, father Danny Aielo bans his son-in-law from his home; Holly sticks up for her husband and it seems a serious rift has occurred. The next scene shows the May-December couple having their baby baptized by a Lithuanian priest, alone in the large, cavernous Boston cathedral. Suddenly the family rushes in, exchanging effusive kisses, hugs and a warm joyous reunion. As the ceremony draws to a close, Dreyfus has a heart attack, contrasting the blessed beginning of a new life and the inevitable ending of an old life. The church serves as site for uniting a broken family, for healing temporary wounds, for preparing for death, for dedicating a child to God with *traditional* significance. When even family seems to desert, or death tiptoes in to take away life, the church is there.

In another cinematic church that is *just* there, death also plays a key element, but in exposing how far short the institution as mere social organization falls in relieving real problems. In Chabrol's *Les Cousins,* a law student depressed at failing his exam, wanders to a church for solace. On its door a sign has been posted announcing that the Church is closed between 7 p.m. and 7 a.m. It is not helpful in times of need.

So, too, *Terms of Endearment* views the church as seemingly irrelevant to modern people and their problems. When two children flee from the turmoil of their mother and home, they wander to a curb and sit down. A vast monumental cathedral hangs in the background as a distant canvas for the two small children. The impressive spires have nothing to do or to say to a troubled, divorced world and its victims.

The church building is used most frequently in films as the scene of wedding celebrations. In fact, weddings are the primary *raison d'etre* for a church in comedies. In numerous films like *Splash,* the church is merely the location for weddings, allowing for a comic incongruity of a gloomy groomsman, Tom Hanks, at his former girlfriend's wedding. Or, in *Semi-Tough,* it is the site of nuptial indecision and reversal, and a chaotic knock-down fight.

Where the wealthy sot Dudley Moore decides to sacrifice his life of luxury and liquid to marry the poor girl he loves (Liza Minelli) is in the church. Even inebriated in the sanctuary, he has the revelatory good sense to announce that he doesn't really love the prospective bride ("You see, I don't really love her. Oh, she's all right and all that, but I don't *love* her!"). At the altar, where one is admonished not to enter the wedding vows unadvisedly, but soberly and in the fear of God, Arthur does wake up. He goes for the pearl of great price, sacrificing his inheritance and everything else for this love. In Blake Edwards' *10,* Dudley Moore clandestinely slips into the church where Bo Derek goes through the motions of a marriage. Hiding behind strategically placed flora, lusting after this seemingly perfect woman, Moore is appropriately stung by a latter representative of the birds and bees. The presence of the church occurs simply because people go to the chapel to get married.

The newspaper advertisement that Buster Keaton takes out in *Seven Chances* informs any interested woman who wishes to marry a man who will come into a very large fortune to meet him at a church. His early arrival at the church offers Keaton a chance to sleep in the front pew. He wakes into a living wedding nightmare, for hundreds of prospective brides have congregated to claim him. Church is not a safe place to sleep.

Mike Nichols indicts the church as co-conspirator of a corrupt and hypocritical social structure in his classic dark comedy, *The Graduate.* In a desperate attempt to rescue Katharine Ross, Dustin Hoffman crashes into her wedding ceremony (shades of Harold Lloyd's last minute rescue of his girl in *Girl Shy*). The church is opulent and modern, constructed with glass, and a reflection of the "plastic" moneyed society of which it serves. Grabbing his beloved and eluding his pursuers, Hoffman locks the affluent, phony wedding party in one of its own social institutions, the church, by blocking the door, literally and symbolically, with a cross.

Finally, even the bizarre cultic *Rocky Horror Picture Show* opens with Brad and Janet leaving their friends' wedding as the quintessential middle class event, mocking its virginity, cleanliness, and normality (Tim Curry is surreptitiously hid in the wedding family portrait as the minister of the Denton Episcopal Church). The legitimate structures of a bourgeoisie society are gaily subterfuged. In contrast, *Cinema Paradisio* portrays the church and its prissy and censorial but comic and affectionate priest as the moral center for community and the arts. Without its religious anchor, the cinema sinks into a den of exploitative immorality, of public masturbation and prostitution, and eventually into its rueful demise. The church as place in these last three films, however, moves from the basically innocent topoi of social structure into a realm of political and ideological implications.

Political Force

As the church increasingly became the primary vehicle for transmitting culture, particularly Roman culture, the forms of the administrative hierarchy of the Roman civil and imperial offices naturally transferred into the establishment of Church government and councils. The church, becoming organized, became political. Such films as *The Cardinal*, *Godfather III*, and *The Verdict* could easily manipulate the financial shenanigans and political duplicity that were part of the legacy of a rich and powerful organization.

The mixings of religion and politics are as valorized as they are varied. In *Cool Hand Luke*, Paul Newman gets trapped in a church. As a sixties' Christ figure, he is imprisoned by the institutions of society; the church being the one prison in which he meets his anti-heroic death. On the other hand, the simple, rustic church set off against the bucolic Scottish landscape is the local and merry meeting place of the villagers (and the comical figure of an African minister in the highlands) eager to make money off the invading capitalists in *Local Hero*. *High Noon* pictures a congregation of cowards and pacifists who hold their town meeting in the church, and decide to do nothing but hide.

In his book on *Christ and Culture*, Niebuhr argued that the church may become so entwined with the political and cultural forces that one cannot distinguish the religious and the secular. The symbol of the church mixed with complete patriarchal authority, obedience, and discipline is well illustrated in the military school film, *Taps*. The formal chapel services inform the young cadets of duty more than grace. Drill and decorum may take precedence over preaching, yet the military state and the church are not separate. They are indistinguishably one.

Niebuhr's conception of Christ against culture is enacted in *The Strong Man*, Capra's last film with the sad, baby-face Harry Langdon. In this Prohibition era film, the innocent fool, whose only ally is God, is pitted against the saloon forces. In the denouement, a vigorous congregation marches Jericho-style around the saloon, bringing down places of evil, drunkenness, and debauchery in apocalyptic Biblical fashion.

Silent films could easily juxtapose goodness and evil in melodramatic fashion. Yet William S. Hart's classic *Hell's Hinges* offers a complex study of human morality in the realm of the polis. (Numerous early films like *Bronco Billy's Redemption* portray the outlaw hiding, quite by providential design, in a church, and being converted.) The church contrasts with a Western saloon, as good confronts evil. But corruption comes from within the church, the young pastor succumbing to the charms of a wayward woman. However, his fall is balanced by the salvation of Hart, seeing a vision of goodness in the church, even if that image of God is a good, and good-looking, woman, the sister of the impressionable pastor. Hart uses his temporal means of gun and force to effect God's judgment after the church is burned down, also bringing down the saloon. The church however is not the mere building that the congregation puts up and tries to defend; it is the remnant of people themselves, who ultimately brush the dust off their boots and leave Hell's Hinges behind them, as Lot leaves Sodom, not looking back.

In a reverse fashion, Franky Schaeffer, son of one of the predominant evangelical spokesmen of the twentieth century, pits a free-wheeling rock and roll culture as the antidote against corrupt, political religion, especially that of organized religious television evangelists (a tip of the hat to Robertson, Swaggart, Falwell, and Bakker) in *Rising Storm*.

The notion of Christ and culture in tension appears in the neorealist masterpiece, *Rome, Open City*, in which priest and communist both struggle against the Nazis, both sacrificing their lives (as a thematic harbinger of *The Mission*); one man dying by the sword and the other surrendering himself to martyrdom. While their ideologies differ radically, a common truce holds them together until this other enemy and evil is vanquished. A similar dialectic is played out in the French comedy, *The Little World of Don Camillo*, in which the titular Fernandel plays the titular village priest at constant war with his childhood friend,

, communist mayor. God continually speaks to Camillo in the church, not to shoot communists from the bell-tower, to give .ctuary to the referee who gave the soccer match to the communist's .eam, and to show charity. The church competes with the local politicians, and provides a steady, humanizing influence, despite Camillo's impatient desire to bonk his enemies and his neighbors (the same people, which may be why God told us to love both groups) on the head with a candlestick.

Rural and southern churches intersect dramatically with politics and racism in several films set in the 1950s and 1960s. *Norma Rae* attacks the social injustice meted out for blue collar mill union workers. The white Southern church leaders throw out their own Norma Rae, Sally Field, when they discover what she's up to, the organization of oppressed workers through the cooperation of an outside "Jewish agitator." Ruben Washafsky of New York finds a meeting place in the local black church and presents his offer of help via the pulpit, leading them out of their misery though self-help. Breaking down social barriers, the churches are vital, significant institutions in this southern community. Martin Ritt contrasts the poor, shabby black church, with its small pine pulpit and gaudy, tasteless, fabrics decorating the altar, which is located on the outskirts of town with the prim and proper white church situated in the center of the community, meticulously painted and groomed, with a manicured lawn. Like the Pharisees who have cleaned the outside of the cup, but left the inside full of greed and arrogance, their hearts are painted corrupt and full of grime. Blacks open up their place to anyone who comes. They are the true Good Samaritans, accepting those of different ethnic and social standing. The white church shows its hypocrisy in its clerically collared minister painting the outside banister *white*. The church according to him is that it is a "house of God"; Norma challenges him to prove it by asking that the church go against social norms and allow the next union meeting to be held there, as a symbol of God's justice for all men and women. However, the sanctuary remains closed to all outsiders, including the viewer. The status quo and the cult of respectability rule the building. It rejects the social and political responsibilities that the film expects it to have and hold. Yet social justice is made possible, as well as a new political consciousness for the former flying nun, after being rejected by her own congregation, through the kindness to strangers proffered by the black church.

Unlike *Mississippi Burning* in which churches mostly explode and burn, *The Long Walk Home* delineates one of the most potent illustrations of a active and fervent church in political action. The black community in Montgomery, Alabama, in 1955 found the church as the center of its source of inspiration, justice and hope. Religious icons and artifacts decorate the church: stained glass windows, big Bibles, hand-clapping worship, a preacher's microphone. Whoopi Goldberg is a maid in a country club developer's home and, due to the Montgomery decision by the black community to boycott the buses, walks an arduous distance to and from her job. Although her feet blister, she determines to walk to church with her family. Her husband explains to their son, that even with the pain, going to church will make her feel better. They arrive at the meeting and stand outside listening through loud speakers. An overflow crowd presses in tightly to hear the Reverend Martin Luther King's exhortation to walk and fight until justice runs down like water. While the walk to the double-steepled church bloodies the soles of her feet, there is no doubt to revival of her spiritual soul. It is in church that life is reaffirmed and resolve continually strengthened. It is in church that row after row of the congregation sings vigorously "Do Not Pass Me By," pleading with the Saviour to hear their humble cry for justice. It is in church that they hear of Reverend King's house being bombed. It is in church that they go to celebrate Christmas service after the family gives their mother a new colorful coat and new pair of shoes. It is in church that the bus boycott is organized. After her son and daughter are beat up by three white boys, they sit in church moving from anger to singing "Marching to Zion." With his battered lip and bruised face, and his father's arm around his shoulders, the elder son shows his courage and faith by painfully, but bravely, singing. It is in church that the family joins in, following the valor of their blessedly meek child. It is in and through the church that political and social justice builds upon a spiritual foundation.

The black church is honored as well in *The Five Heartbeats*, in which a strung out brother is saved in a Motown version of the prodigal son parable is enacted.

No such hope or justice occurs in a more modern time in *Country*, where the church exists as a meeting place to deal with death, with economic uncertainty. The church does not provide the impassioned faith of the Montgomery congregation. The struggle for survival of the clinging Ivy family finds no aid coming from a traditional church, antiquated, modest, wooden, and outdated. Well used pews and hymnals are antique reminders of the hymn the depressed congregation sings: "Faith of our Fathers." As David Duplessis was wont to say, "God has no grandchildren, only children," yet here, there is no deep personal faith. The old religious times are bygone, even as the days of the independent farmer are passing. Weary, defeated farmers assemble without the passion and faith of true believers; they are people with practical problems that seem to find no answers in the communion that they share nominally. When a mentally disturbed boy bursts out in laughter during the singing of a hymn, one feels the sad inadequacy of the church to answer the madness of a rigid social system that cannot respond to the problems of individual people.

One final film uses the image of the church in politically symbolic ways that are subtle and searing. The Fordian antinomy of city vs. garden is revisited in Altmann's bleak, dismal, moody, and resigned *McCabe and Mrs. Miller*, where civilization crawls into the rough wilderness of the untamed West. When hired gunmen from the big mining company come to kill him in the snowy winter weather, McCabe (Warren Beatty) first runs to hide in the unfinished Presbyterian Church, a symbol of the new middle class town emerging in the fading West. He oversees the primitive and undeveloped town from atop the church tower, being provided a vantage point from which to see impending death. He is chased out of the incomplete building by a clergyman holding McCabe's own shotgun, who tells him "This here's the House of God, get out!" It is by his own weapons of violence and pride that McCabe is sequestered from the sanctuary, from the refuge of grace and life that could be his salvation. The steeple towers over all the action, and, when the recruited rogues seemingly set fire to the church, they do so to divert the townpeople's attention from the fight between the free-enterprise capitalist pioneer, McCabe (protecting the bordello and "his" town) and the big business mercenaries. The town rallies to salvage the burning church, but lose their morally loose leader. The new community of Chinese, blacks, storekeepers, whores and regular citizens celebrate and drink to the success of their cooperative work to save the church. The church as the constructed axis of the emerging city does not have room for the maverick individual nor the corporate ownership. Yet one has the sense that the latter cannot be so easily expunged from its domain.

Hypocritical Center
        The greatest charge leveled against the church has consistently been the sin of hypocrisy. As a cultural as well as spiritual entity, it bears the smudge and smell of humanity much more than it shows forth the divine image. The self-righteous and Pharisaical do thrive in an environment in which sinners seek to be like God; yet these often try to be more spiritual than even God Himself. The presence of hypocrites in a church does not make the church itself hypocritical, as one can see in *Footloose*, in which John Lithgow, as the pastor of a rural midwestern community, undergoes a social/spiritual awakening in regards to the

value of dancing. His parishioners may be narrow religious, book-burning bigots, but he provides an oppositional signifier as an enlightened leader. The church may look like a museum of out-dated social and moral values, but just turn on the music and discover the freedom of dancing.

The first script by Anita Loos was directed by D.W. Griffith. *The New York Hat* (1912) concerned a young girl orphaned and slandered by a hypocritical battery of religious women. This delegation of church gossips whispered against the innocent Mary Pickford and the young pastor assigned to care for her. In an era of social reform and creeping censorship, Griffith astutely, and tactically, portrayed the ministerial leadership as honorable and good, thereby deflecting official concern about ridiculing of the clergy, but was also able to attack what he saw as busy-bodyism from socially active females. Griffith's church people were drawn according to degrees of charity. The hypocrisy of *certain* church people and reformers was repeated in his melodramas like *Way Down East*. What is curious about the silent films' representation of the church is the general probity and integrity of the leadership, while its membership slips and sins quite predictably, usually as hypocrites.

In contrast, Charlie Chaplin was kinder to the simple people of religious missions than to their leadership. The ones who worked in the slums such as *Easy Street* not only delivered sermons, but sought to counsel and enable the lost to find their right way around the mean streets of the inner city. Once Chaplin as the tenderfoot cop cleans up the violent, drug-infested ghetto, he leads them into the mission and a middle-class courtesy. Such a portrayal of the mission house and its devoted workers is neither ironic nor satiric for Chaplin, but nostalgic and sanguine. The church makes a difference by being in the midst of the needy. (A mission house with signs of "Jesus Saves" is the site of rescue for Douglas Fairbanks—known as the energetic, gymnastic Billy Sunday of the movies—as well, in the comic *Flirting With Fate*, as it occasions the conversion of an assassin hired by Fairbanks to kill himself.) In the silent film era, both *Easy Street* and *Flirting With Danger* actually portrayed the street ministries and rescue missions of the early twentieth century in a remarkably favorable light. The two comedies incorporated the image of the unrefined, reform-minded church as key narrative codes. The simple pews and wall decorations calling for people to repent and be saved, as well as the kindness of a pretty woman and the rescue from danger, shaped and directed the narratives of both films. It provided the incentive to do good for Chaplin, and it was the cause of good for Fairbanks, when the hired killer for a suicidal Fairbanks, is converted and refuses to kill. Even in such broad comedies, the goodness and good work of those identified with the mission is convincingly evident. The mission chapel is inhabited by people of grace, whose work is to do God's pleasure. A mission house is used cleverly in Harold Lloyd's *For Heaven's Sake*, where the ruffians and thieves of skid row (in a precursor to *Guys and Dolls*) chase Harold into the mission; yet the police show up and want to inspect the criminal element for stolen goods. Lloyd quickly passes the offering plate to each crook one step ahead of the investigating officer. What is remarkable is not the refuge from the law that the mission provides, but the merry inclusion into its humble, hallowed walls of the thieves, publicans and other tipsy sinners.

The Pilgrim allows Chaplin to dismantle the small-minded hypocrisy and double standards of a church even while championing the faith of children. Chaplin, a convict disguised as a minister, mistaken for the Reverend Pim, is welcomed off the train in Dallas, Texas. He is brought directly into the Sunday morning service, awkwardly conducting himself as preacher, acting out the story of David and Goliath for the hilarious delight of a single freckle-faced boy. The members of the congregation sit stunned and expressionless in their pews. The only true life in the church is kindled in the outcast and the child.

Mary Pickford was to encounter such Pharisaism as well in *Tess of the Storm Country*, in which a church elder, aptly named Mr. Graves, refuses to allow her illegitimate baby to be baptized. The plucky heroine nevertheless marches to the altar and sprinkles her baby with holy water.

Irene Dunne's paradigmatic screwball comedy, *Theodora Goes Wild*, sets a subdued and proper, but not particularly repressed, Connecticutt church organist over against the forces of small town America. Writing a sexy serial entitled *Sinner* under a pseudonym, Theodora is "liberated" by Melvyn Douglas in the wicked, wealthy city of New York. She flees his apartment in one scene only to be shown playing "Rock of Ages" in a Sunday morning church service in the next. Two spinster aunts, who are transformed from critical protective concern for her image into devoted defenders of her freedom, march into church after the identity of the writer is made public by the local paper. The congregation leaves off singing its hymn, but the dauntless aunts pick up the lyrics and sing heartily, even lustily, "Onward Christian Soldiers." When Theodora, like Pandora, is opened, she goes wild (though not bad or silly), telling off the gossipy old biddies of the church and literary community. Their stoneage, New England Puritanism is challenged by the blending of author and person of Theodora, whose name aptly means God's gift. Her wildness also exposes the scandal-sensitive, patriarchal political machine as well, where a governor is photographed by the press with this scandalous woman, not unlike present Virginia politics. The political hypocrisy is equal to that of the religious people.

In Frank Capra's *Miracle Woman*, Barbara Stanwyck lambasts the congregation for aggravating her father's heart attack. She denounces them as insensitive and cruel. As a figure based on Aimee Semple McPherson, she then begins her own church of healing as money-making showmanship, until she discovers the fruit of even feigned ministry. Burt Lancaster brought a similar house of God down in flames in *Elmer Gantry*, a modern version of the story of the sons of Eli who mix religion and sex.

In the films of Luis Bunuel, the structural image frequently conjures up the height of civilized decadence or the depth of human hypocrisy. Magnificent church spires mock the aspirations of men who would build the tower of Babel, seeking to climb to God. Instead of attaining the heights of the cathedrals they build, humanity slips and falls short (i.e. *hamartia* or sin), even of the standards it constructs for itself. The awesome cathedral is supplanted by the excessive bourgeois house, filled with possessions that possess the owner. Many of the vices imputed to the Church stem from the contamination of the world and politics invading it. So is the church identified with bourgeois home in Bunuel's *Exterminating Angel*, a vicious satire against a social and political system with religious complicity. Trapped at a dinner party, the discrete bourgeoisie finally escape, only to be trapped like literal sheep in a cathedral, from which these bored and vacuous people, we are led to believe, cannot escape. Like the economic structures of society, Bunuel indicts the church as a prison of the modern man.

Portraying television as both a tool of Satan and his subsequent prison, *The Witches of Eastwick* opens with a shot of a quaint little New England (probably Congregational) church, as a hypocrite talks about keeping values and faith in God. However, three sexually and romantically frustrated women of the village pray for more than they bargain for. While the church sings the hymn, "Lead on O King Eternal," the lonely female trinity call for the prince of darkness. Darrel Van Horn stomps into the church, showing no spiritual efficacy inherent in the building itself and excoriates the people on the subject of women in the church. His own practice is less than emulatory. Nevertheless, he shows up the limp, soggy faithlessness of the congregation.

Satiric caricatures of the church as an inadequate institution continue in such films as *Fletch Lives, Mosquito Coast, The End*, and Woody Allen's *Hannah and Her Sisters*. The latter two use attempted deal making with God as last resort efforts to avoid an impending death.

An irony in Woody Allen's *Interiors* unfolds as a husband meets his wife in the sanctuary of a beautiful, almost posh, gothic cathedral in downtown New York. Everything is neat and tidy, in its proper place, even too orderly. Lack of communication leads the wife to project that the husband has come to end their separation and be reunited, when in fact, he has come to end the separation, with divorce. The spiritual emptiness and hollowness of this relationship is contained in this vast, spacious, vaulted ceiling cathedral, with its flickering candles, in which the prayers of the self-deceived crash against the brass heavens. The interior of the church offers no aid or salvation to the cold interior of a human heart. It was as worthwhile as an empty building.

Empty Building

An old nursery rhyme uses a child's hand to verse: "This is the church; this is the steeple; open the door (undo the hand); and see all the people (fingers enclosed within)." Then one repeats the rhyme, with the hands clasped, and when opened, there are no people. Thus the church in contemporary cinema is frequently portrayed, as a sort of abandoned museum of old, conservative values or as an institutional husk or shell, a sort of an ideological antique.

When Kermit the Frog and his friends enter a country church in *The Muppet Movie*, they find it empty, almost a barn. (In one of the film's running jokes, the outdoor church sign repeats a gag line: "Lost? Have you tried Hare Krishna?") It is a modest, well-kept frame building in the middle of rural America. The Electric Mayhem band (an early Stryper) has found it vacant and decided, with reference to the Presbyterians, to transform it into a coffee house, a sixties sort of relevant happening. Doctor Teeth, the band's leader, views this establishment as a place "so fine, mellow, and profitable" with special emphasis on the profitable. Seeking rest on their way to Hollywood, the Muppets find it useful as a rehearsal site for their musical talents. (Fozzie the Bear does show respect for the church upon entering as he removes his hat, but as soon as he sees the occupying band, he replaces it.) In *Alice's Restaurant*, an unused church is deconsecrated for secular use, with motorcyclists racing through its aisles. In the postmodern, God-is-Dead movement of the late sixties, counterculture groups essayed to establish their own utopian communes out of the traditional one.

An ironic sense of the church as both empty building and sanctuary occurs in a bombed out church in DeSica's film, *Two Women*, with Sophia Loren in an Academy Award winning performance. Loren and her virginal daughter are returning to a liberated Rome, i.e. the center of the Church and the place where her daughter had been educated by nuns, when they stop in an abandoned, and shell-shattered, church, with its roof gutted by bombs. Fatigued, they lie down and are immediately assaulted and raped by Moroccon soldiers. They are literally and symbolically under the eyes of heaven, as the church roof has a hole and the light streaming down into the sanctuary falls upon the victims. Loren, more interested in returning to her business and lover in Rome, has deserted her original home, a place of community and security. The wartime church in which Loren seeks rest, however, has been abandoned by the very people who would make it a refuge in time of trouble. Being a site of absence it invites the invasion and profanation of violence.

In *Die Hard II* an abandoned chapel near the airport is invaded by terrorists, who kill the old caretaker and set up their sophisticated computer system. The church, contextualized by a light snow storm on Christmas eve, is desecrated and violated by the specialized technology brought in to establish a command and surveillance center for works of death. The silent and holy night is broken by uzis blasting through stained glass windows. The empty church turns into a temple possessed by a legion of demons after the Holy Spirit has departed.

In an empty, cavernous and skyscraping Gothic cathedral in Gotham, fantastic gargoyles dominate the finale of Tim Burton's stylized version of *Batman*. Batman and the Joker battle in the church tower, with a most fitting "bat" in the belfry. One grotesque figure entombed in the very stones of the cathedral becomes the means by which the Joker is ultimately crushed and conquered. The Scriptures assure that if the people of God no longer praise God, the very stones will cry out. And as the cathedral is deserted (it seems no one in Gotham goes to church), so the stone gargoyles do the work of goodness, the work that even Batman is unable to effect in his struggle. It is the ugly grinning stone, upon which the Joker's foot is caught, which carries the deceiver down from the heavens. "And I saw Satan fall from the heavens." Evil, as the Prince of the air, the Joker, the great Pretender, is plucked from the skies and hurled to the earth. And it is the church that brings him down, an act not even the champion of justice can execute. Those that mock will find that God has the last laugh.

The church Alice invades in *Nightmare on Elm Street; Part IV; The Dream Master* is not only empty, but cobwebbed and decrepit. In this once holy place she confronts the notorious, seemingly eternal, Freddie Krueger, who had swallowed the souls of other dreamers. From a stained glass window with a prominent cross behind her, Alice is backed into a corner, where she gathers a piece of the broken glass as a final protection. Neither might nor supernatural powers enable her to defend herself. Then an eerie chorus of haunted children sing a version of an old prayer, "Now I Lay Me Down to Sleep" and advise her to show evil its reflection in the mirror, against which it cannot stand. Holding the glass to Freddie's face, the souls encased within him break out in prosthetic special effects, bringing him to judgment and hell. Within the hallowed aisles and pews of this wonderland chapel, Alice conquers, at least till the next sequel, evil. (Curiously in *Young Sherlock Holmes*, a kinder and gentler film, an intimidating figure in a stained glass comes to life to threaten the young hallucinating detective.)

Supernatural Fortress

In the transition into the Renaissance (with an Italian critic applying the term Gothic to describe the vulgar, barbarous style of that era) great artists joined to contribute to the construction of places like St. Peter's. An exalted, even flamboyant, baroque and dramatic style of building in the Counter Reformation, (the internal reform and renewal movement of the Roman Catholics) served to overwhelm the worshippers with pomp, wealth, display, power, pageantry, and grandeur of the doctrines of the true Church. It was usually weighted down with imagery, especially of the Madonna, Mother of God. Mystery and piety were suggested through allegorical, but festive and ornate, scenes of faith. This style conveyed a "naturalism of the supernatural," wherein the universe is filled with more than the senses suggest; it teems with unseen life.

Communication between earth and heaven was not only possible, but occurring, and this theologically significant baroque architecture would try to capture these mysteries. H.R. Rookmaaker revealed that

A visitor to [a baroque church] will often find the dead body of a saint, exposed on or under the altar. Death seems to be at the centre. The whole show is meant to reassure us in the face of the death that will surely come. These shrines are often too much geared towards a superstition in which the saints and their relics play a magical and protective role. The system—the rich and powerful church—rather than Christ, is at the centre. (Dowley 432)

The vault of heaven has been opened for us to catch a glimpse of its fantastic glories, or at least its cherubs, saints, and angels, including the fallen ones, settled on clouds. And if the good spiritual beings did not inhabit the churches, then the evil ones would make themselves at home.

Even when a building was apparently vacant, it could yet inhere and hold some supernatural power. Ancient Indian spirits in the form of ferocious wolves roam the city in *Wolfen*, wreaking revenge on land developers. They hole up in a decaying and run-down church structure which is their holy ground and the crumbling reservoir of their stealthy, but terrible, supernatural powers. From this burnt out, dilapidated ruin in the heart of the South Bronx spreads this savage and spooky retribution against an encroaching technological society.

Historically, the sanctuary was often built near or over some sacred ground, upon which a saint or martyr had been buried. The sacred spots often became associated with the tombs, leading to dark and dim mysteries. As some of the first meeting places were in catacombs as well as homes, the underground burial places tied the facts of death and resurrection with cemetery church yards. One remembered the death of the Saviour as well as the death of the saints with the constant reminders of tombs, marked with crosses and hovering moss-covered angels. Chapels over the tombs of martyrs and saints could inspire the sleepy, but wild, human imagination to contemplate the corpses, relics, and worms underneath the pews. In the nineteenth century, the Victorian cemeteries abounded in weighty and ostentatious memorials, revealing a fascination with death and *memento mori*. Superstition of miraculous and magical burying grounds, as well as the relics of passed saints, could possess the curious minds sensing the marvelous and craving the Numinous. The celtic activity that surrounded the fourth and the nineteenth centuries' fascination with the dead was, in part, tainted by various pagan and romantic ideas crowding into the sanctuary. Such ideas continue to thrive in the horror genre of film. Spirits and ghosts in the courtyard would soon enter the back door.

The most obvious examples of the supernatural powers' relations to the church buildings appear in the vampire films. The Hammer studio films of Terence Fisher and others were remarkably conservative and gothic in their emphasis on maidens in distress, sexually perverse villains, and the role of religious symbols to ward off evil. *Taste the Blood of Dracula*, Peter Sasdy's bosomy film stars the incomparable Christopher Lee as the long-toothed vampire. The living dead is brought back to life by the sacrilege of Lord Courtley, who drinks blood and pretends, in a chapel, to be the evil creature. He is murdered by his outraged companions. Later in the chapel, Dracula rises from the murdered noble's body. At the end, Dracula is, of course, destroyed in the chapel, being trapped by the rising of the sun's rays.

In John Carpenter's misty, ominous *The Fog*, a 100-year old curse returns to the sleepy coastal California town, to bring vengeance on those responsible for the death of sailors seeking safety. As the maggot-infested dead from the bottom of the sea push into this oblivious village, the radio DJ beams instructions from the top of a Lighthouse as a West coast Paul Revere, directing people to flee the fog by retreating to the Old Church (constructed of stone and round arches) on Beacon Hill. A drunken Episcopal priest, Hal Holbrook, laments that the Day of Judgment is at hand and one "can't hide any longer," even in the sanctuary. Trying to find sanctuary in a church which has lost its faith as well as its parishioners, departed spirits swarm and violate the holy grounds in a "just" raid of spiritual vindication for past sins. (The theft of a large gold cache, now forged into a large cross, motivates part of the attack.) The sea zombies crash into the church, breaking through stained glass windows with cheap effects and blasphemies, such as knocking a crucifix off the church wall. Father Malone confesses his *mea culpa*; he is the thief and God's Temple is the tomb of gold; his grandfather stole it and he must answer for it. The dead must be remembered and the sin against them expunged; otherwise, the unconfessed sin rots like old flesh in the heart of the sinner. This is especially fitting if the hypocritical heart is in the Pharisee, in a white-washed sepulcher. As soon as the Captain of the dead possesses the cross, which burns away the riff-raff, the church returns to "normal." Fortunately, the dead come back to pick up Holbrook as interest on his theft. The beleaguered church and lighthouse (parallel correspondences?) stand as weak defenses against stronger spiritual powers, such as Justice. The wickedness of the clergy cannot be hid behind the stone walls of a building, no matter how sacred.

Another film which pits a mortal clergyman against the forces of evil, this time a succubus, is *The Unholy*, a libidinous exploitation of spiritual warfare, in which the devil takes on voluptuous female form to seduce the vulnerable priest. The battleground is the aisle of the church, with the Satanic woman (or the woman in satin) standing at the altar.

Nicholas Roeg's *Don't Look Now* locates Donald Sutherland as an architectural artist, working with slides of a Venice church stained-glass window he is to repair, when his daughter drowns. Lured by an elderly woman who claims she can see the lost daughter, his wife (Julie Christie) seeks help at a seance and is warned of danger to her husband, who subsequently is almost killed in a fall while working on the church window. Their search for spiritual sight, even occultic, is eerily conducted within the context of a church, which has become a structural object and an aesthetic delight rather than a source of direction. The obsessive search proves fatal.

John Carpenter again utilizes the location of a deserted church, out of which loudspeakers spout hymns like "Rock of Ages," as the clandestine center for underground rebels fighting a futuristic capitalist tyranny in *They Live*. Concealed in the old church, near a shanty town for the homeless, are spiritual weapons: ordinary sunglasses that enable a wearer to see through or beyond the surface images of the postmodern propaganda, subliminal advertising and media. These visual instruments of seeing empower the user to discern good and evil. The spectacles for seeing truth through all the trappings of technology are stored in the house of God. True perception and knowledge come through these symbols of holy vision, even the gift of discriminating the falsehood in advertising and television.

The church in *Strange Invaders* finds aliens, rather than revolutionaries, using it; in this case, to conduct laboratory experiments in the basement of a church and to invade and inhabit human bodies. Ultimately the humans are released back to their homes as small transparent globes floating out the front doors of the church. In two other fantasy films, the church is make-shift: a revival tent in the remake of *The Blob* and a wooden lean-to in *Dragonslayer*. Both are managed by crazy old prophets, predicting doom, apocalypse, and judgment on humanity. The church in the latter film is consumed by dragon fire.

Generally, however, the forces of evil that assault and hammer the church do not prevail against this symbolic bulwark of God's power and righteousness, as evidenced in a pessimistic apocalypse film like *The Omen*. While everything and everyone else fails to destroy the offspring of Satan, Damien, the sight of a church causes the diabolical tyke to recoil and throw his nastiest tantrum in the movie. The fact that even the sight of the edifice causes the demon to shudder may indicate an enduring function of the church, even without its people, as a supernatural site for fear and trembling.

Sanctuary

In the style of church building known as the basilica, one received an impression of formidable strength, however grim, dense, solid, firm, and even defiant. It stood as a symbol of the Church Militant—the Church wrestling with the powers of Satan. The light, however dim in these churches, would yet shine in the darkness. It invited in the poor, the frightened, the needy, and oppressed, and many who merely wanted to hide. And the Hunchback of Notre Dame is not the only one, who cries "Sanctuary! Sanctuary!" Jean Valjean finds refuge in the church inspite of his sin in *Les Miserables*. And the whole von Trapp family finds the best way to freedom and safety in Switzerland is through the underground church.

Comic films like *St. Benny the Dip* and the recent *We're No Angels* establish the church as the place where convicts and crooks can find refuge. Bad men are driven to seek the shelter of the church, and then find themselves changed by their contact with the holy place.

In *Flashdance*, Alex (Jennifer Beale) finds a bit of peace and quiet. In contrast to the loud environments of iron welding and pulsating flesh and sweat dancing she finds a momentary refuge with the sweet organ music of a church sanctuary. The church has no ethical or truly spiritual import in the film; she could have just as easily found the solace she sought in a grassy meadow, with bubbling brook, if this were not Pittsburgh. The church serves as only an audio sanctuary, no heavy noise or music intrudes into personal reflection and ambition.

Clint Eastwood frequently identifies the role of the church with helping the oppressed and needy. A right-wing liberation theology underlies his *Joe Kidd*. A village of Spanish people have been interned by bad gringo Robert Duvall in the adobe town church. He threatens to sacrifice them one by one unless Luis Chama, their charismatic leader, turns himself in. Eastwood, representing the law, wrangles with the roughhouse gang, only to be put in with the beleaguered flock, whom he finds praying for God's deliverance at the altar. "Well, the fun's over and he's gone to church," the villains jeer. "Why don't you go to church and pray until this [business with the rebel] is done?" Duvall mockingly suggests.

The humble, docile, and helpless parishioners gather and pray with the Padre, who provides the scowling Eastwood not only with holy water to quench his thirst, but with an antique and empty, but functional, gun with which to overcome the corrupted lawmen and protect the people. The grace of the Kidd overcomes the law. The old mission house, with statues of saints ("This is the day of St James, one of the first martyrs who was beheaded rather than deny his faith," Eastwood is told, not comfortingly), cross and bell watch tower, is a fragile, uncertain sanctuary for the Spanish. The Padre will not send his people outside to be sacrificial lambs. They are arbitrarily dragged from their prayers to a firing squad. The human "saviour" they await will not, even cannot, save them, ruefully acknowledging: "We wanted a savior but we only got someone interested in himself." Chama, as the human savior, is inadequate. Only the Kidd can save them. He feeds the people and protects them. With the tanned Pale Rider in the church, it is as good as a sanctuary.

The Catholic sensibilities of Francis Ford Coppola are played out in his adaptation of Hinton's novel, *The Outsiders*. Young greasers hide from the law in an abandoned church outside of town. It is a place to sleep peacefully and undisturbed. They rise early to enjoy the sunrise. They while away the hours playing cards and joking. In the church, their identity is changed, as they wash the grease out of their hair; they are baptized into a new life. Their sanctuary provides both a physical hideaway from society and a site for personal regeneration. Later, when they return to their "home," it is in flames, with several young children trapped inside. The outcasts rush in where angels fear to tread and rescue the kids. One of the outcasts, Johnny, is burned and dies in the process. In this hierophanous moment of a baptism of fire, he becomes a Christ figure. At the end of his pitiable life, Johnny, a young man of sorrows, is given a new beginning. By losing his life for his neighbor, he is born anew.

Atheist H.G. Wells did acknowledge the work of God in his novel, *War of the Worlds*, but George Pal highlighted the divine providence in destroying the Martian invaders. Populations, devastated, hopeless and panicking, flee to churches, the last fox hole where atheists do become believers. As the world comes literally crashing down about them, the multitudes pray with all earnestness and devotion. Then, with church in the foreground, we watch the demise of the first strange invader, a demise brought about by a simple organism of a germ, against which the Martians have no immunity. The image left is one of the prayers of men and women being answered by divine care and eternal sovereignty. God foreordained that this protection, *deus ex machina* that it is, should be secured. As all other military weaponry fails to arrest the invasion, the film essentially preaches that it was neither by might or power, as the Lord says, but by His Spirit. The people in the besieged sanctuary find the desperate salvation and rescue which they direly sought.

Not so fortunate were the poor patriots and frightened citizens in the Tavini brothers' *Night of the Shooting Stars*. Italian peasants were rounded up and dumped in a church, which speciously promised safety. Yet they were called out and brutally massacred by the Nazis. The church in wartime granted not a place of safety, but one of slaughter of the naive and vulnerable.

Personal, rather than political, sanctuary pops up in Chris Columbus' slapstick comedy, *Home Alone*, where the church stands as a refuge from evil and a source of comfort and grace. When two inept burglars pursue Homer Macauley, the abandoned boy hides in a creche among the true worshippers, disguising himself as a poor shepherd.

A terrible and awesome old man lives next door to him and appears dangerous and threatening. Yet his impression of this frightful neighbor changes when he encounters him in the church where the lonely boy wanders. Sitting still in his pew, he is approached by the spooky neighbor, who looms over him and then dramatically and unexpectedly utters: "Merry Christmas." The old man befriends the kid, sits beside him, and through his gentle love and kindness, chases away fear. He tells the boy that he is refused welcome at the Christmas concert. "You're not welcome in the Church?" the boy asks. "No," the old man responds, "Everyone is welcome in the Church; it is my son who does not want me." "Why don't you call him up," the kid asks.

Misperceived as a singularly wrathful God who could destroy with the power of his right arm, the neighbor (whose meeting the boy in the church proves providential) does become the child's protector, delivering the kid from the two intruders with a biblically mighty blow of a snow shovel. The palms of old man's hands, incidentally, have been pierced, according to the scriptures of the script, and they are only healed at the end of the film when he is reconciled to his estranged son, his chosen people. It is a most curious theological statement for a popular, wacky comedy.

Locus of Romance

When Eric Rohmer's protagonist sees a lovely woman in church in *My Night at Maud's*, it initiates not only a romance, but also kindles up the strength for him to resist carnal temptation at Maud's house on a long snowy night. Andrzej Wajda brings together his lead characters in *A Generation* in a church. A young man wishing to join the Polish Resistance fighters meets the local leader of the Fighting Youth in a church while a wedding is being conducted. The leader is a woman to whom he is attracted and falls in love. Luis Bunuel's Mexican production, *El*, begins with Don Francisco seeing in a church and falling in obsessive love with a woman aptly named Gloria; he haunts the church frequently to ogle her beauty. He eventually steals her from her fiance, marries her and becomes pathologically possessive, cruel and jealous. Separated from her, he enters a monastery where he is supposedly cured, but Bunuel shows otherwise, this middle-aged don has gone bonkers. Cinematic romance begins in one of the most overlooked sites of the mating ritual: the church. When sermons are slow and boring, the lovely image of God may easily detract and engage the attention of the less absorbed worshippers. As noted earlier, even a carnal devotee like Dudley Moore in *10* may be drawn to a church to gaze upon beauty, however superficial.

The church not only inaugurates the romance of a man and a woman, it may also reconcile the brokenhearted. In *Starting Over*, the church basement serves as the locus of group therapy for two motley groups of divorced people, one for men and one for women. Folding chairs replace pews and bulletin boards supplant the hymnals and scripture readings. This room is set apart, made holy, by its openness to confession, emotional healing, renewal, and forgiveness. (Often however, the men in their inchoate ways of communicating, still cannot hear over the loud organ music.) The men are constantly browbeaten by the aggressive women who, at their designated time, literally chase the intimidated men out of their sanctuary. It is richly satisfying then, when on Christmas Eve, the harridans and shrews and the wimps and rejects converge, each group respectively softening and gaining courage. The women invite the beleaguered men to a potluck supper in the basement. On a holiday that augers loneliness for the many single people of our culture, warring factions cast aside their swords and feast together in the belly of the church.

The mighty fortress of the Greco-Roman cathedral in *Ladyhawke* harbors wickedness in the walled city of Aquila, with its high arched ceilings, impregnable walls and thick pillars. Many pilgrims flock to be blessed by the Bishop in his long flowing robes, but this particular man of the cloth is decidedly greedy and lascivious. The full scaled settings of the 13th century milieu utilized cinematographer Vittorio Starato's "sunny pre-Raphaelite" images to create a fully romantic style of two star-crossed lovers, separated by night and day. Cursed to be hawk and wolf, the two must find the cure to their separation at the church. Romantic and sacrificial love combine to conquer the wanton forces of bent religious leadership. The huge stone medieval architecture communicates the cold corruption of the church hierarchy, with its evil bishop steering the church into the darker ages. Yet this church of stone resists the contamination of a reprobate clergyman. in the climax of the movie inside the sanctuary, the evil spell is banished, the villain violently dispatched, justice is restored and, most importantly, the two lovers are reunited. Eros and agape enable a restoration of goodness.

Few films show the reconciliation and rebuilding of trust in a marriage as the scene in Murnau's silent classic film, *Sunrise*. Having been tempted to murder his sweet wife (Janet Gaynor), husband (George O'Brien) is found out. Fully fearful and fully repentant are the two mates. They wander tearfully into a church where a wedding is being performed, and with deep sobbing and heart-felt apologies, renew their vows. It is a joyous reunion in the church and one of the most poignant to be found not only in silent film, but all film.

Source of Healing and Transcendence

The artistic construction of churches, Gothic or other, is subordinate to the task of communicating the Word of God, of telling the sacred stories of the faith for the understanding, encouragement, and edification of the faithful. The church naturally fits into the scheme of being represented as a place for healing or a place where transcendence invades the ordinary and realigns a sense of priorities for the common person. The Atlanta church in *Gone With the Wind* serves as the site for gathering the wounded and dying, as a hospital. Scarlett and Melanie help the doctor attend to the multitude of men sheltered from the storm of Sherman's apocalyptic march of death and destruction. The church is transformed from its grand status in Southern society into an infirmary for the purposes of taking in the sick, the suffering, the dying.

The quest of fourteenth-century villagers to plant a cross on a modern church in *The Navigator* aims to "save" their people from the imminent black plague by taking an odyssey across time. These simple and devout peasants are offered the challenge to escape the plague by burrowing through the earth and planting a copper spire on the highest church steeple on the other side of the world, which turns out to be a modern church in the twentieth century. The younger brother, who is gifted/cursed with prophetic insight and terrifying dreams, sees a man with a glove climb the steeple and fall. Knowing that one shall fall from the church, he substitutes his life for his older brother and his people. Under the ageless cross of the church is paid the precious sacrifice of an innocent life, enacting the gospel of "Greater love hath no man than he who would lay down his life for his brother." To heal the many, the one dies under the symbol and shadow of the church's cross.

The building of a cathedral in David Lynch's *Elephant Man* celebrates life and grace in the midst of pain, suffering, and death. The hideously deformed and freakish John Merrick (John Hurt) seeks love, companionship, acceptance, in his journey of neglect, rejection, and pain. When he astonishes his keepers by quoting the entire 23rd psalm, it marks a new beginning in his communication with the outside world. The only image outside his hospital window is of a single church steeple; this vision inspires him to build a miniature church, a model of the one outside. Its construction is a reflection and a working out of his own spiritual travels, the founding of his own soul. However the model church is not to be completed, as thieves and kidnappers break in to carry him away, destroying the good foundation he has labored to erect. He does escape his freak show captors and returns to his work. As he puts on the finishing touches, he crosses over to a transcendent reality; he himself is taken up into the house of God, pronouncing as his last words and his last work: It is done. His humble efforts signify not simply the work of building Christ's church, but of being Christ's church, of being broken and rebuilt by grace, of demonstrating life over death in the enduring symbol of the cathedral beside his still body.

In the midst of misery, sweating on a chain gang, prisoners become guests of a truly humble and gracious black congregation in Preston

Sturges' classic *Sullivan's Travels*. In the Southern church, it is movie night and the convicts, locked in chains, shuffle into the pews. The sympathetic people sing "Let My People Go," as a shared reminder of oppression. After this idealized display of social unity, a movie shines on the makeshift screen: Walt Disney's Pluto. In one accord the audience laughs heartily. As the body of this congregation suffered when the suffering stumbled into the church, so now all rejoice as one rejoices. The moment eclipses the misery of the prison. The church offers, even in its optimistic American sermon of Disney, laughter, comfort and hope.

The sense of a place of goodness like Sturges' rural church usually occurs in the realm of grace. The church is reconstituted as an earthly Utopia, *eu topia*, literally a good place. The church as a good place may carry a utopian promise. The utopian representation of the church usually carries the viewer into the realm of the fantastic. So in *Heavens Above*, Peter Sellers lives out a parable of an idealistic little parish priest, whose work of seeking to bring the kingdom of God on earth falls short because of the basic sinfulness of all human beings, including the poor. The church, taking in the indigent, is taken advantage of by the same people it hopes to help, and appears to be totally impractical. Its vision is portrayed as idealistically utopian (rather than satirically dystopian in Bunuel's *Viridiana* and *Nazarin*); and even though such holy positive faith may find its proper place in space, in the heavens above, it is worth attempting. The utopian is not utilitarian.

Protestant architecture, onward from the eighteenth century Age of Reason, summoned worshippers to reflect with dignity and solemnity upon Scriptural matters, rather than see visions conjured up by decorative images. The pulpit, where the Scriptures were read, took preeminence over the altar. The transcendent thus makes itself audible in the church through its proclamation of the Word. It comes through preaching. Sermons in films like *Sergeant York, The Getting of Wisdom, Matewan, Chariots of Fire, Manon of the Spring,* and *Au Revoir, Les Enfants* reaffirm the centrality of preaching, of Roman Catholic as well as evangelical denominations, as a mission of the church. Both pastoral and prophetic, the parables and exegeted texts fit the diegetic motive; they move the story by punctuating its moral and spiritual dimensions. As one example, *Sergeant York*, Hawks' bio-drama of W.W. I hero Alvin C. York, pivots on the role of the little country church (with Walter Brennan as Pastor Rosier Pile who preaches repentance and guides him in his spiritual quest for righteousness), the divine intervention of lightning, and Gary Cooper's radical conversion, walking down the sawdust trail to the altar to become a new man.

House of God/People of God
     Herein intertwines the image of the meeting place and the notion of the assembled community of God's people. The saints and their buildings are closely identified in the films themselves. Ecclesiastical events involve people in their representation, for evangelism and preaching, for worship, for struggling with the call of God upon their lives, and for salvation and personal change. The nature of the religious loci is inextricably mixed with the nature of its parishioners. Woven into the tapestry of the church is the fabric of the characters' lives, who, as voluntary members, have tied themselves to the cloth. The church thus turns from organization back into organism, as it were, from death into life. Perhaps the church in *Brother Sun, Sister Moon* best signifies the association of people with the church building. Saint Francis and his outcast brothers and sisters seek to rebuild an old stone chapel, broken and run-down, and deserted. In their simple labors, this motley mass of unwashed and run-down peons are identified as living stones of a spiritual house (*I Peter* 2:5). The church is constructed with the poor, the leprous, the rejected, the lesser and feminine, assembling together to build a stone structure and themselves as a body with many, diverse members.
     John Ford's 1935 Irish tale of betrayal and grace, *The Informer*, follows the temptation and fall of another sinner, the strong, stupid Gypo Nolan, who sells out his best friend for money. Discovered for his treachery, Gypo flees his revolutionary friends and escapes, although fatally wounded, to the church where the family of his dead friend are mourning and praying. Bleeding and dying, he begs their pardon, and they forgive him. The church stands as the ground of absolution and hope for even the most unfortunate of misbegotten sinners such as an Irish Judas. The people who suffer and are comforted in and by the church are those who actually forgive and comfort their brother sinner.
     The acceptance of others who suffer by members of the church is gently played out in Bruce Beresford's *Tender Mercies*. Alcoholic country and western singer Max Sledge (Robert DuVall) falls in love with a young Viet Nam widow, Rose Marie (Tess Harper). Sledge's awareness of his own failings and needs and his friendship with Rose Marie lead him tenderly to the fundamentalist little church. Mack and Rose Marie's Sonny are baptized into the community of sinners, yielding to the power of God. After being washed of their sins, the boy asks the man if he feels any differently. The church community is amazingly gracious and unpretentious. His act of penitence, being born again, and timid steps of faith into a new life sketch a portrait of the conversion process. Even after stumbling and struggling, Max, in the church, as the church, still clings to God's grace and tender mercies.

The people of the church accept sinners of all kinds, including the prodigal daughter in *The Color Purple*. Juxtaposed with the raucousness and brazenness of the "juke house" is the simple, bright and holy (set apart) church of blues singer Shug Avery's father. As a flashy vamp, Shug swigs home-made juice, swivels her hips and dizzies the best of men. Her rebellion against the old time religion succeeds only so far, as she, like Mrs. Watts (Geraldine Page) in *Trip to Bountiful*, is softly and tenderly called home, across the metaphorical bridge, to the little white chapel and its worn pews. The church centers as the scene of reconciliation, hope and new life when Shag renounces her wicked ways and does come "home" to her earthly father, the pastor, and her Heavenly Father, in a gloriously musical climax with choirs uproariously singing, clapping, and dancing. The angels themselves have rarely had such fun.

A rough and sinful man enters the utopian, pacifist community of the Amish in *Witness*. Here is a community truly set apart from the world, that yet takes in a contaminated member of that violent world, Harrison Ford. The film begins with a funeral scene inside an Amish church, a plain meeting hall. Here the church are people, envisioned as devoted members of one another. All things are held in common, and if one needs a barn built, all contribute their talents for the building and lifting up of one.

When wicked Harry (Danny Glover) enters a home in *To Sleep With Anger*, he brings strife between two grown sons in a version of the Cain and Abel story. He is invited to stay by the goodly mother, a good woman who yet dabbles in a few hoary superstitious habits. (The fan of horror films will recognize this old code that evil cannot trespass into a place where it is not been formally invited.) As tragedy befalls the family, the mother also invites in a born-again friend, a former paramour of Harry, and a devout church fellowship. They march in quoting Scriptures that warn how a family shall be divided, mother against daughter-in-law, etc. Later, this pious choir of saints parade in to pray for the patriarch of the family, mysteriously felled by an illness, of which Harry seems to be the cause. They surround the bed and combat the evil with their prayers and Scriptures, eventually triumphing.

Carl Dreyer manages to delineate the minute distinctions of theology between two Scandinavian religious communities in *Ordet* (the Word). The more conservative sect emphasizes holiness and conversion more passionately; while the other stresses the loving of God and neighbor. Of course, neither patriarch loves the other, but seeks to save his soul or damn him to hell. It is the death of a beloved daughter-in-law which brings them together, with a mad son (who read too much

Kierkegaard in seminary) returning to the funeral bier, denouncing all for their lack of faith. He speaks the Word, the name of Jesus Christ, and an almost imperceptible miracle takes place, the raising of the woman from her death. Yet although that miracle takes dramatic center stage, it is the miracle of fighting congregational leaders being united in shared forgiveness, awe and worship that overwhelms. The church divided is people estranged; the church united is people brought together in love, grace and joy.

The location of *Places in the Heart* turns out to be where we lived as children, the places of our roots, our faith, our Christian love. As a symbol of the cultural heritage of America, the church appears at the beginning of the narrative and the church appears at the end of the narrative. In between are natural disasters, death, racism, adultery, greed, cruelty and desperate trials and tribulations. Before the strains of "Blessed Assurance," we arrive into a place and time (in the past and in rural America—away from sophisticated urban life) steeped in and holding on to the Christian faith. The huge church building looms and hovers over the sleepy 1935 Texan town of director Robert Benton's Waxahachie hometown. The sun rises on the church regularly in the film, reassuring the viewer of divine providence for the poor, the oppressed, and the needy. After the tornado, this idealized church remains unscathed. A sense of transcendent unity descends in the finale, where the townspeople are gathered together in the indestructible church. As a spiritual, almost mystical, trope, both the living and the dead characters of the film are assembled in the pews, awaiting the Sacrament of the Lord's Supper and its sign of forgiveness, grace and restoration. Through the fucharist, black and white, poor and rich, enemies and neighbors are united into one Body.

The church is rendered as the symbolic Bride of Christ (*Ephesians* 5:25) in the Academy Award winning *Babbette's Feast*. Embodied in two sisters who give up their talents (beauty, romance, music) for the simple duties of the church is the notion of a holy marriage to God of the people of God. It is to the church their father pastored, a body of eccentric and cantankerous old sinful saints, that the two talented daughters devote themselves. Rather than marrying a noble suitor or promoting one's artistic, God-given, musical ability, the women wed the work of God and sing his hymns. The sacrifice to feed the hungry and visit the sick is done willingly, gladly, by these sisters. Like early versions of Mother Teresa, they labor in love. Director Gabriel Axel personifies the church in flesh and action in the devotion and quiet joy of these two sisters of faith.

Conclusion

It is curious that the church rarely inhabits postmodern landscapes, even as an anachronism. The presence of an exotic cult of Hare Krishna in *Blade Runner* merely offers a pastiche religion to a pastiche architecture and schizophrenic culture. The church belongs to the ages; its spatial and temporal components are rooted in history; it is connected to the crux of history itself—the work of Christ on the Cross, even in its counterfeit and hypocritical manifestations. Its alignment with progressive industrial and reform movements at the turn of the twentieth century brought the church into political association with capitalist society, and by becoming part of the status quo for bourgeois society, it lost some of its prophetic power. Its complicity with colonialism and imperialism or its involvement in personal and social changes such as with Mother Teresa has supplied raw data to be used in the fictional narratives of film. Thus, as the church in history is characterized by both vice and virtue, by cruelty and grace, so too would its filmic counterparts find an appropriate or strategic model for the filmmakers' bias.

Film constitutes its view of the real church by its symbolic uses. Whether as stylistic embellishment, the decoration of part of the neighborhood, or critical simulacrum of a corrupt society, images serve as structuring principles for conveying a sense of place. They are rhetorical devices for focusing attention on particular angles or elements of a phenomenon like the church, while disregarding or even concealing other aspects. And these images advise how we are to view the church, recommending our attitudes and actions toward it.

As this cursory study has illustrated, there is no single, consistent cluster of meanings provoked by cinematic images of the church. Visual treatments vary from film to film, across genres, and even within particular films (*Norma Rae*). Thus a descriptive iconographic analysis of the church as a unique locus in the atlas of the film world maps out a diverse collection of functional points. The images are portable and transcend the genres—all have their steeples and crosses or religious markings. Yet rarely is the church building (or the people of the church) treated neutrally or without rhetorical significance. The church is often seen negatively as an icy, distant or hypocritical institution, viewed with suspicion as a corruption (*The Verdict*), an anachronism (*A Boy and His Dog*), or as inhumane and demonic (*The Church*). Surprisingly, a vast number of films do present kind, positive, sympathetic, and even gracious representations. The emblematic significance has been shown to be not circumscribed in any isomorphic, conforming fashion. Rather its variety, openness and ambiguity in real life allows the image to accrue a host of meanings dependent upon context and character association.

At the closing of the *glasnost* film *Repentance*, an old lady wandering down a road stops by a window where a woman is baking and asks if the road she is on will lead to the church. She is told there are no churches in that village. Then, in the final line of the film, she challenges this information: "What good is a road if it doesn't lead to a church?" This paper has hopefully shown that of the many roads leading to Hollywood, churches have been planted along the way like assorted signposts pointing in other, less material and commercial, directions.

Works Cited

Allan, John. *The Gospel According to Science Fiction*. Milford, MI: Quill, 1975.

Bieler, Andre. *Architecture in Worship*. Philadelphia: The Westminster P, 1965.

Butler, Ivan. *Religion in the Cinema*. New York: A.S. Barnes, 1969.

Dowley, Tim, ed. *Eerdmans' Handbook to the History of Christianity*. Grand Rapids: Eerdmans, 1977.

Drew, Donald. *Images of Man*. Downers Grove, IL: InterVarsity P, 1974.

Friedman, Lester D. *Hollywood's Image of the Jew*. New York: Ungar Publishing, 1982.

Gombrich, E.H. *The Story of Art*. New York: Praeger Publishers, 1972.

Heath, Sidney. *The Romance of Symbolism and Its Relation to Church Ornament and Architecture*. Detroit: Gale Research Company, 1909.

Holloway, Ronald. *Beyond the Image*. Geneva, Switzerland: World Council of Churches, 1977.

Keyser, Les and Barbara Keyser. *Hollywood and the Catholic Church*. Chicago: Loyola UP, 1984.

Kreuziger, Frederick A. *The Religion of Science Fiction*. Bowling Green, OH: Bowling Green State University Popular Press, 1986.

May, John R. and Michael Bird. *Religion in Film*. Knoxville: U of Tennessee P, 1982.

May, Rollo, ed. *Symbolism in Religion and Literature*. New York: George Brailer, 1960.

Schrader, Paul. *Transcendental Style in Film*. Berkeley: U of California P, 1972.

Stowe, Everett M. *Communicating Reality Through Symbols*. Philadelphia: Westminster P, 1966.

Stafford, Thomas Albert. *Christian Symbolism in the Evangelical Churches*. New York: Abingdon P, 1962.

Filmography

Year	Film	Director
1969	*Alice's Restaurant*	Arthur Penn
1981	*Arthur*	Steve Gordon
1987	*Babbette's Feast*	Gabriel Axel
1985	*Back to the Future*	Robert Zemeckis
1989	*Batman*	Tim Burton
1983	*Big Chill, The*	Lawrence Kasdan
1980	*Blues Brothers*	John Landis
1932	*Boudu Saved From Drowning*	Jean Renoir
1975	*Boy and His Dog, A*	L.Q.Jones
1973	*Brother Sun, Sister Moon*	Franco Zefferelli
1981	*Chariots of Fire*	Hugh Hudson
1990	*Cinema Paradisio*	Guiseppe Tornatone
1970	*Cold Turkey*	Norman Lear
1985	*Color Purple, The*	Steven Spielberg
1984	*Country*	Richard Pearce
1958	*Cousins*	Claude Chabrol
1990	*Die Hard II*	Renny Harlin
1973	*Don't Look Now*	Nicolas Roeg
1981	*Dragonslayer*	Matthew Robbins
1989	*Dream Team*	Howard Zeff
1917	*Easy Street*	Charlie Chaplin
1952	*El*	Luis Bunuel
1980	*Elephant Man*	David Lynch
1978	*End, The*	Burt Reynolds
1962	*Exterminating Angel*	Luis Bunuel
1991	*Five Heartbeats, The*	Robert Townsend
1983	*Flashdance*	Adrian Lyne
1926	*Flesh and the Devil, The*	Clarence Brown
1990	*Fletch Lives*	Michael Ritchie
1916	*Flirting With Fate*	W. Christy Cabanne
1980	*Fog, The*	John Carpenter
1984	*Footloose*	Herbert Ross
1926	*For Heaven's Sake*	Harold Lloyd
1954	*Generation, A*	Andrezj Wajda
1977	*Getting of Wisdom*	Bruce Beresford
1924	*Girl Shy*	Harold Lloyd
1939	*Gone With the Wind*	Fleming, et al.
1988	*Grand Highway, The*	Jean-Lap Hubert
1990	*Hard to Kill*	Bruce Malmoth
1988	*Heathers*	Michael Lehman
1963	*Heavens Above*	John Boulting
1916	*Hell's Hinges*	Charles Swickard

1986	*Highlander*	Russell Mucahy
1990	*Home Alone*	Chris Columbus
1923	*Hunchback of Notre Dame*	Wallace Worsley
1939	*Hunchback of Notre Dame*	William Dieterle
1935	*Informer, The*	John Ford
1978	*Interiors*	Woody Allen
1972	*Joe Kidd*	John Sturges
1985	*Ladyhawke*	Richard Donner
1963	*Lillies of the Field*	Ralph Nelson
1990	*The Long Walk Home*	Richard Pearce
1971	*Macabe and Mrs. Miller*	Robert Altman
1986	*Manon of the Spring*	Claude Berri
1987	*Matewan*	John Sayles
1935	*Miserables, Les*	Richard Boleslawski
		Lewis Milestone
1986	*Mosquito Coast*	Peter Weir
1979	*Muppet Movie, The*	Jim Henson
1971	*My Night at Maud's*	Eric Rohmer
1989	*Navigator, The*	Vincent Ward
1912	*New York Hat, The*	D.W.Griffith
1988	*Nightmare on Elm Street, IV:*	Wes Craven
	The Dream Master	
1979	*Norma Rae*	Martin Ritt
1978	*North Avenue Irregulars*	Bruce Bilson
1973	*O Lucky Man*	Lindsay Anderson
1991	*Once Around*	Lasse Hallstrom
1955	*Ordet*	Carl Dreyer
1980	*Ordinary People*	Robert Redford
1985	*Out of Africa*	Sydney Pollack
1983	*Outsiders, The*	Francis Ford Coppola
1985	*Pale Rider*	Clint Eastwood
1923	*Pilgrim, The*	Charlie Chaplin
1984	*Places in the Heart*	Robert Benton
1985	*Prizzi's Honor*	John Huston
1987	*Repentance*	Tengiz Abuladze
1975	*Rocky Horror Picture Show*	Jim Sharman
1945	*Rome, Open City*	Roberto Rossellini
1990	*Russia House, The*	Fred Schepisi
1941	*Sergeant York*	Howard Hawks
1925	*Seven Chances*	Buster Keaton
1985	*Silverado*	Lawrence Kasdan
1965	*Sound of Music*	Robert Wise
1984	*Splash*	Ron Howard
1979	*Starting Over*	Alan J. Pakula
1983	*Strange Invaders*	Michael Laughlin
1987	*Street Justice*	Richard C. Sarafian

1926	*Strong Man, The*	Frank Capra
1941	*Sullivan's Travels*	Preston Sturges
1927	*Sunrise*	F.W.Murnau
1981	*Taps*	Harold Becker
1969	*Taste the Blood of Dracula*	Peter Sasdy
1979	*10*	Blake Edwards
1983	*Tender Mercies*	Bruce Beresford
1983	*Terms of Endearment*	James L. Brooks
1914/22	*Tess of the Storm Country*	Edwin S. Porter/
		John S. Robertson
1936	*Theodora Goes Wild*	Richard Boleslawski
1988	*They Live*	John Carpenter
1960	*Two Women*	Vittorio deSica
1989	*Unholy, The*	Camilo Vilay
1982	*Verdict, The*	Sidney Lumet
1952	*War of the Worlds*	George Pal
1988	*Witches of Eastwick*	George Miller
1985	*Witness*	Peter Weir
1981	*Wolfen*	Michael Wadleigh
1985	*Young Sherlock Holmes*	Barry Levinson

The Ballpark:
Out of the Shadows and Indistinct Background and into the Heart of the Baseball Film

Douglas A. Noverr

The American baseball park has been variously characterized as an architectural and cultural icon, a "consecrated" place or space that, according to Michael Novak, is "not only familiar but also awesome," a place of national memory and a repository of mythic deeds and ignominious misdeeds, and a signifier of urban history as well as the rural past (Novak 122-25). Other than Revolutionary War and Civil War battlefields and historical sites, no other location or cluster of locations has been invested with as much meaning or significance as the ballpark or stadium. Some of this signification can be understood as nostalgia or the effort to recover a lapsed or disappearing past, but clearly more significant issues and cultural conflicts are operative.

As the essential locus of action in the baseball film, the ballpark presented serious problems of production and treatment of this subgenre of the sports film. From the beginning baseball films as feature entertainment were saddled with numerous constraints that limited their development and sophistication.

First, baseball films (and all sports films for that matter) were hampered by the kinds of story genres applied to them. Baseball stories were routinely connected with comedy, romance, capers and hijinks usually involving gamblers or attempted fixes, melodrama, farce and misadventure, fantasy, and the simplistic big-league success story. The *Baseball Bill* series, produced by Universal Film Manufacturing Co., Inc. (which included a series of six silent comic melodramas) and released from June 22, 1916 to November 9, 1917, created a film counterpart to the popular *Baseball Joe* series of novels by Edward Stratemeyer. Even when well-known professional ballplayers werc featured as actors in films, such as the notorious Hal Chase in *Hal Chase's Home Run* (1911), or Frank "Home Run" Baker in *'Home Run' Baker's Double* (1914) and *A Short-Stop's Double* (1913), the formulaic plot dominated (Mote 20-21). Professional ballplayers saw these films as opportunities to pick up some quick and easy income in the off-season, as a means of popularizing themselves in a new mass medium, or as a means of satisfying modest and often misdirected aspirations to another career. In an era when actual images and pictures of baseball stars were extremely limited and confined to local fans or to tobacco trading cards, the motion pictures offered baseball enthusiasts a chance to see their heroes in their domain and field of endeavor (however staged or artificial), and to see them perform acts of throwing, hitting, and running. Beyond this the viewers could see how handsome, self-assured, spirited, and professional were the demeanor and appearance of the star they could only read about or see in occasional static images. Seeing Ty Cobb in *Somewhere in Georgia* (1916), Christy Mathewson and John McGraw in *Breaking into the Big League* (1913), Frank Chance in *Baseball's Peerless Leader* (1913), Hal Chase, or Frank Baker was a thrill in itself, especially for those who would never see a major league game and who could only dream of what a professional looked like or how he performed physically. Starting with the Essanay Company's "World Championship Baseball" series in 1908 (until 1912) and continuing with the Selig Polyscope Company's coverage of the World Series in 1913 (up through 1920), moviegoers could see World Series highlights (Mote 55-59). But these were shot at a distance and did not offer close-up and personal views of individual players as the feature films did.

The film companies saw baseball films as having limited appeal and income potential and thus relegated them to low budgets, tight shooting schedules, ready-made story formulas, and the constraints of studio skepticism. Stars and box-office draws could be made in the western film or in comedy, but the baseball player could not be made into a star due to the vagaries of success within the game, the decline of careers or teams, and the limited appeal or recognition of even the biggest name baseball stars. The studios relied on generic stories by unknown and undistinguished screenplay writers for the most part, or they counted on a certain box-office draw of a Babe Ruth in such films as *Headin' Home* (1920) or *Babe Comes Home* (1927).

Besides the studio executives' attitude that sports films were "box-office poison" (undoubtedly a self-fulfilling prophecy), other problems and conditions hindered the early development of the baseball film. With the notable exception of Ring Lardner's baseball fiction, there was the lack of good available baseball stories. The technical problems of producing realistic action sequences and covering multiple and simultaneous points of focus were substantial and required innovation as well as multiple cameras. Thus, the early technical conventions of the baseball film were determined by practical production considerations as well as by the limited budgets and shooting schedules that were dictated by the expectations of limited box-office returns.

As a result, the style and treatment of earlier baseball films became that of a kind of shorthand method of depiction as well as an attenuated and segmented approach. The game itself was reduced to limited and staged action sequences that could be cut together into a montage of dramatic highlights. The focus was put on the dugout, clubhouse, or off the diamond scenes with reaction shots (rather than on direct action) or with the commentary on the action. The focus on the individual player allowed for close-up shots of at-bats or dramatic moments in the clubhouse locker room or dugout.

The movie ballparks were generic, with just enough background shown to give some authenticity to the setting. No strong concern was given to accuracy or authenticity of setting, since it was assumed that moviegoers were not particularly concerned about this element, or were not even especially knowledgeable about it. The ballpark existed in the shadowy out-of-focus background. Unlike dramatic scenery in the western genre, the ballpark was not thought to have any dramatic potential for meaning or significance in and of itself. A baseball film could be shot almost anywhere, in any ballpark, since it was assumed that moviegoers were looking for diversion and entertainment rather than factual accuracy or authenticity of setting, or at least some semblance of it.

In the 1930s and after, Hollywood studios utilized other methods of bringing the ballpark more into focus as the central locus of drama in baseball films. The use of historical newsreel and documentary footage, intercut with studio scenes or staged action scenes, had the effect of giving factuality and some measure of authenticity. However, such a method also created inevitable problems and often glaring disparities. The documentary footage of actual baseball players in action could be quickly and even laughingly compared with the unskilled and unathletic efforts of an actor trying to portray a Lou Gehrig (Gary Cooper) or a Babe Ruth (William Bendix). The joints and seams of such editing and intercutting easily showed through. In *The Jackie Robinson Story* (1951) there is a nice sequence of historical footage showing the exterior of Ebbets Field and the fans entering the ballpark, but once the action moves inside the park, the location is obviously not Brooklyn's Ebbets Field. In fact, the ballpark used was LaPalma Park in Anaheim, California, which is also used to represent the Jersey City ballpark where Jackie Robinson made his International League debut in April, 1946 with the Montreal Royals (Benson 7).

Occasionally baseball films could overcome these glaring limitations and visual mismatches, as in *The Pride of the Yankees* (1942) when Lou Gehrig comes out of the dark shadows of the dugout, a solitary figure who emerges from the tunnel and into the bright sunlight, publicity, and touching and memorable occasion of Lou Gehrig Appreciation Day. The recreation of Gehrig's famous farewell speech, with his refusal to indulge in self-pity and his self-immortalizing in his simple words, is well done and moving, and his exit back into the darkness of the tunnel back to the clubhouse provides one of the great memorable sequences in baseball films. Sam Wood directed this film for RKO Radio Pictures, which featured Babe Ruth, Bill Dickey, Bob Meusel, and Mark Koenig as themselves. Wood also directed *The Stratton Story* (1949), which featured Gene Bearden, Jimmy Dykes, Mervyn Shea, and Bill Dickey as themselves.

The baseball film also had demonstrated definite potential in the 1930s with a series of comedies starring Joe E. Brown: *Fireman, Save My Child* (1932), *Elmer the Great* (1933), and *Alibi Ike* (1935). The latter two films were based on the writings of Ring W. Lardner, and Joe E. Brown was not only an avid baseball fan but an active and regular player who required that Warner Brothers supply him with a regular baseball team. Brown showed that baseball films could be fun and that action sequences could be well done. He was a part owner of a minor league club and counted many of baseball's greats among his personal friends (Bergan 55).

For decades, however, the baseball film suffered from a combination of factors that hindered its potential: low budgets and quick production schedules used to capitalize on a dramatic story or tragedy, unconvincing studio action sequences or play sequences reduced to montage highlights or to commented-upon rather than shown action, indifferent or poor writing based on hackneyed formulas, sentimentalism, the cameo role exploitation of well-known ballplayers, and the method of intercutting stock footage or brief documentary establishing scenes of ballparks, crowds, and even action sequences. The game was exploited and co-opted for stories or biopics, which could occasionally rise above the mediocrity of the average baseball film and reveal its potential.

The turning point for the baseball film came in 1973 with *Bang the Drum Slowly*, directed by John Hancock with the screenplay written by Mark Harris from his 1956 novel. With this remarkable film the ballpark as the central scene of action and the locus of the player's identity and performance comes out of the attenuated and shadowy background to become a presence and an enclosure of action and meaning. The ballpark becomes a place of beauty and drama, a field upon which human endeavor is observed. For the ballplayers, the ballpark is home; it is where their careers are played out, where they succeed and fail, where they create the meanings and significance of the game through ritualistic action.

In the opening sequence of *Bang the Drum Slowly* Henry Wiggen and Bruce Pearson come out on to the home field of the New York Mammoths and jog leisurely around the outfield, circling the inside perimeter of the park as they talk and laugh. The camera follows them around in a circle, with the sound of their spikes heard while the theme song, "The Streets of Laredo," is played on a flute. The ballpark, which is Shea Stadium, is empty and beautiful in its combination of the green turf and the blue stands in the background. We see two athletes in their prime, although soon we learn that Bruce Pearson is afflicted with Hodgkin's disease and is "doomed" to die during this, his last, season.

Henry Wiggen keeps the knowledge of Bruce's condition to himself until he needs the help of Goose, a catcher on the Mammoths, and Horse, the first baseman. In the most memorable and elegiac sequence of the film, after the team's manager, coaches, and management have learned about Bruce's condition, the team is in the clubhouse waiting out a rain delay. We see the umpires call the team in from the field, and the grounds crew covers the field with the tarp. Piney Woods, a young catcher brought back up to the club, is playing his guitar and begins to sing "The Streets of Laredo." At first, those who know about Bruce's condition, and who know the song is a lament for and by a dying cowboy, try to persuade Piney to sing another song. But he persists, and as Bruce sits by his locker with his catcher's mitt on his hand, Piney sings a song that acknowledges early death and the painful separation from the realities and pleasures of an all too brief life. As the song concludes, the camera shifts outside to an empty ballpark in an overhead shot, with the rain falling heavily and then a framed shot within the grandstand. As the inclement weather has intruded on the game, the reality of death has intruded into the lives of these athletes who are pursuing a pennant and time-bound dreams of success and glory. This is an evocative and profoundly elegiac sequence that connects the team in the clubhouse with the field of play and the ballpark. In his perceptive review of the film Jim Bouton noticed that the tarpaulin was "being pulled over a rainy field in the Washington, D.C. Stadium" but that when the camera cut back to the field the ballpark was "Yankee Stadium. The idea being that it's raining on this catcher's life no matter what town they're in" (Bouton 45). This, of course, is only part of the complex meanings evoked by this sequence. All the players are connected to Bruce's impending death, for a ballplayer can "die" in many ways: a fatal disease, as in Bruce's case; a career-ending injury; a loss of ability or diminution of talent; a ticket to the minors or outright release. John Hancock and cinematographer Richard Shore create a sequence with universal themes set in the context of a clubhouse and ballpark.

In Bruce's final game at home, the game against the Pirates which is no longer significant because the Mammoths have a "big cushion" and "were unstoppable" (in Henry's words), Bruce catches the entire game even though the condition has caught up with him at last. In this sequence, we see the ballpark from his perspective behind the plate with the hitting background in centerfield; the scoreboard in right center; the signs for Coca Cola, Natural Reingold beer, and a New York bank; the marked distances to all the parts of the outfield. While his life is quickly moving behind him, Bruce has the whole ballpark and diamond in front of him, and he gives his best effort to finish what will be his last game. His team rallies behind him, taking care of him between innings. When the plate umpire wonders about Bruce, Henry says "He's all right. We'll take care of him." In the final out of the game, a high pop-up in front of home plate that Horse, the first baseman, catches, Bruce loses sight of the ball and circles dizzily and confusedly as he looks for it. After a brief celebration of what turns out to be a pennant-clinching game, the players go to Bruce and minister to him. The entire scene is shot in slow-motion, with time slowing down for Bruce as he moves outside the circle of time and outside the circle of the game and team. For the Mammoths, this game signifies their ability to care for somebody, to be good to him, to think of him because, as Henry tells Bruce earlier, "Everybody knows everybody is dying. That's why they're as good as they are." Bruce's last request from Henry, as he leaves the team for home in Georgia, is that Henry sent him a scorecard from the World Series, which Henry does not do and for which he recriminates against himself for his thoughtlessness.

Bang the Drum Slowly succeeds for many reasons, but no small part of the film's success is its effective use of the ballpark and its integration of action and meaning within the ballpark. The action sequences are effectively done because the actors function as a team and perform all the motions and plays. It is ensemble acting, and of course, the story is written by a novelist/screenwriter with a love and understanding of the game and its universal meanings. The ritual of baseball is one of fertility and regeneration as well as death and failure. It is a game that requires faith in the talents of the ballplayers, a willingness to give them a chance to succeed and to sympathize and identify with them when they falter or fail.

The stadium in Barry Levinson's *The Natural* (1984) is more the mythical ballpark, although like *Bang the Drum Slowly*, the New York Knights play in a fictional ballpark. Utilizing War Memorial Stadium in Buffalo, built in 1935-37 with WPA funds, Levinson transforms the minor league ballpark into a National League stadium of the 1939 season. This transformation is achieved largely through the installation of period type large sign advertisements on the outfield walls, ranging from one for Zenith radio in left to 5¢ White Owl Cigars in right with signs for Lifebuoy soap ("Zephyr Fresh"), Spearmint Gum, baby food, an automobile, and Jantzen swimsuits in-between. The central scoreboard is topped by an advertisement for Sears Roebuck. This visual effect is similar to the Polo Grounds of the 1930s and up to 1948 when the "outfield walls were covered with advertisements such as Botany clothes, Stahl-Meyer hot dogs, GEM razor blades, Old Gold cigarettes, and Lifebuoy soap" (Benson 261).

The real virtue of Buffalo's War Memorial Stadium is, of course, its distinctive period construction and design, which went virtually unchanged for 50 years, its obstructing roof supports, and its seating capacity of 48,000 since it was built as a football stadium and adapted for baseball (Benson 71).

The appearance of an aging rookie, Roy Hobbs, brings magic, mystery, and excitement to the lowly New York Knights. The sparse crowds that endured the Knights' ineptness and self-defeating play turn into cheering crowds, families, and throngs of young boys who follow a new hero. Levinson manages this transformation effectively with fluid camera work, a variety of shots and camera positions, and dramatic interplay between the stands and the field. He also effectively uses a radio announcer who comments on the action as it is shown and who mythicizes the action and makes it larger than life by sending the play-by-play beyond the confines of the stadium.

In the playoff game for the National League pennant Levinson demonstrates how he has made Knights Stadium the focal point of the film. He starts with a ground level view of the foul lines being chalked, the bases being put in place, and Pop Fisher, the manager, filling out his lineup, crossing out Hobbs and inserting Pat McGee. In an overhead aerial shot of the ballpark, we see all in readiness, except for the one missing piece. However, Roy leaves the hospital and rejoins his team to aid Pop Fisher, who will lose the team to the corrupt Judge if the Knights do not claim the pennant. In the pennant-determining contest Levinson uses multiple points of interest to unify the action dramatically: the ailing but determined Hobbs in his various at-bats, the corrupt trio (the Judge, Gus Sands, and Memo Paris) in the centerfield executive suite, the Knights dugout, Iris and her teenage son (who is Roy's son, as he finds out just before his last trip to the plate), and of course the fans pulling for Roy and the Knights. Caleb Deschanel's cinematography and Stu Linder's editing of this extended, drama filled sequence are superb, and Levinson even has three movie cameras high up on the stadium's roof recording the action. By alternating reaction shots, utilizing a variety of camera locations to show the numerous points of view on the drama, and fluid editing, Levinson brings the action together within the ballpark in a totality of action and setting. The drama culminates in an extended at-bat for Roy Hobbs that is punctuated with a Pirates pitching change to a young fastball pitcher who is a mirror image of the younger Roy, the cracking of Roy's Wonderboy bat on a long foul to right and its replacement by a bat Roy has helped the batboy fashion, blood seeping through Roy's uniform from his stomach wound and surgery, and Roy's titanic home run that smashes into the light tower and sets off a series of explosions in the stadium's lights and a cascading shower of sparks as Roy rounds the bases after a three-run homer that wins the pennant. This sequence effectively dramatizes and visualizes the creation of baseball myth, legend making, and heroic action.

Levinson succeeds in *The Natural* because of his careful attention to period details and because he uses ensemble acting to create a team of believable ballplayers who could carry out extended action sequences (Farber 17H). Further, he understands the mythology and belief system inherent in the National Game as played out within the ballpark that becomes a place of high drama, moments of magic and awe-inspiring joy, and transcendence. When the action shifts to Wrigley Field in Chicago while the Knights are on a road trip, Levinson carefully transforms the same War Memorial Stadium by putting ivy in front of the fences as well as a brick wall around the inside perimeter of the park (Zucker and Babich 30). He stages the crowd scenes in the stadium with as many as 10,000 period dressed fans witnessing the action (Farber 17H). Using Gene Kirby and Richard Cerrone as baseball consultants, Levinson aimed at authenticity in every detail.

Bang the Drum Slowly and *The Natural* have been given such detailed treatment here because they have directly influenced subsequent films and have affected a transformation and elevation of the baseball film into its full potential. The work of Mel Damski in *A Winner Never Quits: The Pete Gray Story* (1986), Martin Davidson in *Long Gone* (1987), John Sayles in *Eight Men Out* (1988), Ron Shelton in *Bull Durham* (1988), David Ward in *Major League* (1989), and Phil Alden Robinson in *Field of Dreams* (1989) illustrates what has happened to what can now be definitely termed a genre. The baseball film has gained increasing respectability and entertainment value for many reasons. Four of these films were written by as well as directed by a single individual: Sayles, Shelton, Ward, and Robinson. Their projects are labors of love and care for the game of baseball gained either by direct experience (Ron Shelton played second base in minor league baseball for five years, and the co-producer of *Bull Durham*, Thom Mount, is the co-owner of the minor league Durham Bulls) or through a life-long passion for the game and its cultural, social, and historical significance. These directors have given careful attention to authenticity and to credibility of action sequences, and they had reasonably substantial budgets to work with, as well as a large degree of autonomy. For example, John Sayles had a budget of over $6 million, and Ron Shelton worked on a budget of $9 million—both directing for Orion Pictures. Even the films made for television (Damski's *A Winner Never Quits* for ABC Television and Davidson's *Long Gone* for HBO Pictures), while obviously made on lower budgets, reflect the higher standards and concerns of the directors. *Long Gone* is an excellent period film (the early 1950s) that focuses on the Tampico Stoogies team in the Alabama-Florida League, and its cinematic use of local ballparks and its treatment of the baseball subculture are evocative as well as authentic.

In all these recent films the ballpark stands out in sharp detail and provides a context of action and rich meanings. They have documented the wide range of interpretations American culture assigns to ballparks: the ballpark as local culture (*Bull Durham* and *Long Gone*, which both feature minor league parks); the ballpark as historical place and fact (*Eight Men Out* and *A Winner Never Quits*); the ballpark as dramatic location and the place of miracles and civic pride (*Major League*); and the ballpark as cultural icon and enduring presence that fuses past, present, and future (*Field of Dreams*).

In *Bull Durham* Crash Davis talks about his 21 days in the "Show" (the major leagues) and tells his Durham Bulls teammates that there "They use white balls for batting practice. The ballparks are like cathedrals. The women all have long legs and brains. The pitchers throw ungodly breaking stuff and exploding sliders." This vision of perfection is, according to Crash, something to respect as well as something to dream and hope for. The game in the "Show" is defined by class, professionalism, and intelligence. If these major league parks are "cathedrals," then the minor league parks, like those in the Carolina League, are the country churches. But the game is the same, and the faith of the fans is still present. Annie Savoy finds the "church of baseball" in Durham, North Carolina. Ray, Annie, and Karin Kinsella, as well as Terrance Mann, find their ideal field of dreams on a simple ball field that Ray has built, tended, and perfected because he trusted the "Voice" and his vision and then acted on his instincts rather than practicality. The "ghosts" of baseball's past (including Shoeless Joe Jackson and the other infamous Black Sox players) find their way to this field, and all are rewarded for believing in it, this former cornfield in Iowa where "dreams come true."

These two examples illustrate how much baseball parks (in all their various forms and relative status) mean to Americans who believe in them. As Terrance Mann tells Ray Kinsella,

The one constant through all the years, Ray, has been baseball. America has rolled by like an army of steamrollers. It's been erased like a blackboard, rebuilt, and erased again. But baseball has marked the time. This field, this game...it's a piece of our past. It reminds us of all that was once good. And that could be again.

Mann sees the ballpark as a place to regain one's childhood when one "cheered their heroes," a place where "They'll watch the game, and it will be as if they'd dipped themselves in magic waters. The memories will be so thick they'll have to brush them away from their faces." After the trial in *Eight Men Out* the unfortunate Buck Weaver tells a group of street kids:

I still get such a bang out of it. Playing ball. You get out there and the stands are full, and everybody's cheering. It's like everybody in the world came to see you. Damn if you don't feel like you're gonna live forever. You couldn't give that up. Not for nothing.

What these recent films have done is to bring "This field, this game" back into congruence and unity and to show that the ballpark and its field are integral to the meanings and national faith involved in the game. While the earlier conventions of the baseball films diminished and segmented the ballpark, and pushed it into a generalized and shadowy background, the more recent films have located it at the center and heart of the action and drama. Every culture needs special places, sacred places if you will, that inspire awe, belief, openness to experience and the possibilities of life, an apprehension of history and tradition. Our ballparks have provided such places of "magic waters" and thick memories, and the baseball films discussed from *Bang the Drum Slowly* on have restored that place to its central focus and made the ballpark dramatically and visually meaningful. As Annie Savoy says in *Bull Durham*, "It's a long season and you gotta trust it." The evolution of the baseball film has been "a long season," but there are those directors and technical talents who trusted its potential and who believed in it, not as the real thing but as a medium that pays homage to baseball and explores dramatically what baseball means to our culture.

Works Cited

Benson, Michael. *Ballparks of North America. A Comprehensive Historical Reference to Baseball Grounds, Yards and Stadiums, 1845 to Present.* Jefferson, NC and London: McFarland, 1989.

Bergan, Ronald. *Sports in the Movies.* London and New York: Proteus Books, 1982.

Bouton, Jim. "Jim Bouton Bangs the Drum Loudly." *The New York Times* 30 Sept. 1973: 11. 1.

Farber, Stephen. "An All-Star Team Puts 'The Natural' on Film." *The New York Times* 6 May 1984: Section 2, 1, 17.

Mote, James. *Everything Baseball.* NY: Prentice Hall, 1989.

Novak, Michael. *The Joy of Sports: End Zones, Bases, Baskets, Balls, and the Consecration of the American Spirit.* New York: Basic Books, 1976.

Zucker, Harvey Marc, and Lawrence J. Babich, comps. *Sports Films: A Complete Reference.* Jefferson, NC: McFarland, 1987.

Selected Films

Year	Film	Director
1932	*Fireman Save My Child*	Lloyd Bacon
1933	*Elmer the Great*	Mervyn Leroy
1935	*Alibi Ike*	Ray Enright
1942	*The Pride of the Yankees*	Sam Wood
1948	*The Babe Ruth Story*	Roy Del Ruth
1949	*The Stratton Story*	Sam Wood
1950	*The Jackie Robinson Story*	Alfred E. Green
1952	*The Winning Team* (biopic of Grover Cleveland Alexander)	Lewis Seiler
1957	*Fear Strikes Out* (biopic of Jimmy Piersall)	Robert Mulligan
1973	*Bang the Drum Slowly*	John Hancock
1976	*The Bingo Long Travelling All-Stars and Motor Kings*	John Badham
1984	*The Natural*	Barry Levinson
1986	*A Winner Never Quits: The Pete Gray Story*	Mel Damski
1987	*Long Gone*	Martin Davidson
1988	*Eight Men Out*	John Sayles
1988	*Bull Durham*	Ron Shelton
1988	*Stealing Home*	Steven Kampmann and Will Adis
1989	*Major League*	David Ward
1989	*Field of Dreams*	Phil Alden Robinson

Setting as a Narrative Convention:
Locales in the Boxing Film

Edward Recchia

The American personality has typically been a paradoxical amalgam of idealism and cynicism. On the one hand, from the Puritans to the Western pioneers, who sought—each group in its own way—to establish their own forms of New Canaan in this continent which promised so much, we have believed in and pursued the Horatio Alger ideal of the individual's capacity to achieve great things, once the opportunity is made available; on the other, from those same predecessors we have also inherited a legacy of hard-headed realism that acknowledges the fact of evil and corruption in the world and in our own society. That blend of American initiative and Yankee cynicism, whether or not it truly exists in today's society, has remained a long-cherished trait that we *like*, at least, to believe has survived into the present, even as the frontier has disappeared and the vision of unlimited opportunities for success for the average individual has dimmed.

No matter what the conditions of our present society, though, our forms of entertainment have, by their very nature, helped us reconcile in some comforting way our sense of the way life *should* be with the way life *is*—if they did not, then we would not have attended them as entertainments and they would have withered and died through attrition. Our modern forms of popular entertainment therefore serve much the same function for us as past forms did for our ancestors. As Stuart Kaminsky points out, "...one can argue that genre film, television, and literature have to a great extent replaced more formal versions of mythic response to existence such as religion and folk tale" (2). Just as comic drama might have allowed audiences in, say, seventeenth-century England to understand their foibles by allowing them to laugh at them, heroic drama to affirm their ideals by raising them to epic proportions, or tragedy to help them cope with the limitations of their own mortal natures, so, too, the dominant present-day American entertainment forms, television and motion pictures, provide us with a way of balancing our beliefs against modern realities.

As one form of our modern visual "literature," then, serious films today attempt in their own particular way to reconcile the *should* with the *is*, and those that have hit upon strains of our deepest cultural and social beliefs have formed our most cherished and original film traditions. In America, for example, the Western and the gangster film might be considered our most indigenous genres and at the same time the ones that represent the twin strains of optimism and hard-headed realism that underlie our collective national character. One other type of film, the sports film, might also be called typically "American." "Sports," Ronald Bergan observes, "have always been part of the American entertainment industry.... Sports create myths and heroes, the very life-force of Hollywood. These myths and heroes, unlike those of the western [sic], are contemporary and relevant to most people's experience" (4).

Although it would appear, Bergan admits, that "...sports, by their very nature, set themselves up against any dramatization imposed upon them [because] the main attraction is their unscripted topicality and the thrill of the unexpected," he also points out that "one does not enter a stadium with the same expectations with which one enters a movie theater" (6). When we enter the stadium or arena, we desperately want our home team to win, but we know that we might be disappointed by the time we leave; when we enter the movie theater, we know that, no matter what the story line and what the fate of the protagonist, in some way the myths that our society has built up regarding sports will, at the least, not be violated, and, at best, will reinforce our most deep-seated and cherished attitudes.

Films about all types of sports may provide that social/psychological reinforcement that we seek through our film viewing; but in many ways, films about the sport of boxing fit most comfortably into our social beliefs while satisfying our entertainment objectives. It may seem strange that our traditionally American idealism about the capability of the individual human being should be embodied in a sport so brutal as boxing; yet it is that very brutality that tests the limits of the individual boxer's physical courage, determination, and endurance. The boxer has no armor, has nothing to hide behind; he is stripped to the waist and vulnerable to the most extreme kinds of physical punishment. We who view a boxing match know that both contestants have achieved a level of mental and physical toughness that transcends normal, everyday human levels. Yet there they are—humans, after all; therefore, the very fact of their being there and doing what they're doing affirms what human beings are capable of. The boxer's exploits become, in their own brutal way, representative of the capabilities that make (or, at least, once made) the American Dream attainable.

Fictional films about boxing multiply this affirmation of the human spirit through the drama we experience as we view the film narrative; for when we see the boxer fighting on screen, we are aware not only of the physical stakes involved, but of the personal, social, and moral ones as well, because we have seen those issues developed as the film's story has developed. When he triumphs, the screen fighter therefore banishes not only his ring foe but the moral demons that have beset him—and, vicariously, us—throughout the film. When he loses, the film nevertheless asserts in some way the rectitude of those values which have become an engrained part of our culture, even as it and we acknowledge that frequently in life, those values do not always prevail.

That acknowledgment makes the boxing film particularly appropriate as a form of entertainment suited to our traditional hard-headed, realistic national character. For the boxing film does not shy away from the fact of evil; rather, it is eager to incorporate the forces of evil as a dramatic component of the film drama. Many boxing films utilize the conniving promoters, the double-crossing managers and trainers, the ruthless gamblers and the corrupt politicians that we know lurk in the background of the real-life sport to represent the forces the boxer must attempt to overcome; they also dramatize the inner forces of corruption—the desire for wealth that might overcome principles, the attractions of the luxurious apartments, the gorgeous blondes, the fine clothes, the parties and the drink—as forces that the individual must overcome in order truly to triumph.

Stanley Solomon's definition of a genre film as "one in which the narrative pattern, or crucial aspects of that pattern, is visually recognizable as having been used in other films" (3) may be arguably broad, but it does point out the importance of convention to any type of traditional film, whether it be labeled a "genre" film or not. Because with the boxing film as with other traditional sports films, the audience becomes accustomed to its conventions—in fact, *needs* them—as a guide to the ritual being played out in the narrative, the test of artistry for the filmmaker is to use the film's accepted hallmarks faithfully yet imaginatively. At the same time, the filmmaker assumes that the viewers are familiar enough with that film tradition's iconography—the tradition's conventional characters, situation, patterns of action—to recognize the value or meaning that has accrued to it, so that those conventions can be utilized as part of the story-telling process. Since film is, as Solomon says, one in which "crucial aspects" of the pattern are "visually recognizable," then just as the landscape itself is a key element in the Western, so there are elements of setting that have become, in effect, icons of the boxing film. Particular locales in the boxing film serve as indicators to the audience of the values inherent in the boxer-protagonist's struggles both outside and inside the ring.

Those indicators have defined themselves over the years, as the boxing film established itself as a distinctive type of sports film; however, they probably achieved their most significant development during the period just before and just after World War II, a time when traditional American optimism was tempered most strongly with strains of cynicism created, first, by Depression-era economic reality and, secondly, by a kind of philosophical *malaise* that beset many American filmmakers following the destructiveness of the Second World War. Within a ten-year period, four films helped define the philosophical and social possibilities for the boxing film; and in many ways, the films that followed—both those that are supremely optimistic like the *Rocky* films and those containing implicit social criticism, like *Requiem for a Heavyweight* in the 1960s or *Raging Bull* in the 1980s—have profited by building upon the legacy of those earlier films.

Of the Depression-era films, probably the most significant is the 1939 adaptation of Clifford Odets' play, *Golden Boy*, which incorporates all of the stereotypical elements of the boxing film into a powerful, if somewhat melodramatic, dramatization of the conflict between the traditional American dream of material achievement and the equally traditional ideal of the sanctity of the individual human spirit. Following the war, during what Harvey Marc Zucker calls "The Golden Gloves decade (1947-57) of the boxing movie" (54), came three films in quick succession: *Body and Soul* (1947), *Champion* (1949) and *The Set-Up* (1949). Coming as they did during the heyday of *film noir*, these films tried to achieve that delicate balance between what the filmmakers of the era saw as "the moral instability of this world" (Cook 469) and the indomitability of the human will. By setting their narratives within locales that have become traditional to the boxing film, the four films demonstrate the depth and range of possibilities available to the boxing film as a significant drama and a critical commentator on American society. In doing so, they substantiate patterns of earlier boxing films and establish patterns for the films that will follow.

Origins: Home and Family

"Papa—I've come home!"
Joe Bonaparte, *Golden Boy*

In John Ford's 1952 film, *The Quiet Man*, retired boxing champion Sean Thornton, played by John Wayne, settles into his ancestral home in Ireland in an attempt to find the peace and fulfillment that a hard life in American steel mills and success in the American boxing ring has finally earned him. He settles into his old family home: a picturesque, thatched-roof stone cottage with a stream bubbling by, in the midst of a lush, green valley. By the end of the film, he has added red-haired Maureen O'Hara to his life and stands in front of his cottage, clay pipe in his mouth and arm around his spouse, waving contentedly at the camera. In the boxing film, such homes are where the heart is. But rarely does the boxer-protagonist realize this fact, until after he has traveled a long and often morally crooked road, and rarely does he receive such bucolic rewards for his realization.

We see Sean Thornton after his career is ended. We have not seen him sweating in the steel mills or seen the grime of the home he shared with his mother back in the United States, nor (save for one brief flashback scene) have we seen him bleeding and sweating in the ring as he fought his way to his championship. Other boxing films—the ones that deal with the actual careers of their protagonists—do, however, blend such unattractive conditions into their dramatic package, so that both the audience's faith in the possibilities for individual success and its acknowledgment of the hard facts of modern existence are satisfied. Even the hero of the most optimistic of modern boxing films, Rocky Balboa, lives in a run-down flat in a shabby Philadelphia neighborhood before he achieves his success in the ring and in his personal life. His situation is a variation of the typical film situation of the young boxer-protagonist, who lives with his parents (or one widowed parent) in a slum or lower-class neighborhood and embarks upon a career to help the family escape poverty. Such settings reflect not only the increasing urbanization of American society but also the shrinking of the American Dream in the twentieth century; and along with that diminution of possibilities comes the acknowledgment of the crippling environmental and economic realities that often beset life in American cities, particularly after the waves of immigration at the end of the previous and beginning of this century. Whatever success the boxing film's protagonist achieves must in some way be reconciled both the reality of such settings and the values represented by the family.

Even before the era of tougher-minded, more realistic films like *Body and Soul*, *Champion* and *The Set-Up*, 1939's *Golden Boy* dramatized the same serious concerns as those three later films, but in a more romantic (and perhaps more didactic) fashion typical of the period and foreshadowing, to a degree, the melodramatic tone of the later *Rocky* series. *Golden Boy* presents before its audience the plight of Joe Bonaparte (played by William Holden), a young New Yorker of Italian heritage, who has exceptional musical talent but who forsakes the violin for the boxing ring. "I love the violin," he explains to his father when he tells him of his decision to choose the ring; "I love it more than anything else. But I've practiced for more than ten years, and where am I?" Earlier in the film, one of his neighbors has made sure the viewers won't miss the point of the film when he asks, "Could a boy make living playing music in our competitive world today?" Joe's solution to his frustration over his current lack of success and to his neighbor's question is the same: "Money's the answer." It won't be, of course; but Joe will have to discover that over the course of the film, as he gradually comes to understand that the values represented by home, family, and his art are the real answer.

In Joe's case, "home" is represented not only by an old-country family but by a father who is dedicated to his son's pursuing a musical career. "Money! Money! We got hearts, we got souls! We gotta take care of that, eh?" replies Papa Bonaparte (Lee J. Cobb) in his heavy Italian accent. As depicted, the home life of the Bonapartes is a stereotype of the classic Italian American family so strong as to approach caricature: The widowed Papa Bonaparte operates the "Italian American Grocery" in a cozy New York neighborhood; he lives above the store with son Joe, daughter Anna and her husband, Ziggy. The flat is colorful and homey, filled with overstuffed couches and chairs covered with chintz, large bureaus and sideboards, both a piano *and* an organ; the walls, decorated in floral patterns, are filled with religious pictures of the Virgin and Child, and religious pictures and icons sit upon every surface. All members of the family love music, and there is one idyllic scene where Joe begins playing his violin for his father, who immediately sits down to listen rapturously; then sister Anna comes into the room and begins to play piano accompaniment for Joe; neighbor Mr. Carp, who is just happening by, slips in to listen; and brother-in-law Ziggy, who had been upstairs in the bathroom shaving, comes down in his undershirt and with shaving cream still on his face, sits on the stairs and listens contentedly.

Family and art versus blood and violence; the young man's inherent artistic sensitivity versus the viciousness of the ring. The reluctant hero ("I love the violin. I love it more than anything else") will eventually find his way back home, but only after he has killed his last ring opponent and broken his left hand, so vital to his violin playing. It is clear that this Depression-era film is more than willing to acknowledge the overwhelming power of economic determinism, even as it affirms, as did many other films of the period, the salvatory worth of the family.

Body and Soul affirms the same old-country values and also ruefully acknowledges economic realities—but in a more realistic, understated manner than does *Golden Boy* and with settings that match the film's darker, starker mood. It uses once again a lower economic-class neighborhood as the jumping-off place for the boxer-protagonist's career. Its hero, Charley Davis (played by John Garfield), is Jewish. He lives in what appears to be the lower East Side of New York in a small flat above the candy store his parents run during the Prohibition era. Across the street from the candy store is the pool hall where Charley and his friends hang out, and as opposed to the old-country richness of the Bonapartes' home, the upper flat Charley shares with his parents has no real warmth or attractive decorative touches to it: the furniture is clean but shabby, the walls relatively bare; a plain board wall with a window—indicating the likelihood that the flat has been expanded or added on to—separates the living room from the kitchen. Those two rooms, the building's rooftop, and its front porch are all we see of Charley's boyhood home. Mama Davis is a far cry from Papa Bonaparte: a grim, unsmiling woman, who knows that life is hard and that the two men in her life may not be tough enough to deal with it—and so has taken on the role of the family "heavy." Even though it becomes apparent as the film moves on that she is capable of loving deeply, she will never sacrifice principle for emotion. The father, on the other hand, is softer. He understands that the happy-go-lucky Charley still has maturing to do, and he's willing to slip his son a few dollars so that he can join his friends at the pool hall.

The initial setting tells the audience everything they have to know about Charley and his family, and the ensuing dramatic conflict is predictable and standard for the boxing film: The Davises are poor but honest—but "poor" will prove to make everything else almost unbearable. Charley's father is accidentally killed when gangsters bombing a speakeasy next to the candy store destroy the store as well. Charley, outraged when his mother must turn to charitable organizations to get by, decides to pursue a boxing career to make money and commands his boyhood friend, Shorty, who will become his first manager, to contact Quinn, a shady fight manager and promoter who hangs out at the local pool hall, to arrange a fight for him. When his mother tries to dissuade him by saying that he might as well get a gun and go shoot someone as beat them up in a ring, he answers, "You need money to buy a gun!" Then he angrily declares, "I want money, do ya understand? I want money, money!" From that point on, he will embark on a journey that will bring him to the championship, but not before he has compromised his principles and alienated his mother and fiancee, Peg (Lilli Palmer); but by the end he will, as did Joe Bonaparte, have traveled full circle and will return to home, family, love, and integrity.

The film's plot comes as close as possible to what Zucker describes as the basic formula for the boxing film: "Most of the plots of boxing films are the same thing over and over again. A slum boy rises to be a contender, but he either loses his virtue to a vamp or is corrupted by gangsters and falls, only to make a comeback at the end aided by the pleas at ringside of the sweetheart he's left behind" (53-54). But as *Shane* is to the Western so is *Body and Soul* to the boxing film: not an attempt to vary the basic pattern of the film tradition it represents but an attempt to authenticate it by deepening every element that makes the tradition meaningful. The film becomes in its own way the embodiment of the spirit underlying the basic fight-film formula, rather than simply a stereotyped copy of the basic pattern. By enriching the conventions of the fight film, *Body and Soul* opens the way for equally rich variations of the formula that will follow. *Champion* and *The Set-Up* provide such variations.

In the case of *Champion,* the film simply reverses the conventional pattern. Midge Kelly, the protagonist (played by Kirk Douglas), will not make a moral "comeback," as Charley does in *Body and Soul.* But he will come from the same deprived circumstances (this time, though, in Chicago, rather than New York, where Joe Bonaparte and Charley Davis were raised) and faces the same corrupting influences. The fact that by the end of the film he is, in fact, corrupted by these influences enforces, through negative example, the same human values that the positive comebacks of Joe, Charley and other, more traditional boxing heroes represent in their respective films. Even though we don't actually see the home where Midge was raised at all in the film and only meet his mother half-way through, the positive power of home and family is made clear—if only by his defection from their humanizing influence.

We see Midge first in the present time, already an established champion; then in flashback we see how he has risen to these lofty heights in the boxing world while declining in every other significant human way. In the first flashback scene, we see Midge in the "home" which brought him—quite literally—on the road to a boxing championship: he is in an empty boxcar, where he and his lame brother, Connie, are attempting to fight off a gang of vagabonds who want to rob them of the few paltry dollars they've saved to travel to California to seek a better life for themselves and their mother. After the robbery, Midge will be bilked and cheated by a variety of other people, until he himself becomes a master exploiter of others, but in these early stages of the film story, the audience has no more difficulty sympathizing with a Midge living in a boxcar as he attempts to find a better home for his mother than they do with a Charley determined to lift his mother and himself out of the poverty of a depressed big-city neighborhood.

In contrast to Charley's salvation in *Body and Soul,* though, Midge's moral decline and eventual fall will reinforce the negative side of the ambiguous values inherent in the poor-but-honest family situation typically depicted in the boxing film by emphasizing the fact that the human spirit can, indeed, fall prey to the corrupting influence of unprincipled wealth and never recover. That sad admission will lead to more film depictions of the hard reality described by Andrew Bergan, when he says, "...for every Cinderella that marries the prince, there are thousands that end up with the impoverished woodcutter, and for every boxer who gets into the big time, there are thousands who end up without a cent" (14). Films like *The Harder They Fall* (1956) and *Requiem for a Heavyweight* (1962) will follow that trend, with the earlier film concentrating on exposing the corrupt forces behind the boxing business and the latter emphasizing the tragedy of the washed-up boxer. But even before these films make their appearance, *The Set-Up,* produced the same year as *The Champion,* combines elements that will appear in the two later films. In *The Set-Up,* as in the later *Requiem,* we see a boxer at the tail-end of a long and not-so-illustrious career; like both Mountain Rivera, of *Requiem,* and Toro Moreno, of *The Harder They Fall,* Stoker Thompson (Robert Ryan), the protagonist of *The Set-Up,* is victimized by unscrupulous promoters, handlers and gamblers; yet he, as do the other two victim-protagonists, demonstrates a level of individual integrity that affirms his worth as a human being, even as it confirms the fact that such integrity is often punished, rather than rewarded, in real life.

Stoker Thompson's "home" reflects both the characteristic fate of many second-rate boxers and, at the same time, their humanity. The locale within which the action of the film takes place could hardly seem more depressing: the film opens by depicting a dark, dingy, honky-tonk street in a dark, dingy, honky-tonk town—apparently named "Paradise City" (if we are to judge by the name of the boxing/wrestling arena in which Stoker is scheduled to fight that night, for the arena's name, "Paradise city A.C.," is advertised in bright neon lights, right next to the sign of the adjoining building, apparently a run-down dance hall/penny arcade named "Dreamland"). Stoker and his wife, Julie (played by Audrey Totter), live in a shabby room at the ironically named "Hotel Cozy," where Julie prepares meals (canned soup and beer) on a hot plate.

Yet, along with the poverty that they share with the Davis family of *Body and Soul* and the Kelly family of *Champion,* the Thompsons also demonstrate the same fierce family loyalty and love. Their only source of conflict is that Julie wants Stoker to quit boxing and get any kind of job, even running a newspaper stand, while Stoker still unaccountably entertains illusions that he'll somehow make it in his chosen profession. Poor and inarticulate as both of them are, they are ennobled by their ability to love; and as the film progresses, Stoker will demonstrate an integrity that will—fortunately for him—force him to give up boxing and to be saved for a better life, even if it is one that is far less glamorous than the one that led him to pursue a boxing career in the first place.

An ironic counterpart to Stoker's fate is that of Mountain Rivera, who, in *Requiem for a Heavyweight,* gives up his only chance to leave the fight game in order to save a member of the only "family" he has left—his conniving manager, who, like Stoker's handlers in *The Set-Up,* has arranged for his boxer to take a dive but without bothering to consult the boxer. To save his manager's life after the fix falls through, Mountain joins a profession in which *every* fight is fixed—wrestling. It is a dire fate, made to seem more pathetic by what Bergan describes as the "tacky" New York background (36) against which the entire film is shot. Littered streets, vacant storefronts, and run-down apartment buildings decorate Rivera's path to the dilapidated gym where he trains and the shabby arena in which he will fight. Everything shouts out decay. Yet that sad setting only elevates Mountain in the viewers' eyes as he shows the same humble dignity in his decision to sacrifice his last chance to escape this stifling environment that Stoker showed ten years earlier, when he defied the odds and the gamblers in order to uphold his integrity.

Louis Giannetti says, "In the best movies..., settings are not merely backdrops for the action, but symbolic extensions of the theme and characterization" (274); and, indeed, in all of these films the locales within which we first see the protagonists not only establish their socio-economic situation but also prepare us for the kinds of conflicts so indigenous to this type of sports film. From the near East Side neighborhood in which Joe Bonaparte and Charley Davis grew up, from the boxcar in which we see Midge Kelly fighting for his brother's and his own survival, from the squalid "Paradise City" in which Stoker Thompson still entertains his dreams, to the even more squalid New York City in which Mountain Rivera ends his, we recognize the inevitable conflict between what we know is the inherent humanity of each individual—that humanity which is most readily illustrated in terms of home and family—and what we must ruefully acknowledge to be the often spiritually debilitating influences that will attack that humanity. Just as settings in slums and boxcars establish motives for the individual's seeking a better life, so settings that follow these locales make clear the conflict of values that will follow.

Gyms and Arenas: Testing and Temptation

Consider the typical boxing gym: it is on one hand a place where the boxer punishes and disciplines his body, ridding it of fat, strengthening it for the battles to come. The quintessential training sequence was probably depicted in the first *Rocky* film (1976), where we see Rocky Balboa transformed within a five-week span from a run-of-the-mill prelim fighter to fit a challenger for his upcoming championship fight with Apollo Creed, as he not only utilizes normal exercises like push-ups and sit ups but also such innovative techniques as using sides of beef in a meat locker as his substitute for heavy punching bags and downing raw eggs at daybreak before embarking on his laborious run through the streets of Philadelphia. As he hardens into fighting shape, he gradually runs faster and faster; the pace of the sequence also picks up; and the stirring music by Bill Conti raises the audience to an emotional pitch, reaching its peak when he completes the final run in the sequence by sprinting up the steps of the Philadelphia Art Museum and raising his hands in triumph. Corny as the sequence might be, the audience is swept along by the increasing intensity of the music and the unusual training methods in its admiration for the typical American underdog who is about to live his own version of their American Dream. In other boxing films, too, training sequences that take place in the boxing gym represent the admirable side of the boxer's existence—his ability to discipline his body, the strength of his will.

At the same time, the gym is the place where cigar-chomping parasites hang out, coldly assessing the laboring boxers as they might pieces of merchandise. As opposed to the seemingly healthy atmosphere of the outdoors, the places in the city where the boxer labors are uncompromisingly dirty, dingy, smoke-filled. Visually, the very appearance of the gym where the film-version boxer is discovered or works out, of the small-time arena where he wins his prelims and builds a reputation, of the shabby locker rooms where he girds himself for battle—these locales tell the viewers, long before they see the corruption that exists there corrupting the mind and spirit of the boxer, the inevitability of the conflicts of spirit that must follow.

Since Stoker Thompson is depicted at the end of his boxing career, we see him on the downhill side of this scenario in *The Set-Up*. The film provides us a view of what may be the seediest locker room ever depicted in a boxing film. Located in the bowels of the "Paradise City A.C.," it represents boxers after they have lost almost everything but their illusions and are even more incapable of withstanding the corrupting influences of those who have the power to manipulate and use them. There is no life in the locker room, unless it is the fungi growing along the surfaces of the locker room's benches, lockers and floors. We see only scar tissue on the faces of Stoker and the other washed-up boxers who populate the room, attesting to the trials they've gone through on their way to a fruitless present and an unpromising future.

In *Body and Soul,* we first see Charley at the beginning of what might be a promising career—but one that hints of dangers, as well: he has just won an amateur fight in the smoke-filled "Algonquin Athletic Club"—a seedy-looking local social club; when, desperate for money, he seeks a professional career, he approaches the small-time manager, Quinn, in a pool hall. Neither place exudes wholesomeness, although, granting the neighborhood that Charley has grown up in, they are natural-enough places to serve as springboards for his career. At the same time, the pool hall in particular bodes nothing promising about the future for Charley or for the alliance between Charley and Quinn. In *Champion,* it is in a small-time boxing arena that Midge Kelly catches the eye of Tommy Haley, the man who will eventually become his manager—but only after Midge has suffered a tremendous beating during his first "professional" fight and then has been cheated out of his agreed-upon fee by the arena's owner. Later in the film, when Midge approaches Tommy and tells him that he'd now like to accept Tommy's previous offer to manager him, Tommy at first backs off and warns Midge to avoid the fight game because it "stinks." "Take a deep breath," he says, looking around the boxing gym where they're both standing: "It stinks in here, doesn't it? And it's not just the sweat."

Yet Tommy finally decides to take Midge on, because "with some guys it's the bottle. Me? I like to watch a couple of good boys in action." And when Midge himself starts training, the film enters into a montage showing the other side of the fight game, the one that films depict as the admirable side of the boxer as he goes through the rigors of training in the gym and fighting prelims at nondescript arenas. The "good boy" doesn't just fight, we find out; the "good boy" must do sit-ups, jump rope, punch bags, shadow box, spar, beat up other "good boys" in preliminary fights and get beaten on himself. He must sweat and bleed to achieve his goal. That other side of the boxer is the one that allows the audience to empathize with him, even as they fear for the reasons that motivate him to take so much physical punishment; and if they did not know even before they entered the movie theater, they usually do know, from those early scenes in the pool hall or the gym, where the conflict will lie. They will root for discipline and determination winning out, yet be well aware that in many boxing films, it's the "stink" that might prevail.

The Train: Breaking Away

Too often the stink does. It is perhaps significant that we see Midge
Kelly in a boxcar when he encounters the first of a series of incidents
that will eventually destroy any goodness in him. The "train montage" is
a convenient way for a film director to cover months of a boxer's career
in a few moments, as he intersperses shots of a speeding train with
calendar pages flipping to show time passing, shots of fight posters
announcing the boxer's upcoming bouts, newspaper headlines, and short
segments of fights that we see the boxer winning. Inevitably, the boxer
arrives back in his home town, but this time as a much different person
and usually to a much different abode than his family home. In *Golden
Boy* it is a different Joe Bonaparte who returns to New York after eight
months on the road. At the time he left, he was still torn between boxing
and the violin, but by the time he returns, he has been as hardened by his
fights as his once-sensitive hands have been hardened by the brine he
soaked them in to make them fighting tough. The scene that immediately
follows occurs in the new, luxurious offices of his manager, Tom
Mooney; but when mobster Eddie Fuselli walks in, it becomes apparent
that the lavishness that has accompanied Joe's achievement of a higher
plateau in the boxing world also will bring him into contact with
stronger corrupting influences. In the resultant narrative, Joe will
become corrupted, until he finally returns to his father's home.

Likewise, Charley Davis goes on the road, and the time sequence is
indicated in the same way: snippets of fight scenes, speeding train shots,
calendar pages, and newspaper headlines. And Charley, too, comes back
a changed man. He is proud of his hard-won success and boisterously
shows off his new, glamorous apartment to his mother and fiancee, Peg.
Yet they immediately sense that he is too caught up in the accoutrements
of his new life style, and they see the danger that his commitment to his
new wealth can bring. Their fear is justified: before the film ends,
Charley will have sold out his integrity in order to make money, even
though he will redeem himself by the film's end.

For Midge Kelly there is no redemption. He is already cut off from the
influence of home when we see him in the boxcar, and even though he
fights valiantly to protect his lame brother, Connie, it is probably no
accident that Connie is physically debilitated; for finally, the family values
that Connie represents prove to be equally handicapped when they must
compete against the lure of personal and financial success for Midge's
allegiance. Joe Bonaparte eventually finds his way back home by his
film's end; so does Charley Davis. Even Stoker Thompson, who has no
real home, finds himself lying within the consoling arms of his wife in the
final shot in *The Set-Up*. But once he embarks on his career, Midge does

not attempt even to visit his mother until he hears that she's dying—and then he arrives too late and unrepentant. By subordinating family to ambition, he also deprives himself of the salvation family can offer.

New Homes, New Values

The reason that boxers like Midge Kelly can't detect the "stink" that Tommy Haley speaks of is that it is usually disguised—at least to the boxer's nose, if not to the audience's—by some very heady perfume in the boxing film. In terms of setting, it is often depicted in two ways: either through the plush offices from which the rich promoters, who will control the boxers' destinies, wield their power, or in the glamorous locales that depict the lush life that the boxer has pursued from the beginning of the film. Both sorts of settings are presented in both *Body and Soul* and *Champion*. When Charley Davis or Midge Kelly is summoned to the center of power—the promoters' offices—depicted in their respective films, each of them is confronted by a wood-paneled, leather-upholstered business suite that sits high above the city, as though dominating it; the promoter sits behind a huge desk, dressed in a rich pin-striped, double-breasted suit and smoking a cigar, while draped across one of the adjacent chairs sits a glamorous blonde—a Marilyn Maxwell (*Champion*) or a Hazel Brooks (*Body and Soul*).

It isn't just a display of money; it's an example of the power that money wields and the kinds of pleasures money can buy. And the boxer, who has already bought into that value system when he first determined to seek his fortune with his fists, will follow suit as soon as he can—even when the inevitable alternative is placed before him: take a dive in this fight or you'll never get a chance at the championship; in fact, you'll never fight in "this town" (the skyline of New York is still visible in the background) again. Both Charley and Midge capitulate and end up with championships. Only Stoker refuses when he has the chance to sell out, and for his reward he ends up in a dark alley with his hands busted.

Yet even though the immediate rewards for Charley's and Midge's sellout seem attractive, the audience already can see, well before the fighter can, what the cost of their moral capitulation will be. Always the "rewards" that the boxer seems to reap seem little too tawdry, a little too glitzy to carry with them any of the substantial human values that the audience feels constitutes true, worthwhile achievement. Envision what kind of life values a Miami nightclub represents, and transfer those values to the Jake LaMotta portrayed in *Raging Bull*. Martin Scorsese didn't have to do much more than show Jake and his swarthy cohorts in the club and have Jake tell a few bad jokes to the vast amusement of the clientele, and his depiction of the emptiness of that boxer's dream was well on its way to being complete.

In case we're in any doubt in *Body and Soul* and *Champion*, the directors make sure we get the message through effective contrasts and commentaries when they show their boxer-protagonists enjoying the fruits of their labors. There is the scene, for example, in *Body and Soul* in which Charley Davis returns to New York from his long and successful tour of road fights. He is now a top contender for the middleweight championship, and he is anxious to introduce his mother to the luxurious apartment that he wants to share with her. It resembles a Versailles drawing room, with high ceilings, elaborate drapery and statuary, and lavish furniture. His mother, though, is unimpressed with the mirrored wall that revolves to reveal a fully stocked bar and instead is put off by the shady manager, Quinn, who seems so much at home in Charley's apartment; likewise, she takes an instant dislike to the manager's languorous blonde girlfriend, who is so entranced by the fur coat that Charley has bought for his fiancée, Peg. The audience, along with Mrs. Davis and Peg, see how skewed Charley's values are becoming, and they know that Mrs. Davis's decision to stay in her own old flat and Peg's lack of enthusiasm over her gift are the film's way of indicating that the values that are more important have little relation to the riches that Charley and other boxer-protagonists pursue as the way to salvation. If we have any doubt, a scene where Charley wakes up one morning after a wild party in the same apartment and picks his way over the strewn bodies of the partygoers who are still sleeping it off in his new "home" drives the point home. If there is still doubt in the audience's mind that Charley has changed, his boyhood friend and co-manager, Shorty, takes Peg aside and pleads with her to marry Charley as soon as possible, hinting that his frenzied pursuit of money has knocked all of his values out of kilter.

In *Champion*, director Mark Robson provides a more subtle contrast, showing Midge only in what appears to be a permanent hotel suite, once he has made it as champion. There he lives in isolated splendor. But Robson contrasts that suite with the comfortable but unpretentious apartment in Chicago that Midge's money has made possible for his mother to move into and in which she lives with Connie and Midge's ex-wife, Emma. It is plain, almost shabby; although comfortable enough, it is closer to the sparsely decorated apartment Charley Davis's mother lives in than the warmly comfortable Bonaparte flat of *Golden Boy*. Midge has done his duty but does not go beyond that; the apartment shows that as much as his failure even to visit her until just moments after she has died. Connie and Emma provide the kind of giving that make the apartment a home, and that's something that Midge is incapable of giving. In the same way, Peg lives with Charley's mother even after her engagement to Charley breaks down. Charley keeps coming back to the two of them for solace, for direction, for a sense of the man he dimly knows he wants to be, no matter how far he has wandered in search of riches.

It is, finally, that human ingredient that Charley is seeking that the boxing films indicate can make a house, an apartment, a hotel room—perhaps even a boxcar—more a home than the most luxurious of apartments. The boxing film's audience knows how to interpret the values that the director depicts as inhering in the locale, and they will not view material well-being as good unless it goes hand-in-hand with strength of character; wealth for its own sake they will view as corrupting. They know, therefore, that the glitz and glamour of Jake LaMotta's Miami nightclub is merely gaudiness; they are prepared when the showiness of Charlie Davis's New York apartment becomes a scene of empty debauchery from which Charlie will wander back to his old neighborhood in search of real meaning and substance; they understand that the tailored suits of the promoters, the fur coats of the blondes are only shells that are inhabited by beings who finally are powerless to satisfy the ultimate needs and yearnings of humans for real love, real fulfillment, real validation.

The Training Camp: Paradise Lost

It is not just romantic poets and philosophers who regard nature as a place of innocence and purity, free from the corrupting effluences of the "civilized" world. In real-life boxing, managers used to hie their charges off into the mountains or the desert, where the fighters could eat simple, hearty food, get plenty of concentrated exercise, discipline their bodies—and, perhaps most importantly, escape the distractions and temptations of the outside world. It is no coincidence that in a variation of the same unorthodox training techniques he used in the original *Rocky*, Sylvester Stallone's Rocky Balboa of *Rocky IV* trains in the midst of Nature (with a capital "N"), lifting tree trunks and chopping wood, while his evil Russian opponent undergoes a mechanized and computerized training routine that emphasizes his lack of humanity—and, by extension, the deficiencies of the political system he represents. For all its modernized embellishments of music, editing, and sound effects, this third sequel to the original *Rocky* still utters all the familiar shibboleths that made the boxing film a popular entertainment in the first place, and the reference to Nature as a place of purification of body and spirit, of refuge from the contamination of society, in this case is simply adapted to become also an encomium to the United States and its ideal of individualism and entrepreneurialism.

Nowadays, real-life boxing champions "train" in rings set up in the middle of Las Vegas gambling casinos, and the system that the Russian boxer represented has proven no match for the realities of supply-side economics. While that latter economic triumph is certainly viewed by Americans as a good thing, we are more reluctant to give up our romantic ideal of pristine nature—whether "Mother" or "human"—remaining sacrosanct from the crass incursions of the material world. Incursions are, nevertheless, what we do see in *Body and Soul* and *Champion*; and the use of the training-camp locale indicates how the films of that era were more anxious to deal with the fact that the boxer's attempts at success are never really safe from the contagion of the corrupt influences that run the boxing business—and, often, the films imply—society as well.

The training-camp sequences in both *Body and Soul* and *Champion* depict the ambivalence inherent in the sport of boxing and dominating the personality of most boxing-film protagonists. In both films we see nature and corruption existing side-by-side. Even though the first scene in *Body and Soul* depicts the training camp where Charley is training for his championship defense, we are to find out later that he has already agreed to throw the fight; that the camp is controlled by Charley's crooked manager, who has promoted both the fight and the fix; that the one individual—an ex-champ who was badly injured when he was double-crossed by that same manager-promoter and who tried to talk Charley out of dumping the fight—has just died; and that Charley's obsessive drive for money has caused him to cast away all of his principles and has driven away his best friend, Shorty (who later dies in an auto accident), his mother, and his former fiancee, Peg. It is a situation not exactly "free" from the corrupting influences of society.

Likewise, although *Champion*'s Midge Kelly is earnestly training for his title defense when we see him in training camp near the end of that film, he has already degenerated in principle so much that he has cast aside his previous manager and best friend, ignored his family, deserted his wife, and dropped his previous blonde golddigger of a girlfriend to carry on an affair with the wife of the upcoming championship fight's promoter. Now, apparently reconciled with his ex-wife and his brother, he has given his blessing to their getting married and they have joined him at the camp; but partly out of boredom, partly to prove to himself that she still must care for him, partly because he can't bear to give up something—no matter how little it means to him any longer—to anyone else, he seduces his ex-wife at the camp while his brother is in town helping set up the title defense.

Chronologically, it is at this point in both *Body and Soul* and *Champion* that Charley and Midge reach their moral nadirs and must either fight their way to salvation or allow themselves to remain lost. Their crises correspond to the varying crises of the protagonists of all other boxing films, who also reach a point where both the dramatic conflict that has been building up throughout the film narrative and the boxing issues will come together and be resolved, either for better or for worse. That resolution will as often as not occur in a final, climactic fight in the ring, and the film will usually tip the balance towards one of the two opposing forces—the inherent goodness of the individual or the powerful, corrupting forces that often lie within society.

The Ring: Paradise Regained—Sometimes

There is a scene in *Raging Bull* in which a defeated Jake LaMotta puts his hands down at his sides in the middle of a fight with Sugar Ray Robinson and invites Sugar Ray to hit him as hard as he can. Robinson obliges, but cannot knock LaMotta out; and at the end of the fight, as he staggers, a bloody but clearly unbowed loser, toward his corner, LaMotta asserts, "But ya couldn't knock me down. D'ya hear me, Ray? Ya couldn't knock me down!" In his mind, he has proven his manhood, just as he did in an earlier scene when, in his own home, he invited his own brother to hit him as hard as he could. To LaMotta, that ability to withstand punishment is a validation of his worth as a human being, and the ring becomes the place where he proves himself. But, rather than just an affirmation of courage or manliness, the film's audience sees something more pathetic and perverted in LaMotta's need to assert his worth in such a way. Although in the most stereotypical boxing films the ring in which the protagonist squares off with his opponent for the climactic battle is the place where he typically redeems himself, cleansing himself with his own blood of any sins he may have committed in the previous one and one-half hours of film action, it is not, as *Raging Bull* demonstrates, always so.

Because the *Rocky* films, despite cosmetic innovations which disguise the fact, actually follow the boxing-film stereotype quite faithfully, Rocky Balboa *does* prove himself in his various fights—even that first one, which he loses to Apollo Creed. The climactic battles in the *Rocky* series are the capstones of the rigorous training schedule he undergoes in each film, ridding his body of any of the excesses of soft living in preparation for the final baptism of blood. The fights themselves, with the sound of punches exaggerated and rousing music cueing the audience as to the pace and direction of the fighters' fortunes, are so orchestrated that they simulate primitive blood rituals in which young warriors prove their manhood, and in terms of the values that the films define, Rocky clearly bleeds enough to prove his.

More subtle treatments of the same stereotype, like *Body and Soul*'s, follow the same pattern, with Charley Davis washing away all his sins (which are considerably more serious than Rocky Balboa's) with one final championship victory. The film compensates for the discrepancy between the amount of blood spilled in this fight and that in a *Rocky* film by having Charley suffer financially, since he loses the money he bet against himself when he decides to win the fight. Where Rocky prepares himself by figuratively going off into the desert to fast and pray for forty days and nights before his salvatory fights, Charley does his penance in retrospect. Both men, though, prove themselves pure enough to be saved through what they do in the ring.

Even Stoker Thompson, who wins in the ring but has his hands smashed as a reward for his honesty and courage, wins, because now he must give up all illusions of becoming a contender and will probably find a less punishing way of making a living, as his wife, Julie, has been begging him to do. At the end of the film, as he lies in the alley where the gangsters have left him after beating him up, he looks up at Julie, who is holding him in his arms, and says, "I won, Julie. I won!" She looks down on his bloody face, knowing that he'll never fight again, and replies, "We both won." The fighters who fight for the right reasons are redeemed—sometimes at the cost of the very things that led them into the fight business in the first place, as with Stoker and Charley Davis, sometimes as an affirmation of those values, as with Rocky. But they are only redeemed when the physical courage and determination they display are aligned with the social and human values that the film and the audience agree are essential to the make-up of a successful human being and that are somehow affirmed within the "squared circle."

Jake LaMotta, Joe Bonaparte, and Midge Kelly have physical courage, too, and a raw, ferocious energy that causes them to fight in the ring like animals protecting their territory. But only one of the trio finds anything close to redemption in the ring. At one point in *Raging Bull*, in fact, Martin Scorsese includes a fight scene that indicates that the blood shed by the fighters is often anything *but* redemptive: he first shows the blood from blows that are striking LaMotta being sprayed on the ringside viewers, as though it is holy water being sprayed on a congregation; then, through LaMotta's eyes, he makes the water being sponged on the fighter seem like blood. The suggestion is that the boxer fights for all the wrong reasons; he bleeds so that the fans, enjoying the fight vicariously, won't *have* to admit that they're satisfying some fairly atavistic tastes through their observance of this "sport."

In *Golden Boy* and *Champion* both Joe Bonaparte and Midge Kelly find themselves alone before their climactic battles: both have been

202 **Beyond the Stars**

forsaken by their families, have alienated their former managers, and have either cast aside or been cast aside by their love interests. Joe speaks for both of them when he declares, "Now I'm alone. I'll show them all! Nobody, nothing stands in my way!" Luckily for him, after he has won his vicious bout with his opponent, Chocolate Drop, he is saved—but only at a price: Chocolate Drop dies from the beating he has received and Joe has broken his left hand, so vital to his violin playing. Filled with remorse over Chocolate's death, he renounces boxing, reconciles with his father and Lorna, his former love, and hopes, as the film ends, to heal his hand and recapture his former musical skills. For Midge there is no salvation. Bloody and beaten, he lies on the canvas in the middle of the last round, until, roused by the ringside commentator's words—"Kelly's through! He's truly washed up! He's finished!"—he struggles to his feet and manages to salvage the only proof he has left that he is anything: his championship. But then he collapses and dies, alone and friendless, on his locker room floor. Even his brother is unable to dredge up any feeling of sympathy for him after he is gone.

When we see an actual fight in an arena or on television, the dimensions involved are primarily physical and psychological. The physical lies within the combatants; the psychological often within us. We like one boxer better than the other, so he's the "good guy." But that layer of meaning we apply to him may have no real basis in fact. He may be "good" because he is from the same town or state that we are, because his quotes are more attractive (or less offensive) than his opponent's; because he fought for our country in the Olympics or because he is old or young or of the right race or religion. In many ways, his "value" to us is as superficial as the home-team uniform our city's or school's football or basketball players wear; if they were to be traded or to choose another institution, they'd be they "bad guys," even though they'd have exactly the same personalities. But with the boxing film, we know more about that individual in the ring; we have lived vicariously through him for one and a half or two hours; we identify with him, even if he's flawed. If he *is* flawed, we see that this fight might be the salvation of him, so the stakes are much higher than in a real-life fight, and we desperately want him—not necessarily to win, but to do the right thing, win or lose. If he is good, we want to see that goodness validated somehow, not just in our minds but by the world depicted in that motion picture. And if he's evil, we want him not just to lose but to be punished in some way for that evil. The boxing ring, then, becomes the place where any of these things can happen, and because we have willingly suspended disbelief, we allow our happiness or sadness to hang on the kind of ending the filmmaker decides to create.

Even though, as Ronald Bergan asserts, "live sports on television or in the stadium have an unwritten screenplay of greater drama and tension than many a written one...," the fictional sports film, when properly done, can add a significant dimension: "In story-features,...the director, if successful, can make the audience react in the same manner to what they are witnessing, thus transmuting news into fable" (6). That "fable's" moral can only come about through the human drama that is depicted through the combined skills of the screenwriter, the director, the actors, the editors, and—as importantly—the scenic designer. For a fable must take "place"; and even though we take that "place" for granted when we watch a film, it is, nevertheless, conveying messages about values to us. As much as the house we live in, the car we drive, the clothes we wear, and the manners we display convey to others the kind of person we are, so are the conventions of place vital to the film's storyteller and essential to our understanding of that story's meaning.

Works Cited

Bergan, Ronald. *Sports in the Movies.* New York: Proteus, 1982.

Cook, David A. *A History of Narrative Film.* 2nd ed. New York: Norton, 1990.

Giannetti, Louis. *Understanding Movies.* 5th ed. Englewood Cliffs: 1990.

Kaminsky, Stuart. *American Film Genres: Approaches to a Critical Theory of Popular Film.* 2nd ed. Chicago: Nelson-Hall, 1985.

Solomon, Stanley J. *Beyond Formula: American Film Genres.* New York: Harcourt, 1976.

Zucker, Harvey Marc, and Lawrence J. Babich, comps. *Sports Films: A Complete Reference.* Jefferson: McFarland, 1987.

Filmography

Date	Film	Director
1939	*Golden Boy*	Rouben Mamoulian
1947	*Body and Soul*	Robert Rossen
1949	*Champion*	Mark Robson
1949	*The Set-Up*	Robert Wise
1952	*The Quiet Man*	John Ford
1956	*The Harder They Fall*	Mark Robson
1962	*Requiem for a Heavyweight*	Ralph Nelson
1976	*Rocky*	John G. Avildsen
1980	*Raging Bull*	Martin Scorsese
1985	*Rocky IV*	Sylvester Stallone

See What the Boys in the Back Room Will Have:
The Saloon in Western Films

Diana C. Reep

> A smelly saloon is my favorite place in the world.
> Scott Glenn, *Silverado*

> Spin the wheel, Eddie. I like to hear it spin.
> Joan Crawford, *Johnny Guitar*

During the first 70 years of American film history, the western film was the dominant genre. Phil Hardy's *The Encyclopedia of Western Movies* does not include silent films but still lists some 4000 westerns made between 1929 and the early 1980s. In most of these films, the saloon is a primary location—a place where characters can easily gather and where human conflicts simmer just beneath the surface noise of the clinking glasses and the thumping piano.

The saloon has been part of the western iconography from the first. One of the first "movies" was *Cripple Creek Barroom* (1898), a vignette only a few minutes long, in which assorted western types in a seedy saloon are served "red eye" by a matronly female bartender. Better known and often called the first real movie, Edwin S. Porter's *The Great Train Robbery* (1903) features a saloon in which the train robbers spend their ill-gotten loot and use their guns to force a tenderfoot to "dance."

As critics have often pointed out, westerns essentially tell the story of the American wilderness and its inevitable clash with encroaching civilization. John G. Cawelti, in *Adventure, Mystery, and Romance,* calls the western landscape "a field of action that centers upon the point of encounter between civilization and wilderness...the epic moment at which the old life and the new confront each other" (193). This wilderness, although dramatically beautiful, is open, unsettled, often barren, subject to extremes of climate, lawless, and dangerous to human life. Oncoming civilization and the inevitable restraints of law and propriety that accompany it are represented in westerns primarily by frontier towns consisting of a cluster of wooden buildings rooted in the middle of the open wilderness like a growth of aberrant cells. With the advantage of historical hindsight, we know that these harbingers of

Eastern civilization, although seemingly insignificant against the backdrop of the savage landscape, will subdue the wilderness in the end.

In a western, the frontier town, no matter how primitive, generally includes a saloon. Initially, the saloon appears to be the opposite of the surrounding wilderness because of its enclosed, sheltered space, bright lights, jostling crowds seeking drinks, cards, and women, and the pounding rhythm of the piano player. But the saloon is actually the indoor setting for the same clash of barbarism and law that is taking place on a grander scale in the outdoor setting. With its lights and music, the saloon gives the illusion of safety, a civilized oasis amid the wild dangers of the open wilderness, but after a while, we see that there are dangers inside this well lighted place in the trigger fingers of the armed men, the easy sexual promise of the bar girls, and the greed of the profiteer come West. Thus, the saloon mixes both the Eastern promise of order—as a commercial establishment providing commodities to customers—and the Western threat of unbridled lawlessness—as a gathering place for the dangerous characters on the frontier.

These forces—order and lawlessness—may clash inside the saloon just as they do in the surrounding wilderness. In *Destry Rides Again* (1939), Brian Donlevy uses his saloon for unscrupulous ends. Ranchers who drink and play cards there find themselves losing their land and homes to Donlevy as surely as if Indians had burned them out. James Stewart, as the the low-key deputy sheriff, must bring a balance of law to the saloon. Seemingly too weak to stop Donlevy, Stewart drinks milk at the bar and dances the square dance with Marlene Dietrich who is Donlevy's accomplice. However, in the end, he also successfully galvanizes the men and women in town to storm Donlevy's saloon and destroy it. Thus, in this film, the saloon's lawless elements are cleared out by the forces of civilization—the townspeople and the sheriff—and both Donlevy and Dietrich die.

The western saloon also provides the stage on which we can discern subtle degrees of savagery and civilized behavior that are not readily apparent in the wilderness. In *Bend of the River* (1952), Arthur Kennedy at first functions much as James Stewart does in the wilderness—guiding the wagon train to Portland and fighting off Indian attacks. But once in the saloon and back at the card table, Kennedy reveals an easy acceptance of killing that contrasts with Stewart's moral code even though both men have a similar outlaw past. Quick on the trigger, Kennedy shoots a crooked card dealer in the saloon as readily as he shoots the attacking Indians in the wilderness. In this film, however, shooting Indians is heroic because, in attacking the wagon train, the Indians are interfering with the process of civilizing the frontier.

Shooting a man in the saloon, however, marks Kennedy as part of the frontier brutality and indifference to progress that must be eradicated by the pioneers as they build their community.

The saloon is also the primary public meeting place when settlers first arrive. Although the church and the school are also meeting places, these buildings seldom appear until the wilderness is largely tamed; at that point, they represent civilization entrenched. The saloon, however, as the first public building, must serve virtually everyone. The fugitive outlaw, the cowboy in from the range, the fallen woman, the sheriff, the banker, the gambler, and the lawman all find their way to the welcoming bar. With this mix of western "types," the saloon becomes a microcosm of the frontier, revealing all the human elements that participated in the Western experience.

Atmosphere

The saloon is usually the only building in the frontier town with a name that is more than a simple identification of the type of business conducted inside. Saloons often have names that promise luxury and fortune—Portland Palace, House of Fortune, Rainbow Saloon, The French Palace, the Alhambra. Other times, the saloon names reveal a self-awareness of the temptations offered inside—The Last Gasp, the Dirty Shame Saloon, The Last Chance Saloon, the Sazerac Saloon, The Road to Ruin. As a private enterprise, the saloon may be named for its owner—Vienna's, Hank's, Mama Malone's, Honest Harry's Chance. The saloon name may also have a local reference as, for example, The Black Nugget in a mining camp, The Long Branch in cattle country, or The Northern in Alaska.

As the names indicate, saloons in westerns are not all alike. While the western landscape looks much the same in film after film—with the burning sands, rugged mountains, sagebrush, winding streams or raging rivers, and the familiar buttes and mesas of Monument Valley—the saloon retains an individual character.

Some saloons represent a level of civilization just barely above the wild open land surrounding them. In *McCabe and Mrs. Miller* (1971), the first saloon we see in the northwest mining town of Presbyterian Church is Sheehan's Saloon and Hotel, an incredibly dirty shack with smokey oil lamps and a grubby bar. The "hotel" is a loft above the bar with several dirty bunks to be shared by the guests. The town itself consists only of a series of shacks perched on a sea of mud, requiring men to walk from place to place over wooden planks and to cross the stream to Sheehan's over a precarious wooden plank bridge. The saloon, in all its filth, is the only place offering human companionship in the midst of this rough country. In *Young Guns* (1988), the outlaws stop at a saloon which is a one-room roadside shack not actually in a town at all. A cow grazes outside while inside a lone prostitute works amid smoke and grime. In *River of No Return* (1954), Marilyn Monroe sings atop a piano in a tent saloon during a gold mining boom. And in *Silver River* (1948), Errol Flynn starts his drive to wealth by destroying and robbing a tent saloon set up outside an army camp. Customers in the saloon in *The Westerner* (1940) line up at a bar made of boards resting on large kegs, and they drink whiskey that, when spilled on the bar, eats into the wood. Primitive as these places are, the saloons offer the first semblance of civilized living in the rough frontier territory and serve the human need to congregate.

As the town grows larger, the saloon takes on more of the "dress" of Eastern establishments. Paneled walls, polished bar, spittoons, mirrors, paintings of nude women, chandeliers, spinning roulette wheels, bartenders in white shirts, and entertainment all imply the increasing influence of civilized tastes. The saloon, as town entertainment center, begins to offer more than the simple drink of raw whiskey. In *Gunsmoke in Tucson* (1958), Gale Robbins, in a lowcut dancehall dress, sings "I Need a Man" to the attentive men leaning on the bar. In *The Spoilers* (1942), dancers and a barbershop quartet perform on a proscenium stage with some of the audience seated in private boxes. Mae West in *My Little Chickadee* (1940) sings on a full stage with an orchestra while W.C. Fields serves drinks in the adjoining bar. In *Heller in Pink Tights* (1960), Sophia Loren's theatrical troupe puts on its version of classical drama in a saloon that includes a full theater and museum. Both *The Mississippi Gambler* (1952) and *The Gambler from Natchez* (1954) are set on the Mississippi River, the eastern edge of the frontier territory. In these films, the saloons are lavishly furnished casinos with customers in evening dress, dining rooms for ladies, and soft background music for the high stakes gambling. Although none of these Eastern refinements totally eliminates the Western lawlessness inherent in the saloon, the increasingly luxurious atmosphere reflects the decline of the primitive forces of the frontier.

The emotional mood established in the saloon setting sometimes mirrors the tensions in the film. The saloon that appears in the opening of *Duel in the Sun* (1946) pulsates with the rhythm of the pounding drums that accompany the sensuous wild dance of the Indian woman performing atop the four-sided bar in the center of the huge hall. Thick smoke hovers over the card games in the alcoves, and an enormous wheel of fortune spins in front of shouting customers. The saloon here is sexually dangerous—Herbert Marshall will not let his daughter, Jennifer Jones, enter it even though her mother is the dancer on the bar. An aura of sexual desire and violence emanates from the provocative dance and the dancer's casual faithlessness as she leaves with a customer. Shortly afterward, Marshall kills both his wife and her lover. This saloon, seen only once, previews the film's theme of uncontrolled sexual desires and the inescapable violence that follows such desires.

The saloons in *The Shootist* (1976) and *The Gunfighter* (1950) are quiet men's clubs, reflecting the established law and order that has left aging gunfighters John Wayne and Gregory Peck without a place in the changing West. The saloon in *Cat Ballou* (1965) consists of a few tables in the general store where elderly gunfighters and hostesses linger as shadows of their own past and symbolize Jane Fonda's inability to find the wild West she has read about. Vienna's Saloon in *Johnny Guitar* (1954) has no customers. The dealers stand behind empty tables; no one plays the piano. Joan Crawford has built her saloon outside of town, on land she intends to sell to the coming railroad. The saloon's emptiness and isolation from the town mirrors Crawford's isolation from the townspeople as she sets herself against them.

Violence

"It's always a mess after a killing," the saloon owner in *Gunfight at the O.K. Corral* (1957) remarks after Kirk Douglas kills Lee Van Cleef with a knife. Killing happens frequently in the Western saloon where the potential for death lurks at every card table. If the wilderness is dangerous because of hostile Indians and the natural risks inherent in every stream, mountain, and desert, the saloon is perhaps more dangerous because human passions are concentrated in that defined space. A game of poker, a woman's smile, a stranger coming through the swinging doors—these are the natural hazards the saloon customer faces. Violence comes to individuals by random chance; groups of men fight political or territorial battles; law and order clash regularly in the small-scale Armageddon of the saloon. So natural is violence in the saloon that in the science fiction film *Westworld* (1973), vacationing Richard Benjamin discovers that one of the popular features of the robot-populated Western theme park is the opportunity for a shootout in the saloon—where the guest always outdraws the robot.

Gambling, always a risky enterprise, carries the threat of death whether one wins or loses. Arthur Kennedy in *Bend of the River* (1952) and Robert Walker in *Young Billy Young* (1969) casually shoot the men they catch cheating in card games. When Kevin McCarthy loses his plantation to Dale Robertson in *The Gambler from Natchez* (1954), he attacks Robertson and dies in the ensuing sword fight—the Mississippi River version of the quick draw. In *The Mississippi Gambler* (1952), Dennis Weaver kills himself after losing his employer's funds in a poker game, and successful gambler Tyrone Power is attacked by a disgruntled loser with a knife.

The plot of *5 Card Stud* (1968) revolves around the afterhours poker game in Mama Malone's Saloon when one man is caught cheating and the furious players immediately drag him outside and hang him. One by one, the poker players then begin to die mysteriously while those still alive meet in the saloon at the original poker table to try to identify the killer who is stalking them. Robert Mitchum, the new preacher in town, exacts revenge for his brother's hanging and finally kills all the card players only to be killed in turn by Dean Martin who did not sit in on the fatal poker hand. The haphazard violence of the first killing—hanging the poker cheat—segues into the systematic killing of the poker players by Mitchum until Martin, a professional gambler, ends the cycle with one more killing. The gambler here enforces order and restores balance to the saloon.

Competition over women sometimes brings quick death in a saloon. Gregory Peck goads Charles Bickford into drawing his gun and then kills him in *Duel in the Sun* (1946) because Bickford has become engaged to Jennifer Jones, and Peck wants her for himself. William Campbell kills a saloon drunk who approaches Jeanne Crain in *Man Without a Star* (1955), and a young thug guns down an old man in *The Good Guys and the Bad Guys* (1969) because Marie Windsor will drink with the old man but not with the young one.

The lone gunfighter stopping in the saloon for a quiet drink probably has too much survival experience to become embroiled in a crooked card game or an argument over a woman. However, he usually cannot get that drink until he has killed someone—often a stranger looking for the notoriety that comes from killing a well known gunfighter. In *Young Guns* (1988), Emilio Estevez kills men in two saloons when they brag how they plan to kill Billy the Kid, not realizing that they are facing him. Jack Buetel, also playing Billy the Kid, kills a stranger in a saloon when the man draws on him (*The Outlaw,* 1943). Gregory Peck in *The Gunfighter* (1950) kills one challenger in a saloon but later is shot in the back leaving another saloon. Ex-gunfighter Glenn Ford in *Heaven With a Gun* (1968) discovers that he cannot easily escape his reputation when an old prison cellmate challenges him in Carolyn Jones' saloon. The two draw on each other under a card table with Ford proving that he is still the faster. Clint Eastwood in *The*

Outlaw Josey Wales (1976) kills a bounty hunter who finds him in a saloon in a ghost town.

Brawls among saloon customers often mirror the conflicts raging outside the saloon. In *Dodge City* (1939), Bruce Bennett's saloon is torn apart when one group of men begins to sing "Dixie" while the other group sings "Marching Through Georgia." The ensuing riot recreates the Civil War in miniature and accelerates the conflict between Bennett and Errol Flynn, the leader of the Southerners. In *Destry Rides Again* (1939), the saloon battle is over ownership of land as the townspeople, including women brandishing clubs, attack the dishonest saloon owner Brian Donlevy and his men.

The saloon may also be the battleground for the hero who singlehandedly must fight the forces of evil. In *Copper Canyon* (1950), Ray Milland comes to the defense of beleaguered copper miners who are being robbed of their mines by MacDonald Carey and others. Milland shoots it out with Carey in Hope Emerson's saloon and then quickly dispatches the other outlaws. The famous fistfight in *The Spoilers* (1942) between independent miner John Wayne and corrupt gold commissioner Randolph Scott reflects the struggle individual citizens must make to protect their rights. Wayne wins the fight on behalf of all the miners.

In *Shane* (1953), gunfighter Alan Ladd takes on the struggle of the farmers versus the cattlemen who want to run them off the range. The saloon in town is attached to the general store—the place for men to have a drink while women shop. But the cattlemen control the saloon, and farmers risk death if they enter. When Ladd walks into the saloon to buy a soda for Brandon De Wilde, Ben Johnson tells him to go back to the store where "it's safe." Gunfighter Jack Palance, hired by the cattlemen, loiters in the saloon while he plans to kill Van Heflin and the other farmers. By his presence, Palance also is holding the saloon as cattlemen's territory in the same way the ranchers hope to hold the range against intrusion by farmers. Later, Palance kills a farmer trying to enter the saloon for a drink and, thus, precipitates the final confrontation with Ladd. Although the film's conflict centers on land, the freedom to patronize the saloon becomes the symbol of the larger struggle, and Ladd's battle with Palance inevitably comes in the saloon where the two gunfighters—neither one actually cattleman or farmer—face each other. Ladd kills Palance, foreshadowing the future victory of the farmers and freeing the saloon from domination by the cattle ranchers.

The saloon as killing ground exemplifies the frontier clash between the Eastern values of restraint, consensus, and negotiation and the Western values of independence and spontaneous action. In *Shane* (1954), the struggle is between farmers who want to fence and plow the land and ranchers who want unrestricted access to the land for their herds. The final shootout, which defeats the ranchers, reinforces the Eastern values and "frees" the saloon from domination by Western forces who want to prevent cultivation of the land. In *Duel in the Sun* (1946), the opposite occurs when Gregory Peck kills Charles Bickford who is planning to marry and raise a family. Here Eastern values are at least temporarily defeated by Peck, a man who indulges every primitive impulse. The saloon in these films provides the arena in which the confrontation between social order and lawlessness can be played out.

Women

Philip French comments in his study of the western that women traditionally have appeared in the genre either as the pure pioneer heroine or as the sexually available saloon girl. Cawelti in *The Six-Gun Mystique* calls women "the primary symbols of civilization" (47) because they bring with them domestic order, schools and churches, and rejection of violence as a means of settling disputes. Cawelti's symbols of civilization are the pure heroines who eschew the saloons that are full of pending violence and accessible vice. The women of the saloons—bar girls, singers, or even owners—imply prostitution, the unrestrained sexuality that is the female version of male violence and, therefore, represents a kind of frontier lawlessness that the forces of civilization intend to eliminate.

Occasionally the pure woman enters the saloon, but, clearly, she does not belong there. When Cathy Downs, just off the Eastern stage and dressed primly in a high collared dress and a wide brimmed hat, enters the saloon looking for Victor Mature in *My Darling Clementine* (1946), she obviously represents a new level of civilization for Tombstone, contrasting sharply with Linda Darnell, the saloon singer dressed in a lowcut blouse.

The famous hair-pulling fight between Una Merkel and Marlene Dietrich in *Destry Rides Again* (1939) occurs when Merkel marches furiously into the saloon because Dietrich, who cheats at cards, has won Merkel's husband's pants in a card game. The battling women draw a cheering mob of male onlookers, but their fight ends in a draw when James Stewart throws water on the combatants after they have thrashed around the floor. That Merkel would even enter the saloon shows how seriously she takes the situation.

On occasion, the woman in a saloon may be a mother figure as is Linda Hunt in *Silverado* (1985) when she listens sympathetically to the cowboys' stories, serves "good stuff" (unwatered whiskey) to her favorites, and persuades corrupt sheriff Brian Dennehy to think twice about killing his enemies. As the masculine violence escalates, however, Hunt's motherly influence wanes.

The saloon, where Western brutality exists side by side with Eastern manners, is not decent enough for a pure woman. Further, a truly good woman is always in the home because her appropriate place is the domestic realm and the private life. The saloon is public. For a woman in a western film, public life in a saloon usually means earning a living through her sexuality. Further the saloon woman is independent and not under the protection of a husband, father, or brother, as is the pure woman. Since independence in a woman erodes purity, the woman in the saloon is always sexually tainted.

The stigma of the saloon is apparent in *Virginia City* (1940). When Errol Flynn and Miriam Hopkins meet on a three-week stagecoach journey, Flynn falls in love with the ladylike Hopkins, but she disappears without a word when they reach Virginia City. Wandering into the smoke-filled Sazerac Saloon, Flynn is shocked to find Hopkins singing and dancing on stage, displaying her legs to a crowd of shouting gold miners. Flynn's amazement clearly shows the accepted division between good women and saloon women. Even more significantly, his manner toward Hopkins, so respectful on the stagecoach, becomes familiar and casual in the saloon. When Hopkins is revealed to be a Confederate spy who is working in the saloon only to gain information about Union operations, her patriotism, albeit for a lost cause, somewhat mitigates her status as fallen woman, and she and Flynn eventually find happiness.

Women who have been tarnished by their contact with saloon life may sometimes be redeemed and restored to the private domestic life. In *Bend of the River* (1952), Jay C. Flippen leaves his daughter, Julia Adams, who has been wounded in an Indian attack, in Portland for recovery and continues with the wagon train to the farming country they plan to settle. On his return to fetch Adams, Flippen knows at once she has fallen sexually (with Arthur Kennedy) because he finds her working in a saloon, managing the gold scales where miners exchange gold for currency. Later, Adams realizes that Kennedy is morally corrupt, and she turns to James Stewart who has supported the pioneers in their efforts to build a settlement. Adams is forgiven her sexual lapse and rejoins the farming community with Stewart who obviously is destined to be her husband. In this film, Adams has the advantage of a loving family. Most women in saloons are on their own.

Marilyn Monroe in *River of No Return* (1954) exemplifies the fallen woman who must be rescued from the saloon because she has no way to free herself. As the film opens, Monroe is singing in a tent saloon in a gold mining camp. She pins her hopes on her lover Rory Calhoun's promise to marry her and take her away, but he leaves her with Robert Mitchum after he steals Mitchum's horse and gun. After a harrowing raft trip down river and Calhoun's death at the hands of Mitchum's young son, Monroe has no option but to return to saloon life to earn her living. As she enters the swinging doors of the Black Nugget Saloon, she glances back wistfully. The film ends when Mitchum strides through those swinging doors and sweeps Monroe off the piano and out into his wagon, rescuing her from her saloon life and taking her home to his farm. Monroe tosses her red shoes into the mud as they drive away. She has held on to those shoes, symbols of her public sexuality, through the perilous journey down river. Now she has been rescued by the right man and can reserve her sexuality for the private life.

Young Billy Young (1969) duplicates this rescue pattern with Angie Dickinson as the singer who wants to be free of the saloon and its owner Jack Kelly who beats her. At the end of the film, Robert Mitchum strides into the Gaslight Saloon and throws Dickinson over his shoulder, taking her out of the saloon and into the respectable—and private—life of a wife. This scene, which duplicates the final scene in *River of No Return* (1954), emphasizes the woman's inability to leave the saloon herself. She must be rescued by a man capable of protecting her.

Although Angie Dickinson in *Rio Bravo* (1959) tells John Wayne that she enjoys earning a living as a saloon gambler, she spends most of her time making his life comfortable and herself indispensable to him. At the end of the film, she models the skimpy outfit she says she will wear to work in the saloon, hoping that Wayne will forbid her to wear it. He does forbid her, thus reserving Dickinson's sexuality for himself in marriage. For these fallen women, the saloon provides an uneasy security, and the women's innate purity shows in their desire to escape the saloon life and reserve themselves for only one man.

Some women in saloons, however, find power through their sexuality and do not want to give that power up. Mae West in *My Little Chickadee* (1940), for example, refuses two marriage proposals in order to remain a saloon singer. West stops all action in the saloon when she enters and walks slowly through the room to ascend the huge split staircase to the stage where she sings with a full orchestra. West enjoys the public gaze of the saloon and the control she has over the men who applaud her.

In *Gunfight at the O.K. Corral* (1957) Rhonda Fleming plays poker better than most men. Her attractiveness, however, brings the usual problems of unwanted attention. When Burt Lancaster, the sheriff, has to talk a drunk out of shooting someone over Fleming, he arrests her because the saloon has a "no women" policy. Lancaster tells her she has no reason to be treated as a lady when she is in a saloon "playing a man's game." Later, he relents and allows her to play poker in a side room. Fleming has built her gambling reputation through success at the tables, and she refuses to accept restrictions that spring from the Eastern concept of women's rightful place in the home.

Women in saloons also have power through their acceptance of male violence as the way to settle conflicts. Although perhaps not personally violent, women in saloons may direct male violence in ways useful to themselves. Rather than appearing vulnerable and needing rescue as Monroe does, women who tolerate male violence have a dangerous edge that can be attractive but also cautionary.

In *Copper Canyon* (1950), Hedy Lamarr is a saloon gambler and the lover of MacDonald Carey, a corrupt deputy sheriff. Lamarr and Carey are trying to seize control of copper mines owned by a group of Southerners who have come to the West after the Civil War. Carey does the killing, but Lamarr joins the strategy sessions. When her romantic attention turns to Ray Milland, a traveling showman and ex-Confederate officer who is helping the miners, Lamarr quickly rejects Carey and helps Milland kill him by dropping the saloon chandelier on Carey when he and Milland are facing each other. She and Milland then move on to San Francisco and presumably bigger saloons.

Marlene Dietrich is the singer in Brian Donlevy's saloon in *Destry Rides Again* (1939) who helps him cheat ranchers at the card tables, swindling them out of their land. When she falls in love with James Stewart, the new deputy sheriff, she changes loyalties and in the end takes the bullet Donlevy means for Stewart. Dietrich dies because she has turned her back on lawlessness, and yet she cannot marry Stewart who epitomizes Eastern values. Dietrich's illegal activities centered in the saloon put her at odds with Stewart's moral codes, and her intense sexuality and unremorseful display of power make her unsuitable domestic material.

For some women, saloons bring out their natural entrepreneurial talents. Julie Christie in *McCabe and Mrs. Miller* (1971) talks Warren Beatty into taking her on as a partner to run the brothel connected to the new saloon he is building. Christie directs the design of the new saloon, demanding paneled walls, mirrors and a level of refinement well above the dirty shacks the town has had thus far. She insists that the men bathe before visiting her prostitutes (Beatty owns the bath house) and takes over the bookkeeping because Beatty cannot handle the accounts. She is also smart enough to know that Beatty cannot outbargain the men who want to buy his saloon, and she warns him that he is facing disaster. Christie's power here stems from her understanding of the forces involved in saloon life and her ability to balance them. Most important, in her control of the saloon and the brothel, Christie is the antithesis of proper womanhood and not at all a symbol of coming civilization.

In *The Spoilers* (1942), the gold miners look to Marlene Dietrich, owner of The Northern Saloon, for help when they are threatened by corrupt gold commissioner Randolph Scott. John Wayne whips Scott in the film's spectacular fistfight, but it is Dietrich who first suspects Scott's dishonesty, who breaks Wayne out of jail, and who keeps Scott in her rooms above the saloon until Wayne arrives to confront him. Dietrich in this film uses her powerful sexuality to combat Scott and the other government officials bent on illegal seizures of mining property; therefore, she supports law and order although she herself represents women who have a public life and lack the "appropriate" dominance of men.

Joan Crawford in *Johnny Guitar* (1954) shows an extreme portrait of the powerful woman in the saloon. Crawford's saloon is on land that she intends to sell to the railroad for enormous profit. The townspeople oppose her plans and her saloon. In this film, the saloon is Crawford's fortress, which she holds in defiance of the opposing townspeople. Her only support is from gunfighter Sterling Hayden, a past lover, and a local desperado, Scott Brady who is a current lover. Crawford wears pants and puts on a gun to protect her territory, but she uses her sexuality to keep Hayden and Brady at her side. When a posse from town—all dressed in black—arrive at the saloon to accuse Crawford of aiding Brady in a bank robbery, Crawford, dressed in white, tells them the saloon is closed and orders them out. Mercedes McCambridge, maniacal in her hatred for Crawford and her repressed sexual longing for Brady (or perhaps for Crawford), burns down the saloon in a spectacular blaze signaling the end of Crawford's power. Crawford survives by killing McCambridge in a gunfight after McCambridge has shot Brady. The film ends with Crawford and Hayden in an embrace, indicating a new start, but clearly Crawford has not willingly given up her saloon and the power it represented for her. This film reverses the usual western film conventions by making McCambridge, the pure woman, fiendish in her quest to destroy the saloon while Crawford, the fallen woman, rejects violence when Hayden offers to shoot the posse members.

For women in the western film, the saloon represents primarily Western lawlessness—that is, the unstrained sexuality of independent women without the constraint of a dominant male. Eastern values for women are outside the saloon in the traditional roles of wife and mother, roles that are subject to the control of a husband and out of the public view.

Community Center

Since the saloon is usually the only meeting place in town until churches and schools arrive, it is often the site of varied activities. In *My Darling Clementine* (1946), for example, Victor Mature performs surgery on Linda Darnell after she has been shot. The saloon turns into an operating room with Darnell lying on two card tables pushed together and whiskey used as the anesthetic.

Civic business may also be conducted in the saloon. Hank's Saloon in *The Man Who Shot Liberty Valance* (1962) is the setting of the town's first election meeting to send representatives to the Capital City statehood convention. Edmund O'Brien, the town newspaperman and habitual drunk, repeatedly asks for a drink while they debate, but John Wayne tells him "The bar is closed." When the election is over, Wayne announces, "The bar is open." In this instance, the Eastern impulse for established government is on the rise and Western debauchery clearly must give way. In other films, the burgeoning civic action in the saloon is not always so successful.

In The Spoilers (1942), John Wayne loses his gold claim in a sham courtroom session conducted by a dishonest judge in the saloon. Walter Brennan as Judge Roy Bean conducts court from behind the bar of his saloon while pouring whiskey in *The Westerner* (1940). Brennan plays cards with the "jury" before they reach a verdict, which he directs. Tony Perkins in *The Tin Star* (1957) tries without success to gather deputies from the crowd in the saloon; instead the saloon patrons form a mob, intent on lynching Perkins' prisoners.

When the saloon is the center for successful civic action, the Eastern values of order and lawful government are clearly becoming dominant as in *The Man Who Shot Liberty Valance* (1962). When support for Eastern values fails, as in the crooked trial in The Spoilers (1942), the struggle between the two forces is still not resolved. The trial in the saloon may imitate the civilized pattern, but the judge and jury are on the side of lawlessness, thereby thwarting justice.

End of the Trail

The gunfighter in westerns is a man isolated from others because of his exceptional ability to kill. He may kill for money or for principle, but in the end he moves on alone after his work is finished. Thus, Alan Ladd in *Shane* (1953) heads for the mountains; Henry Fonda in *My Darling Clementine* (1946) says goodbye to Cathy Downs; Clint Eastwood rides out of town in *Fistful of Dollars* (1964).

The gunfighter, of course, embodies Western savagery and lawlessness since, in his isolation and frequent killing, he is the direct opposite of the pioneers who gather together in communities and embrace government and law. Cawelti in *The Six-Gun Mystique* points out that when the hero of a western film is a gunfighter, the hero has "internalized the conflict between savagery and civilization," and the gunfighter, while he protects and saves the pioneers, also realizes that his own personal qualities are "bound up with the wilderness life" (55). If the gunfighter cannot or will not be assimilated into the community where he must abandon his independent will and natural combativeness, then he reaches middle age tired, lonely, and a target for every young punk seeking a reputation. Once the pioneers subdue the wilderness and develop the towns into bustling communities, the saloon, which contains the last vestiges of the Western ethic, may be the only place where the gunfighter feels he belongs.

In *The Shootist* (1976), John Wayne is an aging gunfighter dying of cancer. Although his reputation still inspires awe, he is a relic of the old West, obviously out of place amid Carson City's trolleys and milk delivery wagons. The Metropole Saloon reflects the turn of the century in its glass doors, dining tables with waiters in white shirts and garters, huge bar, and tile floors. However, a contentious patron may still be shot with impunity if he draws first. Wayne chooses the Metropole as the place where he can direct his own destiny. He sends word to three old enemies to meet him there, and in the final gunfight, he kills them all before he is shot in the back by the bartender. For Wayne, quick death in the saloon is preferable to slow death by cancer. He relies on the Western principles of independent action and personal violence that are still present in the saloon to help him find release.

In *Warlock* (1959), Henry Fonda and Anthony Quinn are gunfighters who are hired by the townspeople of Warlock to rid them of a gang of thugs. Fonda and Quinn also deal faro in the local saloon as a way to supplement their incomes. When the longtime partners have a falling out over Fonda's decision to marry Dolores Michaels and settle down, an enraged Quinn, unable to face the end of the partnership, takes the saloon and its customers hostage. Fonda is forced to kill Quinn, thus supporting order but violating personal friendship. In a Western version of a Viking funeral, Fonda lays Quinn out on the dice table and then burns down the saloon with Quinn's body inside. Realizing that he does not fit in the tame life Michaels offers, Fonda rides out of town alone.

The Gunfighter (1950) centers on Gregory Peck's long wait in a saloon to see the wife and son he left behind years before. Peck, a famous gunfighter, has killed a young gun who challenged him in another saloon. Staying ahead of the boy's avenging brothers, Peck stops in the town where his family lives and waits in the saloon, hoping his wife will see him. As word spreads that the legendary gunfighter is in town, curious crowds gather outside the saloon and children play hooky from school to peek under the swinging doors. Peck is now a curiosity, almost a prisoner in the saloon—the only place where he is welcome. His family typifies Eastern values—his wife is the town schoolteacher—and Peck's presence endangers them, so he cannot stay. After a brief visit, Peck is gunned down while leaving the saloon by another young punk seeking glory. In this film, Peck's wandering life over the Western landscape is broken only by his stops in saloons—he is not acceptable anywhere else.

As gunfighter Doc Holliday, Kirk Douglas in *Gunfight at the O.K. Corral* (1957) is dying of tuberculosis and spends his time in the saloon gambling. Douglas is hoping that he will not have to wait for the tuberculosis to kill him as he eagerly rises to every fight in the saloon. His skill, however, makes it difficult for someone to kill him. After he survives the famous battle at the O.K. Corral, Douglas returns to the saloon and joins another card game, still waiting for death.

After the settlers have made significant changes in the landscape and tamed the wilderness by imposing Eastern values of law and community life, the saloons in these films provide the only haven for the gunfighters whose time has passed.

Conclusion

Peter Homans, in his analysis of western films, comments that the saloon is the most important building in town because it is the gathering place for all the characters and the site of the final shootout between hero and villain. But another building might serve that purpose if the writers directed the story in that way.

The saloon is the most important building in the western because it is the most complex, accommodating as it does both the forces of civilization and of lawlessness. Without the saloon, the wilderness, dangerous and uncontrolled, would be symbolized only by the open landscape—floods, blizzards, mountains, deserts, snakes, and wild animals—surrounding the vulnerable frontier town. Civilization, settled and organized, would be symbolized perhaps by the town's single-purpose commercial buildings, such as the general store. The saloon brings the forces of East and West together in the one commercial building that may serve as battleground or as election site, depending on which force is dominant.

Further, by containing both forces at the same time, the saloon reveals how thin the line is between civilized life and barbarism. The saloon's promise of civilized refuge from the wilderness and its dangers is tenuous at best. The Eastern elements of civilized life—liquor, women, gambling, commercial profit—may trigger the savagery emblematic of the untamed West at any moment. While one drink of whiskey may be comforting, too many will strip the veneer of civilized behavior from any patron at the bar. Female companionship as offered in the saloon violates the concept of monogamy and family, the values that are central to settling the frontier territory. In games of chance, customers and saloonkeepers may pass the time companionably, or they may crave excessive gains and turn to violence.

In the complex world of the saloon, the forces of law and savagery play out the same confrontation that is occurring on the territorial landscape. The saloon symbolically contains that moment of encounter between Eastern law and Western violence. The evolving appearance of the saloon from dirty shack to glittering casino reflects the rise of social order in the frontier, the change from savagery to civilization that, in some measure, is at the heart of every Western film.

Works Cited

Cawelti, John G. *Adventure, Mystery, and Romance.* Chicago: U of Chicago P, 1976.

_____. *The Six-Gun Mystique.* Bowling Green, OH: Bowling Green State University Popular Press, 1970.

French, Philip. *Westerns, Aspects of a Movie Genre.* New York: Oxford UP, 1977.

Hardy, Phil. *The Encyclopedia of Western Movies.* Minneapolis: Woodbury, 1984.

Homans, Peter. "Puritanism Revisited: An Analysis of the Contemporary Screen-Image Western." *Studies in Public Communication* 3 (Summer 1961): 73-84.

Filmography

Because the saloon probably appears at least briefly in 90 percent of the thousands of western films produced since *Cripple Creek Barroom* (1898), directed by W.K.L. Dickson, the following is a selected list of films in which the saloon is the location of significant actions or characters in the stories. Not included are silent films, which are not readily available for viewing, serials, or "modern" westerns set after World War I because the saloon then becomes the modern bar, a location requiring a separate study.

Year	Film	Director
1939	*Destry Rides Again*	George Marshall
1939	*Dodge City*	Michael Curtiz
1940	*My Little Chickadee*	Edward F. Cline
1940	*Virginia City*	Michael Curtiz
1940	*The Westerner*	William Wyler
1941	*Western Union*	Fritz Lang
1942	*The Spoilers*	Ray Enright
1943	*The Outlaw*	Howard Hughes
1946	*Duel in the Sun*	King Vidor
1946	*My Darling Clementine*	John Ford
1948	*The Paleface*	Norman Z. McLeod
1948	*Silver River*	Raoul Walsh
1950	*Copper Canyon*	John Farrow
1950	*The Gunfighter*	Henry King
1952	*Bend in the River*	Anthony Mann
1952	*The Big Trees*	Felix Feist
1952	*Rancho Notorious*	Fritz Lang
1953	*The Mississippi Gambler*	Randolph Mate
1953	*Shane*	George Stevens
1954	*The Gambler from Natchez*	Henry Levin
1954	*Johnny Guitar*	Nicholas Ray
1954	*River of No Return*	Otto Preminger
1955	*Man Without a Star*	King Vidor
1956	*Dakota Incident*	Lewis R. Foster
1957	*Gunfight at the O.K. Corral*	John Sturges
1957	*The Tin Star*	Anthony Mann
1958	*Gunsmoke in Tucson*	Thomas Carr
1959	*Rio Bravo*	Howard Hawks
1959	*Warlock*	Edward Dmytryk
1960	*Heller in Pink Tights*	George Cukor
1962	*The Man Who Shot Liberty Valance*	John Ford
1964	*A Fistful of Dollars*	Sergio Leone
1965	*Cat Ballou*	Elliot Silverstein
1967	*Hang 'Em High*	Ted Post
1968	*5 Card Stud*	Henry Hathaway
1968	*Heaven With a Gun*	Lee H. Katzin
1969	*The Good Guys and the Bad Guys*	Burt Kennedy
1969	*Young Billy Young*	Burt Kennedy
1971	*McCabe and Mrs. Miller*	Robert Altman
1973	*Westworld*	Michael Crichton
1976	*The Outlaw Josey Wales*	Clint Eastwood
1976	*The Shootist*	Don Siegel
1985	*Silverado*	Lawrence Kasdan
1988	*Young Guns*	Christopher Cain

Private Arenas
and
Commonplace
Spaces

Last Bastion of Masculinity:
Men's Rooms in American Popular Film

Linda K. Fuller

Now that their country clubs, private organizations, even their sports locker rooms are legally accessible by women, just about the only place men have left for their "business"—with maybe the exception of Congress, some might argue—is men's rooms. That locale is celebrated, it is discovered, in any number of movies, especially in the 1980s. As a direct backlash against female encroachment, men's rooms in American popular film become the locus for any number of scenarios.

But perhaps the starting point for this essay should be to answer what may be a question you are asking yourself: what is a woman doing, writing about this topic? As a feminist, I consider it a question always to be confronted in academic research; in this instance, as I allude to in the book's Dedication, I have many men in my life, both personally (husband, sons, relatives) and professionally, and they are the ones, in fact, who originally pointed how often men's rooms are featured in film. Lana F. Rakow, writing about "Feminist approaches to popular culture: Giving patriarchy its due" (Rakow 19-41), has argued that while popular culture plays a critical role in patriarchal society, the canon of debaters contains no women, and that the analysis of social power there warrants their input in ongoing discussions. Place and places, for feminists, are important predominantly in terms of experiential and perceptual responses of readers, viewers, listeners, speakers, even filmgoers.

Men's rooms, it turns out, are newsworthy of late. In 1989, *Rolling Stone* voted them the "Hot Location" of the year. The guest column "About Men" of the Sunday *New York Times Magazine* section featured an article entitled "The Men's Room" in the Fall of 1991 (Markulin 30+). And the City Council of Santa Monica, California recently passed an ordinance pronouncing it illegal for men to use women's restrooms or for women to use men's restrooms (except in cases of "urgent necessity")—following "reports of men loitering inside public lavatories to sell drugs or commit lewd acts" (Greene 15).

Aimed primarily at women, Virginia Woolf's 1933 book promoting "A Room of One's Own" has relevance to this day. In this era of working toward equality, it would seem that men should also be allowed their own "space."

Men's rooms in motion pictures most typically are depicted as places of secrecy, where confidences can be exchanged, or where one can seek solace. As early as the original 1972 *The Godfather*, Al Pacino as Michael Corleone, son of the Mafia leader, is instructed to prove his manhood by going into the restaurant bathroom, then "come out shooting." He uses that time in the men's room to gain composure, to calm himself over his agonizing decision to comply. The hero in Roman Polanski's *Frantic* (1988) also has a coming-to-terms with self in the men's room, where he sees himself in the mirror and is appalled at the image projected there. Earlier in the thriller, a Jamaican leads the Harrison Ford character into a bathroom to show him The White Lady—coke, when he thought he was being directed to his missing wife. It's that same notion of trying to get oneself together that Kevin Costner as a morally upright naval hero tries out in the suspense thriller *No Way Out* (1987).

Drug deals in the secrecy of the men's room is also the theme of *The Principal* (1987), where James Belushi in the title role is a renegade sent to lead a high school of hardship cases. At one point, someone is in the bathroom, masked, waiting to attack a teacher—but Belushi intervenes. *To Live and Die in L.A.* (1985) finds the drug dealer fugitive from justice getting caught and busted in the airport men's room.

Two soldiers are cleaning the men's room in Stanley Kubrick's *Full Metal Jacket* (1987), where their secret conversation centers on concern over Fat Leonard, a Private who has been talking to his rifle. As audience, we quickly understand that this intimate sharing really implies their own personal concerns as to whether or not they can handle the war situation. Later, on watch in Vietnam, one of them opens the door to The Head and finds Leonard sitting there with his gun, loading bullets. "I am in a world of shit," he proclaims, then freaks out. The Sargeant arrives, demanding, "What is your major malfunction, numb nut? Didn't Mummy and Daddy give you enough attention when you were a child?" That comment earns him the full metal jacket—bullets of death. "Too easy, man," says the soldier, who then sits down on the toilet and shoots himself.

Secret conversations in men's rooms also figure in other films of the 1980s. Eddie Murphy as the uproarious street hustler Agent Orange in *Trading Places* (1983), who gets groomed to take over Dan Aykroyd's role as a financial wizard, is sitting in the bathroom sneaking a joint when he hears Ralph Bellamy and Don Ameche discuss the whole scheme: "We took a perfectly useless psychopath and made him successful, and a successful man gone mad. Do you really believe I'd have a Nigger running the company?" Maybe the men's room works like our subconscious: we only allow disclosure of our racism when and where we think we can get away with it.

Another interesting conversation takes place in a men's room in *Barton Fink* (1991) when John Turturro as the film's title character, a 1930's-style Hollywood would-be scriptwriter, stands at a urinal when he is distracted by loud groaning noises. Out from a stall comes P. Mayhew (John Mahoney), a famous writer, who acknowledges him simply with, "Sorry about the odor." Barton Fink wants to make a connection—he's suffering writer's block, and has been told to talk to other writers. But right now Mayhew is too busy: "I've got drinkin' to do," he says, offering a swig of his "social lubricant." Yet, he suggests Fink stop by sometime at his bungalow. This first meeting would lead to others.

Robocop (1987), a futuristic super-hero based on the idea of a 24-hour security system, has a scene where one needs to insert special cards to enter the men's room. This conversational confrontation is overheard there: "You've insulted me, and insulted this corporation. You've fucked with the wrong guy." The result—a hired killer and lots of screen violence.

Two professors share intimate thoughts with one another on the "publish or perish" game in the college men's room in *D.O.A.* (1988), an update of the 1949 film noir. Ultimately, that information is used against the Dennis Quaid character, who discovers too late that his confidante has jealously poisoned his liquor.

A more amusing conversation in the men's room is exchanged by the unlikely *Twins* (1988), Jules (Arnold Schwarzenegger) and Vince (Danny DeVito). They leave their dates to go, giggle, flush at the same time, and then share true confessions at the urinals. After the exchange, Arnold reaches down, hoists up his half-pint sibling, and hugs him. Another customer enters, looks over at them disgustedly, and they retort in unison, "We're brothers."

Humor emanates literally from the men's room in a classic scene from the police parody *Naked Gun* (1988) when Leslie Nielsen as Frank Drebin, the toughest—and clumsiest, cop in the world, forgets that he still has his microphone on when he walks out from the stage to the men's room while the mayor ("Queen Elizabeth"/Nancy Marchand) is delivering an after-dinner speech. He groans, whistles, says "whoops," sings, and simultaneously farts and urinates—all the while, with the audience listening in. In *Gremlins II* (1990), Billy (Zach Galligan) rushes little Gizmo the Gremlin into the men's room to make sure he is safe, and the state-of-the-art public address system bellows: "Welcome to the Men's Room. Hey pal, I sure hope you wash those hands." Another funny comment occurs in 1990's *Quick Change*, where bank robbers have no trouble with their heist but encounter all kinds of problems trying to get out of New York City. Dressed in clown outfits, Bill Murray and Randy Quaid as the burglars have strapped the stolen bounty to their bodies, under their clothes. As they rush into stalls of the men's room to re-arrange themselves, they begin oohing and aahing. A well-dressed businessman stands at the sink saying despondently, "I hate this city."

Beyond mere secrecy, men's rooms in films have also become a place for privacy. While at one point Shelley Duvall and her son try to hide out in a deserted hotel's men's room from the deranged Jack Nicholson in the Stanley Kubrick horror classic *The Shining* (1980), the suspense is simultaneously intensified and relieved when Nicholson hatchets his way in, citing the famous line, "Wendy, I'm home!...Heeere's Johnny!" Novelist Stephen King had unwittingly included a foreboding scenario where the Nicholson character hallucinates about a conversation in the bathroom with a former winter hotel resident who reportedly had gone crazy with "cabin fever," and had killed his family with a hatchet.

A gang of thugs goes into the gas station men's room searching for a woman (Demi Moore) in *One Crazy Summer* (1986). But the only person they find is John Cusack, the innocent bystander who only was there to wash his hands. When he reaches up for the towel rack, he finds it stuffed with dollar bills; clearly, *she* had put them there.

Privacy in the pissoir is also a theme in *Let It Ride* (1989), where Richard Dreyfuss as Trotter, a Miami cabbie who wants to make it big at the race track, sits in a stall praying, "God, just let me make this one. I don't belong here with these losers. I belong at the Jockey Club, where they all have teeth." Michael J. Fox as the lead character in Jay McInerney's novel-made-movie *Bright Lights, Big City* (1988) depends upon the men's room as a private place to go snort "Bolivian soldiers." And in *Bad Influence* (1990), James Spader as the greedy Wall Streeter gunning for the title of the company's Chief Accountant, is seen alone in the men's room splashing water on his face to regain composure under the office stress.

Men's rooms have also become a familiar scene for where power plays are staged cinematically. Oftentimes, at issue is peer pressure. In the rash of 1980s teen pics, a number use the men's room at the locus for confrontations, both physical and verbal, of who's in charge. One of the earliest such films was *My Bodyguard* (1980), where 15-year-old Clifford Peache (Chris Makepeace) tries to make the transition from private to public high school. In the school bathroom he is grabbed by a bunch of boys and brought to Moody (Matt Dillon), the group leader, who suggests that he needs a bodyguard to protect himself from Ricky Linderman, the class "psychopath." In this case, it's extortion in the men's room.

For *The Karate Kid* (1984), the school bathroom scene is simultaneously humorous, scary, and bizarre. He too is attending a new place, having moved from Newark to California. All goes well until he makes the mistake of talking to the gang leader's girlfriend—for which event he is beaten up and harrassed. At one point he goes into the men's room and sees the bad guys there, dressed in skeleton outfits and rolling joints. Luckily he makes his exit in time, if after a frightening time of being seen and trying to hide. Fred Savage (best known for his role on television's "Wonder Years") as Charlie, who has changed bodies with his father in *Vice Versa* (1988) is a kind of redemption of these high school confrontations. Charlie as a man breaks into the bathroom where three toughs are smoking. He yells "freeze," frisks them, and tells them to leave kids alone. He then leaves, with the edict to clean the toilet bowls: "I'll be back in a half-hour, and they better be clean." It's our ultimate fantasy: getting the bullies.

Nearly half of *Three O'Clock High* (1987) takes place in the high school men's room. Casey Siemaszko plays the lead role character, Jerry Mitchell, who has a very bad day at school. Mostly, it focuses on the rumors about Buddy Rovelle, a psychotic "touch freak" who reportedly is a murderer. Poor Jerry has been singled out by the authorities to be nice to Buddy. When he finds himself standing next to him at the urinals, he decides to introduce himself, saying he is from the school newspaper and has been assigned to write an article about him. Buddy calls him a fag. He then sees someone in the stalls put his feet up, and when the guilty party touches Buddy, the "psychopath" flushes the offender's foot, then throws him against the bathroom mirror. "Take that newspaper of yours," he warns Jerry, "and wipe your dick with it." But that's not all: he announces that he wants a fight with him, in the parking lot, at three o'clock that afternoon. Jerry panics during a science class documentary on violence in the insect industry, and bolts for the bathroom to regain his senses. He repeats this scenario after an out-of-hand pep rally, but this time Buddy enters the men's room, kicking open all the doors. No, wait—it isn't Buddy, it's the film students, who torture Jerry verbally: "Pain is temporary, film is forever." In a weak moment, Jerry decides to take $450 from the school store to pay someone to defend him. But when Buddy knocks the thug out, it's back to the bathroom as a refuge—this time to vomit. Then, just before the three o'clock deadline, we see Buddy in the bathroom, throwing water on his face before the showdown. The faceoff occurs, the throngs gather and cheer, and the underdog is triumphant.

College students are featured in *St. Elmo's Fire* (1985), named for the bar where the brat pack meets. "Step into my office," says Judd

Nelson, ducking his head into the toilet. The group all goes into the men's room, where they josh and chant—a manhood/friend/buddy understanding underlying the whole atmosphere. These peers don't want a power play, but only to be together.

However, in *True Believer* (1989) James Woods plays a hard-nosed lawyer who is harangued by another member of the legal profession, even in the men's room: "Can't I take a simple piss?" he complains. Before the climatic trial in this thriller is another bathroom scene, where Woods is seen washing his face, then looking at himself in the mirror to prepare himself for the fight.

The men's room mirror figures heavily in *Patton* (1970), when General Montgomery (Michael Bates) first draws hot water to get steam on the mirror, then outlines a map on it to describe the invasion of Sicily. Afterwards, the plan is easily wiped off. World War II is also described in *Biloxi Blues* (1988), the second of Neil Simon's loosely autobiographical triology; here, the men's room is a place for retreat, or retrenchment.

Sometimes too the men's room isn't necessarily where the action takes place, but is used as part of a plot convention. The *Blues Brothers* (1980), for example, post signs there of their upcoming gig, hoping the hype will help them draw a large audience. Unfortunately, a group that they had scammed also spots the sign, and then knows where, and when, to get revenge. Yet a different message appears in *Road House* (1989), where Patrick Swayze plays a bar bouncer in a Missouri saloon: "Don't eat the big white men" hangs over the urinals.

Or things could be much more serious. The men's room is the scene for a murder in Peter Weir's *Witness* (1985). A little Amish boy named Samuel (Lukas Haas) separates from his mother to go the bathroom in the Philadelphia railroad station, where he witnesses a homicide. The accomplices hear something, and recheck the toilets—but Samuel locks the door and climbs underneath to the next stall. There is a dramatic moment when his Shaker hat falls off, but the real cinemagraphic focus is on the young man's enormous, terrified eyes. Harrison Ford as the policeman assigned to the case makes the most of the little boy's vision and memory, and a story of social and cultural commentary evolves.

Comraderie in the men's room has become a commonplace in films. Now, when current movies are dealing with the past, like the 1991 *Barton Fink* story that is set in the 1930s, they include what has become the requisite locale. *For the Boys*, also of 1991, although a retrospective of many wartime benefits since World War II, has its men's room scene.

The men's room in film has become the locus where any number of themes are revealed: secrecy for self and/or with others, privacy to "do one's thing"—whether to do drugs or seek solace, humorous plot conventions, power plays, war wrangling, sheer comraderie, even murder. From the more than two dozen films listed here, one can see support for the argument that men's rooms might truly be the last bastion for masculinity.

Works Cited

Greene, Bob. "Controversy over restrooms and gender crosses the line." *Union-News* 11 Dec. 1991.
Markulin, Joe. "The Men's Room." *New York Times Magazine* 15 Sept. 1991.
Rakow, Lana F. "Feminist approaches to popular culture: Giving patriarchy its due." *Communication* Vol. 9, No. 1 (1986).

Filmography

Year	Film	Director
1970	*Patton*	Franklin Schaffner
1972	*The Godfather*	Francis Ford Coppola
1980	*My Bodyguard*	Tony Bill
1980	*The Shining*	Stanley Kubrick
1983	*Trading Places*	John Landis
1984	*The Karate Kid*	John G. Avildsen
1985	*St. Elmo's Fire*	Joel Schumacher
1985	*To Live and Die in L.A.*	William Friedkin
1985	*Witness*	Peter Weir
1986	*One Crazy Summer*	Savage Steve Holland (and Writer)
1987	*Full Metal Jacket*	Stanley Kubrick (and Producer)
1987	*No Way Out*	Roger Donaldson
1987	*The Principal*	Christopher Cain
1987	*Robocop*	Paul Verhoeven
1987	*Three O'Clock High*	Phil Joanou
1988	*Biloxi Blues*	Mike Nichols
1988	*Bright Lights, Big City*	James Bridges
1988	*D.O.A.*	Rocky Morton and Annabel Jankel
1988	*Frantic*	Roman Polanski (also Co-writer)

1988	*Naked Gun*	David Zucker
1988	*Twins*	Ivan Reltman
1988	*Vice Versa*	Brian Gilbert
1989	*Let It Ride*	Joe Pytka
1989	*True Believer*	Joseph Rubin
1989	*Road House*	Rowdy Herrington
1990	*Bad Influence*	Curtis Hanson
1990	*Quick Change*	Bill Murray, Howard Franklin
1990	*Gremlins 11*	Joe Dante
1991	*Barton Fink*	Joel Cohen
1991	*For the Boys*	Marty Dell

Newsroom Cityscapes:
Filming the Fourth Estate

Norma Fay Green

A 1903 journalism handbook acknowledged the occupational mystery and lure of the newsroom locale: "There are few things concerning which the general public is more curious, and about which it knows less, than the inside of a metropolitan newspaper office" (Shuman vii). Just a few years later, any secrets surrounding newsroom operations were revealed in what became one of the most popular settings for American films.

In Charlie Chaplin's 1914 debut in *Making a Living*, the viewer is shown a division of news labor between staff and management in their occupational space. The editor's spacious office is furnished with oriental rug, gilt-framed painting and safe. Later, we see the more proletariat composing room when would-be reporter Chaplin rushes in with copy and photographs of an automobile accident. It is a crowded shot with men dwarfed by mammoth machines which they somehow manipulate to spew out hot metal type. The movie short has a decided factory feel as it peels away any romantic illusions to offer a peek at the increasingly industrialized news production process.

By the talkies era, filmgoers got more than a glimpse at the newsroom locales. More casual than courtroom settings and slightly less chaotic than hospital emergency scenes, movie newsrooms were designed to convey a sense of the atmosphere in which journalists attempted to produce a publication or newscast. Typically, the films involving urban reporters and editors began in one of two ways—either with a shot of the finished product or with a pan of the newsroom. Motion pictures of the 1930s often started with a glimpse of the freshly printed newspaper or live broadcast—the part of journalism most familiar to audiences—and then worked backward to show how it was put together. Exterior shots of the building would dissolve to the interior to reveal the nerve center of media operations—the newsroom. It soon became a cinematic journalism cliche to open with the visual icon of print journalism—rolling presses—all giant gears and well-oiled metal cylinders rotating in properly inked precision around rolls of newsprint the size of sequoias. These films would then dissolve to a vast open room where an assembly line of reporters and copy editors seemed to be pounding out and polishing copy for the next edition. To vary the opening, some films cut to the core of media activity and begin in the newsroom.

Newsroom set dressing normally called for the usual array of office furnishings such as desks, chairs, file cabinets, coat racks, fans, clocks, calendars, bulletin boards, assorted desk accessories as well as typewriters or computer terminals and tape recorders and videocassettes (depending on the era and media to be depicted). What distinguishes cinematic newsrooms from other offices are the little touches such as those found in the opening scene of the 1932 *The Roadhouse Murder.* The camera's sweep of the newsroom stops momentarily for the audience to read the sign below the clock: *"The New York Star* expects you to watch your jobs and not the clock!" before passing a stoop-shouldered white-haired man blowing up an inner tube (presumably for his hemorrhoids exacerbated by years of sitting on stiff wooden chairs), going to a drunken reporter (wearing the requisite snap brimmed hat) trying to type a letter of resignation and finally coming to rest on the prone body of cub reporter Chick Brian asleep on his desk with a newspaper covering his face. Signage also sets the tone for the 1937 cornball comedy *They Wanted to Marry* in a newsroom full of admonishments such as "Keep It Brief!" and the rhetorical "Is It News?" along with a huge banner "Look Out for Libel" over the exit signs as a friendly reminder of the litigious world outside.

Michael Curtiz's *Mystery of the Wax Museum*, a color film from 1933, starts with an aerial shot of the newsroom. The camera sweeps over the jacketed backs of a chorus line of male reporters tapping their typewriters and barking into telephones with choreography to rival Busby Berkeley. With newsrooms as establishing shots, the viewer is shown an open floor plan—known as the bullpen[1]—where people are sitting, standing, walking or running. On first glance, it may appear to be just another business setting but several elements of the *mise en scene* usually distinguish the newsroom from other offices. Visual cues such as the posture and costuming of stock characters—people, often dressed in outerwear such as hats and coats (are they coming or going?), may be seen leaning back in chairs with feet propped up on desks or using desks to sit on, stand on or lie down on—as well as their behavior in motion—slamming telephone receivers, ripping paper out of typewriters or running around—and the sound—talking fast and loud above the din of communications equipment—all contribute to a sense of urgency and lack of typical business decorum. Films set in newsrooms offer one of

the few places where the audience is just as likely to see men typing as
women, or taking dictation for rewrite. The cinematic news operation is
an equal opportunity slavemaster to the deadline. Some shots have the
feel of a transportation terminal at rush hour. This is not accidental. By
the time Canadian director Phillip Borsos was researching the rhythm of
newsrooms for his 1985 film, *Mean Season*, filmmakers had developed a
certain savvy about creating the drama of deadlines:

I wanted to know what goes on a 3 p.m., at 5 p.m. There's a wonderful flow of
traffic at different times of the day...Gradually, the room fills up. Later, there's
a ferocious attack at the computer terminals. A lot of newspaper movies have 10
people in the background, or 50, but there's always the same level of action. If
the script said 3:10 p.m. and the first edition was an hour off the streets, I
wanted to know what would be happening. (Gross 19)

   Former journalist Robert Darnton claims that the structural
hierarchy of such a room is self evident to anyone who has ever worked
as a journalist (62-63) but general viewers were usually helped to find
order in the chaos as the camera panned the frenzied landscape and then
honed in on key characters or action. Normally, the editor who assigns
stories and decides how news will be used is shown in a power
position—the middle of the room or in a glass-walled corner office with
a view of the whole newsroom. A key underling may be seated nearby at
the head of a horseshoe-shaped table where copy editors sit hunched
over manuscripts or illuminated VDTs like modern-day monks.
Reporters may be scattered about the room or clustered in rows of desks
demarcating beat assignments such as sports or crime news. Publishing
executive Michael Korda contends that the bullpen arrangement with
reporters out in the open is an obvious way for news executives to
exercise control over their print and broadcast staffs:

The rationale for an open office is democracy and sociability, but the fact is that
chief executives...don't trust their senior employees...executives are out in the
open at their desks like typists in the Army, but their boss is in a position to see
all of them, like a master sergeant. One of the first steps toward giving people
autonomy was to give them privacy and deprived of it, they are reduced to the
role of clerks in a Victorian counting house. (71)

In Fritz Lang's 1956 *While the City Sleeps*, we see the multi-media
conglomerate Kyne Inc. presented as a rabbit warren of glass-walled
enclosures separating the newspaper, television station and wire service
enterprises. Ceiling ductwork is exposed with pneumatic tubes sending

234 Beyond the Stars

copy between the newsrooms and typesetting floors. With all the see-through vistas, the journalists have nowhere to hide. Reporter Dana Andrews is first seen shaving at his desk before a telecast and later, after a hangover, he returns to his too-neat desk and dumps pencils out of a cup so he can get a drink from the water cooler. The only person who seems to have any privacy is dying media mogul Walter Kyne who is shown in a hospital bed next to his beloved ticking wire service machines in his wood-paneled office. Kyne's news managers are depicted as typical mid-level executives. Print editors and broadcast news producers in journalism movies are often in the middle of newsroom settings—in the middle of the action and the middle of the corporate hierarchy as internal managers between owners and workers as well as buffers between the news products and their consumers.

At newspapers, the office of the managing editor or editor-in-chief is more private that the newsroom but not nearly as plush as the publisher's inner sanctum or as grimy as the press room. Editors often have couches which are convenient for the naps we see them taking such as Walter Matthau in the 1974 *The Front Page*, Hume Cronyn in the 1974 *Parallax View* and Burt Reynolds in the 1988 *Switching Channels*. Managerial sofas were handy rest stops for underlings in the 1929 *Big News* and the 1957 *The Great Man*. They are less conspicuous than newshawker Michael J. Pollard who sleeps under the pinball machine in the counterculture newspaper office of the 1977 *Between the Lines* and not as grandiose as the mattress and filigreed headboard of Charles Foster Kane hauled to his newly acquired *New York Inquirer* by a driver who protests, "There ain't no bedroom in this joint." Some editors even have bathrooms and bars. The sink in the office closet is handy for Edward G. Robinson to do his Lady MacBeth ritualistic hand washing as tabloid editor in the 1931 *Five Star Final*.

Even some popular columnists rate separate quarters complete with private secretaries like gossipmonger Lee Tracy in the 1932 *Blessed Event*. Another Walter Winchell-like character Ricardo Cortez writes "Keyhole to the City" from a wood and opaque-glass walled office in the 1932 *Is My Face Red?* A barber and manicurist come to his confines and in one of the opening scenes, we see him mixing moonshine to put in his water cooler. In the 1957 *Sweet Smell of Success*, the nightclub banquette is where columnist J.J. Hunsecker gets most of his information which he writes up at home but we do see the newspaper office where his secretary holds down the glass-walled fort. In a hallway outside is a billboard promoting Hunsecker with a huge pair of his signature spectacles looking in, almost spying, on his assistant who shows some advance copy to press agent Tony Curtis.

By the 1980s, the status of certain columnists and star reporters may not have been rewarded with a room of their own as much as proximity to their mentor-bosses. The Royko-like columnist has no real office in the 1981 *Continental Divide*, which was filmed on location at the *Chicago Sun-Times*. Souchak, played by John Belushi, sits in the newsroom surrounded by stacks of paper as he types his latest exposé into the computer system and waves at his editor. He seems to thrive on being close to the madding crowd both in the newsroom and out on the street, until his apartment is bombed. He is urged to keep a low profile and eventually leaves town. There is little elegance in his exit or the work habitat he left behind. Not nearly as visually dramatic as reporter Jimmy Stewart's niche in the *Chicago Times* newsroom set of the 1948 *Call Northside 777*, Souchak's newsroom is functional and drab—a no-frills utilitarian office space, much like the fluorescent-lit work habitats shown in the 1984 *Fletch* and the 1986 *"Crocodile" Dundee*.

Despite the impersonality of open space in the newsroom, journalists often demarcate their territory with personal items such as posters and photos. In the 1987 *Broadcast News* producer Holly Hunter occupies a corner spot and while she has no walls per se (just an exterior window), she creates her own barriers in her professional demeanor. As the ambitious city editor in the 1936 comedy, *Wedding Present*, Cary Grant has no special amenities. There was no glass-walled office, just a symbolic knee-high railing to separate him from the rest of the bullpen. The viewer can catch a glimpse of a Rivera-like Machine Age mural in the background but the editor's space lacks any distinct artwork until would-be painters are hired to decorate his desk and nearby support column with blackboard graffiti symbols such as a cat, heart, flower, house and beer stein. Leaving no stone or journalistic prop unturned, they even paint his hat and hand it back to the incredulous Cary. But furnishings alone can't keep a newsroom locale interesting. Directors often mix frenzy into the formula.

Conditioned by years of fast-paced action in the movie newsrooms, Russell Baker was disappointed by his first encounter with the real space:

I had seen plenty of city rooms in the movies. They were glamorous places full of exciting people like Lee Tracy, Edmund Lowe, and Adolph Menjou trading wisecracks and making mayors and cops look like saps...I had expected the newsroom to have glamour, but this place had nothing but squalor. The walls hadn't been painted for years. The windows were filthy. Desks were heaped with mounds of crumpled paper, torn sheets of newspaper, overturned paste pots, dog-eared telephone directories. The floor was ankle deep in newspaper print, carbon paper, and crushed cigarette packages. Waist-high cans overflowed with trash. Ashtrays were buried under cigarette ashes and butts...Ugly old wooden chairs looked ready for the junk shop. (19)

Staging the work of a reporter and making editing look exciting has always been a challenge to filmmakers. One author complained that "writers are always treated foolishly by movies, unless they're journalists, folks of action" (Reed 109). One advance man for the 1976 *All the President's Men* visited the *Washington Post* and reported "For action purposes, the newsroom was about as exciting as an insurance office and might look almost too dull on film" (Clein 25). To overcome the static look, actors were directed to move about the set more frequently and quickly than was observed in real life newsroom situations. A reviewer of the 1987 *Broadcast News* noted that "moving camera and quick cuts enliven our view of office space, so that we end up watching people with desk jobs as raptly as if they were tightrope walkers" (Mesic 114). Directors often walked a thin line themselves by trying to make the newsroom authentic and yet action-packed to hold the audience's attention.

Even the 1941 *Citizen Kane*, which was lauded for its innovative cinematography, got mixed reviews when it came to the newsroom. Film critic Pauline Kael grumbled that "most of the newspaper-office scenes looked as clumsily staged as ever..." (54) while film designer Leon Barsacq called the "newspaper city room...memorable (64). By the time *Teacher's Pet* opened in 1958 with a scene of a public tour of the newsroom, the filmgoers no doubt knew the route by heart for as Deac Rossell said: "For three decades before television, newsrooms and the intrigues of reporters chasing a story were a Hollywood staple" (68). But by the end of the 1950s, newspapers were declining and so was attendance at movies about them. Growing accustomed to realistic visual images of reporters *in situ* on the television nightly news, audiences expected more in terms of fictional fare about the occupation as well. So, in the 1960s and 1970s, film directors tackling stories about journalism sought out more semblances of truth in newsroom locales.

Verisimilitude probably reached its peak in the 1976 *All the President's Men* which Robert Redford called "the most overresearched project anyone could do" (Clein 26). Considering all the cover-ups that had been exposed in the actual investigation of the Watergate burglary and subsequent resignation of a U.S. president, the filmmakers searched for newsroom authenticity. Because it was not possible to film on location—something that was later done at the *Miami Herald* for both the 1981 *Absence of Malice* and 1985 *Mean Season*—producers turned to a time-honored motion picture trick and created a *Washington Post* newsroom replica in a Burbank, California studio. The attention to detail was almost as incredible as the press attention which documented the quest for exactitude in the filming of their vocation. In a tie-in Warner book on the making of the Warner Bros. movie, author Jack Hirshberg described the dressing of the newsroom locale:

Down to the graphics on the walls and numbers on the telephone extensions, it was an identical twin...The Post had generously shipped dozens of packing crates crammed with refuse from its newsroom—old galley proofs, wire service copy, unopened mail, directories from Government bureaus—and these were distributed among the 200 desks, along with 1972 Washington telephone directories; 1972 calendars were on the walls, the dates changed daily according to the scene being shot. The Post even re-set all the type and photos for front pages of seventeen 1972-73 editions so that if, say, a scene took place on August 3, 1972, copies of the Post strewn around the newsroom in that scene were the authentic editions for the date. (114)

Hirshberg chronicled the invasion of the real newsroom by various members of the film cast and crew who observed, took notes, taped and photographed the fifth floor room and its inhabitants. Writing about the production in *American Film*, Harry Clein quoted director Alan Pakula as insisting that the "set was not modified to make it easier to photograph. It was the other way around; I wanted to push myself into solutions dealing with reality."[2] Designer George Jenkins and second assistant director Charles Ziarko are credited with the laudable look of the newsroom replica described as "a set that will show more realistically the workings of a major newspaper than any other film ever made" (Clein 25). Jenkins' meticulousness was legendary:

...he moved into the *Post* and started measuring floors, walls, windows, doorways, supportive pillars, ceiling-light fixtures. He took over 1,000 color slides, borrowed the original building blueprints from the architects, and consulted with the original decorating firm. The position of each desk, Teletype machine, Telex, wirefoto receiver, even each waste basket, was plotted so these items could be properly placed in the make-believe newsroom. (Hirshberg 111)

Ziarko was sent to Washington to observe the present staff. Clein reports that Ziarko expected more journalists would smoke than he actually found. "He noted the number of those who wore glasses, the racial mix...and the difference in dress between reporters, editors, and copy aides" (25). Hirshberg noted that Ziarko plotted the newsroom traffic flow "according to the day of the week and hour of the day, and (made) copious notes of reporter's routines. Thus the actors, few of who had ever been inside a newspaper office, were able to move about and function as if they were veterans" (114). Pakula even had a *Post* reporter meet with actors and "lecture the cast on the niceties of newsroom etiquette and indoctrinate them in the varied duties of editors, writers, and supportive personnel" (Hirshberg 114). Clein said that the actors ad libbed in journalistic jargon that was "picked up on an eight-track recording system for judicious inclusion in final dubbing" (26). Nothing about the *mise en scene* was left to chance. Jim Webb, who won an Academy Award for his production sound for the film, explained why he was hired for the journalism film project:

When "President's" came along, one of the reasons I got the show was because of the big newsroom scene. They were going to use what they called "deep focus," split diopters, so you could see and hear things going on in several rooms simultaneously. They reasoned that if I could record all these simultaneous conversations in "Nashville," I could do something similar for them. It turned out they didn't quite need that much sound. But it got me the job. (Brouwer and Wright 438-39)

Did the meticulousness pay off? The film won several Academy Awards and was erroneously credited with increasing enrollment at the nation's journalism schools.[3] A journalism trade magazine hailed the film as an occupational image watershed stating, "It helped to soften the public perception of the newsroom as a stable of the irascible, a notion compounded through the century by previous films and television."[4] In addition, the technical standards set by the film seemed to raise the stakes for future studio productions involving newsrooms. Also, the pressure was put upon filmmakers to replicate the open newsroom format that viewers were conditioned to see thanks to the local TV news show formats popularized across the country in the 1970s.[5] Les Brown noted, "Because everyone is now witness to the process of journalism, filmmakers and tv producers must offer more sophisticated and varied fare" (qtd. in Gouveia 12F).

This challenge was apparently taken to heart in the production of the 1985 *Mean Season*. Film critic Jane Gross noted the significance of actually using the *Miami Herald* newsroom rather than attempting to duplicate it. She quoted producer David Foster on his decision:

I don't think we could have had the aroma, the feel we had at the *Herald*. It had a tone, that city room. I had no idea news reporters were that sloppy. The clutter on the desks—dirty utensils, tottering stacks of books, tangled computer printouts—was not tampered with...Reporters use the plastic ballpoint pens that are standard issue in newsroom supply cabinets and bulky, outdated tape recorders crusted with grime. (19)

Gross explained that the production used actual members of the staff as on-locale "consultants and extras, filming in the middle of the night to prerecorded soundtracks of the noisy crescendo of afternoon deadlines" (19). Fellow critic Vincent Canby proclaimed, *"Mean Season* is awfully good in depicting the routine of the fictional Miami Journal, the crises and tensions of daily deadlines, the sense of life being lived in 24-hour installments" (17). It's interesting to note that films set in newspaper newsroom locales were still being praised in the 1980s, one decade after public opinion polls indicated that most Americans declared television as their news medium of choice. The depictions of broadcast newsrooms were slow to match those of their print predecessors and, because of different news presentation equipment, the films often began differently as well.

Instead of rolling presses, films portraying television journalism usually begin with television monitors of paternalistic-looking anchormen and fresh-faced women reporters. In the 1976 *Network*, we see the windowless newsroom with light linoleum floors, gray metal desks and chairs, and lots of adjustable industrial shelving overflowing with book-like videocassette boxes. It looks like it could be mopped up and moved on a minute's notice. News director William Holden's office is carpeted, full of mementoes and glass walled with a good view of Manhattan and the newsroom. When programming executive Faye Dunaway starts to seduce Holden, she comes into his incandescently-lit office after the evening newscast and sits on the edge of his desk—invading his personal space. Both the actor's behavior to the furniture and the lighting are significant in this scene. Michael Korda observed that executives tend to use desks as fortresses:

Many people feel more comfortable and secure behind a huge, heavy wooden desk, and it is easier to do business with such people if you can tempt them out from behind it...If you can't, then put your hat or brief case on the desk if you want to make them nervous...Once they have taken refuge behind five-hundredweight of mahogony, you can't argue... (17)

Illumination, or lack thereof, is another important status symbol for executives.

The less power people have, the more strongly lit their space or office is, the extreme of nonpower being a desk in the open, lit from above by banks of fluorescent lights in the ceiling. With each step in, the amount of light tends to decrease, the assumption being that since truly powerful people don't need to type, write or even read very much, they don't need bright working lights. In most offices this pattern is easy to observe from the open spaces which are lit like operating rooms and the more private offices, in which a certain ambiguous dimness is maintained, to the inner executive offices, which are paneled in dark wood, have curtains instead of Venetian blinds and are lit by shaded lamps, the dark private caverns of the powerful. (Korda 102)

Bright lights are important to those on camera to present the news. But if there is power in shadows, such influence is portended in *Network* when viewers are shown the darkened stage where Peter Finch will deliver the news. Any sense of urgency or global outreach, however, symbolized by six clocks and three phones (two red, one black) in the pine-paneled backdrop is lost on the movie audience who see it for the prop it really is, just scenery like the audio-enhanced clatter of wire service machines played as background sound at the beginning of each broadcast. Ratings and marketshare have become the determinant of TV news show content and format. This is never more evident than in the guillotine-like aerial shot of the back of network executive Robert Duvall's balding head looking down on a butcher block-topped desk.

The 1979 *China Syndrome* offers a minimalist newsroom with fluorescent lighting and requisite furnishings but little clutter as Jane Fonda prepares her copy on a manual typewriter. The newsroom is seen in the distance with people moving about occasionally through the picture window of the editing room where Sigourney Weaver spends more time in the 1981 *Eyewitness*. The open newsroom set is quite visible in the 1988 *Switching Channels* which spoofs CNN headquarters with its post-modern news factory look featuring open industrial beamed ceilings, photogenic blue walls and banks of TV monitors in the background, and lots of cables and electronic equipment strewn about the hangar-like space. Searching for the boss, reporter Kathleen Turner is informed he's "in the pit." Indeed, the vast room does have the look of a trading room where news is the commodity being brokered. While none of these films about TV journalism begin in the newsroom, the 1987 *Broadcast News* makes it clear that the newsroom is home base.

The network bureau newsroom is the place where the staff of *Broadcast News* characters gather before the frenzied rush of preparation, actual airing and, for post-mortems. There is a partial opaque glass wall between the photocopy and wire service machines in the middle of the room but otherwise it is an open space unlabeled save for a white sign locating the bureau as "Washington." Recessed fluorescent ceiling lights supplement gooseneck lamps on desks set on white flooring. At least twice during the movie, cameras pan the newsroom to show yellow canvas film bags (stenciled with the international message, "Urgente") laying around like so many sacks of flour at a mill. Despite huge cylindrical wastebaskets on wheels and countless shelves, there doesn't seem to be enough space or inclination to put things away after every newscast. In the darkened editing room, producer Holly Hunter shows her real power. We see her at best workhorse speed, swigging from an Evian bottle. A t-shirt, photos and a sampler embroidered "If you can't stand the heat, get out of the kitchen" are on the wall behind her and in front is an editing console, with a red-lit digital clock showing how many seconds to airtime. While Humphrey Bogart whipped out a whiskey bottle from under his typing table in the 1952 *Deadline U.S.A.*, anchor William Hurt opens his desk drawer in *Broadcast News* to reveal a natural bristle hairbrush, a box of clean shirts and an array of neutral ties. Times had certainly changed in terms of newsroom necessities. Appearance is important in TV news and the value of looking professional has colored decisions about real-life newsrooms as well.

When the CBS-TV affiliate in Chicago revamped its news set from what one critic described as the "gritty working newsroom that had doubled as the station's on air set since 1973" (Feder 45), the station's general manager was quoted as explaining the necessity for the change:

I thought long and hard about it, because the newsroom format has been the signature of this television station for a long time. It wasn't a matter of wanting to "break with the past." It was simply that the newsroom environment made it very, very difficult to light the set and shoot it—not to mention audio problems. It wasn't physically practical to function in that environment. (Feder 45)

While the real stations may be jettisoning the newsroom set for a no-nonsense, less busy-looking background, the newsroom locale still seems to work in American motion pictures where it has become visual shorthand for deadline drama. *NBC Nightly News* senior producer Cheryl Gound (rumored to be a prototype for Jane Craig, the Holly Hunter character) complimented *Broadcast News'* director for his simulation of network news operations. She said she most enjoyed the "newsroom gallows humor and its depiction of the 'crash and burn mentality' of getting a piece on the air" (Behrens 2).

Even though the frantic pace of movie portrayals of journalism has continued seemingly unabated since Chaplin's time, there have been changes in the cinematic newsroom look. Sparsely decorated newspaper office furniture, for instance, has shifted from bulky wooden slatted chairs designed in the nineteenth century to more space-age metal and plastic ergonomically-correct upholstered seating. Despite the praise for the modern architecture details featured in magazine and radio office interiors, little of the avant-garde designs ever filtered down to the lowly newsroom which was rarely featured in films about the more affluent and upstart cousins of the metro dailies.[6] Elegant touches were usually the preserve of magazine executives like Clark Gable's streamlined suite newly redecorated by his assistant Jean Harlow in blond woods that match the color of her hair in the 1936 *Wife Versus Secretary*. Even in the 1987 *Street Smart*, more scenes take place in the editor's floor-to-ceiling windowed corner office than the nondescript modern newsroom. (The see-through uncluttered desk in the magazine mogul's office seems symbolic of the vacuousness of the character played by Andre Gregory. He is shown getting his hair cut and sitting toad-like in a huge, overstuffed black leather chair. A single green plant in his office is a cactus, which may mirror his prickly nature as reporter Christopher Reeve struggles to save his career.) With minimal architectural details, the depictions of cinematic newsrooms evolved from the thigh-high wooden gates designating public and private sections of the bullpen such as those seen in the 1940 *His Girl Friday* to the armed guard at the cable station prepared to tackle unwelcome visitors in the 1988 remake, *Switching Channels*. Even the sounds changed in the newsroom. Bird-like chirps of electronic telephones and plastic pecks at computer keyboards have replaced the heavy-handed hammering of manual typewriter keys to paper and clanging candlestick phones. Modern motion picture newsrooms have become more insulated—with carpeted floors and upholstered chairs in artificially bright, windowless rooms—more self contained and detached from the outside work that journalists are assigned to cover.

Supposedly representing benign way stations in the news process where information is merely assembled, these movie newsrooms often have been transformed into exciting locales for newsmaking confrontations including jilted bride Jean Harlow marching down the aisle of the newsroom, not the church, in full wedding regalia to chew out fiancé Spencer Tracy in the 1936 *Libeled Lady*. Newsrooms have been the scenes of everything from floods (1937 *They Wanted to Marry*) to fistfights (1952 *Deadline U.S.A.*) and fires (1958 *Teacher's Pet*). Disgruntled readers have stormed newsrooms and threatened staffs with guns and lawsuits in films from the newspaper-noir-looking 1931 *Five Star Final* to the sunless city room in the Miami-based 1981 *Absence of Malice*. Death and destruction occur when informants plunge from metal catwalks into the roaring presses as in *Deadline U.S.A.*, when editors are poisoned with tainted carry-out food in the 1974 *Parallax View*, when magazine writers trash editor's offices with baseball bats as in the 1985 *Perfect* or when terrorists decimate Perry White's office and much of the Daily Planet newsroom in the 1980 *Superman II*. (Other bad guys come back to swoop away takeover publisher Mariel Hemingway—right through the ceiling of her office—in the 1987 *Superman IV*.)

Despite all the mayhem brought into the newsroom, the locale is regenerated over and over again by able-bodied studio carpenters working under the direction of artful eyes conditioned to design such mythic space. If all the world's a stage, the newsroom has managed to be in the eye of the cinematic *Sturm und Drang* for much of the twentieth century. While the inner sanctum of American journalism is no longer the enigma it once was, newsroom cityscapes continue to be used regularly in popular films to convey comic and tragic, profound and prosaic aspects of the occupation and the urban life it covers. Even in the age of remote satellite feeds, facsimile transmissions, cellular phones and amateur videocamera footage, it is difficult to imagine that the centralized newsroom will become obsolete after decades of dedicated service as a stock locale.

Notes

[1]Dictionaries disagree as to the origin and exact sequence of usage of "bullpen," but most claim the term is derived from police or baseball references—either of which would have been familiar to reporters covering crime or sports. It has been defined as "an enclosure for prisoners or a place where relief pitchers warm up"; also sleeping quarters at a lumber camp. Snoozing reporters are shown occasionally in movie newsrooms so that latter definition is valid. However, no films have been found showing actual bulls brought in the newsrooms, so the literal meaning cannot be validated!

[2]Pakula wanted to become an eyewitness to the traditional eyewitnesses of history. Clein quotes Pakula as saying: "It was the little objects that literally brought down the most popular men in the world. I'm using the camera as the reporters' eyes; thus the detail has to be exact; the camera sees what they see" (26). An interesting spoof of this technique is found in the opening newsroom scene of the 1978 *Superman*. We see the room fuzzily and jerkily through the viewfinder of Daily Planet cub photographer Jimmy Olson's camera as he moves about the bullpen snapping candids of fellow workers.

³Journalism educator Richard Cole corrected a popular misconception: "...it should be pointed out that all the growth was taking place *before* Bob Woodward and Carl Bernstein became famous. Many people have said that their reporting of the Watergate affair in the *The Washington Post* was a major factor in drawing students into the study of journalism and mass communications in college. But their book...was not published until 1974, and the movie...did not appear until 1976. By the mid-1970s, the mushrooming of journalism enrollments had already taken place" (5).

⁴Roberts, 80. For many journalism aspirants, though, it helped to reinforce what Noel Carroll calls "the reciprocal relation between picture recognition and object recognition" (83). Case in point is found in a journalist's recall of the first time at the Washington Post: "I was escorted through the hubbub of the immense newsroom, a replica of the set in 'All the President's Men' (journalism imitating art?)..." (Collins 138).

⁵In an assessment of the various news show formats such as happy talk, formal, eyewitness and tabloid styles, "in-the-newsroom" set was defined as "on-air personalities reporting from their natural working habitat—the busy newsroom (include cluttered desks, ringing phones and clacking wire machines) or the appearance to the viewer of an actual newsroom which may be staged." WLWC-TV (Columbus, Ohio) news producer Scott Lynch is quoted as saying that the open set "gives the viewers the feeling of being close not to where the news is made but where it is put together" (Czerniejewski and Long 23, 28).

⁶Design critic Albrecht noted "the majority of offices seen in film interiors of the 1920s and 1930s pertained to the prosperous industries of fashion, finance, and especially the media." He claimed that the actual relocation of NBC headquarters to the Art Deco Rockefeller Center was the catalyst for many radio journalism films. The architecture of Paramount's "Big Broadcast" series of musicals was noteworthy: "the quality of modern details—glass walls, marquees with translucent soffits, tubular furniture—is remarkable throughout the company's suites of svelte offices and public reception areas." He also cites the publisher's offices in *Gentlemen of the Press*, which "combines the characteristic vertical piers, setback profiles, and chevron motifs of the new style of skyscrapers. Even the supports of the desk use the zigzag profiles Art Deco designers favored" (all 124). Howard Mandelbaum and Eric Meyers also mention the interior elegance shown in *Gentlemen of the Press* and *The World Moves On*. But little of this geometric style appeared in newsrooms. Indeed, once viewers get past the Art Deco doors at Amalgmated Broadcasting System in the 1957 *The Great Man*, Jose Ferrar shows a rather prosaic radio newsroom with a big clock, many file cabinets arranged under hanging lights and newspapers clipped to a rack like laundry hanging on a line.

Works Cited

Albrecht, Donald. *Modern Architecture in the Movies.* New York: Harper & Row, 1986.

Baker, Russell. *The Good Times.* New York: Penguin Books, 1990.

Barsacq, Leon. *Caligari's Cabinet and Other Grand Illusions: A History of Film Design.* Ed. Elliott Stein. Rev. ed. Bowton: New York Graphic Society, 1976.

Behrens, Leigh. "Producer Finds She's News." *Chicago Tribune* 14 Feb. 1988: sec. 6:2.

Brouwer, Alexandra and Thomas Lee Wright. *Working in Hollywood.* NY: Crown Publishers, 1990.

Carroll, Noel. "The Power of Movies." *Daedalus* 114: 4 (1985).

Canby, Vincent. "A Journalism Movie that Raises Tough Questions." *New York Times* 3 Mar. 1985: 17.

Clein, Harry. "Progress Report—All the President's Men, Verisimilitude: A New Formula." *American Film* 1: 1 (1975): 25-26.

Cole, Richard. "Much better than yesterday, and still brighter tomorrow." *Journalism Educator* 40: 3 (1985): 4-8.

Collins, Nancy. *Hard to Get: Fast Talk and Rude Questions Along the Interview Trail.* New York: Random House, 1990.

Czerniejewski, Halina and Charles Long. "Local Television News in 31 Different Flavors: The Happy Medium." *Quill* May 1974: 21-28.

Darnton, Robert. *The Kiss of the Lamourette.* New York: Norton Publishing Co., 1990.

Feder, Robert. "Channel 2 will transform its news set 'slowly'." *Chicago Sun-Times* 28 Mar. 1991: 45.

Gouveia, Georgette. "Movies, TV Taking Harder Look at Journalists." *Lansing State Journal* 15 Feb. 1987: 12F.

Gross, Jane. "An Actor Explores the Fourth Estate." *New York Times* 10 Feb. 1985: H19.

Hirshberg, Jack. *A Portrait of All the President's Men: The Story Behind the Filming of the Most Devastating Detective Story of the Century.* New York: Warner Books, 1976.

Korda, Michael. *Power! How to Get It. How to Use It.* New York: Random House, 1975.

Mandelbaum, Howard, and Eric Meyers. *Screen Deco: A Celebration of High Style in Hollywood.* New York: St. Martin's, 1985.

Mesic, Penelope. "Jane's Big Job: In Broadcast News Who You Are Is What You Do—Even if You Don't Dress for Success." *Chicago Magazine* Mar. 1988: 114.

Reed, Joseph. *American Scenarios: The Use of Film Genre.* Middletown, CN: Wesleyan UP, 1989.

Roberts, Jerry. "Newspaper Videos." *Editor & Publisher* 22 Apr. 1988: 80-81, 112-13.

Rossell, Deac. "On the Set: Absence of Malice—Sally Field Knits while the First Amendment Burns." *Esquire* July 1981: 68.

Shuman, Edwin L. *Practical Journalism.* New York: Appleton, 1903.

Filmography

Year	Film	Director
1914	*Making a Living*	Mack Sennett
1929	*Big News*	George LaCave
1931	*Five Star Final*	Mervyn LeRoy
1932	*Blessed Event*	Roy Del Ruth
1932	*Is My Face Red?*	William Seiter
1932	*Roadhouse Murder*	J. Walter Ruben
1933	*Mystery of the Wax Museum*	Michael Curtiz
1936	*Bride Comes Home*	Wesley Ruggles
1936	*Libeled Lady*	Jack Conway
1936	*Mr. Deeds Goes to Town*	Frank Capra
1936	*Wedding Present*	Richard Wallace
1936	*Wife Versus Secretary*	Clarence Brown
1937	*They Wanted to Marry*	Lew Landers
1940	*His Girl Friday*	Howard Hawks
1941	*Citizen Kane*	Orson Welles
1942	*Woman of the Year*	George Stevens
1948	*Big Clock*	John Farrow
1948	*Call Northside 777*	Henry Hathaway
1948	*June Bride*	Bretaigne Windust
1952	*Deadline—U.S.A.*	Richard Brooks
1956	*While the City Sleeps*	Fritz Lang
1957	*Great Man*	Jose Ferrer
1957	*Sweet Smell of Success*	Alexander Mackendrick
1958	*Teacher's Pet*	George Seaton
1959	*—30—*	Jack Webb
1969	*Gaily, Gaily*	Norman Jewison
1974	*Front Page*	Billy Wilder
1974	*Parallax View*	Alan J. Pakula
1976	*All the President's Men*	Alan J. Pakula
1976	*Network*	Sidney Lumet
1977	*Between the Lines*	Joan Micklin Silver
1978	*Superman*	Richard Donner
1979	*China Syndrome*	James Bridges
1980	*Superman II*	Richard Lester
1981	*Absence of Malice*	Sydney Pollack
1981	*Continental Divide*	Michael Apted
1981	*Eyewitness*	Peter Yates
1983	*Superman III*	Richard Lester
1984	*Fletch*	Michael Ritchie
1985	*Mean Season*	Phillip Borsos
1985	*Perfect*	James Bridges
1986	*"Crocodile" Dundee*	Peter Faiman
1987	*Broadcast News*	James L. Brooks
1987	*Street Smart*	Jerry Schatzberg
1987	*Superman IV*	Sidney Furie
1988	*Switching Channels*	Ted Kotcheff

Venus on a Chaise Lounge (Mars Doing Laps):
Poolside Sex and Death
in American Popular Films

Greg Metcalf

> Okay! That's It! Everybody outta the pool!
>> God's response to Original Sin,
>> according to Bill Cosby

Sigmund Freud gave us the pairing of Eros and Thanatos as the basic drives of Life and Death within the human psyche. Hollywood gives us the pairing of Sex and Violence, the basic narrative drives for much of American popular film. In examining the uses of swimming pool locale in American popular film, Freud's broader drives can be seen to lie just beneath the surface of those narrative drives. The swimming pool will be seen to be a location of fantasies of sexuality, death and rebirth, all within a set of conventions which link Eros and the Female, Thanatos and the Male.

There are practical reasons for the swimming pools being a common locale in American popular film. Ownership of a pool signifies that a person has achieved a type of success that Hollywood films often record. Swimming pools are a common feature of California homes which are available for location shooting. At a baser, market-oriented level, a swimming pool setting can justify presenting swimsuit-clad beauties to the movie-going audience.

But still waters—even chlorinated ones—run deep. Beneath these practical considerations lies the fact that swimming pools have become the locale for some very specific sorts of gender-based behavior in American film. The swimming pool has most consistently been presented as a sensual space of female sexuality. When the right couple is present at the pool—especially at night— sexual and romantic fulfillment are almost inevitable. When too many men are present at the pool without female dilution, destruction and death are almost inevitable. Under certain circumstances the swimming pool can become a fertile location for birth and rebirth, and under the wrong circumstances the swimming pool is debased

247

into a sterile—and largely masculine—location for spiritual and actual death.

> You look like the type that goes in for swimming, huh?
>
> Joan
>
> Why not, when the world is so generously supplied with water?
>
> Ned, *The Swimmer*

On the basis of its title alone, it seems natural to begin this discussion with the 1968 film, *The Swimmer*. While the film, based on a John Cheever short story, was not a great box office success, it offers the most complete catalog of the locale's uses. In the course of the film we are exposed to the swimming pool as the location of sexuality, virility and rebirth. We are also shown the consequences of male and female presence in the "female space" of the swimming pool.

Burt Lancaster plays Ned Merrill, an advertising man who, on a glorious Sunday afternoon, decides to swim home through his suburban neighbors' pools. In swimming home, we soon realize, Ned is attempting to swim into his fantasy of the past.

At first, Ned's attempt appears successful. The swimmer seems reborn, radiating a youth and virility that set him apart from other men. But as the film progresses, as reality seeps into his fantasy, Ned is overcome by chills, his body is stooped by his efforts and even his bald spot becomes more apparent.

The Swimmer makes a clear linkage of the swimming pool and the sexual female. The pools are defined almost exclusively as female-controlled spaces. Ned's receiving permission to swim in a young woman's pool carries clear sexual overtones. First, older non-sexual women and then, as the film continues, all women reject and attack Ned at poolside. In the pool of his ex-mistress, Ned is forced to confront the reality of his failure as a lover ("We made love in this pool and you loved it, remember?"—Ned. "I lied."—Shirley). Lest we miss the connection between sexuality and swimming, Ned cannot swim across this pool.

Likewise, the film utilizes the conventions of male behavior at poolside. From the first of the pool parties, non-swimming men begin to destroy Ned's fantasy. In the two cases where a pool is clearly controlled by men, the swimmer ends up coming to blows with them.

On its way to showing us that Ned has lost his attributes of (suburban) masculinity, *The Swimmer* makes use of most of the conventions of the swimming pool locale. It is in the private pools that Ned's fantasies of virility exist. While swimming he is reborn, however briefly. The more public the pool, the less life-giving it is. Perhaps the most central of pool conventions is the pool's definition as a female space. As the film comes to revolve around Ned's relationships with the women in his life, the centrality of the pool locations becomes obvious. When the film concludes with Ned's recognition of the loss of his mistress, his wife, and his daughters coinciding with his having no pools left in which to swim, *The Swimmer* makes the connection unavoidable.

> Dry, she ain't much. Wet, she's a star.
>
> Harry Cohn on Esther Williams

The linkage of the bodies of women and bodies of water can be traced back through world mythologies, represented visually in such paintings as Boticelli's *The Birth of Venus* (1482). More recent popular culture placements of the bodies of beautiful women in swimsuits can be found in "bathing beauty" pageants staged near bodies of water from the 1920s to today's Atlantic City-based Miss America "scholarship competition" still centered around a swimsuit competition. Hollywood's focus on the beachside and poolside bathing beauty, from early newsreels to *Hardbodies: 2* (1986), falls into this simultaneously mythic and commercially-pragmatic linkage of women and water.

While there were undoubtedly synchronized swimming buffs in the audiences for the films of Esther Williams and some of the Busby Berkeley extravaganzas, the fantasy swimming pool scenes function largely as stylized presentations of interchangeable female sexuality. While an Esther Williams could provide a focus for this sexual energy, the massed Busby Berkeley-style production of undifferentiated female bodies helped attach the sexuality of the moment to the mass and the location, helping to fuel the sexual linkage of "girls" and "swimming pools."

The pool-based female sexual extravaganza has become so established as a convention of American popular film that it can be parodied in both American and foreign films. *The Muppets Take Manhattan* (1984) made puppet lust-object Miss Piggy the center of her own fantasy pool extravaganza. The Australian film *Starstruck* (1982) inverted the cliche of "female sexuality as synchronized swimming" by reveling in the same routines performed by a male swimteam for a woman's gaze. Most powerfully, Jean-Luc Godard's *Alphaville* (1965) used the convention to highlight the linkage of sex and violence that lies near the heart of much of America's popular film. Godard turns the synchronized handmaids of Eros into erotic charnelmaids of Thanatos. The film's female swimmers recover the corpses of male political prisoners when their divingboard executions propel them into an indoor pool.

As the bathing beauty has been incorporated into films with a more linear narrative, the interchangeable bathing beauties increasingly have moved out of the pool to be draped upon towels and chaise lounges around the pools of wealthy men. No longer the cogs in a swimming machine of female energy, the bathing beauty becomes a "staffage" figure. In the same manner that American Indians were placed in landscape paintings to signify their American locales, the bikinied females lie exposed at poolside in films like *Goldfinger* (1964), *For Your Eyes Only* (1981), *Star 80* (1983), *Dragnet* (1987), *Road House* (1989) and *The Hard Way* (1991) as a means of establishing the power of a male character who controls the pool (and therefore the women).

Which is not to say that individual women do not exist in swimming pools. In fact, the pool is often the place where the female object of desire is first seen by both the hero and the film-viewer, or first seen as desirable. This dramatic presentation of the love object can be seen as an extension of Boticelli's *The Birth of Venus*—a painting liberally quoted as a "private pool" piece by Terry Gilliam for Venus's entrance in *The Adventures of Baron Munchausen* (1988)—in *Harper* (1966), *The Cool Ones* (1967), *The Swimmer, Marlowe* (1969), *Raging Bull* (1980), *Fletch* (1985), and the soft-core film within the film *Slaughterhouse Five* (1972). In *Earth Girls are Easy* (1988), Valerie (Geena Davis)'s lounging bikini-clad body is capable of attracting men from another solar system to crash into her pool. On occasion, the convention is altered to allow a swimming male to look up from the pool to see the love object, as in *My Tutor* (1982) and *Taking Care of Business* (1990). In both cases she eventually joins him in the pool.

Another significant variation within the convention is the addition of nighttime nudity which can be seen in *My Tutor, National Lampoon's Vacation* (1983), *Black Widow* (1986), *Children of a Lesser God* (1986), *Something's Got to Give* (Marilyn Monroe's unfinished last film), and *The Seduction* (1982), where Jamie (Morgan Fairchild)'s pool—also the site of her lovemaking—seems as central to the film as the actress herself, with the crazed fan's rising passion often signaled by the wash of reflected pool lights on Jamie's house.

Some filmmakers have had it both ways with the fantasy of poolside female sexuality by both presenting and critiquing the fantasy. *National Lampoon's Vacation* allowed Clark (Chevy Chase) to achieve his sexual fantasy when his lust object (Christy Brinkley) invites him to swim naked with her in the very public motel pool, but the reality is a public humiliation. Later Clark and his wife repeat the experience to more pleasurable, off-screen results. *National Lampoon's Christmas Vacation* (1989) debunks the fantasy by interrupting Clark's dream of having a lingerie saleslady in his fantasy backyard pool with the needs of his pathetic niece. This fantasy critique is most clearly seen in juxtaposing *My Tutor* with *Fast Times at Ridgemont High* (1982). After watching Terry (Caren Kaye), his French teacher, taking her nightly nude swim, *My Tutor*'s Bobby (Matt Lattanzi) has a fantasy of pool-sex with her which blends into actual pool-sex. In *Fast Times at Ridgemont High* we see Brad (Judge Reinhold)'s masturbational swimming pool fantasy but he, and we, are abruptly interrupted by Linda (Phoebe Cates), the disgusted object of his desire.

Perhaps the most telling inversion of the convention is seen in the character of Gordon Breedlove, played by Jack Nicholson in *Terms of Endearment* (1983). Breedlove is the drunken, sybaritic next-door neighbor of Aurora Greenway (Shirley MacLaine). While the overweight, balding ex-astronaut is seen as a skirt-chasing buffoon, he is also the object of Aurora's denied desire. We know this through Aurora's attention to Breedlove's swimming pool and the sounds emanating from it. Aurora watches Breedlove walk a bevy of young women to his pool. From the solitude of her gazebo, Aurora hears him screaming and splashing in his pool and complains. Soon we see Aurora going out to her garden and listening to the sounds from Breedlove's pool. Aurora finally interrupts Breedlove's nighttime swimming to take him directly from his pool into her bedroom.

> Just you and her? Alone? By the pool?
>
> Jack, *My Tutor*

The swimming pool as a location for shared sexuality has been interpreted in a variety of ways, most of which confirm the idea of the pool as a female space which the male is allowed to visit. Such films run the gamut from a carnivorous female sexuality, seen in Brantley's (Michael J. Fox's) near-rape by his aunt (Margaret Whitton) in her pool—accompanied by the signature music from *Jaws*—in *The Secret of My Success* (1987), to the female-dominated pool party of *Fresh Horses* (1988), to the sensuality of John (William Hurt)'s penetration of Sara (Marlee Matlin)'s world in *Children of a Lesser God*. In the latter film, the darkened pool is established as her space as we see her swimming, nude, at night. When John enters the pool Sarah is naked, he is fully dressed. As Sarah undresses him, the soundtrack suggests that John is making a transition to her non-hearing world. A similar scene occurs in the showing of affection in *Cocoon* (1985) when the nude alien female Kitty (Tahnee Welch) "shares" herself with the nude human male Jack (Steve Guttenberg), revealing her world to him through a lightshow in the pool. When the frustrated lover, Walter (Bruce Willis) and Nadia (Kim Basinger), finally get together in a pool in *Blind Date* (1987) the mix is sanctified by the addition of a priest. A more extreme disruption visits the adulterous pool coupling of romance novelist Mary Fisher (Meryl Streep) and Bob (Ed Begley, Jr.) in *She-Devil* (1989) when Bob's wife Ruth (Roseanne Barr) drops off their kids.

For the more symbolically inclined, Jim McBride's version of *Breathless* (1983) gave us the iconic image of Jesse (Richard Gere) extended off the end of a diving board to lift Monica (Valerie Kaprisky) out of the pool for a kiss. In a scene that reflects the complications of her lesbian relationship, *Lianna* (1983) (Linda Griffiths) interrupts her public lap-swimming to discuss her passion with her lover and, lacking the intimacy of a private pool, the two describe what they are doing to the other in their imagination. Even more abstractly, the orgiastic relationship between the three women and Van Horne in *The Witches of Eastwick* (1987) is represented, in part, as the women float *over* the pool.

The idea of the swimming pool as a private, sensual space seems central to its conventional use in American film. At a purely symbolic level, there is little difference between the nighttime hot tub lovemaking of Dale (Mel Gibson) and JoAnn (Michelle Pfeiffer) and their final full-bodied daytime embrace in the surf in *Tequila Sunrise* (1988). What difference exists is a matter of degrees of intimacy. The swimming pool takes the public ocean of *Beach Blanket Bingo* (1965) and *From Here to Eternity* (1953) and turns it into a controlled, intimate space. The hot tub and jacuzzi intensify the intimacy in pools big enough for only two in films like *Tequila Sunrise*, *Switch* (1990), *A Change of Seasons* (1980) and *Amazon Women on the Moon* (1987).

> It is our duty to suppress. Suppression is our vaccine. Suppression is civilization.
>
> The Doctor, *Investigation of a Citizen Above Suspicion*

Issues of artificiality and naturalness also tend to float around the edges of pool films. *The Swimmer* makes much of the increasing artificiality of the swimming pool as location of parties and public rowdiness in contrast to the ideal river of Burt's youth. *Club Paradise* (1986) and *The Mighty Quinn* (1989) both juxtapose pools and ocean beaches to underscore the unnatural racial and class-based separations that occur at the Caribbean poolside. The central romantic scene in *Little Vegas* (1990) takes place at a private natural pool (smaller, but reminiscent of the commune pool in *Easy Rider* [1969]) specifically in contrast to the community's noisy public pool. (As in *Fast Times at*

Ridgemont High, in *Little Vegas*, the sexual-swimming connection is made when Lexi [Katherine O'Hara]'s invitation to Carmine [Anthony John Denison] to join her in swimming is also an invitation to join her in sex.) *Whore*'s (1991) only "romantic" scene takes place between whore and pimp in a swimming pool complete with its own waterfall.

A student of these films would gather that the swimming pool is seen as natural when it is intimate, a private space for lovers. Artificiality becomes a factor as the pool becomes public, with increasing numbers of people (generally, and inappropriately, dressed) and increasing formality. By these standards we see that the epitome of artificiality, the debasement of the swimming pool, is to be found in the ritualized non-sensuality of the business-oriented poolside party.

In a "pure" party form, the swimming pool is a location of libidinous excess—for example in the Christmas skinny-dipping party in *The Last Picture Show* (1971) or the drunken debauchery of the Australian *Don's Party* (1976) or the students' chaotic party in a swimming pool built in a college lecture room in *Real Genius* (1985). (The fact that the poolside is the one calm male refuge at *North Dallas Forty's* [1979] opening bacchanalia is a warning that something is wrong.) A sliding scale of artificiality can be established, with these sensual examples at on end, moving through the purchased image of sensuality in the pool-centered sex club of *Night Shift* (1982), the premeditated fully clothed pool-hopping of *Down and Out in Beverly Hills* (1986) and *It's a Wonderful Life*'s (1946), ripe with untapped sexuality, into the staid—and dry—extreme of poolside cocktail parties in films like *The Swimmer, Seconds* (1966), *The Star Chamber* (1983), *The Secret of My Success* and *Dead Again* (1991) (in which a fountain is transformed into a swimming pool through its use in a brief Busby Berkeley-esque passage). In the poolside cocktail party, sensuality is toweled-off and sublimated into stylish female gowns, male verbal combat toward eventual power and position, and a tended bar.

In such scenes, the pool functions as a student's highlighter, reminding us of the sensuality, conflict and chaos which lurks beneath the black tie, ready to explode as it does when Roman Strauss (Kenneth Brannagh) knocks a sleazy reporter (Andy Garcia) into the pool for looking at his wife's anklet in *Dead Again*. With suppression comes fetishization; the pool—repository of sexuality—represents the power and wealth of those who possess it. The vulgarity of actually showing the flesh, acting out the violence or sexuality is no longer necessary. In such scenes all takes place at a symbolic level, exploding only when a character like Strauss forgets to sublimate his response and "acts naturally."

> Just when I thought it was safe to go back in the water...
>
> Brantley, *The Secret of My Success*

It is at points such as these that the pool can become a threatening space. As long as it remains a female space, the threat remains clearly sexual. In a comic example, we see the sexually carnivorous Aunt Vera "devouring" Brantley in *The Secret of My Success*. A more serious, though still sexual, threat is seen as female threatens female in Paul Schrader's 1982 remake of *Cat People* as Irena (Natasha Kinski) stalks the topless Alice (Annette O'Toole) in a darkened swimming pool. In *Black Widow* (1987), the battle between the two female protagonists is finally acknowledged in a nighttime, poolside scene during Katherine's wedding celebration. Beside the same pool in which Katherine seduced Alex's lover, Katherine declares her victory over Alex (Debra Winger) and then roughly kisses her in a hostile and erotic coda. Female aggression at poolside takes an explicitly sexual overtone, even in cases of murder. Consider the dead gigolo-narrator (William Holden) of *Sunset Boulevard* whose corpse floats in a pool after being killed by his "spider-woman" lover, Norma Desmond (Gloria Swanson), whom he has tried to leave. The exception might be Melina (Carole Bouquet), the avenging daughter who kills a man at a bikini-dense poolside in *For Your Eyes Only*, but even she is quickly reduced to a passive sexual object by the removal of her crossbow and the standard framing of a James Bond film.

However, when the swimming pool becomes a male domain things get out of balance and physical aggression and competition increase. In its more sublimated states the male competition is seen in Thornton (Rodney Dangerfield)'s diving competition in *Back to School* (1986) and the poolside repartee of *Beverly Hills Cop 2* (1987) where Axel Foley (Eddie Murphy's con-man cop) is able to float but Sergeant Taggart (John Ashton's by-the-book cop) slips and falls fully clothed into the pool. In *It's a Wonderful Life*, male jealousy leads to the prank that dumps George (Jimmy Stewart) in the pool. (Steve Martin)'s embarrassment over his perceived failure as a father and a money-maker compared to his daughter's future father-in-law (Peter Michael Goetz) in *Father of the Bride* (1991) culminates in a doberman-driven dousing in the man's pool. Psychological threats and actual violence visit the heroes of *My Bodyguard* (1980) and *Ordinary People* after all-male swimming. The hostility between the drill instructor (Louis Gossett) and his officer candidates in *An Officer and a Gentleman* leads to the near-drowning of a terrified candidate during a crash drill in the base swimming pool. The competition quickly escalates in a film like *The Osterman Weekend* (1983) in which an all-male water volleyball game quickly degenerates into a near-drowning of the host. A mini-convention of male-based pool violence may be emerging in the "person falling from great heights in to a pool" as seen in *Diamonds are Forever* (1971), *Stick* (1985), *Lethal Weapon 2* (1989), and *Harley Davidson and the Marlboro Man* (1991). A recent innovation in this field can be seen in the "entire car falling from great heights into a pool" of *The Last Boy Scout* (1991).

Generally men outnumbering women at the pool means violence unto death. It is in the all-male pool therapy of *One Flew Over the Cuckoo's Nest* (1975) that the threat to McMurtry (Jack Nicholson)'s freedom and life is first revealed. By the end of *The Osterman Weekend*, the women have left, the surface of the pool has been set aflame, and the hero is under water dodging bullets. Actual testosterone-heavy swimming pool murders can be found in *Gorky Park* (1983), the British *The Long Good Friday* (1980), *The Brotherhood of the Yakuza* (1975), *Goldfinger* (a woman is gilded to death for failing to help Goldfinger cheat at his poolside cardgame), *Sunset Boulevard* (1950), *Alphaville*, *The Seduction*, *The Amateur* (1982) twice in *Lethal Weapon* (1987) (one is shot at poolside and drowned, one is blown up on a diving board), four times in *The Last Boy Scout* (one is killed by broken nose at poolside, one is shot at poolside, one is shot while submerged in the pool, and one is blown up at poolside), and in an archetypical literary-based example, Gatsby (Robert Redford)'s death in *The Great Gatsby* (1974).

Sometimes the result is not death but just wrongness. In *Barton Fink* (1991), the Coen brothers manipulate this conventional male tension to generate additional threat in the poolside meeting between the crazed studio head (Michael Lerner) and Fink (Jon Turturro), the screenwriter. Fink wakes up next to the corpse of his lover, only to be hustled to his boss's poolside to account for his unfinished film script. Three overdressed men meet in a scene in which the inevitable violence emerges on a sado-masochistic pivot as the boss's irrational humiliation and firing of his assistant to show his power segues immediately into his self-abasing foot-kissing before the writer to show his love. Over-dressed men at a poolside party in *Seconds* manhandle Cary Grant and destroy his illusions of love and a second chance at life. *North Dallas Forty* and *The Falcon and the Snowman* (1985) also use the men conferring at poolside to foreshadow unpleasantness to come. In *Bugsy*, Mickey (Harvey Keitel)'s vulgar threats to Ben Seigel (Warren Beatty) are made at an all-male poolside; the men move into a bar and quickly become conciliatory.

The one place where potentially positive male-male swimming pool relationships exist is in the paternal tutor role. While the empty pool in *The Swimmer* foreshadows the death of Ned's fantasy, it also offers him the chance to teach the abandoned boy how to swim—a metaphor for how to survive in a hostile world. Such a scene is implied at the end of *Terms of Endearment*, when Breedlove takes Aurora's problem grandchild to his pool to teach him the "internationally famous Breedlove crawl." Both of these examples point to another distinctly male metaphor in the swimming pool, lap swimming. From Ben (Dustin Hoffman) in *The Graduate* (1967) to Conrad (Timothy Hutton) in *Ordinary People* (1980), grinding away through the water seems to reflect an unsatisfying loss of identity that might connect more broadly to the roles they are being called upon to assume in society.

> The pool doesn't work anymore. It's too late.
>
> Walter, *Cocoon*

Some pools are unused. Just as an empty pool foreshadows the death of Ned's fantasy in *The Swimmer*, the unused pool foreshadows discord, death and impotence. In *Rebel Without a Cause* (1955) the kids declare the empty pool of the abandoned mansion to be a "sunken nursery" for the disposal of unwanted children, only to have the abandoned child Plato (Sal Mineo) end up battling three gang members there as the prelude to his armed dash toward death, all because his fantasy of a perfect teen family has collapsed. It is in the poolhouse and at the chilly side of a covered pool in *Crimes and Misdemeanors* (1989) that Judah Rosenthal (Martin Landau) discusses having his brother (Jerry Orbach) arrange the murder of Judah's mistress, Dolores (Angelica Huston). In *Ricochet* (1991), a dry pool is used by the villain (John Lithgow) to torture the hero (Denzel Washington), addict him to heroin, film him participating sex with a dominatrix—all to the end of destroying his career before killing him. Through the wrong sexual adventure in the darkened poolhouse of an unused pool, Warren Beatty's hairdresser loses the key woman in his life in *Shampoo* (1975) (a location and result repeated with less permanent consequences in *Fast Times at Ridgemont High*). As if to underline Kane's fragility after being left by his second wife, the newsreel section of *Citizen Kane* (1941) shows a bundled Charles Foster Kane, framed by statues, sitting next to an unused pool.

But even in the death-filled male pool world, women can restore the balance. Christopher Reeve's *Superman* (1978) in the eponymous film almost dies from death-by-kryptonite in Lex Luthrop's partially filled swimming pool. It is Miss Teschmacher (Valerie Perrine), the very sexual bad-female-gone-momentarily-good, who purifies the pool (by removing the kryptonite) and allows the rebirth of the Superman.

A much more ambiguous approach to the reinvigorating power of women at swimming pools is found in Robert Altman's surreal *Three Women* (1977). The film revolves around issues of birth, and rebirth, healing and swimming pools in a world of women inaccessible to men. The central characters work at a desert health spa where they use pool therapy to attempt to restore their elderly patients. Pinky (Sissy Spacek) attempts to drown herself in another swimming pool only to be, perhaps, reborn in the image of Millie (Shelly DuVall).

In fact, in the struggle between Eros and Thanatos, the pool often becomes a place of birth and rebirth. In the broad sense of the sense of the terms, the Erotic birth is pure and life-affirming, but at the more Thanatic extreme, the event is a polluted death-parody of birth.

> C'mon, you'll be a new man, believe me!
> Art tempting Bernie to join him in the swimming pool in *Cocoon*

At the death end of the poolside spectrum, *Gremlins* (1984) uses a darkened high school swimming pool as the site of the single-sexed reproduction of the swarms of vile gremlins who almost destroy the quiet town. While allegedly comic, the vision of polluted mass birth is clearly horrific. The heroes spend the rest of the film tracking down and killing these unnatural babies. Only slightly less literally, the climax of *Poltergeist* (1982) offers a violent "rebirth" that fills the swimming pool with corpses exploding out of their graves.

For the most part, though, the swimming pool births and rebirths are positive and nurturing. There is, of course, *The Swimmer'* temporary rebirth through swimming. Sergeant Taggart of *Beverly Hills Cop II* is reborn as a more-relaxed anti-authoritarian in style and substance after being doused in the pool. The rebirth of Claire (Mary McDonnell)'s maternal identity in *Grand Canyon* (1991) is announced in a scene featuring Claire lying on a chaise lounge at poolside with an abandoned baby she has decided to adopt. As she cuddles the rescued baby, she speaks to her drifting husband by phone, beginning the resurrection of the couple's marriage.

The clearest transformation of the pool into a womb occurs in *Cocoon* in the placement of the alien cocoons in a swimming pool near a Florida retirement home. The pool serves as both the literal womb for the aliens and as a fountain of youth for elderly residents of a nearby home. Swimming in the pool's "life force" causes first a sexual, then a physical, and possibly a spiritual rebirth among the elderly swimmers.

This same sort of metaphorical rebirth occurs more dramatically when Jerry (Nick Nolte), a street-person, tries to drown himself in the

Whitemans' (Richard Dreyfus and Bette Midler) backyard pool in *Down and Out in Beverly Hills*. Jerry is dragged kicking from his fetal drowning position into a new life. Reborn as a functional member of the society, he becomes a sexual savior to the family, satisfying the wife, the daughter and maid, instilling the son with a confidence in his own creative and sexual identity and bringing a new life to Mr. Whiteman as well.

It is in the fantasy of sexuality and rebirth of *Down and Out in Beverly Hills* that we return to the conventional uses of the swimming pool to which *The Swimmer* responds. While Ned must leave the pool and ends the film a broken and pathetic man, the more commercially successful Hollywood film offers us a happier resolution. While there are negative variations upon the theme, the swimming pool of American popular film is an edenic life spring that offers a space for fantasies of sensual fulfillment, where women are more female, men are more macho, and the promise of rebirth is perpetually within reach.

Filmography

Year	Film	Director
1941	*Citizen Kane*	Orson Welles
1946	*It's A Wonderful Life*	Frank Capra
1950	*Sunset Boulevard*	Billy Wilder
1955	*Rebel Without a Cause*	Nicholas Ray
1964	*Goldfinger*	Guy Hamilton (British)
1965	*Alphaville*	Jean-Luc Godard (French)
1966	*Harper*	Jack Smight
1966	*Seconds*	John Frankenheimer
1967	*The Graduate*	Mike Nichols
1967	*The Cool Ones*	Gene Nelson
1968	*The Swimmer*	Frank Perry and Sydney Pollack
1969	*Marlowe*	Paul Bogart
1971	*Diamonds are Forever*	Guy Hamilton (British)
1971	*The Last Picture Show*	Peter Bogdonavich
1972	*Slaughterhouse-Five*	George Roy Hill
1974	*The Great Gatsby*	Jack Clayton
1975	*The Brotherhood of the Yakuza* (a.k.a. *The Yakuza*)	Sydney Pollack
1975	*One Flew Over the Cuckoo's Nest*	Milos Forman
1975	*Shampoo*	Hal Ashby
1976	*Don's Party*	Bruce Beresford (Australian)
1977	*Three Women*	Robert Altman

1978	*Superman*	Richard Donner
1979	*North Dallas Forty*	Ted Kotcheff
1980	*A Change of Seasons*	Richard Lang
1980	*The Long Good Friday*	John MacKenzie (British)
1980	*My Bodyguard*	Tony Bill
1980	*Ordinary People*	Robert Redford
1980	*Raging Bull*	Martin Scorcese
1981	*For Your Eyes Only*	John Glen
1982	*The Amateur*	Charles Jarrott (Canadian)
1982	*Cat People*	Paul Schrader
1982	*Fast Times at Ridgemont High*	Amy Heckerling
1982	*My Tutor*	George Bowers
1982	*Nightshift*	Ron Howard
1982	*An Officer and a Gentleman*	Taylor Hackford
1982	*Poltergeist*	Tobe Hooper
1982	*The Seduction*	David Schmoeller
1982	*Starstruck*	Gillian Armstrong (Australian)
1983	*Breathless*	Jim McBride
1983	*Lianna*	John Sayles
1983	*Gorky Park*	Michael Apted
1983	*National Lampoon's Vacation*	Harold Ramis
1983	*The Osterman Weekend*	Sam Peckinpah
1983	*Star 80*	Bob Fosse
1983	*The Star Chamber*	Peter Hyams
1983	*Terms of Endearment*	James L. Brooks
1984	*Gremlins*	Joe Dante
1984	*The Muppets Take Manhatten*	Frank Oz
1985	*Cocoon*	Ron Howard
1985	*The Falcon and the Snowman*	John Schlesinger
1985	*Fletch*	Michael Ritchie
1985	*Real Genius*	Martha Coolidge
1985	*Stick*	Burt Reynolds
1986	*Back to School*	Alan Metter
1986	*Black Widow*	Bob Rafelson
1986	*Children of a Lesser God*	Randa Haines
1986	*Club Paradise*	Harold Ramis
1986	*Down and Out in Beverly Hills*	Paul Mazursky
1986	*Hardbodies: 2*	Mark Griffiths
1987	*Amazon Women on the Moon*	Joe Dante, Carl Gottleib, Peter Horton, John Landis, and Robert K. Weiss
1987	*Beverly Hills Cop 2*	Tony Scott
1987	*Black Widow*	Bob Rafelson
1987	*Blind Date*	Blake Edwards
1987	*Dragnet*	Tom Mankiewicz

1987	*Less Than Zero*	Marek Kanievska
1987	*Lethal Weapon*	Richard Donner
1987	*The Secret of My Success*	Herbert Ross
1987	*The Witches of Eastwick*	George Miller
1988	*Adventures of Baron Munchausen*	Terry Gilliam
1988	*Casual Sex?*	Genevieve Robert
1988	*Earth Girls are Easy*	Julian Temple
1988	*Fresh Horses*	David Anspaugh
1988	*Tequila Sunrise*	Robert Towne
1989	*Crimes and Misdemeanors*	Woody Allen
1989	*Lethal Weapon 2*	Richard Donner
1989	*The Mighty Gun*	Carl Schenkel
1989	*National Lampoon's Christmas Vacation*	Jeremiah Chechik
1989	*Road House*	Rowdy Harrington
1989	*She-Devil*	Susan Seidelman
1990	*Switch*	Blake Edwards
1990	*Taking Care of Business*	Arthur Hiller
1990	*The Hard Way*	Richard Donner
1991	*Barton Fink*	Joel Coen
1991	*Bugsy*	Barry Levinson
1991	*Dead Again*	Kenneth Brannagh
1991	*Defending Your Life*	Albert Brooks
1991	*Father of the Bride*	Charles Shyer
1991	*Grand Canyon*	Lawrence Kasdan
1991	*Harley Davidson and the Marlboro Man*	Simon Wincer
1991	*The Last Boy Scout*	Tony Scott
1991	*Ricochet*	Russell Mulcahy
1991	*Whore*	Ken Russell (British)

Interiors:
The Space of Melodrama

Thomas Sobchack

Perhaps the ideal medium for melodrama was radio where the soaps prospered for years. On the air it could be what its name originally meant—a play with music—directly transmitting the melodrama's chief concern, the characters' inner emotional states. Dialogue plus sighs, laughs, cries, whimpers, shouts, and silences—all underscored with appropriately affecting music—adequately revealed the loves, hopes, fears, and sorrows of the female protagonists' lives. Essentially a drama of interior life, of choices made or not made concerning social relationships, of feelings expressed or repressed, the melodrama requires no specific spacial context, a particular locale. To make any sense a western must be set in the great outdoors, but a melodrama needs only a generic room, a place where people can talk.

The enunciative power of the visual in film, however, where space is always represented, adds a factor unavailable to radio. Setting, decor, and costume articulate important elements of the complex and conflicting moral dilemmas that constitute the melodrama's core of meaning. Though mute, background in a filmed melodrama often speaks what the characters can not, signifying the inexpressible. The rooms women inhabit in these films not only limit their world, but display the limitations the world places on them. Douglas Sirk said about the characters in his melodramas "their homes are their prisons" (Schatz 252). Although scenes do take place outdoors, interiors—the places where women live and work—remain the privileged spaces of filmed melodrama.

The world of melodrama is small—a woman, her lover, family, a few friends. The larger world of politics, business, and history is rarely presented directly. The characters exist only through and for each other. The only thing that matters is individual emotional happiness, the goal authorized by the culture for the characters in these stories, yet seldom achieved, because that kind of happiness always depends not on what they do, but what others do. Women, confined to their small circle in their small spaces, are portrayed as only capable of reacting to outside forces. Genres featuring male protagonists, on the other hand, take place in a larger world, the exterior location representing a field of action, a site for self-determination. The independent male characters single-mindedly choose a goal, struggle to overcome obstacles, and either succeed or die trying. The literal expanse of horizon in such films represents clear-cut possibilities for action—right or wrong, them or us. The dependent female characters of melodrama, however, enclosed in their interiors, are seldom given the opportunity of even gazing at that horizon, much less given the chance to "go for the gold," to pursue one unambiguous goal, to be active determiners of their lives.

In *Shirley Valentine* (1989), a working-class English housewife who spends much of her time preparing meals for an unappreciative husband occupies her days literally talking to the wall in the kitchen. Shirley dreams of sitting on a beach somewhere where grapes are grown, sipping the wine of the country, watching the sun set across the water. She wants to expand her horizons, to become independent, to have the same options that men presumably have. But women in melodrama are always dependent in some way, held back, restricted, compromised in their search for happiness. The protagonist of *Shirley Valentine* is one of the few who succeeds in escaping the confinement of that domestic interior, though not without a struggle. In most melodramas (*Mildred Pierce*, 1945, for example) such escape is usually punished in some way.

The surface meaning disseminated by melodramas is that women should remain in their interiors and find contentment there. But as most commentators (Byars, Doane, Elsaesser, Haskell, et al) have shown, the films, in fact, articulate the opposite. The illogic of the discourse becomes apparent upon close examination. Women's exclusion from the larger world is registered as an absence of that world from the films. The fact that women seem to have power only over the interiors which predominate in melodrama suggest their disempowerment in the exterior world. The justifiable resentment of women against the dictates of the patriarchal order is patently inexpressible in a main stream commercial film. From D.W. Griffith to the present, this paradoxical narrative thrust creates the peculiar tension found in all melodramas between surface elements and underlying meaning. Women are continually depicted as nobly accepting the limitations placed on them by the culture, but in fact what is actually being shown is the mechanism of the repression itself. Narrative ruptures inherent in the form—protagonists nearly always have to choose between two inadequate solutions, either career or family, for example—continually undermine the surface message of women's willing acceptance of such a situation. But the struggle to speak the truth about women's position is equally visible in the mise-en-scene, in the lightning, sets, and costumes used to materialize the script. In Griffith's *Broken Blossoms* (1919), the contrast between the squalor of the house Lillian Gish is abused in and the soft, comforting room of her Chinese protector is unforgettable. In Griffith's able hands, the interiors of *Way Down East* (1920) and *Orphans of the Storm* (1922) speak volumes about the characters' relations with each other and the world.

Throughout the history of film melodrama, however, evocative interiors appear in the work of unheralded studio directors as well as film artists. This fact leads to the conclusion that telling interiors are part and parcel of the genre. Between the wars, the studios cranked out hundreds of women's films in response to audience demand for the product. John Stahl, seldom mentioned as an auteur, directed a number of melodramas in the thirties—*Back Street* (1932), *Only Yesterday* (1933), *Imitation of Life* (1934), *Magnificent Obsession* (1935), *When Tomorrow Comes* (1939)—most made from popular novels. In each of these films, the interiors consistently register the frustrating limits placed on women's aspirations. For example, Irene Dunne in *Back Street* waits and waits for her married lover in a tiny well appointed apartment, but she waits interminably and alone, fearing to leave lest she miss one of his random appearances. Her obsessive love for John Boles is virtually a prison sentence. Though the windows are covered with fancy curtains, they could as well be iron bars. It is in this way that melodrama speaks "beyond the capacities of representation" (Byars 167), using the interiors of the locale to relay excess and often paradoxical meanings to the primarily female audience who understand the meaning of those spaces all too well. Not surprisingly, many of the art, set and costume directors who literally produced the shape and texture of those spaces during the studio years were women—Bonnie Cashline, Edith Head, Natalie Kalmus (Walsh 30). They couldn't help but imprint the films with their knowledge of the real state of women's lives.

Most commentators have noted the intense identification women have with the melodrama, movies about "dilemmas of moral choice focusing on themes of interpersonal connection and the fear of separation from loved ones" (Walsh 42). Chodorow, Weitzman and other psychoanalysts have suggested separation-individuation is more difficult for women than men and this might account for the practice. Carol Gilligan observes that women focus on moral choice as complex rather than abstract, see personal responsibility more important than being in the right, and value persons over abstractions, all part of the matter of melodrama (Gilligan 73). Linda Williams maintains that it is women's ability to recognize themselves in the bodies of other women that allows them to see through the surface plots of women's films to know the underlying problems addressed (Williams 5-9). These are all valid explanations of the phenomenon, but one can also add that the interiors in which melodramas take place are so familiar to women in their actual lives that identification with the film's diegesis is enhanced by that recognition. The spaces where family and community relations are forged are crucial to the melodrama. The action of the films takes place in women's rooms: the kitchen, the living room, the bedroom in the immediate domestic area; the club, the hospital, the office where people meet and talk in the external social arena.

> In the room the women come and go
> Talking of Michelangelo.
>> T.S. Eliot "Love Song of J.Alfred Prufrock"

Most women live in interiors. Not just physically, but psychologically. Joan Crawford in *Mildred Pierce* says at one point as she bakes yet another batch of pies to help make ends meet, "I think I was born in the kitchen!" In today's world of working women, who more often than not must manage the household as well as the outside job, this sentiment is still echoed by many. A common expression states brides have to "feather their nest" when entering a new domicile, that is, personalize the place by attending to elements of the decor. Though perhaps a time worn cliche, this notion indicates the extent to which women have seen their immediate surroundings—the interiors they will spend much of their time in—as extensions of themselves. That's why the locales of melodrama resonate so profoundly with their intended audience. Men may be attracted to the wide open spaces of the western or thrilled by the exotic quality of a strange planet in a Star Trek film, but they do not live in those places everyday. "Melodrama expresses a reality experienced by most of the people most of the time" (Byars 18), a reality known intimately by women.

Though the milieu of the melodrama is primarily middle class, modestly affluent, white, professional, suburban, the sort of homogenized mainstream America figured in the vast majority of movies from Hollywood, the melodrama has on occasion made use of its interior settings to represent class differences. A number of women's films feature mothers who sacrifice themselves for their children's entry into a higher station in life. In the 1937 *Stella Dallas*, the young and ambitious Stella (Barbara Stanwyk) is shown chafing under the yoke of having been born in a mill worker's family. The interiors of her childhood home are dark, narrow, low ceilinged, and ill furnished, suggesting both a lack of money and a lack of taste. The churlish mother and weak-willed father match the rooms. Upwardly mobile, Stella charms a company manager into marriage. From a high-class Eastern family, Steven Dallas (John Boles) loves Stella's raw vitality, but intends to raise her up to his status by teaching her how to act like a lady. The interior of their first apartment is clearly high-class: spacious rooms, fine furniture, rugs, crystal, lace tablecloths and so on. But Stella finds the social life of the uptight, upright, well-to-do boring, and turns to the more lively company of people from her original milieu.

The country club is one of the choice interiors of the melodrama because it is a site where social status is easily represented: the camera can quickly isolate people in one part of the room gossiping about people in another part of the room, inadvertent meetings between rivals and lovers plausibly occur in such a place, and characters can acquit themselves properly by obeying the rules of social decorum or fall from grace by behaving badly in public. Though a pivotal scene at the country club in *Stella Dallas* actually takes place on an outdoor patio dance floor, it functions like any interior scene where people sit around at small tables and have the opportunity of watching and commenting as other characters dance. Stella refuses to sit quietly at the table of stuffed shirt corporation bosses as her husband commands. Instead she dances the night away with a local gambler who's also out of his element in the refined atmosphere of this meeting place of the small town's aristocracy. Embarrassed by her choice of rowdy friends, Steven departs for New York and a return to the high toned social circles he had known as a youth, leaving behind a daughter, Lolly.

Stella, supporting herself as a seamstress, makes a comfortable home for herself and her child, but she never gets over her taste for loud clothes, bright colors, and unpretentious acquaintances—all earmarks of a lower class, but lively world. Yet she sends her daughter to private school in hopes that Lolly will have "all the advantages" in life she was denied. When Lolly's friends at school realize what kind of background she comes from, they snub her. In a most poignant scene, we see the over-dressed Stella presiding over an over-dressed birthday party table in her extravagantly ornate dining room as she and Lolly await the arrival of the school chums. Instead they are treated to a series of polite notes indicating not a single other child is going to attend the party. Here the interior is more than background that needs to be filled; it places the character firmly in her lifestyle.

The paradox of Stella Dallas is that she clearly prefers her crude and vulgar lifestyle, but wants something far different for her daughter. She feels guilty about her choice, knowing it is not considered the right one by society. This paradox, like so many in melodramas, is never adequately explained. The life that Stella desires for her daughter is represented visually, however, in scenes in the mansion of Steven Dallas' high society girlfriend (later his wife) where Lolly goes to spend holidays with her father. Long sweeping staircases, elegant draperies, thick expensive carpeting, crystal chandeliers, large and spacious rooms portray the comfort and beauty available to the wealthy, old line families, the "advantages" in Lolly's future if she marries into this world. The price, of course, is giving up a mother's companionship. Stella realizes she can never fit into that world, never feel comfortable in those rooms. Overdressed as usual, Stella visits the mansion to make a deal with Dallas' poised and elegant intended. Looking out of place, Stella is presented as a woman who could never walk in those rooms speaking of Michelangelo. In the famous last scene of the film, Stella, forever barred from easy commerce with her daughter, stands outside the residence and looks in at those well manicured rooms where Lolly is being married, caught between the desire for her daughter's well being and her own.

Melodramas in the early 1940s shifted to more patriotic themes, but interiors still functioned as barometers of the protagonists' lives. With the end of the war and the rise of film noir, melodrama frequently took on a more menacing tone. The possible range of interiors, both domestic and public and their uses is illustrated fully in *Mildred Pierce* (1945). Kitchens, living rooms, bedrooms, restaurants, bars, dance floors—all are evident in this classic film. The plain, dowdy, suburban home of the Pierces seen at the beginning of the film justifies the attempt by Mildred to make life materially better for her children. At first she need only bake pies in that kitchen to supply the daughters with piano and voice lessons. After the father walks out on the family, however, Mildred is forced to find work to support the family, something her status conscious daughter Veda despises. Mildred is one of those stock mothers in melodrama who sacrifices herself to give her children all the "advantages." After the younger daughter dies of pneumonia, Mildred throws all her energy into making a better life for Veda, the social climber. In a significant scene in Veda's bedroom, the young girl manipulates her mother into compliance with her wishes by saying, "I love you," though it is clear she's a self-centered, selfish brat. The ambience of the room subtly attests to Veda's self-absorption.

The small, but homey "kitchen" seen in that first house (the kind Mildred declares she was "born" in) is replaced by the fried chicken restaurant she eventually builds into a lucrative chain. Though characters mention the business is doing well, most of the time Mildred appears in the restaurant, she is working, fixing up the place, checking on the waitresses, watching over the cooks. Though it's a much larger and more impressive space, Mildred is still doing domestic work. Her ambitions for her daughter and her own attraction for the neér-do-well playboy Monte Beragon come together when she visits the mansion he needs to sell for quick cash. There is a funereal aspect to the dusty, dark wood paneled interior, redolent of decay. Perhaps Mildred should have been forewarned by the gloomy atmosphere, but she plunges on in her efforts to make a better life for Veda and marries the heel. Our next shot of the house after she's moved in shows what a little sprucing up can do. Neat curtains, lighter furniture, flowers on every table make the place seem bright and airy, though the presence of Zachary Scott's moody Beragon never seems to match the new, bright and optimistic look brought by Mildred.

Eventually Beragon is murdered at the Malibu Beach house where Mildred and he first met. A blend of melodrama and film noir, the film's dark and shadowy interiors and gloomy outdoor scenes at night stem from the noir tradition. At the same time the interiors consistently reflect or comment on the characters' inner feelings. From those first images of Mildred sweating over her pies in a typical, unpretentious, suburban kitchen through the bright and sunny moments in the restaurant when Mildred is at the height of her business success to the climactic moments in the shadowy police detective's office, the kitchens, the bedrooms, the livingrooms all lend their distinctive atmospheres to fill in the nuances of character the figures on the screen exhibit.

Several male directors of melodramas in the classic Hollywood period whose work spans the 40s and 50s—George Cukor, Vincente Minnelli, Otto Preminger and Douglas Sirk—are easily identifiable as sympathetic to women's concerns. They self-consciously manipulated the mise-en-scene of their pictures to create a rich, visual accompaniment to the plot that worked like music supplying non-verbal emotional overtones. Sirk, in particular, is noted for his use of decor to amplify the nature of the characters, to represent aspects of their inner lives repressed in the script. In *Written on the Wind*, for example, Sirk recalled employing "deep focus lenses" to give the effect of "harshness to the objects and a kind of enameled, hard surface to the colors. I wanted this to bring out the inner violence, the energy of the characters which is all inside them and can't break through" (Elsaesser 1). The relationship between the lighting, composition and decor of the interiors of melodrama and the meaning constructed by the viewer in response to the films should be clear. Emotional realities are evoked through the seemingly unimportant background material.

In 1930s melodrama, the difference depicted between classes had seldom suggested the lower class might have some value. In a world still reeling from the Depression, the lives of the upper classes were to be envied and aspired to. In the 1950s, when rampant materialism gripped the country, the melodrama could more easily be ambivalent about such assumptions and often quite critical. In films like *All That Heaven Allows* (1955), *Rebel Without a Cause* (1955), *Giant* (1956) and *Picnic* (1955), the materialism of the Eisenhower years comes under fire. The wealthy are seen as either decadent, warped, and impotent or rule-bound, stultified, insensitive, and heedless of natural human values. Interiors almost self-consciously proclaim these films' attitude toward the upper class. The gothic mansion brooding over an empty landscape in *Giant* is redolent of deep seated psychological problems inherent in the traditions of the wealthy Texans. The ghosts of the frontier past—when men were men and women played their submissive role—haunt the members of the Benedict clan. The antique quality of their value system is echoed in the antique filled rooms of the house. The new bride from the landed gentry of the East, Elizabeth Taylor, a stranger to those hide-bound ways, is not allowed to make any changes either in the decor or in the way people relate to their lower class neighbors. Sal Mineo's neurotic rich kid in *Rebel*, abandoned by his family, lives in a dreary, but expensive modern house, empty of any human warmth. His bedroom, a jumble of books, knick-knacks, posters and souvenirs suggests the way he's tried to surround himself with material goods to make-up for the loss of family, but his eventual, unnecessary death critiques his class and its hollow values.

William Holden's jobless drifter in *Picnic* is presented in sharp contrast to Cliff Robertson's successful small town businessman (a member of the local ruling class) by showing Holden unconfined by interiors. He works shirtless in a garden, displays poise and ease at the Labor Day picnic on the grass in the afternoon, and moves gracefully and powerfully at the outdoor dance that evening. The natural man, potently sexual, Holden attracts Robertson's sensual and lusty fiancee, Kim Novak, to change alliances. Robertson, though an ardent pursuer of Novak, always looks uncomfortable in the outdoors, more at home in the busy and efficient office that represents his family's grain elevator business which dominates the community. Unlike Holden who is free to hop the next freight, Robertson is imprisoned by his commitment to the material world.

Douglas Sirk uses the same constellation of conflicting values in *All That Heaven Allows* to attack the complacency, rigidity and unfairness of the traditions of social decorum set by the local aristocracy in any community, and particularly the way they imprison women. In this film Rock Hudson plays Ron Kirby, the man of nature influenced by Thoreau, a gardner who becomes a nurseryman, more interested in growing living things than making money or becoming a part of the social set. Jane Wyman is Cary Scott, an attractive middle-aged widow who has lived all her life in affluence, dependent on her husband's care and attention. The house she lives in is full of stylishly furnished but rather ordinary rooms; she wears expensive, but tasteful clothes. She spends her evenings at the "club" properly escorted by a comfortable, reliable, and sexless longtime friend of hers and her husband's, playing bridge, drinking cocktails, and gossiping. Sirk portrays Cary as imprisoned by her material surroundings, her soul choked lifeless by the string of expensive pearls (undoubtedly a gift of her late husband) always draped around her neck. Significantly his portrait hangs strategically over the fireplace in the living room of the Scott house where many of the scenes take place, still dominating her life even after his death.

Kirby enters Cary's life like a breath of fresh air. He drives an old, beat-up station wagon, wears checkered shirts and work shoes, and speaks his mind with candor. The interior of the cluttered nursery, the warm and inviting casual quality of his best friends' house, and the old barn waiting for just the right woman to become a wonderful country home all suggest Ron's freedom from the rat-race and his determination to walk to the beat of a different drummer. Soft colors, textured surfaces, comfortable design fill the spaces Ron occupies with an ambience of shared enjoyment of people's idiosyncrasies and individualities. By contrast the interiors of the club and Cary's home are hard edged, metallic, unyielding, portraying an atmosphere that forces people to conform to what is considered proper. Quite rightly, Cary sees in Ron a rescuer from the shallowness of her current life.

Unfortunately true love and justice never run smooth. The community, exemplified by Cary's college-age children, by its insistence that Ron is not the right sort, and far too young besides, opposes the impending marriage. The barn, now remodeled into a beautiful, cosy, warm home seems unlikely to ever give lodging and comfort to the now separated couple. But finally, through a series of accidents (Sirk's films frequently suggest the only way anyone can really overcome the force of public opinion, the weight of the traditional, conservative value system, is through some external twist of fate, something very rare except in the movies), Cary is installed in the new interior, though not without circumstances that in typical Sirk fashion, add an ambivalence to the "happy" ending. Ron has been hurt in a fall, and it is unclear how long he will be bed-ridden. Cary has come to his side, not as an eager bride ready for love (as she had intended earlier in the story), but to nurse him back to health. And yet the force of the final scene with Ron lying on the sofa, a fire burning merrily in the fireplace, and Cary looking out of the large picture window at a deer (nature comfortably intersecting with the social matrix) provides hope that this new interior, the charming and livable barn, corresponds to her new interior. At least she has been able to throw off the burden of that other house—the legacy of her first husband and his stature in the world of commerce—and find a freer, more generous life in a new home with a man she loves. Cary may have only traded one male ruler for another, but Ron's life style stresses individual choice and personal values over material goods. There is the potential their coming together may lead to a more fulfilling life for both of them, and the image of that lovely interior complements this idea. The barn was once a dilapidated ruin. But with hard work it has become a beautiful place in which to live. Perhaps a similar dedication to refurbishing the relationship between the couple will prove successful.

A less positive but perhaps more realistic view of the effects lower class life has on people's emotional well being is found in George Cukor's *The Marrying Kind* (1952). Aldo Ray, a post office employee, and Judy Holliday, a secretary, meet, fall in love and marry. Though devoted to each other, their economic woes tear the marriage apart. Two interiors dominate the film. The first is the inside of an empty courtroom where the couple, now contemplating a divorce, tell their story to a woman judge who sympathetically tries to understand their conflicts and see if she can keep them together. The second is the small apartment they can barely afford on his salary, what had been imagined as a first temporary step toward a real home of their own, but which turns out to be the best they can ever have. The courtroom is dark, full of shadows, weighted down with the sense of finality that the contemplated divorce entails. In that setting the couple express anger, frustration and anxiety. Each half of the couple alternates telling some part of the history of their marriage—their very different emotional responses to the same incidents is made clear, though neither the man's nor the woman's view is privileged over the other.

As Ray and Holliday talk to the judge, their stories are dramatized as a series of flashbacks which take place chiefly in the apartment. For the newly married couple, it seems adequate, but hardly large enough to give Holliday a sense that it needs fulltime management. Yet her husband refuses to let her work now that she's a married woman. Ray sees much of his ego wrapped up in being able to support her. But after a couple of children are born, the situation becomes worse. In these scenes the apartment's minimal size becomes a metaphor for the limitations placed on the family income by the job Ray has and his adamant refusal to let Holliday work. The dining nook in the kitchen in which one vicious argument erupts between husband and wife with the five-year-old daughter in the middle underscores the effect the interior has on the couple. The table is wedged between the two counters in a space so narrow that the adults can scarcely squeeze past each other as they fix their toast and coffee. Seated at the table, nose to nose and jaw to jaw, they harangue each other over the issue of her going back to work to bring in the much needed money. The cramped quality of their lives is mirrored in the dimensions of that cramped apartment.

Even with strict adherence to the Breen Office code until the sixties, Hollywood melodramas were able to use the bedroom as a focal point for scenes depicting the emotional precariousness of couples. In *The Marrying Kind*, Ray comes home drunk early in the morning after flirting with a floozy at a dinner dance (there's the dance floor or club interior again where husbands or wives can meet an "other" who spells trouble) only to fall asleep half dressed as Holliday vents her jealous rage over his behavior from the other twin bed. Though Rock Hudson never appears in the same bedroom with Jane Wyman in *All That Heaven Allows*, his presence is felt strongly in a scene where the grown-up daughter tells her mother how humiliated she would be if the proposed marriage to the gardener were to take place; the scene effectively cuts Hudson out of the bedroom picture at that moment in the plot as Wyman measures the depth of her family's opposition.

Though the relationship of interior settings to lives of both the characters and the audience of melodrama is a convention of the genre, it is one capable of extensive elaboration. Rooms with beds are often pivotal places in melodramas. Bette Davis's hospital room in *Dark Victory* (1939), for example, functions quite differently than Debra Winger's in *Terms of Endearment* (1983), and Douglas Sirk gives the whole locale an ironic twist when Rock Hudson is confined to a hospital bed in his remake of *Magnificent Obsession* (1954). Davis's vivacious young socialite uses the occasion to flirt with her doctor (George Brent), though the audience already knows she has a fatal tumor, a fact being kept from her. Winger comes to terms with her feelings about her mother, Shirley Maclaine, during her stay in the hospital amidst a great deal of flowers and tears. Hudson's macho, playboy millionaire is made to appear a spoiled brat as he is bossed around by Agnes Moorhead's nurse. Hudson's contentiousness in his scene is recalled later as a reverse image of Jane Wyman's hospital room scene near the end of the film where she portrays the long suffering, but noble woman who ruins her health by refusing to marry Hudson because she is blind. In each of these cases except Hudson's the sight of the attractive and brave protagonist laid up in the stark, white-walled, impersonal room is designed to evoke copious amounts of sympathy from the viewer, but each works in subtly different ways.

After the demise of the studios, of course, the bedroom (now without the obligatory twin beds) could be used for a variety of ends. In *9 1/2 Weeks* (1986), the bed is the arena for the couple's dissolution. Even as early as *Cat on a Hot Tin Roof* (1958), significant scenes take place in the bedroom, where Paul Newman's sexual impotence can be alluded to rather directly. Elizabeth Taylor as the tough-willed, strong, sexually vibrant character eventually instills some emotional backbone in Newman so he can stand up to his father and finally become a man in all senses of the term. Bedrooms are visible everywhere in *The Turning Point* (1977), a later addition to the genre. Shirley Maclaine and her husband talk in bed trying to resolve their relationship; coming in late at night, Anne Bancroft has a heart to heart with Maclaine's daughter, an up-and-coming ballerina, in a bedroom; the daughter lustfully romps in bed with Mikhail Barishnikov as she learns about the wayward ways of men.

Though the interior is the favored locale of melodramas, the external world does occasionally appear as a site of narrative action. When it does, it is usually treated as symptomatic of the emotional turmoil taking place between characters. For example, in melodramas that feature a family patriarch trying to keep control of his domain—*The Long Hot Summer* (1958), *Home From the Hill* (1960), *From the Terrace* (1960), *Written on the Wind*—outdoor sequences function like interiors indicating the degree to which the family dominates the socioeconomic reality of the community. "The dramatic action may be confined exclusively to the family's mansion and estate, as in *Cat on a Hot Tin Roof*, or it may extend to the larger social community, as in *Written on the Wind*...where the community is an extension of the family estate" (Schatz 236). There the town is actually named for the oil rich Hadley family whose business built it. In *Giant* it almost seems as if the entire state of Texas is part of the Benedict ranch. The small town in Kansas featured in *Picnic* is similarly dominated by Alan's family. In all these films, though, the outdoor sequences only serve to confirm the decay and corruption that such male power inevitably succumbs to when it is not informed by the healing power of woman's nurturing abilities. Men, too long accustomed to having things their way, stuck in the traditional modes of male behavior, heedless of the rewards close cooperation with the females in their lives can bring, eventually lose control of that outside world.

Such a fate for Alan in *Picnic* can only be surmised. Madge (the Harvest Queen) departs from his life, however, suggesting that his future in the family business may not be as fruitful as it might have been if he had been able to keep her by his side. The marriage of the older couple in the story, Rosemary and Howard, and the impending marriage of Madge and Hal, on the other hand, gives credence to the idea that mutual respect and admiration between men and women may lead to a union that has the potential to rejuvenate the world in some way. The final image of the film, shot from the air, shows the freight train Hal is riding and the bus Madge has taken moving on converging lines towards an intersection where metaphorically they will meet to begin a new life in another location. In this last shot the outdoor scene represents escape from the confinement of small town mores, an escape as desirable for men as it is for women.

Though all melodramas seem to inherently register the characters' value systems through architecture, decor, and costume, nowhere is it more obvious than in Woody Allen's non-comic *Interiors* (1978). This aptly named film, almost a paradigm of the strategies practiced by the genre, demonstrates how interior settings can articulate a range of important thematic elements operating in melodrama. Eve, the mother of three grown daughters, compulsively organizes the decor of her and their homes, seeking order, quiet and timelessness through the use of muted gray, cold, lifeless tones. Though she has done this for years, the attempt to ward off the clutter, noise and anxiety of the world outside becomes totally obsessive when her husband Arthur decides to leave her and live a life of his own. He eventually marries a widow named Pearl who is the very opposite of Eve—lively, warm, spontaneous, most frequently dressed in bright colors; Pearl intends to redecorate the family beach house to "liven it up." The extended family is tested by Arthur's wedding: the three daughters in one form or another come to terms with their new stepmother, but Eve, shattered by the realization the perfectly organized and controlled existence of the family unit she believed in would never return, drowns herself in the ocean.

The contrast between the two women and their attitudes toward life, spouse, and children is unmistakably manifest in the setting and decor of the interiors each prefers. It is noticeably evident in Eve's attempt to ban the outside world with all its messiness from the clean, well-lighted places she has designed inside. Windows are not to look out of, but exist to block the outside world from coming in. In a first unsuccessful suicide attempt, Eve is seen taping the windows of her apartment shut, slowly, carefully, precisely, before turning on the gas. The sound track amplifies the grating noise of the tape until it drowns out the street noise beyond the panes. The camera pulls back and we see the room has been re-done, everything in it now arranged symmetrically.

Even in death, Eve attempts a formal closure, seeing herself as part of an abstract composition. Though full of pretty decorative objects, this interior is colorless, empty of life, mirroring Eve's inner reality.

When Pearl enters any of these spaces, on the other hand, she brings color to the scene. Generous, fun-loving, noisy, more interested in food than art, she bubbles over with enthusiasm, transforming the muted tones of the decor into something richer, even before she takes paper and paste and paint to the walls. The way she dresses—bold colors, nubby textures, lots of flashy jewelry—indicates what the interiors of her house will look like, reflecting her enthusiasm for living, even with the heartbreaks and frustrations that includes.

Over the years, without someone like Pearl to give expression to the idea that life must be embraced totally and completely, the three daughters' interiors have been drained by their mother's penchant for abstraction and control. Each has sought refuge in some area of art, presumably the realm of order: Renata is a successful poet married to an unsuccessful novelist which causes marital friction; Flyn, the family beauty, is a television actress without much ambition and a deep seated contempt for her shallow life; and Joey, untalented and fretting over her failure to become an artist, aborts her child rather than marrying the documentary filmmaker with whom she lives. None of the women appear to be able to move outside themselves, to engage with life.

In a well worn cliche of countless melodramas, women are seen at windows, staring out at a world they are powerless to control. Sometimes waiting for a loved one to "come home;" sometimes mourning lost opportunities; sometimes thinking of the uncertainties of life. A convention of the genre, the shot emphasizes women's place in the "interior" world, the domestic world, rather than the social and political world of action outside the home. *Interiors* supplies many examples of this image. Frequently the three daughters stand next to a large window in a pale, well-composed room. The light from the outside models their faces in a melancholy image, as they stare offscreen at the world through the window, but we realize they see nothing, only their own introspective ruminations (Yacowar 190). The interiors of the rooms created by Eve visible on the screen are powerful signifiers of the invisible interiors of her daughters. Only Pearl's arrival may with her change of decor put some life in these empty vessels.

Woody Allen is, of course, well-known for his conscious use of film elements in all of his movies, and therefore the complex use of setting in *Interiors* to stand for the character's inner lives is certainly intentional. The interiors of melodramas, however, whether made by famous directors or studio hacks, have always revealed as much about the characters and their real relations with the world as plot and dialogue. Invariably these spaces are enclosed, interior spaces—even outdoor scenes in melodramas are shot as if they were interiors. In *Picnic* the climactic harvest dance sequence takes place on a rectangular wooden platform that holds the characters like a room. No breeze or sun's shadow mars the perfect stillness at the studio back lot pond in *Written on the Wind* where Rock Hudson and Dorothy Malone meet to remember old times. All the locales in these films, interiors or exteriors, reveal the characters as enclosed, circumscribed, confined. And since women are the chief protagonists of the melodrama, this means the genre defines women as confined to these spaces. Even when the film is produced on the Hollywood assembly line, the constricting spacial element produces a dense diegetic framework that mirrors the oppression of the characters.

It seems clear that the melodrama over the years has by and large displayed surface values that are prosocial and supportive of the status quo reinforcing the banishment of women to the domestic area—the "interiors" of the home and the world. And at the same time this ideology of submission to the patriarchal order is undercut by the very conventions of the genre. In effect the films always critique themselves by setting up an ambiguous value system. Women protagonists, unlike their male counterparts in other genres, are never allowed a clear-cut, unalloyed resolution of the conflicts in the film (Elsaesser 14). They are always constrained by the terms of the equation: "damned if you do, damned if you don't." Stella can either increase the possible happiness for her daughter or for herself, but she can not do both. The heroine of all the versions of *Back Street* can have either love or a career, but not both. In *The Turning Point*, both of the protagonists must choose between being ballerinas and having families. They can't really do both except through intermediaries or surrogates like children and students. Such limitations on female options appear patently unfair, but the representation of those limitations has been the staple of the melodrama from early in film history, reflecting the situation of women in the world outside the theater. It takes an extraordinary effort for a woman, even in today's more liberated times, to juggle the responsibilities of being wife, mother, lover and career person. The interiors of the filmed melodrama have always served as an indicator of the trap, the prison, the barriers women have had to face seemingly forever. Hopefully those barriers are coming down today and contemporary women will be able to see the interior space as merely one of the options in a wide panorama of spaces in which to act out a life.

Works Cited

Byars, Jackie. *All That Hollywood Allows: Rereading Gender in 1950s Melodrama*. Chapel Hill: U of North Carolina UP, 1991.

Elaesser, Thomas. "Tales of Sound and Fury: Observations on the Family Melodrama." *Monogram* 4 (197): 1-15. Reprinted in Grant, ed., *Film Genre Reader*. Austin: U of Texas UP, 1986.

Gilligan, Carol. *In a Different Voice: Psychological Theory and Women's Development*. Cambridge: Harvard UP, 1982.

Schatz, Thomas. *Hollywood Genres: Formulas, Filmmaking and the Studio System*. New York, Random House, 1981.

Walsh, Andrea. *Women's Films and Women's Experience, 1940-1950*. New York: Praeger, 1984.

Williams, Linda. "'Something Else Besides a Mother': *Stella Dallas* and the Maternal Melodrama." *Cinema Journal* 24, no. 1 (Fall 1984): 2-27.

Yacowar, Maurice. *Loster Take All: The Comic Art of Woody Allen*. New York: Ungar, 1979.

Filmography

Year	Film	Director
1927	*Sunrise*	F.W. Murnau
1927	*Seventh Heaven*	Frank Borzage
1932	*Back Street*	John Stahl
1934	*Imitation of Life*	John Stahl
1937	*Stella Dallas*	King Vidor
1940	*Rebecca*	Alfred Hitchcock
1942	*Now, Voyager*	Irving Rapper
1945	*Mildred Pierce*	Michael Curtiz
1946	*It's a Wonderful Life*	Frank Capra
1948	*Best Years of Our Lives*	William Wyler
1949	*Letter to Three Wives*	Joseph Mankiewicz
1952	*The Marrying Kind*	George Cukor
1954	*Magnificent Obsession*	Douglas Sirk
1955	*All That Heaven Allows*	Douglas Sirk
1955	*East of Eden*	Elia Kazan
1955	*Picnic*	Joshua Logan
1955	*Rebel Without a Cause*	Nicholas Ray
1956	*Giant*	George Stevens
1956	*Written on the Wind*	Douglas Sirk
1958	*Cat on a Hot Tin Roof*	Richard Brooks
1958	*The Long, Hot Summer*	Martin Ritt
1958	*Some Came Running*	Vincente Minnelli
1959	*Imitation of Life*	Douglas Sirk

1960	*Home from the Hill*	Vincente Minnelli
1977	*The Turning Point*	Herbert Ross
1978	*Interiors*	Woody Allen
1983	*Teams of Endearment*	James Brooks
1989	*Shirley Valentine*	Lewis Gilbert

Contributors

Jay Boyer teaches courses in American film and literature at Arizona State University.

Mark J. Charney is Assistant Head of the English Department at Clemson University, where he teaches classes in contemporary literature, film genre studies, film theory, and writing. He earned his Ph.D. from Tulane University in 1987 and his M.A. from the University of New Orleans in 1980, in spite of the dangerous and corruptive influence of New Orleans life. He has just published a book on Barry Hannah for Twayne Publishers and is working on an intellectual biography of D.W. Griffith for the University Press of Virginia's Minds of New South Intellectual Biography Series.

Carlos E. Cortés is a Professor of History at the University of California, Riverside. The recipient of two book awards, he is currently working on a three-volume study of the history of the U.S. motion picture treatment of ethnic groups, foreign nations, and world cultures. A former guest host on the PBS national television series, "Why in the World?," he received his university's Distinguished Teaching Award and the California Council for the Humanities' 1980 Distinguished California Humanist Award.

Norma Fay Green, who has worked in eight different newspaper and magazine newsrooms, is a Mass Media Ph.D. candidate at Michigan State University. She has taught a variety of journalism courses at MSU, Northwestern University and Columbia College-Chicago and continues to practice what she preaches as a freelance journalist.

Kathy Merlock Jackson (Ph.D., American Culture, Bowling Green State University) is an associate professor of communications at Virginia Wesleyan College, where she teaches courses in mass communications. She is the author of *Images of Children in American Film: A Sociocultural Analysis* (1986) and *Walt Disney: A Bio-Bibliography* (1993).

Terry Lindvall is Professor of Film at Regent University in Virginia Beach, Virginia. He received his BA from Southern California College,

M.Div. from Fuller Theological Seminary, and his Ph.D. from the University of Southern California. He is currently writing *The Silents of God: Church and Cinema from 1896-1922*. He has published numerous articles and reviews for CHOICE and various religious journals, and is the Editorial Consultant for *Sync: The Regent Journal of Film and Video*. He and his wife, Karen, have one son, Christopher.

Greg Metcalf makes his home in American Studies at the University of Maryland, College Park, where he also teaches Film and Government courses. He has given the odd lecture on Art-related Film and Literature at the Smithsonian Institution. He continues to write on issues of adaptation to film, Victorian culture, and Marlovian detectives, while compiling a "post-post-modern" book of film quotations and creating art historical snow domes.

Douglas A. Noverr is a Professor in the Department of American Thought and Language at Michigan State University and teaches in the Graduate Program in American Studies. With Lawrence E. Ziewacz he has published *The Games They Played: Sports in American History, 1865-1980* (1983) and *Sport History* (1987). With Erik S. Lunde he has published *Film History* (1989) and *Film Studies* (1989). He has published a number of articles on sports films and sports history, reviews sports books for the *Journal of American Culture, the Journal of Popular Culture,* and *CHOICE*, and contributed numerous articles to the five-volume *Biographical Dictionary of American Sports*.

Barbara Odabashian is an Assistant Professor of English at John Jay College—The City University of New York, where she has created and directs a Film Studies Minor in the Department of English. She received a Ph.D. in English and Comparative Literature from Columbia University, and publishes in the area of Renaissance literature as well as film studies.

Edward Recchia is a Professor of American Thought and Language at Michigan State University and has explored literary and film subjects in publications as diverse as *Studies in Short Fiction, Literature/Film Quarterly*, and *Literatur in Wissenschaft und Unterricht*. Recent publications include "The American Western Film in the 1980s" and "Martin Scorsese's *Raging Bull*: In Violence *Veritas*?"

Diana C. Reep is Professor of English at The University of Akron where she teaches popular culture and professional writing. Her studies in television and audience response have appeared in such journals as

Journalism Quarterly, Sex Roles, Family Perspective, and *Communication Research.*

Brooks Robards is the author of *Arnold Schwarzenegger* (1992). She does research on Film & TV and has published articles on the TV cop genre and on innovation in TV programming. She is Professor of Mass Communication at Westfield State College in Massachusetts.

Jack G. Shaheen, an internationally recognized specialist on stereotypical portrayals of Arabs in mass media, is a professor of mass communications at Southern Illinois University at Edwardsville and a professional journalist. Dr. Shaheen, selected by the Department of State as a Scholar-Diplomat, is the author of *Nuclear War Films* and *The TV Arab*. At present, he is at work on *The Hollywood Arab* and *The Comic Book Arab*.

Thomas Sobchack teaches in the Film Studies Program at the University of Utah. Co-author of *An Introduction to Film* and *Introduction to Film Criticism*, he is currently doing research on the work of Andrei Tarkovsky, Post-war British Comedies, and the Family Melodrama.

Colleen M. Tremonte recently completed her Ph.D. in American Literature and Women's Studies at Texas Christian University. Her previously published articles include "Recasting the Western Hero: Ethos in High-Tech Science Fiction" and "The Poet-Prophet and Feminine Capability in Walker Percy's *The Second Coming*."

Carol M. Ward teaches film in the English Department at Clemson University. *Mae West: A Bio-Bibliography* was published by Greenwood Press in April 1989. Her critical biography of Rita Mae Brown was published by Twayne.